ENABLING THE BUSINESS
OF AGRICULTURE 2017

ISBN (paper): 978-1-4648-1021-3
ISBN (electronic): 978-1-4648-1022-0
DOI: 10.1596/978-1-4648-1021-3

Cover image: "Farmers Market #15" © Julie Ford Oliver, www.juliefordoliver.com. Used with the permission of Julie Ford Oliver. Further permission required for reuse.

Cover design: Base Three

Library of Congress Cataloging-in-Publication Data has been requested.

Contents

ENABLING THE BUSINESS OF AGRICULTURE 2017

Sunflowers. Sofia, Bulgaria.
Photo: Boris Balabanov / World Bank.

Foreword

Sustainable agricultural development is one of the most powerful tools to end extreme poverty and boost shared prosperity. Agriculture is the economic and social mainstay of some 500 million smallholder farmers, and in developing countries, the sector is the largest source of incomes, jobs and food security. Sustainable, inclusive growth in the agriculture and food sectors creates jobs—on farms, in markets, cities, towns and villages, and throughout the farm-to-table food production and consumption chain.

Seen against the backdrop of an increasing world population that is expected to reach nine billion by 2050, rising food demand is estimated to increase by at least 20% globally over the next 15 years with the largest increases projected in Sub-Saharan Africa, South Asia and East Asia. Boosting the productivity, profitability and sustainability of agriculture is essential for fighting hunger and poverty, tackling malnutrition and boosting food security. In short, the world needs a food system that can feed every person, every day, everywhere with a nutritious and affordable diet, delivered in a climate-smart, sustainable way.

To achieve this goal, we need to be more productive and efficient in the way we grow food, while building the resilience of both farmers and food supply chains while simultaneously reducing the environmental footprint of the agriculture and food sectors. This process requires policies and regulations that foster growth in the agriculture and food sectors, well-functioning markets, and thriving agribusinesses that make more food available in rural and urban spaces.

In pursuit of these objectives, we are pleased to present the World Bank Group's *Enabling the Business of Agriculture (EBA) 2017*, the third in a series of annual reports. The predominant focus of the EBA project is to measure and monitor regulations that affect the functioning of agriculture and agribusinesses. This year's report provides analysis and results for 62 countries representing all regions and income groups, and covers the following topic areas: seed, fertilizer, machinery, finance, markets, transport, information and communication technology, and water. Two additional topics—land and livestock—are being developed, and initial results are presented in this report. Two overarching themes—gender and environmental sustainability—are included in the EBA analysis with a view to promoting inclusive and sustainable practices.

Despite the inherent complexity of agricultural systems and the differing regional and country contexts in which agriculture and agribusiness performance needs to be evaluated, globally comparable data and indicators offer meaningful tools that can enable countries, policy makers and stakeholders to identify barriers that impede the growth of agriculture and agribusinesses, share experiences and develop strategies to improve the policy environment anchored in local contexts. The EBA indicators and analysis presented here not only help strengthen the information base that can be used for informed policy dialogue but can also encourage regulations that ensure the safety and quality of agricultural inputs, goods and services while minimizing costs to make more food available to more people.

Robust, effective and efficient regulatory systems are essential components of well-functioning agriculture and food markets. In turn, such systems can help achieve the twin goals of the World Bank Group—ending poverty by 2030 and boosting shared prosperity—as well as the Sustainable Development Goals. In keeping with the objectives of earlier reports, we offer these findings as a public good that can help advance knowledge and understanding of the critically-important role that the agriculture and food sectors can play in accelerating sustainable development for the benefit of all.

Augusto Lopez-Claros
Director, Global Indicators Group
World Bank Group

Juergen Voegele
Senior Director, Agriculture Global Practice
World Bank Group

Acknowledgments

Enabling the Business of Agriculture 2017 was prepared under the leadership of Preeti S. Ahuja and Federica Saliola, with the support of César Chaparro-Yedro, Tea Trumbić and Farbod Youssefi, working under the general direction of Augusto López-Claros, Ethel Sennhauser and Juergen Voegele. During this cycle, Farbod Youssefi led the operationalization of the *Enabling the Business of Agriculture* indicators, working with client facing teams across a number of Agriculture Global Practice client countries. The team would also like to acknowledge the support of Melissa Johns. Current and former team members included Yulia Amanbaeva, Dinah Bengur, Liwam Berhane, Arturo Francisco Bonilla Merino, Lila Melissa Cardell, Rong Chen, Dariga Chukmaitova, Davida Louise Connon, Cyriane Coste, Klaus Deininger Nealon Devore, Sarah Diouri, Raian Divanbeigi, Soha Eshraghi, Leopoldo Fabra, Pilar Fernández, Felix Frewer, Fernanda Barros Gabbert, Arnau Gallard-Agusti, Bill Garthwaite, Tulia Gattone, Slavena Georgieva, Lucia Gruet, Graham Hamley, Maureen Itepu, Edna Massay Kallon, Marina Kayumova, Milan Kondić, Maksat Korooluev, Alva Kretschmer, Robert de l'Escaille, Jean Philippe Lodugnon Harding, Wisambi Loundu, Valerie Marechal, Thibault Meilland, Julia Navarro, Esperanza Pastor Núñez de Castro, Nina Paustian, Aditi Poddar, Ana María Santillana Farakos, Sara Savastano, Kateryna Schroeder, Justin Lee Schwegel, Gabriel Simoes Gaspar, Bungheng Taing, Samjhana Thapa, Geyi Zheng and Yucheng Zheng.

Assisting with data collection were: Joshua Ahyong, Rebecca Louise Barnes, Vinicius Beraldo, Sabhanaz Siddharth Dixit, Rashid Diya, Ranjia Duan, Fadia Hayee, Luka Kalandarishvili, Kenan Karakulah, Garri Kasparov, Yousra Khalil, Gregory La Rocca, Atul Menon, Behrad Nazarian, Teresa Peterburs, Lochard Philozin, Jason Pierce, Gaurav R. Pradhan, Rustam Rakhmetov, Juan Manuel Ramírez Roldán, Leekyung Shim, Charnae Supplee, Nan Tang, Alexander Troncoso, Xinyu Weng, Kristina Wienhöfer, Dou Zhang and Yang Zhao. The team is grateful to local consultants who supported data collection or helped the team during country visits: Faiza Hesham Hael Ahmed (Jordan), Kali Sankar Ghosh (India), Jocellin Kye Hoan Lee (Republic of Korea), Krit Pattamaroj (Thailand) and Macarena Vio (Chile).

Punam Chuhan-Pole, Richard Colback, Carlos A. da Silva, Andrais Horvai, Ed Keturakis, Oksana Nagayets, Harideep Singh and Patrick Verissimo reviewed the full draft report and provided feedback. The team received additional written comments from Oliver Braedt, Juan Buchenau, Poonam Gupta, Julian Lampietti, Daniel Lederman, Mohamed Medouar, Michael Morris, Balakrishna Menon Parameswaran, Sajjad Ali Shah, Raju Singh, Adama Toure and Martien Van Nieuwkoop. The team is also grateful for valuable comments and reviews provided by colleagues across the World Bank Group, in particular those in the 62 World Bank Group country offices and those working on several key areas investigated by the report. The team would especially like to acknowledge the hard work of the following individuals in the country office who helped distribute questionnaires and validate the data: Asma Ben Abdallah, Abimbola Adubi, Arusyak Alaverdyan, Mustafa Alver, Amadou Ba, Mariam Bamba, Julia Barrera, Husam Beides, Sylvie Bossoutrot, Blessings Botha, Melissa Brown, Nabil Chaherli, Mudita Chamroeun, Ladisy Chengula, Purna Bahadur Chhetri, Youjin Choi, Kevin Crockford, Catherine Doody, Svetlana Edmeades, Yanina Ermakova, Time Hapana Fatch, Noreen Grace Fernandes, Xavier Furtado, Augusto García, Andrew Goodland, Sameer Goyal, Artavazd Hakobyan, Alexandra Horst, Geeeun Jang, Chakib Jenane, Kwang Chul Ji, Frauke Jungbluth, Min Jae Kang, Katie Kennedy Freeman, Wansup Kim, Hans Kordik, Sobir Kurbanov, Soo Yeon Lim, Thomas Lubeck, Omar Lyasse, Seenithamby Manoharan, Chanhsom Manythong, Mohamed Medouar, Michael Morris, Aimee Mpambara, Joyce Msuya, Linda Mukwavi, Alex Mwanakasale, Valens Mwumvaneza, Srinivasan Ananthan Nallappa, Jan Nijhoff, Aifa N'Doye Nione, Dorota Agata Nowak, Patience Nyenpan, Francisco Obreque, Pierre Olivier, Balakrishna Menon Parameswaran, Fernando Paredes, Manivannan Pathy, Doina Petrescu, Nodira Pirmanova, Tatyana Ponomareva, Maria Theresa Quinones, Tim Robertson, Marina Sahakyan, Sheu Salau, Yeyande Sangho, Elena Savinova, Manievel Sene, Bekzod Shamsiev, Animesh Shrivastava, Sarah Simons, Rita Soni, Heinz Strubenhoff, Raquel Orejas Tagarro, Hardwick Tchale, Talimjan Urazov, Bela Varma, Griselle Felicita Vega, Son Tanh Vo, Bobojon Yatimov and Sergiy Zorya.

The team also benefited from comments and discussions with experts from both inside and outside the World Bank Group. The team is especially grateful to Simeon Djankov, who provided extensive comments on the report draft and methodology. Comments were also received from: Ulrich Adam, Guillaume Agede, Esteban Alcade, Oya Pinar Ardic Alper, Jamie Anderson, Patrice Annequin, Maria Antip, Joshua Ariga,

Jackie Atkinson, Ken Bagstad, Jennie Barron, Todd Benson, Julio Berdegue, Franck Berthe, Stephen Biggs, Jos Bijman, Zhao Bing, Florentin Blanc, Dave Bledsoe, Ademola Braimoh, Carl Bruch, Juan Buchenau, Balu Bumb, Stefano Burchi, Francois Burgaud, Jacob Burke, Christina Katharina Busch, Peter Button, Fabrizio Cafaggi, Thomas Cantens, David Casanova, Rita Cestti, Lawrence Clarke, Rick Clayton, Joseph Cortés, Gilly Cowan, Gaspar Csaba, Barney Curtis, Richard Damania, Valerie D'Costa, Morgane Danielou, Roger Day, Arsala Deane, Walter de Boef, Theo de Jager, Bénédicte Leroy de la Brière, Alejandro Álvarez de la Campa, Philip de Leon, Erik De Ridder, Romano DeVivo, Brigitte Dias Ferreira, Eugenio Díaz-Bonilla, Luz Berania Díaz Ríos, Cheryl Doss, Ian John Douglas Gillson, Carel du Marchie Sarvass, Marsha Echols, Hanan El-Youssef, Ijeoma Emenanjo, Natalia Federighi, Stephane Forman, Francis Fragano, Carlos Francia, Bill Gain, Pierre Jean Gerber, Tanja K. Goodwin, Jean-Christophe Gouache, Rodrigo Gouveia, Lars Nikolajs Grava, Alison Griffith, Caren Grown, Nora Ourabah Haddad, Adelaida Harries, Nagaraja Rao Harshdeep, Terhi Havimo, Catherine Hayes, Paul Hazen, Martin Hilmi, Stephen Hodgson, Nathalie Hoffman, David Hong, Mombert Hoppe, Ivo Hostens, Jens Hügel, Wilfried Hundertmark, Ankur Huria, Sarah Iqbal, Robert Ireland, Krista Jacobs, Ishrat Jahan, Peter Jeffries, Chakib Jenane, Scott Justice, Benjamin Kaufman, Jari Kauppila, Rochi Kemka, Elshad Khanalibayli, Josef Kienzle, Kaoru Kimura, Henriette Kolb, Holger Kray, Charles Kunaka, Andrea Kutter, Andrzej Kwiecinski, Abdelaziz Lagnaoui, Ingo Lang, Steven Lawry, Francois Le Gall, Isabel López Noriega, Youlia Lozanova, Antonio Francisco Lucas, Valerio Luchessi, Javier Mateo-Sagasta, Fran McCrae, Leslie McDermott, Madeleine McDougall, Emma McInerney, Gerard McLinden, Ruth Meizen-Dick, Hailu Mekonnen, Grant Milne, Michael Morris, Victor Mosoti, Goeffrey Mrema, Mohinder Mudahar, Ajai Nair, Claudia Nari, Patricia Neenan, Trevor Nicholls, Alan Nicol, Marion Niland, Beatriz Oelckers, Francois Onimus, Jean-Pierre Orand, David Orden, Theresa Osborne, Washington Otieno, María Claudia Pachón, María Pagura, Roy Parizat, Judith Payne, Douglas Pearce, Ana Peralta, Marco Pezzini, Patrick Philipp, Stephen Francis Pirozzi, Caroline Plante, Natalia Pshenichnaya, Justin Rakotoarisaona, Douglas Randall, Maurice Rawlins, Jean Regis, William Rex, Claudia Ringler, Ben Rivoire, Felipe Targa Rodríguez, Loraine Ronchi, Jiang Ru, Eliana Carolina Rubiano Matulevich, Ignacio Ruiz Abad, Philippe Sabot, Sebastián Sáez, Salman M. A. Salman, Namal Samarakoon, Bexci Sánchez, Daniel Mario Saslavsky, Aguiratou Savadogo-Tinto, Rachel Sberro, Carl-Stephan Schaefer, Susanne Scheireling, Harris Selod, Bambi Semroc, Orlando Sosa, Jitendra Srivastava, Sanjay Srivastava, Victoria Stanley, Leanne Stewart, Nancy Sundberg, Simon Sunderland, Tahira Syed, Sanna Liisa Taivalmaa, Virginia Tanase, Michael Tarazi, Jessica Troell, Muhabbat Turdieva, Kees van der Meer, Panos Varangis, Peter Veit, Francesco Versace, José Viegas, Martin Ward, Hugo Wilson, Julie Wojtulewicz, Justin Yap, William Young, Winston Yu and Andrew Zaeske.

The *Enabling the Business of Agriculture* program was developed in partnership with several donors, whose funding and support makes this report possible: the Bill and Melinda Gates Foundation, the Department for International Development (DFID), the Danish Ministry of Foreign Affairs, the United States Agency for International Development (USAID) and the Government of the Netherlands.

The *Enabling the Business of Agriculture 2017* outreach strategy is being executed by a communications team led by Indira Chand and Sarwat Hussain, supported by Zia Morales. The development and management of the Enabling the Business of Agriculture website and technical services were supported by Andrés Baquero Franco, Fengsheng Huang, Kunal Patel, Vinod Kumar Vasudevan Thottikkatu and Hashim Zia.

The report was edited by Dina Towbin and designed by Base Three LLC.

Enabling the Business of Agriculture 2017 benefited from the generous input of a network of more than 3,932 local partners, including legal experts, business associations, private sector representatives, farmers' organizations, academics, government officials and other professionals actively engaged in the policy, legal and regulatory requirements in the 62 countries covered this year. Please note that the data published in the report and online represent a unified response based on the answers the team received from various respondents and sources, and are not attributed to any particular respondent. Wherever possible, answers were corroborated by official fee schedules, laws, regulations and public notices. The names of those wishing to be acknowledged individually are listed at the end of the report and are available at: http://eba.worldbank.org.

About *Enabling the Business of Agriculture*

Since 2013, *Enabling the Business of Agriculture* (EBA) has collected data on laws and regulations that impact the business environment for agriculture. The analysis has yielded some important results, such as: EBA country data have been used to open dialogues on regulatory reform with governments across several countries in Sub-Saharan Africa and East Asia; indications of interest from other development agencies in joining forces with the World Bank; engagement with a range of vital stakeholders from the private sector to civil society to academia; and continued enhancement of the methodology.

Enabling the Business of Agriculture 2017 is the third report in the series. The data can be used by governments, investors, analysts, researchers and others interested in this component of the enabling agribusiness environment to assess countries' performance on the topics measured, as well as to identify regulatory good practices that can be found around the world.

Enabling the Business of Agriculture builds on the *Doing Business* methodology and quantifies regulatory practices and legal barriers that affect the business of agriculture. *Doing Business* has pioneered a unique approach for comparing countries' performances on the regulatory environment; the results are noteworthy—more than 2,900 regulatory reforms have been documented since 2004 in 190 countries around the world. But the *Doing Business* focus has been on small and medium enterprises located in the largest business cities.[1] Businesses that operate in and around agriculture face additional constraints to enter and operate in the market and often deal with stricter regulatory controls related to registration and quality control of their service and/or goods. Recent shifts in population and food demand have made it all the more paramount that a country's regulatory frameworks and institutions enable farmers to produce and deliver more and safer food.

How does regulation impact the agriculture sector?

What can governments do to improve the access of farmers to essential inputs and services that increase their productivity in an environmentally sustainable manner? How can smallholders be helped to raise their socio-economic well-being while facilitating their integration with value chains? What can governments do to facilitate entrepreneurs and agribusinesses to thrive in a socially and environmentally responsible way?

Governments can help by establishing appropriate regulatory systems that ensure the safety and quality of agricultural goods and services without being costly or burdensome overall so as to discourage firms from entering the market. Excessive regulation makes firms move to the informal economy[2] and generates high unemployment.[3] Poorly-designed regulations impose high transaction costs on firms thus reducing trade volumes,[4] productivity[5] and access to finance. Creating an enabling environment for agriculture is a prerequisite to unleash the sector's potential to boost growth, reduce poverty and inequality, provide food security and deliver environmental services.[6] Among other factors, government policies and regulations play a key role in shaping the business environment through their impacts on costs, risks and barriers to competition for various players in the value chains.[7] By setting the right institutional and regulatory framework, governments can help increase the competitiveness of farmers and agricultural entrepreneurs, enabling them to integrate into regional and global markets.

Over the past decade a branch of economic literature has highlighted the significant impact of business regulations on economic performance.[8] It is crucial to have regulations that can lower risk by enabling farmers to operate in a context where the outcomes of their decisions are more predictable. Governments need to strike the right balance between correcting market failures through regulations and minimizing the costs that those regulations impose on economic agents. This balance is essential for agriculture, but it is also particularly challenging. It is not unusual for governments to implement too-stringent agricultural regulations,[9] which impose excessive compliance costs for agricultural firms and make them more prone to remaining (or becoming) informal.[10] The agriculture sector's dependence on land, which is a finite resource and binds its growth to productivity gains, underscores the impact of regulations on areas such as land tenure and price volatility. Farmers face considerable risk due to their susceptibility to exogenous elements and from extreme or erratic weather, insects, rodents and other pests, and diseases. What's more, this uncertainty is exacerbated by the inherent volatility of agricultural markets.[11]

Reducing transaction costs imposed by regulations is imperative in agriculture. Transport costs can make up one-third of the farm gate price in some Sub-Saharan African countries and can prevent farmers from specializing in the goods where they have a competitive advantage.[12] In addition to transport, improving access to reliable and affordable information and communication technology (ICT) services is vital to a global food and agriculture system that is able to achieve its potential.

Regulations that can lower risk by enabling farmers to operate in a context where the outcomes of their decisions are more predictable are crucial. In fact, successful regulatory reform has contributed to increased supply and lower prices in the seed and mechanization markets in Bangladesh and Turkey, in the fertilizer sector in Bangladesh, Kenya and Ethiopia, and in the maize industry in Eastern and Southern Africa, among others. A series of legal, institutional and administrative reforms in the 1990s led to a wide range of improvements in Mexico's water resource management. Vietnam introduced Land Use Rights Certificates in 1993, which increased the security of land tenure for farmers and gave rise to more land area devoted to long-term crops.

Agricultural production has unique and evolving dimensions through which it interacts with relevant laws and regulations. These dimensions include, for example, regulations of agricultural input markets such as seed and fertilizer, and regulations that enable small-scale and remote farmers to access finance as well as quality, sanitary and phytosanitary standards and trucking licenses.[13]

What does *Enabling the Business of Agriculture* measure?

Enabling the Business of Agriculture 2017 presents data that measure legal barriers for businesses operating in agriculture in 62 economies and across 12 topic areas. It provides quantitative indicators on regulation for seed, fertilizer, machinery, finance, markets, transport, water, and ICT (table 1). Two overarching themes—gender and environmental sustainability—continue to be included in the report analysis to ensure that the messages developed by EBA encourage inclusive and sustainable practices. This year scoring was piloted for the land topic for 38 countries in which data were collected. The data for the remaining 24 countries will be collected next year and the team will refine the methodology further. EBA also collected data on the livestock topic, focusing on veterinary medicinal products (VMPs). The report explains the methodology and provides some insight from data collection for VMPs, but future editions will expand the topical coverage to include the areas of animal feed and genetic resources.

Two types of indicators emerge: *legal indicators* and *efficiency indicators*. *Legal indicators* are derived from a reading of the laws and regulations. In a few instances, the data also include some elements which are not in the text of the law but relate to implementing a good regulatory practice—for example, online availability of a fertilizer catalogue. *Efficiency indicators* reflect the time and cost imposed by the regulatory system—for example, the number of procedures and the time and cost to complete a process such as certifying seed for sale in the domestic market. Data of this type are built on legal requirements and cost measures are backed by official fee schedules when available.

Table 1 | What *Enabling the Business of Agriculture* measures—12 areas of regulation studied

TOPIC	WHAT IS MEASURED
SEED	> Time, cost and requirements to register a new seed variety > Protection and licensing of plant breeder rights > Quality control of seed in the market
FERTILIZER	> Time, cost and regulation for fertilizer registration > Quality control of fertilizer in the market > Requirements for importing fertilizer
MACHINERY	> Time, cost and requirements for tractor registration, inspection and maintenance > Time, cost and requirements for tractor testing and standards > Requirements for importing tractors
FINANCE	> Requirements for establishing and operating deposit-taking microfinance institutions and financial cooperatives > Requirements for third-party agents to provide financial services and provision of e-money by nonfinancial institutions > Use of agriculture relevant assets as movable collateral and availability of credit information on small loans and from non-bank institutions
MARKETS	> Establishment and operation of producer organizations > Phytosanitary requirements on management and control of pests and diseases > Documents, time, cost and requirements for domestic trade and export of agricultural goods
TRANSPORT	> Time, cost and requirements to operate commercial trucks > Time, cost and requirements for cross-border transport
WATER	> Water use permits > Water resource management
ICT	> Licensing of mobile operators
LAND	*(pilot scoring for 38 countries)* > Coverage and relevance of land records > Public land management > Gender disaggregation of land records > Leasing of land between private parties > Procedural safeguards in case of expropriation
LIVESTOCK	*(not scored)* > Requirements to register veterinary medicinal products > Requirements for importing veterinary medicinal products > Requirements for labeling of veterinary medicinal products
ENVIRONMENTAL SUSTAINABILITY	*(not scored)* > Conservation of plant genetic resources > Access and sustainable use of plant genetic resources > Water quality management > Soil health management
GENDER	*(not scored)* > Availability of gender-disaggregated data > Restrictions on women's employment and activity > Women's participation and leadership in collective institutions > Non-discrimination provisions

Sources: EBA database; Doing Business database.

How are EBA indicators selected?

The choice of the indicators developed for the eight scored topics was guided by a review of academic literature. The scoring choices of each indicator were informed by extensive consultations with key stakeholders, including civil society organizations, partner institutions, practitioners, public and private sector representatives, researchers and technical experts. The team is working on developing background papers for each topic to establish the importance of the regulations that EBA measures in each topic area for important outcomes such as agricultural output.

The *Enabling the Business of Agriculture* methodology provides a quantitative assessment of the regulations in each of the selected topics. The methodology, however, considers more than the number of regulations and does not promote deregulation. For example, higher scores are given for stricter labeling and penalty rules related to fertilizer or seed quality control since the laws and regulations need to set appropriate standards in these areas to ensure health and food safety. Higher scores are also given for the efficient application of regulations, such as affordable and timely tractor registration requirements. Countries that perform well on the EBA topics are those that balance proper enforcement of safety and quality control while avoiding burdensome and costly requirements that could discourage private sector development.

Going forward, it is envisaged that the selection of topics and related indicators will build on the current indicators and include the following additional measures: expansion of the livestock topic to include areas of animal feed and genetic resources; expansion of the gender cross-cutting area; refinement of the land scoring methodology; and development of an "Implementation Efficiency Index" to complement and provide additional policy insights alongside the current regulatory indicators. The refinement and selection of indicators will undergo a thorough internal review and collect feedback from various stakeholders from within the World Bank Group as well as from external participants. Already in place is a broad-based technical advisory committee with specialists from the private sector, academia, governments and the World Bank Group.

How are countries selected?

Enabling the Business of Agriculture 2017 covers 62 countries in seven regions (map 1). Selection criteria have been used to determine the countries included in the study, ensuring adequate representation of all regions and different levels of agricultural development. To select a sample of countries where an assessment of regulatory framework for agribusiness would be meaningful, the team did an analysis of the agriculture sector's importance by looking at two contributions—to GDP and to employment. Countries with small agricultural sectors (defined as less than US$1 billion) were excluded unless the population employed in agriculture is more than 100,000 people. The countries were then grouped by geographic regions (using World

Map 1 | Geographical coverage of *Enabling the Business of Agriculture 2017*

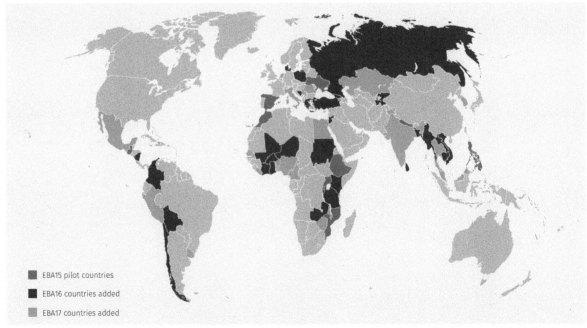

- ▇ EBA15 pilot countries
- ▇ EBA16 countries added
- ▇ EBA17 countries added

IBRD 42732
FEBRUARY 2017

This map was produced by the Cartography Unit of the World Bank Group. The boundaries, colors, denominations and any other information shown on this map do not imply, on the part of the World Bank Group, any judgment on the legal status of any territory, or any endorsement or acceptance of such boundaries.

Table 2 | Example of calculating Colombia's distance-to-frontier (DTF) score for fertilizer

TOPIC/INDICATOR	DATA	DTF SCORE		FRONTIER
Fertilizer		81.58		
Fertilizer registration index (0-7)	6	85.71		7
Time to register fertilizer a new fertilizer product (days)	45	96.39	97.73	11
Cost to register a new fertilizer product (% GNI pc)	7.83	99.07		0
Fertilizer quality control index (0-7)	6	85.71		7
Fertilizer imports (0-7)	4	57.14		7

Source: EBA database.

Bank country classifications) and agricultural transformation (grouping inspired by the *World Development Report 2008*). This process produced the following geographic groups: Eastern Europe and Central Asia; East Asia and Pacific; Latin America and the Caribbean; Middle East and North Africa; South Asia; Sub-Saharan Africa; and Organisation for Economic Co-operation and Development (OECD) high-income countries. The agricultural transformation groups developed are defined as either: *agriculture-based countries* (where agriculture employs more than 25% of the workforce and agriculture value added contributes more than 25% to the GDP); *transforming countries* (where agriculture employs more than 25% of the workforce and agriculture value added contributes less than 25% to the GDP); or *urbanized countries* (where agriculture employs below 25% of the workforce and agriculture value added contributes less than 25% to the GDP).

In selecting the first 10 pilot countries, and for subsequent expansion of the dataset to 40 and to 62 countries this year, the team aimed to include as many agriculture-based, pre-transition and transition countries, with a few important urbanizing and high-income countries from diverse geographical regions to allow EBA to measure and showcase good regulatory practices for each of the topic areas.

How is the distance-to-frontier score calculated?

A significant development in this year's report is the refinement of the scoring methodology. For the first time, *Enabling the Business of Agriculture 2017* presents both topic scores, using the distance-to-frontier (DTF) method pioneered by *Doing Business* and topic rankings. The DTF score benchmarks countries with respect to regulatory best practice, showing the absolute distance to the best performance on each *Enabling the Business of Agriculture* indicator, and can help in tracking the countries' absolute level of performance and how it improves over time. The DTF score measures the distance of each country to the frontier, which represents the best performance observed in each indicator for eight *Enabling the Business of*

Agriculture topics (seed, fertilizer, machinery, finance, transport, markets, water and ICT). For legal indicators, the frontier is set at the highest possible value, even if no country currently obtains that score. For efficiency indicators, the frontier is set by the highest performing country.

Enabling the Business of Agriculture uses a simple averaging approach for topic indicator scores to arrive at the topic score. Each topic measures different elements of the enabling agribusiness environment and the DTF scores and rankings for each topic vary considerably. Colombia, for example, has a DTF score of 92.10 for finance, 88.89 for ICT, 85.52 for water and 81.58 for fertilizer—indicating it is very near the frontier in these topics (see table 2). At the same time, it has a DTF score of 73.92 for transport, 70.08 for markets, 63.19 for seed and 38.16 for machinery—showing areas where better regulatory practices can be adopted.

The topic DTF scores are sorted from highest to lowest and assigned a ranking from 1 to 62. The ranking complements the distance to frontier by providing information on the country's performance on EBA topics relative to the other countries' performance on the indicators in this particular year. It should be noted, given the composition of the indicators, that the scores and rankings are measurements of a particular set of regulations and do not necessarily assess the sum of all elements that shape the regulatory framework studied.

How are the data collected?

Enabling the Business of Agriculture indicators are based on primary data collection through standardized questionnaires completed by expert respondents in each country as well as the team's own analysis of the relevant laws and regulations. Once the data are collected and analyzed, several follow-up rounds address and clear up any discrepancies in the answers the respondents provide, including conference calls, written correspondence and country visits. Each year the team travels to the countries where it is hardest to collect data remotely. For the last two years, the team has traveled to about 20% of the sample countries. During the *EBA2017* data collection period, the team visited these 13 countries: Armenia, Côte d'Ivoire, India, Jordan, Republic of Korea, Kyrgyz Republic, Liberia, Malawi, Morocco, Nepal, Russian Federation, Sri Lanka and Tajikistan. The data are then reviewed using desk research and follow-up with respondents. The preliminary data are validated through World Bank focal points in each country office. The data are then aggregated into indicators which allow for further analysis and comparisons, and contribute to the report writing phase. The report undergoes peer review with internal and external reviewers, as well as all relevant global practices and regions before it is released to the public (figure 1).

Chosen from the private sector, the public sector and civil society, respondents include firms, academia, financial institutions, professional associations, farmer organizations and government ministries and agencies. These individuals and organizations are chosen because of their knowledge of their countries' laws and regulations. Involving various experts increases the data accuracy by balancing the possible biases of different stakeholders. Reaching out to both the private and public sectors helps compare the perspectives of all parties. Those wishing to be recognized are acknowledged in the *Local Experts* section at the end of the report.

Enabling the Business of Agriculture data are collected in a standardized way to ensure comparability across countries and over time. Following the methodological foundations of *Doing Business,* questionnaires use a standard business case with assumptions about the legal form of the business, its size, its location and the nature of its operations for each topic applied for all countries (table 3). Assumptions guiding respondents through their completion of the survey questionnaires vary by topic (see appendix B). In addition, in the interest of comparability, the values in the assumptions are not fixed values but proportional to the country's gross national income (GNI) per capita. The data in this report are current as of June 30, 2016, and do not reflect any changes to the laws or administrative procedures after that date.

What does *Enabling the Business of Agriculture* not measure?

Many elements affect a country's enabling environment for agribusinesses. The political situation in a country, for example, can greatly influence its attractiveness to business and investors. Social aspects, such as literacy and overall education levels and life expectancy, are also important indicators. A country's economic performance, measured by factors such as inflation, unemployment, income growth, government revenues and expenditures, is also very influential when determining a country's overall enabling environment. In many countries around the world, foreign exchange restrictions can be a major impediment to doing business. These factors are not captured by the *Enabling the Business of Agriculture* indicators but are well covered by other data initiatives that should be used together with the data presented to present a fuller picture of the enabling environment.

In many developing countries, many aspects of agricultural activity, from employment to the production and sale of goods, occur through informal channels. Burdensome regulations and lack of transparency, could be one reason for this, as could the quality of institutions, extension services and physical infrastructure. For example, regardless of the quality of transport regulations, lack of road infrastructure is a major barrier to transporting agricultural goods from the farm to markets. However, these elements are also not measured by the *Enabling the Business of Agriculture* indicators.

Enabling the Business of Agriculture has deliberately chosen to focus the indicators presented in this report on measuring laws and regulations that affect agribusiness firms that provide agricultural inputs, goods and services. The indicators constructed reflect elements that are under the direct influence of the government and can be compared across countries.

The chosen methodological approach has its benefits and limitations. The data presented are comparable and based on standardized assumptions. This methodology has proven to be successful in stimulating reform activity and allows countries to compare their performance on specific areas to other countries but also to monitor progress over time. Using standardized scenarios, however, can generalize and exclude some important context-specific information. To address some of these limitations, the data presented in this report and any recommendations that stem from it must be interpreted together with other important datasets as well as country relevant information.

What's next?

Enabling the Business of Agriculture 2017 presents scored indicators for eight topics in 62 countries around the world and introduces initial data collected for livestock, land, gender and environmental sustainability. The team will use the 2017 year to disseminate the data and findings, refine and synthesize indicators, expand topic and country coverage, and hold discussions with various stakeholders on the best ways going forward. The main areas for development identified relate to strengthening the processes for obtaining relevant feedback on: indicator

Figure 1 | Data collection, review and analysis

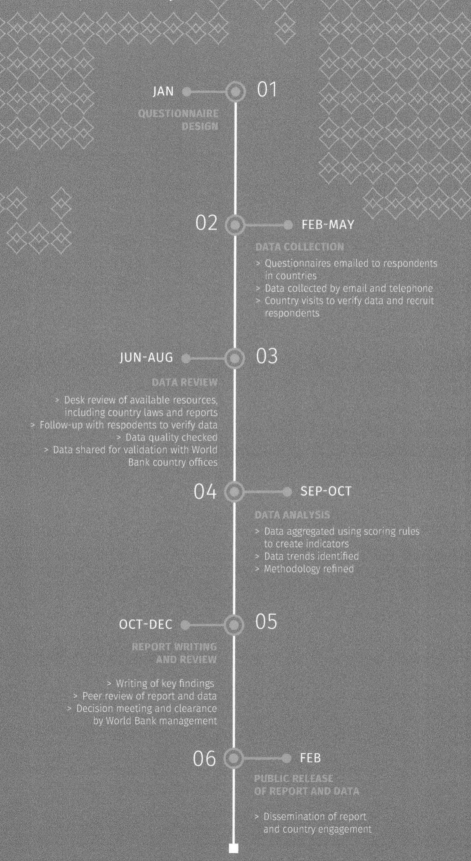

JAN ● ◎ 01

QUESTIONNAIRE
DESIGN

02 ◎ ● FEB-MAY

DATA COLLECTION

> Questionnaires emailed to respondents
  in countries
> Data collected by email and telephone
> Country visits to verify data and recruit
  respondents

JUN-AUG ● ◎ 03

DATA REVIEW

> Desk review of available resources,
  including country laws and reports
> Follow-up with respodents to verify data
> Data quality checked
> Data shared for validation with World
  Bank country offices

04 ◎ ● SEP-OCT

DATA ANALYSIS

> Data aggregated using scoring rules
  to create indicators
> Data trends identified
> Methodology refined

OCT-DEC ● ◎ 05

REPORT WRITING
AND REVIEW

> Writing of key findings
> Peer review of report and data
> Decision meeting and clearance
  by World Bank management

06 ◎ ● FEB

PUBLIC RELEASE
OF REPORT AND DATA

> Dissemination of report
  and country engagement

development and refinement; country selection and criteria used for future scale up; identifying countries where subnational analysis would be relevant and developing a subnational methodology.

Future reports will allow the team to monitor progress of countries in each of the topic areas by tracking regulatory reforms that affect the indicators measured.

Country coverage is also expected to expand and eventually cover between 80 and 100 countries.

Feedback is welcome on the data, methodology and overall project design to make future *Enabling the Business of Agriculture* reports even more useful. Feedback can be provided on the project website: http://eba.worldbank.org.

Table 3 | *EBA* questionnaires use a standard business case with assumptions

	ASSUMPTIONS USED TO STANDARDIZE THE BUSINESS CASE
SEED	*The seed variety:* > Is a maize variety developed by the private sector. > Is being registered for the first time in the country. > Has not been registered in any other country.[a]
FERTILIZER	*The business:* > Is a private sector company. > Is domestically registered in the country. > Imports fertilizer to sell in the country. > Has registered at least one new fertilizer product in the country. *The fertilizer product:* > Is a new chemical fertilizer product. > Is produced in a foreign country. > Is being registered for marketing purposes.
MACHINERY	*The business:* > Is a private sector company (manufacturer, dealer or distributor of agricultural machinery). > Is registered as a business in the country. > Imports agricultural tractors into the country. *The machinery:* > Is a two-axle/four-wheel drive agricultural tractor designed to furnish the power to pull, carry, propel or drive implements.
FINANCE	*Microfinance institutions (MFIs):* > Can take deposits, lend and provide other financial services to the public. > Are licensed to operate and supervised by a public authority. > Countries identified as having a high level of financial inclusion are not measured under the MFI indicator.[b] *Financial cooperatives:* > Are member-owned, not-for-profit cooperatives that provide savings, credit and other financial services to their members. *Agent banking:* > Is defined as the delivery of financial services through a partnership with a retail agent (or correspondent) to extend financial services to locations where bank branches would be uneconomical. > Countries identified as having a high level of financial inclusion are not measured under the agent banking indicator.[b] *Electronic money:* > Is stored and exchanged through an electronic device and not associated with a deposit account at any financial institution.

MARKETS	*The business:*

> Performs general agricultural trading activities.
> Does not directly engage in agricultural production, processing or retail activities.
> Does not operate in a special export processing zone.

The export product and trading partner:

> Is a combination of a plant-based agricultural product group and a partner country which represents the highest five-year average export value, based on UN Comtrade 2009–13 data.

The shipment:

> Is transported via a 20-foot full container-load.
> Weighs 10 metric tons or US $10,000, whichever is most appropriate.
> All packing material that requires fumigation (such as wood pallets) is assumed to be treated and marked with an approved international mark certifying that treatment. |
| **TRANSPORT** | *The business:*

> Is a private business entity or natural person whose core business is transporting goods by road for commercial purposes.
> Has met all formal requirements to start a business and perform general industrial or commercial activities.
> Has a maximum of five trucks; each truck has two axles and a maximum loading capacity of 15MT (metric tons). Trucks comprise a traction unit and a trailer.
> Transports agricultural products within the country, including perishable products. It does not transport fertilizers, pesticides, hazardous products or passengers.
> Carries out cross-border transport services with its largest agricultural border-adjacent trading partner.
> The company's main office is located in the country's largest business city.
> The trucks were first registered in the largest business city less than six months ago.
> All employed drivers have the domestically required driver's license to drive a 15MT vehicle.

The transported product:

> Is based on UN Comtrade's 2009–13 five-year average export value of major plant product groups.

The cross border trading partner:

> Is based on UN Comtrade's 2009–13 five-year average trade value of major plant product groups, as well as on a border-adjacent criterion. |
| **WATER** | *The water user:*

> Is a farm growing crops.
> Is a medium-size[c] farm for the country, with land area that falls between 2 and 10 hectares.
> Uses mechanical means to individually abstract water for irrigation.
> Is not located in a broader irrigation scheme.

The water source[d]:

> Is a river located 300 meters away from the farm; or
> Is a groundwater well located on the farm. |
| **ICT** | *The mobile operator:*

> Is a private company.
> Provides telecommunications services such as voice, SMS (Short Message Service) and data. |

Note:

a. If maize varieties are not being developed by the private sector in the country, an imported maize variety is considered, which may have been previously registered elsewhere.

b. High level of financial inclusion is defined are those countries that score 0.8 or higher, as measured by the average of the normalized value of the FINDEX variables "account at a financial institution (% of rural adult population)" and "account at financial institution (% of adult population)." Countries under this classification are as follows: Denmark, Greece, Italy, Korea, the Netherlands and Spain.

c. If medium-size farms in the country, as prescribed in any official farm-size classification system, deviate significantly from this given range, any exemption from permit requirements that may otherwise apply to small farms (for example, exemptions for smallholders or subsistence farmers) are not considered.

d. The choice between surface water and groundwater as a source for irrigation water is made based on the predominant irrigation water source for the country, based on the most recent available data from FAO Aquastat for the percentage of area equipped for irrigation by surface water and groundwater.

NOTES

1　Djankov 2016.

2　Bruhn 2011; Branstetter et al. 2014.

3　Amin 2009.

4　Djankov, Freund and Pham 2010; Hoekman and Nicita 2011.

5　Barseghyan 2008.

6　Byerlee, de Janvry and Sadoulet 2009.

7　Cullinan 1999; Diaz-Bonilla, Orden and Kwieciński 2014; Hafeez 2003; Christy, Mabaya, Wilson, Mutambatsere and Mhlanga 2009.

8　Djankov, McLiesh and Ramalho 2006; Jalilian, Kirkpatrick and Parker 2007; Loayza and Servén 2010.

9　Diaz-Bonilla, Orden and Kwieciński 2014; USAID 2015; Divanbeigi and Saliola 2016.

10　Loayza, Servén and Sugawara, 2009.

11　Aimin 2010.

12　World Bank 2007; Gollin and Rogerson, 2014.

13　Divanbeigi and Saliola 2016.

REFERENCES

Aimin, H. 2010. "Uncertainty, Risk Aversion and Risk Management in Agriculture." *Agriculture and Agricultural Science Procedia* 1: 152–56.

Amin, M. 2009. "Labor Regulation and Employment in India's Retail Stores." *Journal of Comparative Economics* 37 (1): 47–61.

Barseghyan, L. 2008. "Entry Costs and Cross-Country Differences in Productivity and Output." *Journal of Economic Growth* 13 (2): 145–167.

Branstetter, L. G., F. Lima, L. J. Taylor and A. Venâncio. 2014. "Do Entry Regulations Deter Entrepreneurship and Job Creation? Evidence from Recent Reforms in Portugal." *The Economic Journal* (July 16): 805–32.

Bruhn, M. 2011. "License to Sell: The Effect of Business Registration Reform on Entrepreneurial Activity in Mexico." *Review of Economics and Statistics* 93 (1): 382–86.

Byerlee, D., A. De Janvry and E. Sadoulet. 2009. "Agriculture for Development: Toward a New Paradigm." *Annual Review of Resource Economics* 1 (1): 15–31.

Christy, R., E. Mabaya, N. Wilson, E. Mutambatsere and N. Mhlanga. 2009. "Enabling Environments for Competitive Agro-Industries." In *Agro-Industries for Development*, edited by: C. Da Silva et al., pp. 136-85. Wallingford, UK: CABI.

Cullinan, C. 1999. "Law and Markets: Improving the Legal Framework for Agricultural Marketing." *FAO Agricultural Services Bulletin* 139, Rome.

Diaz-Bonilla, E., D. Orden and A. Kwiecinski. 2014. "Enabling Environment for Agricultural Growth and Competitiveness: Evaluation, Indicators and Indices." OECD Food, Agriculture and Fisheries Papers, No. 67. OECD, Paris.

Divanbeigi, R. and F. Saliola. 2016. "Regulation and the Transformation of Agriculture." Working Paper presented at FAO Conference on Rural Transformation, Agricultural and Food System Transition.

Djankov, S. 2016. "The Doing Business Project: How It Started: Correspondence." *Journal of Economic Perspectives*, 30 (1): 247–48.

Djankov, S., C. Freund and C. S. Pham. 2010. "Trading on Time." *The Review of Economics and Statistics* 92 (1): 166 –73.

Djankov, S., C. McLiesh and R. M. Ramalho. 2006. "Regulation and Growth." *Economics Letters* 92 (3): 395–401.

Gollin, D. and R. Rogerson. 2014. "Agriculture, Roads, and Economic Development in Uganda." In *African Successes: Sustainable Growth*, edited by S. Edwards, S. Johnson and D. N. Weil, chapter 2. Chicago: University of Chicago Press.

Hafeez, S. 2003. *The Efficacy of Regulations in Developing Countries*. New York: United Nations.

Hoekman, B. and A. Nicita. 2011. "Trade Policy, Trade Costs, and Developing Country Trade." *World Development* 39 (12): 2069–079.

Jalilian, H., C. Kirkpatrick and D. Parker. 2007. "The Impact of Regulation on Economic Growth in Developing Countries: A Cross-Country Analysis." *World Development* 35 (1): 87–103.

Loayza, N. and L. Servén, eds. 2010. *Business Regulation and Economic Performance*. Washington, D.C: World Bank.

Loayza, N., L. Servén and N. Sugawara. 2009. "Informality in Latin America and the Caribbean." World Bank Policy Research Working Paper Series. World Bank, Washington, DC.

USAID (United States Agency for International Development). 2015. "Agribusiness Regulation and Institutions (AGRI) Index." USAID, Washington, DC.

World Bank. 2007. *World Development Report 2008: Agriculture for Development*. Washington, DC: World Bank.

Abbreviations

AML/CFT	Anti-Money Laundering and Combatting Financing of Terrorism
ANTAM	Asian and Pacific Network for Testing of Agricultural Machinery
CAR	capital adequacy ratio
CDD	customer due diligence
CEMA	Comité Européen des groupements de constructeurs du machinisme agricole
CGAP	Consultative Group to Assist the Poor
CSAM	Centre for Sustainable Agricultural Mechanization
DTF	distance-to-frontier
DUS	distinctiveness, uniformity and stability
EAC	East African Community
EBA	Enabling the Business of Agriculture
ECA	Europe and Central Asia
ENTAM	European Network for Testing of Agricultural Machines
ePhyto	electronic phytosanitary certificate
FAO	Food and Agriculture Organization (of the UN)
FOPS	falling object protection structures
GHz	gigahertz
GNI	gross national income
ICID	International Commission on Irrigation and Drainage
ICT	information and communication technology
ICTA	Instituto de Ciencia y Tecnología
ICWE	International Conference on Water and the Environment
IFAD	International Fund for Agricultural Development
IFFCO	Indian Farmers Fertilizer Cooperative Limited
IFPRI	International Food Policy Research Institute
INERA	Institute for Environment and National Research (Burkina Faso)
IPPC	International Plant Protection Convention
IRU	International Road Transport Union
ISF	International Seed Federation
ISTA	International Seed Testing Association
ITPGRFA	International Treaty on Plant Genetic Resources for Food and Agriculture

IWMI	International Water Management Institute
IWRM	integrated water resources management
KYC	know your customer
LPI	Logistics Performance Index
MENA	Middle East and North Africa
MFI	microfinance institution
NASFAM	National Smallholder Farmers' Alliance of Malawi
NGO	nongovernmental organization
OECD	Organisation for Economic Co-operation and Development
OIE	World Organisation for Animal Health
PBR	plant breeders' rights
PCGS	partial credit guarantee system
PRA	pest risk analysis
RML	Reuters Market Light
ROPS	roll-over protection structures
SACCO	savings and credit cooperatives
SDG	Sustainable Development Goal
SMEs	small and medium enterprises
SMS	Short Message Service
SSA	Sub-Saharan Africa
TFP	total factor productivity
UNEP	United Nations Environment Programme
UNIDO	United Nations Industrial Development Organization
UNESCAP	United Nations Economic and Social Commission for Asia and the Pacific
UPOV	International Union for the Protection of New Varieties of Plants
VCU	value for cultivation and use
VMP	veterinary medicinal products
VRC	variety release committee
WAMU	West African Monetary Union
WTO	World Trade Organization
WUOs	water user organizations

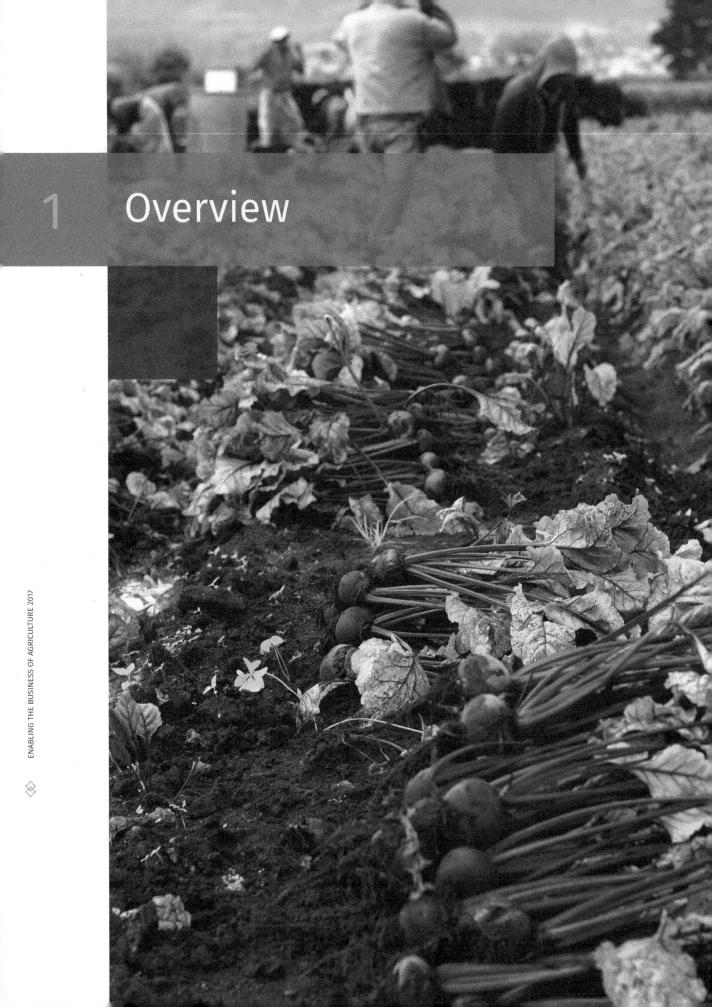

1 Overview

The global food system plays a central role in meeting the World Bank Group's twin goals of eliminating extreme poverty and boosting shared prosperity. Ending poverty will not be possible without raising the incomes of the rural poor, which account for 78% of poor people worldwide.[1] Schultz remarks that "most of the world's poor people earn their living from agriculture, so if we knew the economics of agriculture, we would know much of the economics of being poor."[2] Moreover, some 800 million people currently suffer from hunger across the globe[3] and the demand for greater variety and better quality food from a growing, urbanized population continues to increase. Agriculture has a strong record as an instrument for poverty reduction and can lead growth in agriculture-based countries.[4] In fact, growth originating from agriculture has been two-to-four times more effective at reducing poverty than that originating from other sectors.[5]

To meet the challenges ahead, food systems must not only be able to provide food security to the growing world population but they must also deliver diverse, nutritious diets that are affordable and accessible to all. Improved agricultural productivity must be coupled with increased resilience to climate change and reduced greenhouse gas emissions. In addition, for agriculture to deliver on its full potential, value chains must be strengthened, smallholder linkages to markets improved and agribusiness expanded.[6]

The agricultural sector is a significant source of employment, even as countries traverse different stages of agricultural structural transformation. Globally, 30% of all workers are employed in farming, while in low-income countries the share is 60%. As economies grow and develop, the importance of agribusiness relative to farming increases, leading to significant opportunities for employment growth and value added.[7] Central to achieving this will be the investments, performance and success of key players across agricultural value chains—from farmers, to input and service providers, to large and small agricultural businesses.

Enabling the Business of Agriculture 2017 (EBA17) aims to foster a more conducive environment for agribusiness. By providing key data on regulatory frameworks that are globally comparable and actionable, it strengthens the information base that can be used for policy dialogue and reform. Such efforts can stimulate private sector activity and lead to more efficient and effective agricultural value chains.

A produce farm in Chimaltenango, Guatemala.
Photo Maria Fleischmann / World Bank.

Table 1.1 | List of EBA indicators

	"LEGAL" INDICATORS	"EFFICIENCY" INDICATORS
SEED	> Plant breeding > Variety registration > Seed quality control	> Time and cost to register new varieties
FERTILIZER	> Fertilizer registration > Quality control of fertilizer > Importing and distributing fertilizer	> Time and cost to register a new fertilizer product
MACHINERY	> Tractor operation > Tractor testing and standards > Tractor import	> Time and cost to obtain type approval > Time and cost to register a tractor
FINANCE	> Branchless banking > Movable collateral > Non-bank lending institutions	
MARKETS	> Producer organizations > Plant protection > Agricultural trade	> Documents, time and cost to export agricultural goods
TRANSPORT	> Trucking licenses and operations > Cross-border transportation	> Time and cost to obtain trucking licenses > Time and cost to obtain cross-border licenses
WATER	> Integrated water resource management > Individual water use for irrigation	
ICT	> Information and communication technology	

EBA focuses on legal barriers for businesses that operate in agriculture in 62 countries and across 12 topics, including seed, fertilizer, machinery, finance, markets, transport, water, information and communication technology (ICT), environmental sustainability, gender, land and livestock. EBA's dataset features two types of indicators (table 1.1). Legal indicators primarily reflect the text of laws and regulations[8] and assess their conformity with a number of global regulatory good practices. Efficiency indicators measure the transaction costs that firms have to bear to comply with national regulations on the ground. Transaction costs are expressed in time or monetary units, such as the time and cost needed to comply with requirements on agricultural exports.

After a pilot exercise conducted in 2013–14 covering 10 countries,[9] *EBA16* included 40 countries and six scored topics: seed, fertilizer, machinery, finance, markets and transport. In *EBA17*, country coverage is expanded to 62 countries with two new topics added to the scoring: water and ICT. In addition, efficiency indicators measuring transaction costs are expanded and scored for the first time.

Countries with more agribusiness-friendly regulations

EBA scores countries based on both the quality and efficiency of their regulatory systems, through two aggregate measures per topic: (i) the distance-to-frontier (DTF) score or absolute distance of a country to the best performance on each topic (see appendix A); and (ii) the topic ranking that results from ordering DTF scores (see table 1.2).

Agriculture's relevance varies significantly across countries. Based on the *World Development Report 2008*[10] and combining data on agriculture's contribution to GDP and the share of active population dedicated to agriculture, EBA categorizes countries into three groups: agriculture-based, transforming and urbanized. Urbanized countries are on average at the frontier of good regulatory practices across all EBA topics (figure 1.1). They are followed by transforming countries. Agriculture-based countries have more room to improve the quality of their regulatory frameworks and decrease transaction costs. However, agriculture-based countries have shown on average a

Figure 1.1 | Urbanized countries show better agriculture regulations than transforming and agriculture-based countries

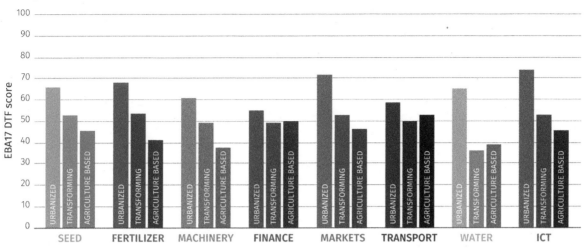

Source: EBA database.

Note: EBA countries are divided into three groups. Urbanized countries have a contribution of agriculture to GDP below 25% and a share of active population in agriculture below 25%; transforming countries have a contribution of agriculture to GDP below 25% and a share of active population in agriculture over 25%; agriculture-based countries have a contribution of agriculture to GDP over 25% and a share of active population in agriculture over 25%. The EBA17 distance-to-frontier (DTF) score is the average of the DTF scores of the following topics: seed, fertilizer, machinery, finance, markets, transport, water and information communication and technology (ICT). The correlation between EBA scores and agricultural transformation phase is 0.61.

better or similar performance compared to transforming countries in the finance, water and transport topics and are closing the gap on markets. Kenya, Malawi and Mozambique have comprehensive legislation regulating water use permits. Burkina Faso, Côte d'Ivoire and Ethiopia are among the top 10 countries in terms of the efficiency in obtaining a cross-border trucking license.

Countries' regulatory quality is associated with economic growth[11] and levels of development.[12] High-income countries have better agribusiness regulations as measured by EBA,[13] and this outcome is shown across all topics. However, there are exceptions; some countries perform better on EBA indicators than what their income level may suggest. That is the case of Vietnam for fertilizer, machinery and transport; Kenya for seed, finance, water and ICT; and Kyrgyz Republic for finance, markets and machinery. On the other hand, despite its very solid regulations on ICT operating licenses and plant protection, Chile does not have a framework for fertilizer registration or tractor type approval.

In terms of regions, OECD high-income countries have on average the most agribusiness-friendly regulation (figure 1.2). They all share regulation that promotes quality control, facilitates trade and enables entry and operations in agricultural markets. Spain ranks among the top six countries globally in all eight EBA-scored topics. However, OECD high-income countries also have room for improvement. Romania is among the top three performers globally in terms of regulations for transport, machinery and ICT, but it takes more than three years to register a new fertilizer product, while the global average is below one year.

This performance is mainly due to field testing (not required in best practice countries) and the delays associated with the Gazette notification. Poland has the most comprehensive and efficient regulations on tractor operation, import, testing and standards, but lacks a regulatory framework for warehouse receipts to complement the existing collateral regime to obtain a loan for agricultural production, as well as legislation on deposit-taking microfinance institutions (MFIs).

Following OECD high-income countries, Europe and Central Asia as well as Latin America and the Caribbean regions show a number of good regulatory practices. For example, all countries in Europe and Central Asia have implemented good regulatory practices on tractor imports, not requiring import permits or importers to register in addition to their general business license. In addition, both Bosnia and Herzegovina and Serbia are among the top five countries globally in the fertilizer area, due to best practice regulation on registration and quality control. The fertilizer registration process takes about one month in both countries, and costs only 0.5% and 5.3% income per capita, respectively. The Kyrgyz Republic ranks in the top 15 for markets and machinery, showing efficient processes for exporting agricultural goods and tractor registration, but it is placed in the bottom 10 for seed and transport due to the lack of regulations on seed quality control and trucking licenses. The Russian Federation performs well in EBA's machinery, water, and ICT topics.

Countries from Latin America and the Caribbean have comprehensive regulation on financial inclusion and water management. In fact, Colombia and Mexico score

Table 1.2 | Country rankings on EBA topics by economies

	SEED	FERTILIZER	MACHINERY	FINANCE	MARKETS	TRANSPORT	WATER	ICT
ARMENIA	28	53	30	52	23	56	5	31
BANGLADESH	54	35	49	23	21	45	56	37
BENIN	55	61	53	41	34	50	38	31
BOLIVIA	25	45	52	13	22	15	43	30
BOSNIA AND HERZEGOVINA	56	1	34	60	11	32	6	31
BURKINA FASO	57	56	32	41	37	12	47	59
BURUNDI	40	42	50	59	55	30	33	52
CAMBODIA	38	26	44	48	46	34	37	43
CAMEROON	58	48	37	51	41	31	44	52
CHILE	29	54	28	46	9	46	28	15
COLOMBIA	27	8	45	1	17	10	3	9
CÔTE D'IVOIRE	30	45	35	18	60	19	49	22
DENMARK	3	3	8	37	6	3	24	6
EGYPT, ARAB REP.	37	33	26	56	49	61	55	57
ETHIOPIA	39	59	25	27	51	21	34	62
GEORGIA	13	21	42	39	19	38	48	6
GHANA	48	34	38	16	54	59	30	22
GREECE	14	9	5	4	5	14	12	1
GUATEMALA	26	10	57	24	14	58	58	21
HAITI	61	58	43	54	57	62	57	43
INDIA	21	18	21	15	43	49	53	18
ITALY	4	6	11	6	4	4	10	6
JORDAN	22	17	33	62	25	22	41	22
KAZAKHSTAN	35	15	9	50	16	55	18	22
KENYA	7	43	29	10	59	16	4	12
KOREA, REP.	8	14	19	12	10	39	9	11
KYRGYZ REPUBLIC	53	19	14	8	13	56	36	43
LAO PDR	59	27	59	47	35	26	40	59
LIBERIA	62	62	60	35	62	59	61	31
MALAWI	50	44	23	20	33	41	19	50
MALAYSIA	45	50	18	28	40	54	45	22

	SEED	FERTILIZER	MACHINERY	FINANCE	MARKETS	TRANSPORT	WATER	ICT
MALI	52	23	61	41	44	44	50	52
MEXICO	24	24	51	9	3	20	2	9
MOROCCO	20	51	17	57	24	8	8	18
MOZAMBIQUE	23	47	47	25	30	33	21	22
MYANMAR	34	30	62	61	53	51	62	37
NEPAL	46	41	36	34	28	52	52	43
NETHERLANDS	1	7	7	17	1	9	20	1
NICARAGUA	44	11	48	36	20	36	23	43
NIGER	49	55	55	45	39	17	39	43
NIGERIA	42	31	16	22	48	43	46	37
PERU	10	52	58	2	27	5	11	15
PHILIPPINES	11	22	13	33	38	37	17	37
POLAND	5	2	1	21	7	24	13	1
ROMANIA	6	28	3	11	12	2	7	1
RUSSIAN FEDERATION	18	20	12	38	18	40	15	15
RWANDA	60	38	41	7	47	27	32	50
SENEGAL	36	60	54	41	36	35	42	37
SERBIA	19	4	2	40	8	13	14	12
SPAIN	2	5	6	3	2	1	1	1
SRI LANKA	47	36	39	58	58	48	54	59
SUDAN	41	56	27	53	61	47	59	57
TAJIKISTAN	51	49	22	55	32	6	35	56
TANZANIA	17	37	40	5	56	25	22	18
THAILAND	32	16	24	29	52	53	60	31
TURKEY	12	13	4	32	29	28	51	31
UGANDA	31	40	31	31	45	18	26	22
UKRAINE	33	32	15	26	26	42	29	43
URUGUAY	9	25	56	19	15	11	25	37
VIETNAM	43	12	10	30	31	7	27	12
ZAMBIA	16	39	46	14	50	23	16	22
ZIMBABWE	15	29	20	49	42	29	31	52

Source: EBA database.

among the top 10 countries globally within these two topics. For example, Colombia has developed comprehensive rules enabling non-bank correspondents to provide financial services on behalf of a commercial bank; Mexico has developed a modern and comprehensive water regulatory framework anchored by the 1992 National Water Law, although some implementation challenges remain. Some countries in the region lag behind in several areas. Guatemala lacks a general framework for tractor type approval and registration, and trucking licenses, despite solid fertilizer quality control and plant protection regulations.

The regions lagging behind on EBA scores are: South Asia, Sub-Saharan Africa, and East Asia and Pacific. On average, countries from these regions have less than half of the regulatory good practices promoted by EBA. This situation mainly affects regulations related to quality control and operations in the different agricultural markets that EBA measures. It is most time-consuming to complete the process of exporting agricultural goods in Sub-Saharan African countries, taking 6.0 days on average, and the documents are most expensive in South Asia and Sub-Saharan Africa, costing 2.5% income per capita. The process for obtaining tractor type approval is the lengthiest and most expensive in South Asia (270 days and 604% income per capita, versus 21 days and 7% income per capita in East Asia and Pacific). This year EBA conducted a pilot study in India for all EBA topics to track subnational differences and will build on it for future data collection and analytical work (box 1.1).

In Sub-Saharan Africa, there is great variation across countries measured and topics. In the region, 7 of the 21 countries do not have a clearly designated government agency to conduct pest surveillance, and only Senegal and Tanzania have a publicly available database with information on plant pests and diseases. However, last year Sub-Saharan African countries adopted more regulatory reforms in plant protection than in other regions. Kenya is the best performer on EBA indicators in the region. It is among the 5 top performers in the water topic, thanks to a series of regulatory reforms on water resource management and a permit system that started in 2002 with the introduction of a new Water Act. On the other hand, the country still has great potential to improve its regulatory framework on fertilizer registration and plant protection, as well as to streamline the process related to exporting agricultural products. In East Asia and Pacific, Vietnam shares international best practices in the areas of fertilizer registration (from the legal and efficiency standpoint), efficiency of tractor registration and type approval, as well as trucking licenses both for domestic and cross-border transportation.

Benin, Arab Republic of Egypt, Haiti, Liberia, Myanmar, Sri Lanka and Sudan are the countries with the greatest room for improvement—on average—in all areas that EBA measures. For example, Haiti, Liberia and Myanmar (all conflict-affected countries) do not have any of the good regulatory practices on plant protection and very few in the areas of integrated water resource management, financial inclusion or trucking licenses.

Figure 1.2 | OECD high-income countries rank highest on EBA, followed by Europe and Central Asia, and Latin America and the Caribbean

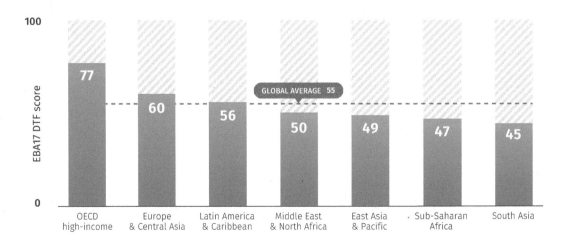

Source: EBA database.

Note: The EBA17 distance-to-frontier (DTF) score is the average of the DTF scores of the following topics: seed, fertilizer, machinery, finance, markets, transport, water and information communication and technology.

EBA and regulatory quality

The EBA overall DTF score provides a synthetic measure of the quality and efficiency of countries' regulatory environment for agriculture. Its results are well correlated with other measurements of regulatory quality for the whole economy, such as the regulatory quality component of the *Worldwide Governance Indicators (WGI)* and *Doing Business*,[14] which measures regulatory quality and efficiency for businesses that perform general industrial or commercial activities.

One potential criticism relates to the fact that what is written in the books does not necessarily reflect what happens in practice. In this regard, the relationship between EBA and the WGI rule of law component[15] was analyzed and noted that where good regulatory measures are in place, laws also tend to be better enforced (figure 1.3).

Efficiency, quality control, operations and trade

Legal indicators in the eight EBA-scored topics can be distributed across three cross-cutting categories, namely: (i) **operations** indicators that measure the requirements for local companies to enter the market and develop agribusiness activities;[16] (ii) **quality control** indicators that assess regulations governing plant protection, water resource management, safety standards for agricultural machinery and quality control associated with seed, fertilizer and truck operators;[17] and (iii) **trade** indicators that measure

Box 1.1 | Subnational EBA study in India

For the first time, EBA conducted a subnational pilot study to assess how sensitive EBA indicators are to differences among different locations within a country. Four Indian states were selected: Bihar, Maharashtra, Odisha and Uttar Pradesh. For topics where EBA considers a case study that assumes that the company operates in the country's largest business city, the following cities were selected on the basis of population data: Patna (Bihar), Mumbai (Maharashtra), Bhubaneswar (Odisha) and Lucknow (Uttar Pradesh). When discrepancies were found across Indian states in specific topics, Maharashtra data were considered as the proxy for India for the cross-country results presented in this *EBA17* report.

The main result of this pilot study is that while the legal and regulatory framework for agriculture and agribusiness is largely harmonized across the country, some differences emerge regarding the implementation of administrative procedures by state-level or local government agencies.

Laws governing entry and operations, quality control and trade for fertilizer, machinery, seed, transport and finance are either federal or state-level with very similar provisions across states. For example, in the finance area, the Federal Guidelines for Engaging of Business Correspondents 2010 and the Payment and Settlement Systems Act 2007 apply to all Indian states, providing global best practice for the branchless banking indicator. However, financial cooperatives are governed by state-level laws; they are similar across the four states analyzed, lacking a deposit insurance system and disclosure requirements.

Some differences exist in the area of water and environment. Under India's Constitution, water management is largely decentralized to the state level. Across the four states, only Odisha has established the legal foundation for a water use permit system that applies to farms that are medium-size or larger. In only two out of the four states (Maharashtra and Odisha) does the legal framework include mandates for the establishment of basin-level institutions, and only Maharashtra and Uttar Pradesh set a legal requirement for the preparation of basin plans and the creation and maintenance of a registry of water users. Within the environmental sustainability topic, plant genetic resources aspects are managed at the national level, but some differences persist in soil health management; namely, only Odisha and Maharashtra have a specific mandate for the development of land use plans. Other areas, such as producer organizations, are regulated by both central and state-level governments.

The time and costs to comply with government regulations vary across the four states in some EBA topics. For example, registering a tractor costs 500 Rupees and takes seven days in Bihar, while it costs only 200 Rupees and takes two days on average in Uttar Pradesh. Also the cost of tractor roadworthiness inspection is higher in Bihar (300 Rupees) than in the other three states (200 Rupees). The cost to obtain a truck-level state permit in Maharashtra is slightly lower (18,300 Rupees) than in Bihar, Uttar Pradesh (both at 20,000 Rupees) or Odisha (23,000 Rupees). While regulations related to plant protection and export documents remain national, phytosanitary certificates are issued by local government offices. There are other specific state-level licenses and permits, such as those related to domestic agricultural markets and inter-state transport.

Figure 1.3 | Higher EBA scores are associated with better performance in other measures of regulatory quality

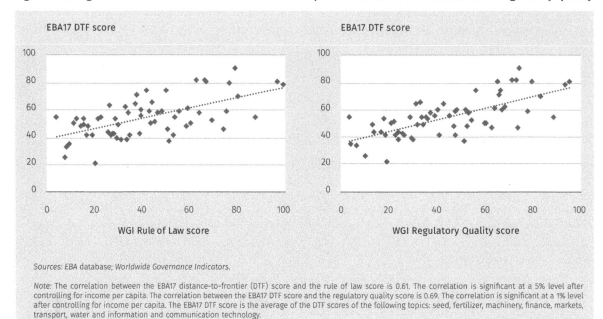

Sources: EBA database; Worldwide Governance Indicators.

Note: The correlation between the EBA17 distance-to-frontier (DTF) score and the rule of law score is 0.61. The correlation is significant at a 5% level after controlling for income per capita. The correlation between the EBA17 DTF score and the regulatory quality score is 0.69. The correlation is significant at a 1% level after controlling for income per capita. The EBA17 DTF score is the average of the DTF scores of the following topics: seed, fertilizer, machinery, finance, markets, transport, water and information and communication technology.

trade restrictions related to the export of agricultural products, the import of fertilizer and tractors, and cross-border transport rights.[18] Efficiency indicators measure the time and cost needed to comply with the processes measured by EBA.[19]

EBA indicators advocate for regulations that promote efficient regulatory processes that support agribusinesses while at the same time ensuring safety and quality control. The importance of the three cross-cutting EBA legal categories plus efficiency indicators has been clearly stated,[20] however, it is not clear whether they are entirely compatible with one another or if success in one may come at the expense of another. Data show that rules that facilitate entry and operations in the market are compatible with regulations that promote safety and quality control (table 1.3). These rules are complements rather than substitutes. And countries with higher scores on operations and quality control tend also to have more effective trade requirements.

There is also a high correlation between the three legal dimensions combined (operations, quality control and trade) and the efficiency of the processes captured (figure 1.4), showing that solid regulatory frameworks tend to be present in countries that also have efficient processes. However, there are exceptions, for example: Malawi has laws related to seed and fertilizer registration containing some key elements on the books, but it is the country where it is most expensive to register both new seed varieties and fertilizer products. In Sri Lanka, on the other hand, while regulatory procedures such as tractor registration and trucking licensing are efficient and affordable, the country's laws and regulations are not robust enough in some areas covered by EBA, as shown by the lack of legislation on agent banking activities or operation of warehouse receipts. Both the quality and the efficiency dimensions of business regulations, as captured by the EBA indicators, show significant correlations with countries' agricultural productivity. On average, agricultural productivity is higher

Table 1.3 | Correlation across EBA cross-cutting dimensions

	OPERATIONS	QUALITY CONTROL	TRADE
QUALITY CONTROL	0.86		
TRADE	0.63	0.67	
EFFICIENCY	0.68	0.70	0.46

Source: EBA database.

Note: All correlations are significant after controlling for income per capita.

Figure 1.4 | EBA regulatory quality and efficiency go hand-in-hand

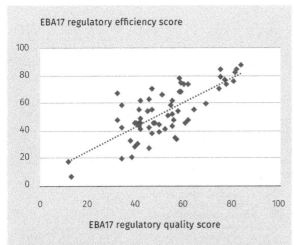

EBA17 regulatory efficiency score

EBA17 regulatory quality score

Source: EBA database.

Note: The correlation between EBA17 regulatory quality scores and EBA17 regulatory efficiency scores is 0.76. The correlation is significant at a 1% level after controlling for income per capita. The regulatory quality score captures the robustness of laws and regulations related to seed registration, fertilizer registration, tractor operation, testing and standards, and agricultural trade, as well as trucking licenses and cross-border transportation. The regulatory efficiency score measures the time and costs to complete the regulatory processes that correspond to the areas covered by the aforementioned regulatory quality score, including registering a new seed variety, registering a new chemical fertilizer product, registering a tractor, obtaining a tractor type approval, acquiring per-shipment agricultural export documents and obtaining domestic and cross-border trucking licenses.

Figure 1.5 | Countries with better regulations on markets also perform better in fertilizer

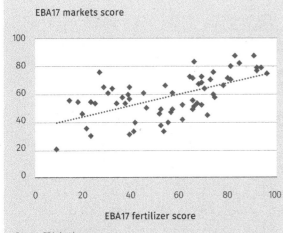

EBA17 markets score

EBA17 fertilizer score

Source: EBA database.

Note: The correlation between the EBA17 markets score and the EBA17 fertilizer score is 0.60. The correlation is significant at a 1% level after controlling for income per capita.

when transaction costs are lower and countries adhere to a higher number of regulatory good practices.[21]

Each EBA indicator measures a different aspect of the agricultural regulatory environment. The DTF scores and associated rankings of a country can vary, sometimes significantly, across indicator sets. However, the correlation among any pair of EBA indicators is positive and ranges between 0.13 and 0.68. For example, solid and efficient rules on plant protection and trade in agricultural products are associated with better rules for importing and controlling the quality of essential agricultural inputs, such as fertilizer (figure 1.5). Reforms in different areas that EBA measures are complementary.

Nondiscriminatory measures

The design and implementation of nondiscriminatory and inclusive laws and regulations are key to encouraging competition, boosting investor confidence and facilitating agricultural investments in the long run.[22]

EBA data assess the existence of nondiscriminatory measures in agricultural laws and regulations that can assist domestic, foreign or small-scale private sector operators in doing business, as well as the ones that can promote women's participation in certain agricultural activities. Such measures include allowing the private sector to register fertilizer, granting plant breeders' rights or transport licenses based on the same rules for domestic and foreign applicants, establishing an affordable capital requirement to create a financial cooperative or creating a quota or mechanism to promote women's participation in leadership roles in producer organizations (see appendix C).

Spain has in place the highest number of the nondiscriminatory measures in agriculture (figure 1.6). Out of the 29 good practices that EBA covered, more than 27 are included in its agricultural laws and regulations, with only a few legal obstacles that prevent domestic or small-sized companies from engaging in operations in the agriculture sector. Sub-Saharan African countries including Tanzania and Zambia are also among the top performers in this area. For example, there is no minimum capital requirement to establish a producer organization in Tanzania, and Zambia grants transport, backhauling, triangular and transit rights to foreign transport companies. On the other hand, countries such as Haiti, Malaysia and Myanmar have greater potential for improvement. For example, in Malaysia, foreign companies are not yet allowed to obtain a trucking license, and in Haiti, non-bank businesses cannot issue e-money.

Figure 1.6 | Spain has the most nondiscriminatory agricultural laws and regulations, while Haiti has the greatest potential for improvement

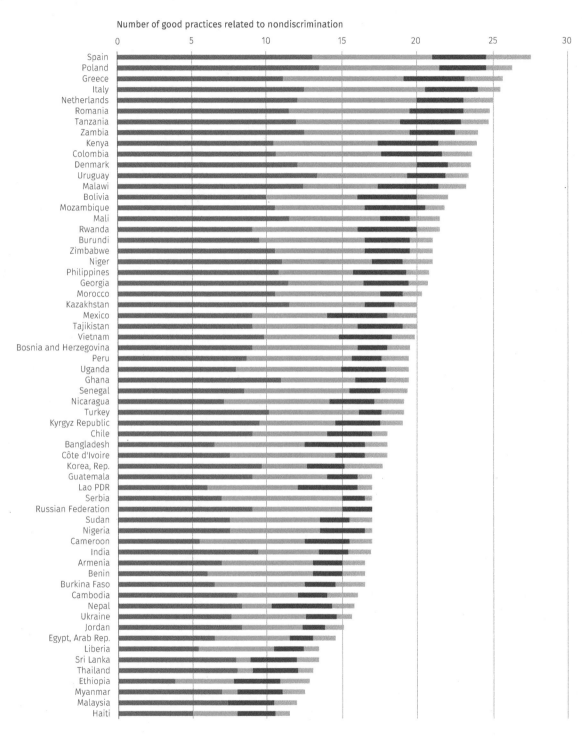

Number of good practices related to nondiscrimination

■ Domestic private sector aspect (number of good practices) (out of 14)   ■ Foreign private sector aspect (number of good practices) (out of 8)

■ Small businesses aspect (number of good practices) (out of 4)   ■ Gender aspect (number of good practices) (out of 3)

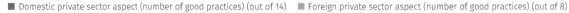

Source: EBA database.

Access to information

Research suggests that easier access to regulatory information is associated with greater quality of business regulation and less corruption.[23] Farmers and agribusinesses, many of them located in remote rural areas, could potentially save significant time and cost if they had the possibility to comply with administrative processes electronically or access information such as registries and official fees online.

EBA measures good practices related to the accessibility of information in the agriculture sector. These practices range from the availability of catalogues, databases and fee schedules that can inform the private sector of regulatory processes and help them make business decisions, to the provision of e-services including online issuance of the phytosanitary certificate or electronic application for the renewal of transport licenses, as well as legal obligations to disclose information including the effective interest rate of loans issued by financial cooperatives (see appendix C).

OECD high-income countries on average have the highest number of good practices related to access to regulatory information (figure 1.7). In all eight countries, there is publicly available information such as water resource monitoring results, regulated quarantine pest lists and official fee schedules for seed certification. In other regions, however, greater effort is needed to make regulatory information more accessible to the public. For example, in Sub-Saharan Africa and the Middle East and North Africa, where 24 countries were studied, half of the countries' laws do not specify a method for calculating the water abstraction charge, and only Kenya and Mozambique currently have an online fertilizer catalogue.

Putting EBA data in context

EBA data are collected and analyzed following standardized case studies, and the same EBA indicators are presented for all 62 countries, aiming at ensuring comparability across countries and time. However, it is essential for policymakers to interpret EBA scores in conjunction with more detailed contextual information to better prioritize the policy areas in need of reform.

For example, among the potential contextual data available for water, the level of inter-annual water variability or the level of water stress could be important factors to consider when defining regulatory priorities on water resources management and permitting systems for irrigation water use, as measured by EBA. In certain cases, reform towards a more comprehensive legal framework could take on higher importance in countries with low EBA water scores and high inter-annual variability, such as Haiti, India and Jordan (upper-left quadrant of figure 1.8, in red), while it may not be the primary focus for countries with an already robust legal framework combined with smaller challenges related to inter-annual water resources variability, such as in Bosnia and Herzegovina, the Netherlands or Vietnam (lower-right quadrant of figure 1.8, in green).

EBA data also relate to the international context through the Sustainable Development Goals (SDGs), adopted by United Nations Member States to guide policies and regulations on the development agenda for the next 15 years. Agriculture connects all 17 SDGs and is at the core of SDG1 and SDG2, which call for ending extreme poverty and hunger. The link between EBA and the SDGs is twofold: on the one hand, the SDG targets were considered in the refinement of EBA's indicators; on the other hand, specific data points from EBA may serve as metrics for tracking countries' progress on SDG objectives (box 1.2).

Conclusion

EBA's main objective is to measure and benchmark regulations that impact agribusiness globally. It can serve as a tool for countries to take stock of their current regulatory environment and promote change. Higher income and urbanized countries tend to have more agribusiness-friendly regulations, although there are numerous exceptions. Most countries have some good practices but EBA indicators also highlight areas that could be improved. A good way to start is through the introduction of regulations that promote quality control and nondiscrimination, efficient administrative procedures and access to information. EBA data demonstrate that all these objectives are compatible. The next chapters show how they can be achieved.

Figure 1.7 | OECD high-income countries on average have the most good practices related to access to regulatory information

Average number of good practices related to access to information

Source: EBA database.

Figure 1.8 | Use of water variability data to inform regulatory priorities

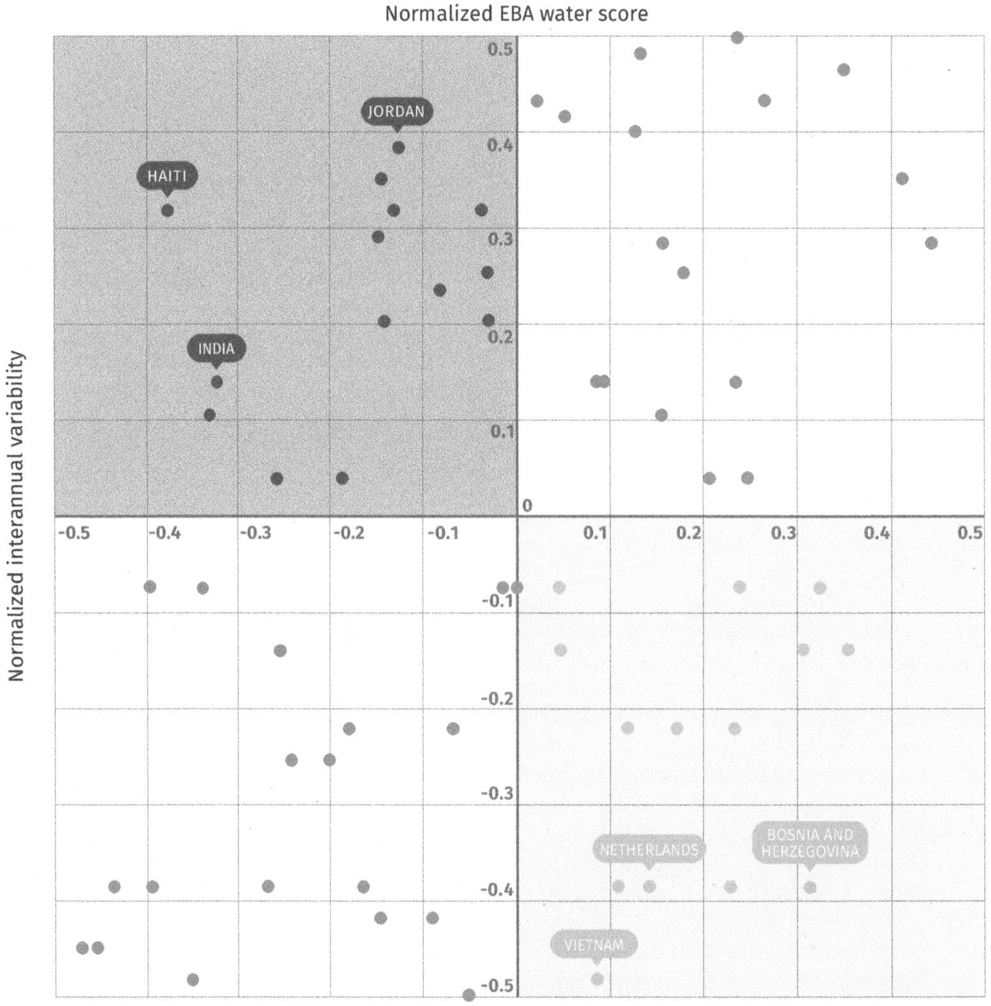

Normalized EBA water score

Sources: EBA database; FAO Aquastat/WRI 2016.

Note: Interannual variability is an indicator of the variation in water supply between years, created by the World Resources Institute (WRI). It ranges from 0–5, where 0 is lowest and 5 is highest (most variable). For plotting, both interannual variability values and EBA water scores have been normalized to a scale between -0.5 and 0.5.

Box 1.2 | Sustainable Development Goals on EBA topics

EBA has links to a number of Sustainable Development Goals (SDGs), including Target 1.4 (Access to Basic Services), Target 2.5 (Genetic Diversity of Cultivated Plants), Target 6.3 (Improving Water Quality), Target 6.4 (Efficient and Sustainable Water Withdrawals), Target 6.5 (Integrated Water Resource Management), Target 9.3 (Enterprise Access to Financial Services) and Target 9c (Access to Information and Communications Technology), among others.

For example, SDG Target 2.5 calls to "maintain the genetic diversity of seeds, cultivated plants...and their related wild species, including through soundly managed and diversified seed and plant banks... and promote access to and fair and equitable sharing of benefits arising from the utilization of genetic resources." EBA measures the existence of a national genebank or collection system for plant genetic resources, their data's availability online as well as the access by private companies to the germplasm preserved in the gene banks (figure 1.2.1).

SDG Targets 6.4 and 6.5 call for efforts to "substantially increase water-use efficiency...and ensure sustainable withdrawals and supply of freshwater" as well as the implementation of "water resources management at all levels." EBA measures the regulation of water use permits, the legal requirements and establishment in practice of basin institutions, basin plans, water resource inventories and water user registries. However, a big gap remains between the legal mandate and the implementation in practice in many countries (figure 1.2.2).

Figure 1.2.1 | Wide regional variations observed in the establishment of national genebanks

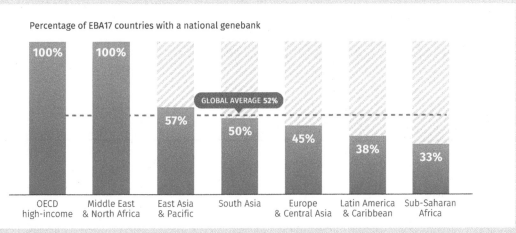

Percentage of EBA17 countries with a national genebank

Source: EBA database.

Figure 1.2.2 | Implementation gap in water information is higher in lower-income countries

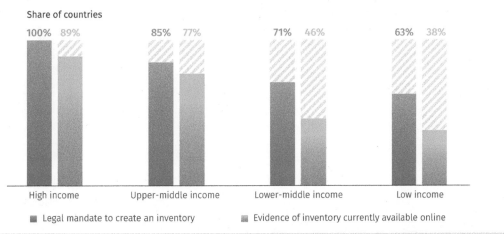

Share of countries

■ Legal mandate to create an inventory   ▨ Evidence of inventory currently available online

Source: EBA database.

NOTES

1 World Bank 2015.

2 Schultz 1980.

3 FAO, IFAD and WFP 2015.

4 World Bank 2007.

5 World Bank 2015.

6 *Ibid.*

7 *Ibid.*

8 Some data points under these indicators refer to good practices related to the accessibility of information in the agriculture sector (see section on "access to information" in this overview).

9 Ethiopia, Guatemala, Morocco, Mozambique, Nepal, the Philippines, Rwanda, Spain, Uganda and Ukraine.

10 World Bank 2007.

11 Eifert 2009; Divanbeigi and Ramalho 2015.

12 Acemoglu, Johnson and Robinson 2005; Aghion and Durlauf 2009.

13 The correlation between the *EBA17* overall DTF score and income per capita is 0.65.

14 The correlation between *EBA17* DTF score and the *Doing Business17* DTF score is 0.75. The correlation is significant at a 1% level after controlling for income per capita.

15 The rule of law indicator captures perceptions of the extent to which agents have confidence in and abide by the rules of society and in particular the quality of contract enforcement, property rights, the police and the courts, as well as the likelihood of crime and violence (http://info.worldbank.org/governance/wgi/index.aspx#doc).

16 The full list of EBA indicators under the operations category is as follows: plant breeding, variety registration, fertilizer registration, tractor operation, branchless banking, movable collateral, non-bank lending institutions, producer organizations, trucking licenses and operations, individual water use for irrigation and ICT.

17 The full list of EBA indicators under the quality control category is as follows: seed quality control, quality control of fertilizer, tractor testing and standards, plant protection and integrated water resource management.

18 The full list of EBA indicators under the trade category is as follows: importing and distributing fertilizer, tractor import, agricultural trade and cross-border transportation.

19 The full list of EBA indicators under the efficiency category is as follows: time and cost to register new seed varieties; time and cost to register a new fertilizer product; time and cost to obtain type approval; time and cost to register a tractor; documents, time and cost to export agricultural goods; time and cost to obtain trucking licenses; and time and cost to obtain cross-border licenses.

20 Ciccone and Papaioannou 2007; Klapper, Laeven and Raghuram 2006; Fisman and Sarria-Allende 2010.

21 Divanbeigi and Saliola 2016.

22 OECD 2014; United Nations 2013.

23 Geginat and Saltane 2016.

REFERENCES

Acemoglu, D., S. Johnson and J. A. Robinson. 2005. "Institutions as a Fundamental Cause of Long-Run Growth." *Handbook of Economic Growth* 1A, 386–472.

Aghion, P. and S. Durlauf. 2009. "From Growth Theory to Policy Design." Working Paper 57. Commission on Growth and Development, Washington, DC.

Ciccone, A. and E. Papaioannou. 2007. "Red Tape and Delayed Entry." Working Paper 758. European Central Bank, Frankfurt am Main.

Divanbeigi, R. and F. Saliola. 2016. "Regulation and the Transformation of Agriculture." Working Paper presented at FAO Conference on Rural Transformation, Agricultural and Food System Transition.

Divanbeigi, R. and R. Ramalho. 2015. "Business Regulations and Growth." Policy Research Working Paper 7299. World Bank, Washington, DC.

Eifert, B. 2009. "Do Regulatory Reforms Stimulate Investment and Growth? Evidence from the Doing Business Data, 2003–07." Working Paper 159. Center for Global Development, Washington, DC.

FAO (Food and Agriculture Organization), IFAD (International Fund for Agricultural Development) and WFP (World Food Programme). 2015. *The State of Food Insecurity in the World 2015. Meeting the 2015 International Hunger Targets: Taking Stock of Uneven Progress.* Rome: FAO.

Fisman, R. and V. Sarria-Allende. 2010. "Regulation of Entry and the Distortion of Industrial Organization." *Journal of Applied Economics* 13 (1): 91–111.

Geginat, C. and V. Saltane. 2016. "'Open for Business?'— Transparent Government and Business Regulation." *Journal of Economics and Business* 88: 1–21.

Klapper, L., L. Laeven and R. Raghuram. 2006. "Entry as a Barrier to Entrepreneurship." *Journal of Financial Economics* 82: 591–629.

OECD. 2014. *Policy Framework for Investment in Agriculture.* Paris: OECD Publishing.

Schultz, Theodore W. 1980. "Nobel Lecture: The Economics of Being Poor." *Journal of Political Economy* 88(4): 639-651.

United Nations. 2013. *World Economic and Social Survey 2013: Sustainable Development Challenges.* New York: United Nations.

World Bank. 2007. *World Development Report 2008: Agriculture for Development.* Washington, DC: World Bank.

——. 2015. *Ending Poverty and Hunger by 2030.* Washington DC: World Bank.

2 Seed

Tests completed in Uganda in 2015 revealed that seeds sold as hybrid maize in local markets were often not as advertised; less than half of the seeds were authentic hybrid seeds. High yielding seed must be made available to and ultimately adopted by farmers to increase their productivity and meet growing global food demand. However, inauthentic and poor quality hybrid seeds can result in smaller harvests, which ultimately affects farmer's profitability. In Uganda, farmers make the decision to invest in hybrid seed expecting an improvement of their yield. This expectation justifies the higher price paid for these seeds compared to traditional varieties. If the expected yield is not met, farmers are likely to reject hybrid seed.[1] To avoid such a scenario, in August 2016 the government of Uganda launched a campaign to reduce counterfeit seed in the market.

Seed is the most important input in crop production. In most countries, seed supply systems are dual, being characterized as informal (or farmer-managed) and formal. Informal systems are based on small-scale farmers' own efforts to save seeds from their crops, and by farmer-to-farmer gifts, exchanges, and trade. Informal seed systems provide a rich diversity of seed, including varieties that are relevant to farmers and adapted to local weather conditions. They also offer dynamic channels of seed distribution that can reach the most remote farming communities. Finally, they are vital to support biodiversity and resilience against climate shocks.[2] Formal seed systems were built on scientific breeding developed at the beginning of the 20th century by academic research and corporate breeding. Breeding associated with these systems led to an increase of yields, due to a considerable improvement of seed's agricultural productivity, a greater resistance to insect pests and diseases, and tolerance to drought or flood.[3] Formal seed systems generate new varieties that are then released for multiplication and distribution. Informal seed systems are also an important source of seed. Since farmers use both formal and informal channels to source their seeds in most regions, points of integration must be identified to achieve seed security in a balanced seed system that includes formal and informal players. The EBA seed indicators focus on the formal seed system due to the greater availability of comparable data. Formal seed systems are more uniform and are centralized around institutions. The activities performed across the system have been covered by treaties and other international standards. In contrast, informal seed systems are defined by the diversity of practices implemented across countries, or even across regions of the same country. Nevertheless, this year the EBA environmental sustainability topic piloted new indicators that measure innovative practices that support the circulation of seed produced by farmer-managed seed systems. This data, available on the EBA website (http://eba.worldbank.org), measure practices relevant outside of the formal seed system.

Sifting seeds in a field along Red River in northern Vietnam.
Photo: Quy-Toan Do / World Bank.

EBA is committed to developing indicators that support an integrated approach to strengthening seed systems and promote economic growth and poverty reduction. In line with this commitment, the seed indicators will be refined in future years to include practices tested this year in the environmental sustainability indicators, as well as expand the coverage of regulatory aspects relevant to the informal seed sector.

What do the seed indicators measure?

Seed indicators measure laws and regulations applicable to the development, release and quality control of seed, all of which are crucial to increasing the availability and quality of seed reaching the farmer (table 2.1). The seed indicators are organized as follows:

Plant breeding: The development of new varieties is essential to the strength of seed systems. Innovative breeding can increase plant resistance to climate change, lead to higher yields and stimulate an increase in private sector competitiveness. Among other factors, having a legal environment that grants intellectual property rights over plant materials is vital to encourage private sector investments in the seed sector.[4] This indicator measures the existence of a regulatory framework granting and protecting breeder's rights, the duration of the protections granted, the existence of discrimination between national and foreign breeders seeking protection, the availability of a list of protected varieties and the right to license protected varieties. In addition, the indicators cover access to materials essential for innovative breeding such as early generation seed developed by the public sector, germplasm stored in publicly managed genebanks, and genetic materials imported for research purposes.

Variety registration: The variety release process should ensure transparent rules for the release of hybrid seed of good quality and avoid unnecessary delays. This indicator measures how functional and inclusive the release process is, and the availability of information on new varieties. In particular, it covers the acceptance of testing data from foreign authorities, the composition of the variety release committee (VRC) and the existence and frequency of its meetings, and the availability and maintenance of an online variety catalogue. In addition, this indicator provides data on the time and cost involved for the private sector when registering a new maize variety with the government, from application to final release.

Seed quality control: The quality of seed is crucial for the adoption of new varieties by farmers. Only hybrid seeds of good quality can increase yields, ensure adaptability to climate change and therefore justify higher prices. The seed quality control indicator focuses on the quality control process that follows the release and multiplication of new varieties. It measures practices such as official fee schedules, the existence of a requirement to perform post-control tests, record-keeping to ensure traceability of breeding materials and labeling. Finally, this indicator measures the existence of third-party accreditation or self-accreditation to allow nonpublic sector actors to complement the government during the certification process.

How do countries perform on the seed indicators?

Overall, countries' performances across indicators are varied. Among the three indicators under the seed topic, the plant breeding indicator has the most regulatory good practices adopted across countries. Plant variety protection laws and registries are in place in countries with the strongest and least burdensome seed regulations such as the Netherlands and Uruguay, as well as in others with weaker seed laws such as Burundi,

Table 2.1 | What do the seed indicators measure?

PLANT BREEDING	• Existence, duration and terms of plant variety protection • Right to license protected varieties and availability of information on protected varieties • Access to germplasm, breeder and foundation seed
VARIETY REGISTRATION	• Legal requirements to register a new seed variety and information accessibility, including time and cost • Acceptance of testing data from foreign authorities • Variety release committee and availability of online variety catalogue listing registered varieties
SEED QUALITY CONTROL	• Breeders' requirement to ensure the traceability of breeding materials • Publically available fee schedule for certification • Third-party accreditation or self-accreditation for certification activities • Labeling requirements and penalties for mislabeled seed containers

Source: EBA database.

Table 2.2 | Where are seed regulations stronger and less burdensome and where are they not?

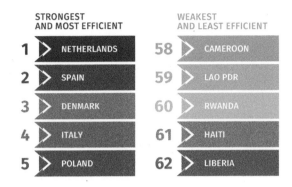

STRONGEST AND MOST EFFICIENT		WEAKEST AND LEAST EFFICIENT	
1	NETHERLANDS	58	CAMEROON
2	SPAIN	59	LAO PDR
3	DENMARK	60	RWANDA
4	ITALY	61	HAITI
5	POLAND	62	LIBERIA

Source: EBA database.

Sudan and Tajikistan (table 2.2). In Burundi, a 2016 decree introduced a legal framework for the protection of plant varieties and created a register of protected varieties administered by the National Office of Control and Certification of Seed. Nonetheless, there is still room for improvement, even in countries with a topic score above the global average such as Georgia, which has adopted most of the regulatory good practices of the plant breeding indicators and the seed topic in general, but does not yet have a list of protected varieties available publically.

Overall, OECD high-income countries perform the best in the EBA seed indicators. Most countries have inclusive release systems. But in Greece and Poland nongovernmental representatives are underrepresented in VRCs. In addition, seed producers applying for registration in these countries need to comply with additional procedures after the VRC's decision to release the new variety. These additional steps affect the efficiency of their registration process, among the longest in the region. For most countries studied, additional efforts are required to have a strong and inclusive quality control process. It is less the case for OECD high-income countries, which have most of the regulatory good practices measured by the seed quality control indicator. Seed producers complying with mandatory certification have access to transparent costs and collaborate with the public authority to perform certain certification activities themselves. In Denmark, Italy and Spain, accredited seed companies perform their field inspections, sampling and lab testing and then label seed themselves. However, in Chile and Korea, plant breeders have not yet been required to retain records on the plant reproductive materials that they use.

Sub-Saharan African countries perform the lowest overall in the EBA seed indicators. Intellectual property rights are often neglected, as one-third of the countries in Sub-Saharan Africa do not grant any protection of plant materials or any access to germplasm

conserved by public authorities. Regarding the region's registration process efficiency, more than one-third of Sub-Saharan African countries studied are not registering any improved seed[5] at all. The registration cost for a new maize variety in Sudan is among the highest across all countries studied, with an average cost representing 621% income per capita. Seed quality control processes lack transparency in the region since many countries do not have official fee schedules for certification activities that the government performs, and in nearly half of the countries, third-party certification is not permitted. Sub-Saharan African countries are closely followed by East Asian and Pacific and South Asian countries, whose performance on the seed indicators is also driven by a limited adoption of the regulatory good practices measured by the seed quality control indicator. However, several countries stand out within the Sub-Saharan Africa region with seed topic scores above the global average. In Kenya, for example, the legal framework provides tools for the protection of new varieties and access to early generation seeds and germplasms. The registration process is not restricted to the public sector and VRCs meet as often as necessary, which results in a registration time that is among the shortest across all countries studied. Furthermore, both Burundi and Rwanda adopted new legislation on the protection of plant varieties this year, which may lead to the creation of publically available registries.

What are the regulatory good practices?

Box 2.1 highlights regulatory good practices and some countries that implement these practices.

Allowing partnerships between the public and the private sector in the performance of seed-related activities

Scaling the formal seed sector is critical for countries wishing to increase the availability of hybrid seed of good quality.[6] To do so, private sector participation must be encouraged. In many countries, public research takes the lead in areas such as pre-breeding, germplasm conservation, and crop and resource management. Therefore, it is essential that the private sector has access to the outcome of public research as well as to the genetic resources that the public sector conserves, to support their own breeding efforts.[7] Seed companies can improve the production of breeder and foundation seed in the case of limited public capacity. Among the 62 countries studied, 38 allow private seed companies to produce breeder and foundation seed of local public varieties and to access germplasm conserved in public genebanks. For example, in Vietnam and Kenya, the law does not include any prohibition for the production of breeder and foundation seed, while in Guatemala, breeders wishing to produce them are required to sign an agreement with the *Instituto*

Box 2.1 | What are the regulatory good practices?

	REGULATORY GOOD PRACTICES FOR SEED	SOME COUNTRIES WHICH IMPLEMENT THE PRACTICE
PLANT BREEDING	Intellectual property rights over plant materials are granted and protected by law without discrimination based on the nationality of the applicant.	ITALY, ROMANIA
	Varieties subject to intellectual property rights are listed in a publicly available document.	CHILE, KENYA, POLAND
	Companies are not legally prevented from producing breeder and foundation seed of local public varieties.	UKRAINE, VIETNAM, ZIMBABWE
	Germplasms conserved in public genebanks are accessible to companies.	DENMARK, GEORGIA, SPAIN
	Intellectual property right over plant materials can be legally licensed to another party for production and sale of the variety.	EGYPT, ARAB REP., KOREA, REP.
	No government testing (other than phytosanitary) is required to import germplasm for the development of new varieties.	ARMENIA, UGANDA
VARIETY REGISTRATION	Testing results from foreign authorities are accepted as official data for registration purposes.	ITALY, MOZAMBIQUE
	A legally established variety release committee meets regularly and balances public and private sector participation in the evaluation and registration of new varieties.	KENYA, SPAIN, URUGUAY
	An up-to-date variety catalogue is available online and includes agro-ecological zones suitable for each variety listed.	NIGERIA, PERU
	Variety registration is efficient and affordable.	KOREA, REP., THAILAND
SEED QUALITY CONTROL	Official fee schedules are available for certification activities that the public authority performs.	CAMBODIA, CAMEROON
	Plant breeders are required to ensure the traceability of their plant reproductive materials for at least two years.	BURUNDI, SERBIA
	Private seed companies and/or third parties may be accredited to perform certification activities.	RUSSIAN FEDERATION, ZAMBIA
	A percentage of certified seed is subject to post-control tests by the national seed authority yearly, and seed is removed from the market if standards are not met.	GHANA, MOROCCO
	The law requires the labelling of seed containers and provides for a penalty for the fraudulent sale of mislabeled seed bags.	BOLIVIA, INDIA, JORDAN

Source: EBA database.

de Ciencia y Tecnología (ICTA). In Benin, Burkina Faso, Cameroon, Lao PDR, Nicaragua and Peru, public research and genetic resources that the public sector conserves are not accessible to the private sector.

Partnership between the public and private sectors should not stop with breeding. The VRC is responsible for testing new varieties for registration and approving it for further commercial production and distribution. To ensure that testing criteria are developed by all stakeholders, nongovernmental representatives (associations of seed companies, nongovernmental organizations [NGOs] or farmer associations) should be included in the VRC routine operations. Among the 62 countries studied, 38 countries require the participation of nongovernmental representatives when deciding whether to release a new variety or not (figure 2.1). Among these countries, nine require an equal or higher number of nongovernmental representatives over governmental ones. In the Netherlands, for example, the largest seed producer in Europe and where there are more than twice as many nongovernmental representatives compared with public sector representatives in the VRC, the time to register a new variety is among the shortest across countries. In Denmark, the largest exporter of seed globally, only one of the 11 members of the VRC is a government representative. In contrast, Ethiopia, Mexico and Russian Federation, which do not have associations of seed companies, NGOs or farmer associations in their VRC, have among the longest registration time.

In many developing countries, the lack of personnel and other resources lead to long delays in seed certification and testing, which impede the delivery of certified seed to farmers in a timely manner.[8] Laws can allow the accreditation of private laboratories, private inspectors and university centers to lessen the burden on the public sector. Among the 62 countries studied, 36 countries have laws that allows private seed companies and third parties to be accredited for certification activities usually performed by the national authority. In Romania, since 2002, individuals and seed companies can be accredited to carry out field inspection and sampling, to test seed quality and to issue certification documents under Ministry of Agriculture supervision. The accreditation is subject to training and to compliance with standards that the Ministry sets. In Cambodia, Nigeria and Sri Lanka, as well as in 16 other countries—mainly low-income and lower-middle-income countries— only the national authority can perform the mandatory certification.

Implementing regulatory good practices

The ideal regulatory environment for the seed sector is a clear legal framework supported by functioning institutions and efficient procedures. The law establishing institutions and granting rights should be enforced in practice. Similarly, practices implemented without a legal framework may not always be beneficial to all seed sector actors in the absence of clear implementation criteria. Among the 45 countries where public research institutes license public varieties to seed companies for production and sale, 13 countries do so in the absence of clear rules. In 2016, the Institute for Environment and National Research in Burkina Faso (INERA) designed a framework agreement on future public-private partnerships for the production of initial classes of seed.

Figure 2.1 | Nongovernmental representation in variety release committees (VRCs)

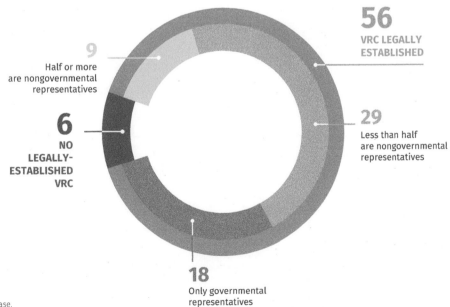

9
Half or more
are nongovernmental
representatives

56
VRC LEGALLY
ESTABLISHED

6
NO
LEGALLY-
ESTABLISHED
VRC

29
Less than half
are nongovernmental
representatives

18
Only governmental
representatives

Source: EBA database.

The release process for a new variety is prescribed in the country's seed law and usually involves an evaluation of the new variety through testing, review of the result by a decision body and registration in an official catalogue. Among the 62 countries studied, 56 establish a VRC tasked with reviewing the test results of any new maize variety, before its registration and release. In Benin, Bosnia and Herzegovina, Burkina Faso, Cambodia, Mali and Rwanda, the VRC provided for in the law does not appear to meet in practice, while they are a prerequisite to the availability of seed in countries where registration is mandatory. With the exception of few countries such as Georgia or Italy, where regulatory good practices go hand-in-hand with a streamlined and low-cost variety registration process, a large number of countries have adopted lengthy procedures that are likely to result in delays in seed delivery to the farmer.

Fourteen countries, most of them in Sub-Saharan Africa, do not have any private seed companies registering new maize varieties, despite appropriate regulations being in place. In Niger, the seed law establishes a strong regulatory framework, which includes a VRC with the participation of all stakeholders and meetings on a quarterly basis, as well as a variety catalogue available online. However, the country still has no private seed companies that register new maize varieties.

In a number of countries, VRCs are functioning with varied stakeholder participation and regular meetings but the registration process is still burdensome to seed producers because of its length or cost (figure 2.2). For example, in Nicaragua the registration regulatory requirements follow most of the good practices identified. The VRC is functional, meets monthly and does not require additional procedures to release the new variety after its decision. Despite these regulatory good practices, however, the variety registration process in Nicaragua is the third most expensive across all countries, equivalent to 787% income per capita, and has the sixth lengthiest procedure that lasts 650 calendar days.

Certification processes designed to ensure seed quality have been identified as having a negative effect and as impeding the development of the seed supply chain,[9] due to delays in the government's performance of certification activities. Accreditation mechanisms are intended to allow seed companies or third parties to assist the public authority in certifying seed. Among the 62 countries studied, more than half of them have created a legal framework for third party or self-accreditation. However, only 31 countries accredit individuals or companies for field inspections, sampling, lab testing or labelling. For example, in Armenia, Serbia and Uganda, seed companies or third parties have not been accredited despite the existence of regulation.

Ensuring seed quality in the market

Regulations establish mechanisms that guarantee farmers' access to hybrid seed of quality for their crop production. Hybrid seeds, when used properly and together with other inputs like fertilizer, have proven to increase farmers' yield by 12–15%.[10] A registered seed's genetic purity, identity and a given minimum quality level must be found in the seed sold if that seed is ultimately to reach the farmer's fields and improve

Figure 2.2 | Few countries have both strong registration regulations and an efficient registration process

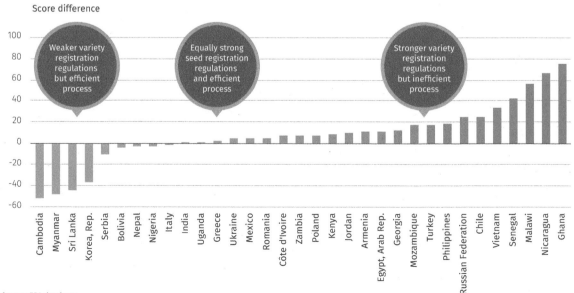

Source: EBA database.

Farmers harvest their crops near Kisumu, Kenya. Photo: Peter Kapuscinski / World Bank.

yields. Research has shown that farmers will not adopt new technologies such as improved seed varieties when they do not expect any economic return due to low-quality seed.[11] Post-control tests assess the quality of certified seed to verify that the seed's varietal purity has been maintained. Among the 62 countries surveyed, half of them require the performance of these tests whether in the field or in laboratories. Among them, 10 countries have seed laws that require the national authority to test a minimum percentage of certified seed annually (Burundi, Denmark, Ghana, Greece, Morocco, the Netherlands, Poland, Romania, Spain and Turkey).

Labelling standards and sanctions for the fraudulent sale of mislabeled seed containers can also improve seed quality at the retail level. A labelling system allows farmers to know what they are buying and from whom, making producers and distributors accountable for the seed container content. Standardized labels can improve farmer's confidence in the seed in circulation. Among 62 countries studied, 5 do not have a legal requirement to label seed containers for sale. Most of them require labels to include the producer name and address, the crop name, the class of seed and the minimum germination percentage, which is necessary for the farmer to make an informed decision on which variety to purchase. Other information such as the production year, the minimum purity percentage or the existence of a chemical treatment may also be required, such as in Ghana, Mexico or

Zimbabwe. By contrast, more than half of the countries studied do not require labels to include information relating to repacking or relabeling of seed containers. Repacking and relabeling information allows the buyer to retrace certified seeds to their seed lots. Finally, a large majority of countries have seed laws that include a penalty for sale of mislabeled seed to discourage the circulation of fake seeds.

Conclusion

Introducing and implementing seed quality and assurance are challenging. This process requires a robust legislative framework, sufficient financial resources, well-trained inspectors, capable laboratories and relevant legal mandates to conduct post-control tests and market inspections. Countries that implement such systems take a significant step towards a more competitive and commercially-oriented agricultural sector that has access to improved varieties and increased crop yields. Moreover, such countries reduce the risk of fake and low-quality seed entering the market, which can otherwise undercut crop yields and lead to reduced food supply or even shortages.

NOTES

1   Bold et al. 2015.

2   Keith Virgo 2016.

3   Fita et al. 2015.

4   Fernandez-Cornejo. 2004.

5   Only maize seed is considered for the hypothetical case study assumption used to standardize the variety registration indicator.

6   Prabhala et al. 2015.

7   Bishaw and van Gastel 2009.

8   USAID 2016.

9   Smale et al. 2011.

10 Abate, de Brauw, Minot and Bernard 2015.

11 Bold et al. 2015.

REFERENCES

Abate, Gashaw Tadesse, A. de Brauwm, N. Minot, and T. Bernard. 2015. *The Impact of the Use of New Technologies on Farmers' Wheat Yield in Ethiopia: Evidence from a Randomized Controlled Trial.* IFPRI Discussion Paper 01462. International Food Policy and Research Institute, Washington, DC.

Bishaw, Zewdie and A. J. G. van Gastel. 2009. "Variety Release and Policy Options." In *Plant Breeding and Farmer Participation*, edited by S. Ceccarelli, E. P. Guimarães and E. Weltizien, 565–88. Rome: FAO.

Bold, T. et al. 2015. "Low Quality, Low Returns, Low Adoption: Evidence from the Market for Fertilizer and Hybrid Seed in Uganda." Kennedy School Faculty Research Working Paper Series. Harvard University, Kennedy School, Cambridge, MA.

Fernandez-Cornejo, J. 2004. "The Seed Industry in U.S. Agriculture: An Exploration of Data and Information on Crop Seed Markets, Regulation, Industry Structure, and Research and Development." United States Department of Agriculture, Washington, DC.

Fita, A., A. Rodríguez-Burruezo, M. Boscaiu, J. Prohens and O. Vicente. 2015. "Breeding and Domesticating Crops Adapted to Drought and Salinity: A New Paradigm for Increasing Food Production." *Frontiers in Plant Science* (6): 978, November. doi: 10.3389/fpls.2015.00978.

Prabhala, Pr. et al. 2015. "Early Generation Seed Study." Bill & Melinda Gates Foundation for the United States Agency for International Development (USAID). USAID, Washington, DC.

Smale, M., D. Byerlee and T. Jayne. 2011. "Maize Revolutions in Sub-Saharan Africa." World Bank Policy Research Working Paper 5659. World Bank, Washington, DC.

USAID (United States Agency for International Development). 2016. "Southern Africa Regional Seed Sector Assessment." USAID, Washington, DC.

Virgo Keith. 2016. *Correspondence*, December 20. United Kingdom.

3 Fertilizer

In Western Kenya most farmers grow maize, predominantly for subsistence. The average farmer plants just under one acre of maize during the "long rains" from March to July, and again during the less productive "short rains" from August until January. Using only one-half teaspoon of fertilizer per plant would increase yields by about $26 per acre and cost only $20 per acre. After accounting for the extra labor associated with fertilizer use, the fertilizer rate of return is around 70% a year, a worthwhile investment.[1]

Fertilizer is credited with increasing global yields of food crops by 40–60%,[2] and no region has been able to boost agricultural growth without increasing its use.[3] The Green Revolution, which can be attributed to the use of fertilizers and improved seeds, has had a dramatic impact on the food supply and incomes of many developing countries. During the past 40 years the world witnessed an extraordinary period of crop productivity and was able to overcome chronic food deficits. However, the use of fertilizers and other chemical inputs has increased soil erosion and acidification and groundwater pollution.[4] To counter this unwelcome development, care is necessary to prevent soil damage, environmental pollution or adulterated fertilizer use, while continuing to increase the much-needed use of fertilizer in certain regions.

Low productivity in regions such as Sub-Saharan Africa is associated with the limited adoption of fertilizer.[5] In West Africa, for example, where soil nitrogen and phosphorus contents are low, fertilizer use between 2002 and 2009 was at an average of 5 kg/ha, significantly less than the recommended 50 kg/ha.[6] While fertilizer use has dramatically increased in some countries such as Burkina Faso, from 0.4 kg/ha of arable land in 2002 to 14.3 in 2013, and in Ghana from 3.7 to 35.8 during the same time period, little change has occurred in other countries such as Niger, which has barely moved up from 0.6 to 0.7kg/ha.[7] Furthermore, low fertilizer use not only restricts yields today, but also promises future productivity declines due to the ongoing depletion of soil nutrients.[8]

27

Portrait of Abou amid millet stalks in southwest Niger.
Photo: Stephan Gladieu / World Bank.

Fertilizer use in developing countries is constrained by a number of factors, particularly high prices and unavailability that often reflect unsatisfactory procurement practices, inefficient administrative procedures and inadequate infrastructure. Limited understanding among farmers of fertilizer use hampers more widespread fertilizer uptake.[9] Some major challenges that impact farmers stem from the lack of new and innovative fertilizer products in the market, cumbersome import procedures that can discourage businesses from importing and adulterated or contaminated fertilizer products. Adulteration or contamination can lead smallholders to doubt the value and importance of fertilizers if their potency and effects are compromised.[10] In more serious cases, fertilizer adulteration can reduce crop growth, affecting output in ways that lead to food and income insecurity and may be environmentally harmful.

Policies and regulations that enable the sector to grow and producers to maximize their potential, for example, can often come into conflict with concerns regarding soil health and water contamination. Nevertheless, strong regulations that enable increased fertilizer access are essential to increase yields. As a result, as in any other industry, the debate remains on appropriate regulation levels.

What do the fertilizer indicators measure?

The fertilizer indicators measure laws and regulations on the registration, import and quality control of fertilizer products, all of which are crucial to increasing fertilizer access (table 3.1). The indicators cover the following areas:

Registering Fertilizer: In most countries, fertilizer cannot be imported, manufactured, distributed, sold or used unless it has been registered with a designated authority. Registration of fertilizer products ensures the safe entry of new products into the market as governments are able to provide market oversight through a registration scheme and test the fertilizer's impact on soil, human health and the environment. Moreover, product registration gives farmers confidence in the products that they are using. This indicator measures the following:

Registration requirements. The requirement to register fertilizer products, the types of entities required to register products, types of fertilizer products required to be registered and any time-limitations on fertilizer registration.

Registration procedures. Procedures, time and cost to register a new fertilizer product.

Fertilizer catalogue. The existence of an official fertilizer catalogue with a list of registered fertilizers, and its availability online.

Re-registration of fertilizer products. The requirement to re-register a product previously registered in another country.

Importing and Distributing Fertilizer: Fertilizer production is energy intensive, and the industry benefits from economies of scale as well as low costs of raw materials. It is no surprise, therefore, that the world's production capacity is concentrated in a few countries. With just five countries[11] producing half or more of the global supply of the most common types of fertilizer, simple and uncomplicated import procedures are essential to fertilizer access in the majority of countries around the world. This indicator focuses on:

Table 3.1 | What do the fertilizer indicators measure?

REGISTERING FERTILIZER	• Legal requirements to register a new fertilizer product and information accessibility • Time and cost to register a fertilizer product
IMPORTING AND DISTRIBUTING FERTILIZER	• Entities allowed to import fertilizer products • Requirement for a company to register as a fertilizer importer • Requirement of import permits to import fertilizer products • Entities allowed to distribute fertilizer products
QUALITY CONTROL OF FERTILIZER	• Labeling requirements for fertilizer bags • Prohibition and penalties for the sale of mislabeled and open-bag fertilizer

Source: EBA database.

Entities that are allowed to import and distribute fertilizer: Entities allowed to import and distribute fertilizer, including the private sector, nongovernmental organizations, and producers organizations.

Import registration: The requirement to register as a fertilizer importer and any time limits on the validity of the import registration.

Import permits: The need to obtain an import permit to import fertilizer products, any per-shipment or volume limitations applicable to the permit, any time limits on the validity of the permit and total time and cost to obtain the permit.

Quality Control of Fertilizer: The potential damage caused by adulterated fertilizer, typically not apparent until months after application, undermines trust in fertilizer quality and discourages farmers from using fertilizer at all.[12] Quality control and inspection methods, as well as punishments for breaking laws, vary significantly across the world. However, a minimum set of standards to increase fertilizer quality control can be applied in all countries and across regions and income groups. This indicator measures:

Labelling and packaging requirements: The obligation to label fertilizer bags and specific labeling requirements, including language and label content.

Mislabeled and open-bag fertilizer: The prohibition of and establishment of penalties against the sale of mislabeled and open-bag fertilizer.

How do countries perform on the fertilizer indicators?

Bosnia and Herzegovina performs the best on the fertilizer indicators this year, due to strong regulations in all areas; it has one of the most inexpensive and least burdensome fertilizer registration procedures, and registration also does not expire and is not subject to periodic fees. In addition, all registered fertilizer products are included in a catalogue that is accessible online, creating further transparency for industry stakeholders. Bosnia and Herzegovina performs particularly well on the importing and distributing fertilizer indicator; for example, importer registration is a one-time-only requirement and no per-shipment import permits apply. On quality control measures, fertilizer bags must comply with comprehensive labeling requirements in at least one of the country's official languages, and mislabeled and open bags are prohibited and subject to penalties, encouraging further fertilizer quality control. EU countries also performed well across all fertilizer indicators, with Denmark, Greece, Italy, Poland and Spain all receiving among the top 10 scores, principally due to strong rules adopted and harmonized

at the EU-level.[13] OECD high-income and Europe and Central Asia countries demonstrate strong regulations applicable to importing and distributing fertilizer—high-performing countries typically only require a one-time import registration at the company level and do not require any per-shipment import permits.

The countries, from lowest to highest, with the worst performance on the fertilizer indicators include Liberia, Benin, Senegal, Ethiopia, Haiti, Sudan, and Burkina Faso, along with Niger. These countries have rudimentary regulatory frameworks for registering fertilizer. Countries that performed poorly with respect to regulations for importing and distributing fertilizer are primarily located in Sub-Saharan Africa and the Middle East and North Africa regions, where the renewal period for importer registrations are shorter and import permits are expensive and valid for a shorter period of time. Ethiopia received the lowest score of all 62 countries on importing and distributing fertilizer because the private sector is prohibited from engaging in any such activities. The lowest scores in the quality control indicator, also found predominantly in the Sub-Saharan Africa region, are driven by the absence of laws prohibiting mislabeled and open-bag fertilizer, the lack of appropriate penalties and the absence of labeling requirements in at least one of the official languages of the country (table 3.2).

Significant variation was found across countries with respect to the efficiency and complexity in registering fertilizer products. The time and cost to register a new fertilizer product are lowest on average in OECD high-income and upper-middle-income countries, and highest in low-income countries (figure 3.1). For example, it takes on average 330.7 calendar days to register

Table 3.2 | Where are fertilizer regulations strong and least burdensome, and where are they not?

STRONGEST AND MOST EFFICIENT		WEAKEST AND LEAST EFFICIENT	
1	BOSNIA AND HERZEGOVINA	58	HAITI
2	POLAND	59	ETHIOPIA
3	DENMARK	60	SENEGAL
4	SERBIA	61	BENIN
5	SPAIN	62	LIBERIA

Source: EBA database.

a fertilizer product in the 62 countries sampled, ranging from 1205 days in Romania to 11 days in Uruguay. This stark difference in time is driven principally by lengthy field testing. Across the 62 countries sampled, the average cost to register a new fertilizer product is 171.7% of income per capita, and it is most expensive in Malawi, totaling 3030.5% of income per capita. It is cheapest in Spain where it is free.

What are the regulatory good practices?

Box 3.1 highlights regulatory good practices and some countries that implement these practices.

Reduced field testing for fertilizer registration

Registering new fertilizer products is a good practice because it ensures that a country has control over what fertilizers are used within its borders. Registration schemes and the oversight they provide are helpful in giving farmers assurance that inadequate nutrients, heavy metals or other residues found in fertilizer products do not contaminate crops, animals and the environment. However, registration procedures should be time and cost efficient to ensure that new products can reach the market in a timely manner. Although controls are necessary to prevent soil damage, environmental pollution or adulterated fertilizer use, certain lengthy

Figure 3.1 | Low-income countries have the most inefficient and costly processes to register a new fertilizer product

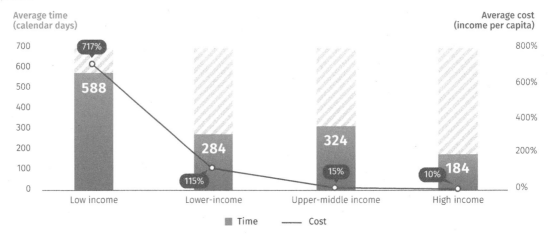

Source: EBA database

Figure 3.2 | Countries with field-testing procedures tend to have higher time and cost to register fertilizer products

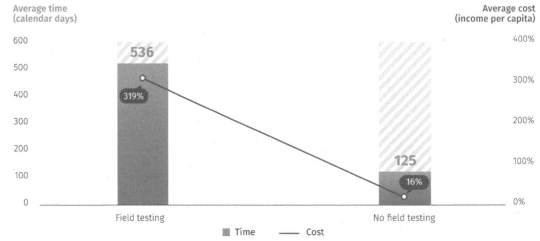

Source: EBA database.

Box 3.1 | Example of regulatory good practices for fertilizer

	REGULATORY GOOD PRACTICES FOR FERTILITZER	SOME COUNTRIES WHICH IMPLEMENT THE PRACTICE
REGISTERING FERTILIZER	Fertilizer product registration is inexpensive, is not subject to periodic fees and does not expire.	DENMARK, SERBIA
	An official fertilizer catalogue listing all registered fertilizers is available online.	INDIA, SPAIN
	Chemical fertilizer registration includes an application to register and lab sample analysis, and excludes field testing due to limited additional benefits.	BOSNIA AND HERZEGOVINA, POLAND
	Re-registration of a fertilizer product is not required if it is already registered in another country that is part of a regional agreement or approved in the regional catalogue.	GREECE, ITALY
IMPORTING & DISTRIBUTING FERTILIZER	All entities, including the private sector, nongovernmental organizations and producer organizations, can import and distribute fertilizer.	CHILE, KENYA
	All entities are required to register as importers, and registration is inexpensive and does not expire.	COLOMBIA, KOREA, REP.
	Import permits are not required or they are imposed only at the trader level, with no volume, shipment or time limits, and they are inexpensive and simple to obtain.	RUSSIAN FEDERATION, SPAIN
QUALITY CONTROL OF FERTILIZER	Fertilizer must be packed in sealed bags and labeled in at least one of the country's official languages, including details such as brand name, content, origin, manufacturing and expiration date, safety instruction, etc.	MEXICO, SERBIA
	Regulations prohibit the sale of mislabeled and open fertilizer bags, and impose penalties on those who fail to comply with set standards.	MOROCCO, ROMANIA

Source: EBA database.

and expensive procedures such as field testing are not deemed necessary as part of an effective registration process. Three complimentary nutrients (nitrogen, phosphorus, and potash) have been extensively tested and used for over a century, with general agreement on the required balance that will maximize production.[14] Practitioners report that a simple soil analysis can be used to determine if the product is suitable for that agro-ecological zone, and there is general consensus on which fertilizer to use for particular crops. As a result, field tests for these ingredients only drive up the time and cost of fertilizer registration, with little added value (figure 3.2).

Of the 48 countries that actually practice fertilizer product registration, 21 require field testing, the majority of which are in Sub-Saharan Africa (7), South Asia (4), and Europe and Central Asia (6). In countries requiring this procedure, the average cost in income per capita is 319% (63% if outliers Malawi, Nepal, Tanzania and Ukraine are excluded), compared to 16% in countries that do not require field testing. The average time to register a new fertilizer product in countries requiring field testing is 536.35 days, in contrast to 125.1 days in countries where this requirement does not exist.

Streamlined import permit requirements

Among the 62 countries studied, 22 countries do not impose any import permit requirements, nine of which are in Europe and Central Asia, and six are OECD high-income countries.[15] Several countries in Sub-Saharan Africa (Cameroon, Côte d'Ivoire and Kenya) and in Latin America and the Caribbean (Haiti and Peru) do not require an import permit and can serve as good examples for other countries.

Fertilizer in bags, preparing for rice growing in rice field, Bangkok, Thailand. Photo: Shutterstock.

In 20 of the 39 countries that require import permits, those permits are valid for less than 12 months. If an import permit is required, the least burdensome option are blank permits with no volume, shipment or time limits that are affordable and simple to obtain. Blank permits with time validities of 12 months or more grant importers flexibility in terms of the departure and arrival time of shipments, and allow companies' decisions with respect to the volumes and prices to be based on commercial interests. Twelve countries impose blank permits with no volume restrictions, the majority of which are in Sub-Saharan Africa (5) and the Middle East and North Africa (3). The majority of these countries have a permit validity of more than 12 months.

Per-shipment import permits with short time validities pose several problems. First of all, they limit the importer's negotiating power, as the import permit is attached to a specific shipment (and therefore volume) that cannot be changed once the permit is issued. Furthermore, short time validities force companies to negotiate purchases within very specific time periods and, in some instances, they also present logistical complications, such as the permit expiring before the fertilizer is shipped from one place to another.

Twenty-three countries still impose per-shipment import permits, and four countries impose permits by volume. Burundi and Sudan require a per-shipment import permit with a two-month validity, whereas Bolivia, Nicaragua, Tanzania and Vietnam require a per-shipment import permit that expires within a month. Bangladesh and Nigeria impose a different kind of restriction by requiring per-shipment import permits with a particular volume quota that is valid for 12 months. Not all 23 countries impose such limited time frames—Senegal requires a blank permit that is valid for 48 months and Benin's blank permit is valid for 24 months.

Closing the gap between fertilizer registration law and practice

Of the 62 countries studied, 48 legally require fertilizer products to be registered before they can be imported and sold in the country. Some countries, such as those in the EU, perform well on the fertilizer registration indicator because they have strong legal frameworks in place *and* there is a low-cost process to register fertilizer products that is streamlined and efficient. However, many other countries lag behind despite a strong legal framework, either because businesses do not register fertilizer products in practice or because the registration process is so onerous as to discourage the registration of new fertilizer products altogether.[16]

Six countries either have no observable practice in terms of the registration of fertilizer products or only allow the public sector to register fertilizer products. In Burundi, Mozambique and Tajikistan, although the private sector is permitted to register new fertilizer products, no products were registered last year. In

Figure 3.3 | Few countries have both strong fertilizer registration regulations and an efficient registration process

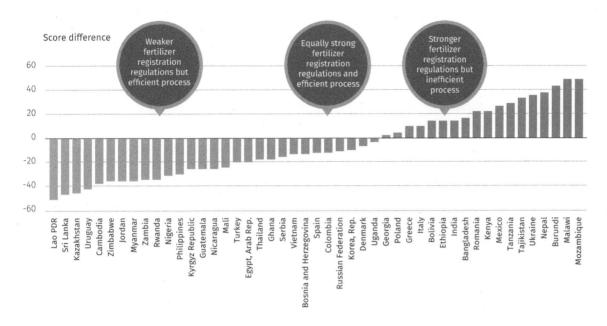

Source: EBA database.

Bolivia, Ethiopia and Kenya, the law permits only the public sector to register new fertilizer products.

Several other countries have strong legal frameworks in place for registration but use complicated registration processes, including the total time (in calendar days) and cost (as a percentage of income per capita) to register a new fertilizer product (figure 3.3). For example, although Malawi's regulatory framework performs above average as compared with other countries, the practical experience for private sector actors registering fertilizer products in the country results in it receiving one of the lowest ratings on this component. Malawi follows regulatory good practices such as requiring fertilizer product registration and having no time limitation to the fertilizer product registration. However, Malawi has the fourth lengthiest and the most expensive fertilizer registration process out of all 62 countries, taking 913 days and 3030.48% of income per capita to register. Similarly, while Nepal's registration laws also perform above average, their practical application is relatively lengthy and costly; it takes 1,125 days, and 645.2% of income per capita to register a new fertilizer product in Nepal.

Conclusion

There are many opportunities for countries to implement laws and regulations that improve access to fertilizer, promote fertilizer use, and increase agricultural productivity. Regulatory best practices may be difficult to achieve in certain regions in the short term due to a mix of factors, including the absence of laws and lack of institutional capacity for implementation. However, certain practices can facilitate regulatory and market efficiency and thus increase fertilizer access. While fertilizer registration ensures the safe entry of fertilizer products into the market, efforts should be made to make the process as efficient as possible, while maintaining quality control. Ensuring that fertilizer registration is not held up by procedures such as field testing, which has been deemed unnecessary in most cases, can go a long way in cutting time and cost and encouraging the entry of new fertilizer products into a market. Furthermore, streamlining import permits can facilitate timely fertilizer entry into a country and help avoid time-consuming paperwork and logistical complications.

NOTES

1 Duflo et al. 2011.

2 Hoyum 2012.

3 African Union 2006.

4 Savci 2012.

5 Gregory and Bumb 2006.

6 Keyser et al. 2015.

7 World Development Indicators: Agricultural Inputs, Fertilizer Consumption (kilograms per hectare of arable land), (accessed November 7, 2016), http://data.worldbank.org/indicator/AG.CON.FERT.ZS.

8 Beaman et al. 2013.

9 Duflo et al 2008.

10 Pullabhotla and Ganesh-Kumar 2012.

11 Canada, China, India, the Russian Federation and the United States are the largest fertilizer producers in the world.

12 Pullabhotla and Ganesh-Kumar 2012.

13 Council Regulation (EC) No 2003/2003 of 13 October 2003 of the European Parliament and of the Council relating to fertilisers [2003] OJ L 304/1.

14 World Bank 2016.

15 Import permit data are not presented for Ethiopia because only the public sector is allowed to import and distribute fertilizer products.

16 *Ibid*.

REFERENCES

African Union. 2006. "Abuja Declaration on Fertilizer for an African Green Revolution." African Union, Abuja, Nigeria.

Beaman, Lori et al. 2013. "Profitability of Fertilizer: Experimental Evidence from Female Rice Farmers in Mali," *American Economic Review*, 103 (3): 381-86.

Duflo, Esther et al. 2011. "Nudging Farmers to Use Fertilizer: Theory and Experimental Evidence from Kenya." *American Economic Review* 101 (6): 2350–390.

Duflo, Esther et al. 2008. "How High are Rates of Return to Fertilizer? Evidence from Field Experiments in Kenya." *American Economics Review* 98 (2): 482-88.

Gregory, D. I. and B. L. Bumb. 2006. "Factors Affecting Supply of Sub-Saharan Fertilizer in Africa." Agriculture and Rural Development Discussion Paper 24. World Bank, Washington, DC.

Hoyum, Raymond. 2012. "Nepal Fertilizer and Nutrient Assessment." Summary report. United States Agency for International Development, Washington, DC.

IFDC (International Fertilizer Development Center). 2010. "Rapid Appraisal of Fertilizer Quality in Cambodia." IFDC, Muscle Shoals, Alabama, USA.

Keyser, J. C. et al. 2015. "Towards an Integrated Market for Seeds and Fertilizers in West Africa." Working Paper 93630. World Bank, Washington, DC.

Pullabhotla, H. and A. Ganesh-Kumar. 2012. "Review of input and output policies for cereals production in Bangladesh." IFPRI (International Food Policy Research Institute) Discussion Paper 01199. IFPRI, Washington, DC.

Savci, S. 2012. "An Agricultural Pollutant: Chemical Fertilizer." *International Journal of Environmental Science and Development* 3 (1): 77–80.

World Bank. 2016. *Breaking Down Barriers: Unlocking Africa's Potential Through Vigorous Competition Policy.* Washington, DC: World Bank.

4 Machinery

Each year during plowing season, Leela Rajput used to hire 15 laborers to work from dawn until dusk every week preparing his 10-hectare plot in the northwestern Indian state of Uttar Pradesh. This year, he will use a tractor instead. With the machine, he expects to finish the job in a single day. Indian agriculture is belatedly engaged in a mechanical revolution, boosting productivity in a sector that has long relied on cheap labor to tend crops in the world's second most populous country. Job opportunities in cities have drained the pool of workers in villages. "I just can't find enough people to do the hard work in the fields anymore," says Mr. Rajput. He adds that the tractor helps bring more women into the workforce by making the work less physically demanding.[1]

Farm machines are indispensable to modern agriculture. Some of the most significant increases in farming productivity have been achieved as a direct result of agricultural machines.[2] Agricultural mechanization offers the ability to increase agricultural productivity by bringing more land under cultivation and by improving the timeliness of operations, thereby enabling markets for rural economic growth and improving rural livelihoods.[3] By enhancing the efficient utilization of inputs such as seeds, fertilizers, plant protection chemicals and irrigation water, and expanding cultivated areas, agricultural mechanization can greatly enhance farming profitability and reduce human drudgery. This change can make farming a more viable and attractive commercial enterprise, particularly for youth, and promote rural employment. Furthermore, the benefits of agricultural machinery become particularly important as the demand for food, fiber and fuel continues to rise against a backdrop of expanding urbanization and increased constraints on land and water resources.[4]

Despite its benefits, mechanization levels still vary widely across the globe. In the countries studied for *EBA 2017*, high mechanization levels are observed in European countries, with penetration rates of 1,300 tractors per 100 square kilometers of arable land, as in the case of Poland.[5] By contrast, low mechanization levels persist in many developing countries, particularly in Sub-Saharan Africa, with penetration rates as low as 2.24 tractors per 100 square kilometers of arable land, as in the case of Mali. In many regions, mechanization's low contribution to agricultural development is partly due to the fragmented policy approaches taken by governments on mechanization issues.[6] Despite its high cost and high profile, agricultural machinery is an input like any other and the policies, laws and regulations impacting the industry affect the way in which mechanization inputs are made available on the market, including their accessibility, commercial viability and safety. For example, most countries today leave the importation and sale of tractors to the private sector. However, the public sector continues to be involved in matters related to licensing, inspection and testing, and other areas of regulation regarded as being in the public interest.

MACHINERY

Men stacking hay onto a tractor, Macedonia.
Photo: World Bank.

What do the machinery indicators measure?

Agricultural tractors are used as a proxy to measure laws and regulations that may restrict tractor imports and operations, as well as the quality requirements applicable to imported tractors (table 4.1). Agricultural tractors were chosen for their relevance and comparability, given that tractors are imported and used around the globe, unlike other forms of machinery that are region or crop specific. The machinery indicators are organized as follows:

Tractor imports: This indicator measures aspects related to importing agricultural tractors, including the ability of private sector companies to import and sell tractors, and the procedures for registering as a tractor importer and for obtaining an import permit. Few developing countries manufacture agricultural equipment and machinery domestically. As a result, demand must be met through imports, typically handled by the private sector though sometimes managed through government imports. Even where the private sector is involved, however, tractor importation procedures can be cumbersome and time consuming for businesses, due to unnecessary or inefficient bureaucracy. This inefficiency negatively impacts the process and increases transaction costs and delivery times. An efficient and inexpensive process can greatly ease supply constraints for tractor importers and improve tractor distribution in a country.

Tractor operations: This indicator measures the legal and practical dimensions of registering agricultural tractors and completing inspections of in-use tractors, as well as the requirement that tractor dealers provide after-market tractor service and parts. Registering agricultural tractors not only establishes ownership rights over the purchased tractor but it also facilitates

the enforcement of road, safety and tax regulations. Furthermore, a substantial proportion of the tractor fleet in many countries is not safe for operation due to poor maintenance and a lack of repairs.[7] Therefore, most countries require that tractors be inspected at regular intervals to identify faults and conduct repairs, which can, in turn, improve tractor performance. Agricultural tractors can have a life span of 5 to 30 years, but they can be kept operational only through regular servicing.[8] Therefore, it is essential that farmers have access to tractor service and maintenance, and spare parts. A regulatory framework that promotes efficiency and reduces transaction costs for tractor registration and roadworthiness checks, while at the same time ensuring control and safety, can enhance the uptake of machinery and protect tractor users.

Tractor testing and standards: This indicator measures the legal and practical dimensions of tractor testing, the prevailing tractor type approval[9] process in a country (including the associated procedures, time and costs) as well as tractor performance and operator safety standards. Standardization and tractor testing systems alone cannot boost mechanization growth. However, appropriate testing and streamlined type approval procedures for agricultural tractors—undertaken in conformity with established national or international standards—can increase the safety and technical reliability of tractors, reduce the environmental and social cost inflicted by substandard tractors, and increase farmers' access to safe, reliable and efficient machinery.[10] While the absence of testing and standards may help encourage growth in agricultural mechanization in the short-term, it risks problems emerging in the future.[11] Therefore, a thorough testing and evaluation of a tractor's performance, its quality, durability and safety, should be required.

Table 4.1 | What do the machinery indicators measure?

TRACTOR IMPORTS	• The private sector's ability to import and sell tractors • Importer registration and renewal requirements, including registration validity • Import permit requirements, including permit type, cost and validity
TRACTOR OPERATIONS	• Tractor registration requirements • Roadworthiness inspection of in-use tractors, including inspection cost • Provision of after-market service and parts • Time and cost of tractor registration
TRACTOR TESTING AND STANDARDS	• National and international standards applied in the country • Tractor type approval requirements, including testing, validity and international recognition • Requirement of protective structures and seatbelts • Time and cost of type approval

Source: EBA database.

Figure 4.1 | The number of tractors per 100 square kilometers of arable land is highest in countries that score well in EBA machinery legal indicators

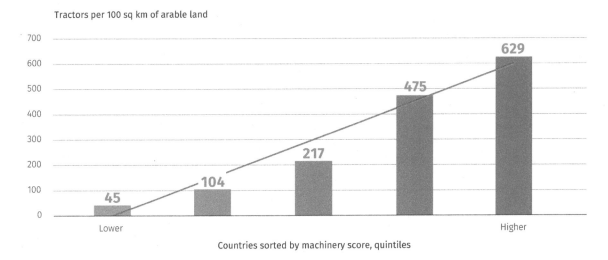

Tractors per 100 sq km of arable land

Countries sorted by machinery score, quintiles

Sources: FAOSTAT, *EBA* database.

Note: The correlation is 0.52 between the machinery score and the number of tractors per 100 square kilometers of arable land from the FAOSTAT dataset. The correlation is significant at a 5% level after controlling for income per capita.

How do countries perform on the machinery indicators?

The countries that score high on the machinery indicators tend to have higher tractor penetration rates (figure 4.1). Certainly, there are several factors—such as specific mechanization policies and market realities—that affect the agricultural machinery sector and contribute to the adoption of tractors for agricultural production. However, the enabling regulatory environment for agricultural machinery and the efficiency with which governments are implementing laws and regulations are important precursors for a well-functioning tractor market.

Countries with the highest score on the machinery topic, such as Poland, Romania, Serbia and Turkey, share many common features (table 4.2). These countries facilitate streamlined import procedures, making it easy for tractor importers to introduce their products to the market, while at the same time promoting adequate control and inspections to ensure that tractors meet quality, durability and safety standards. The countries with the lowest scores, such as Liberia, Mali and Myanmar, each demonstrate room to adopt many of the identified good practices. For example, importing tractors is cumbersome in these countries and standards with regards to quality, performance and safety are not established or followed. Regulations on tractor registration, type approval, roadworthiness inspection and tractor maintenance provision are weak or absent in these countries.

The quality of regulations and practices in the tractor operations and the tractor testing and standards indicators vary greatly across countries. The three countries within the Middle East and North Africa region (Egypt, Jordan and Morocco) and most OECD high-income countries covered have robust regulations on tractor operation that require tractors to be registered and inspected for roadworthiness. Most of these countries also make the provision of after-market parts and services a statutory requirement, ensuring road safety and security to customers. OECD high-income countries and countries in the Europe and Central Asia region score highest on tractor testing and standards,

Table 4.2 | Where are machinery regulations strongest and most efficient?

STRONGEST AND MOST EFFICIENT		WEAKEST AND LEAST EFFICIENT	
1	POLAND	58	PERU
2	SERBIA	59	LAO PDR
3	ROMANIA	60	LIBERIA
4	TURKEY	61	MALI
5	GREECE	62	MYANMAR

Source: EBA database.

as most of them require tractors to be tested and type approved, while at the same time mutually recognizing the certifications issued by other countries. By contrast, countries in the Latin America and Caribbean region score low in this indicator because regulations on tractor testing, as well as tractor performance and safety standards, are not established.

Although the scores on tractor imports do not vary as much across countries as for tractor operation and tractor testing and standards, differences do exist. The 8 OECD high-income countries[12] and the 11 countries in Europe and Central Asia[13] region have implemented all the good practices identified under the tractor imports indicator. For example, these countries do not require importers to register in addition to the general business license, and import permits are not required in these regions. By comparison, countries in Middle East and North Africa and Sub-Saharan Africa regions have lower tractor imports indicator scores.

The data show that countries that score higher on tractor imports and operations also tend to have stronger laws on tractor testing and standards. Scores also indicate that regulatory efficiency on the one hand—as defined by the time and cost involved in complying with target regulations—and tractor quality control regulations on the other, tend to be complements rather than substitutes. Countries with a strong legal framework also often have less burdensome procedures in terms of time and cost associated with tractor registration and tractor type approval (figure 4.2).

What are the regulatory good practices?

Box 4.1 highlights regulatory good practices and some countries that implement these practices.

Safeguard availability and timely delivery of agricultural tractors through streamlined import procedures

Complex import formalities impede the flow of international trade and increase the time and cost to import.[14] Nevertheless, many countries continue to require permits as a prior condition for the importation of tractors. Where permits do exist, the application process should be as efficient and cost-effective as possible, the validity should be unlimited and there should be no restrictions in terms of quantity of tractors or number of shipments.

Among the 62 countries studied, 17 require importers to obtain permits to import tractors. Sometimes, import permits are intended to provide assurance on the shipment quality[15] or to limit the quantity of imports to protect local manufacturing. None of the OECD high-income and Europe and Central Asian countries—many of them manufacturers of tractors—require import

permits. Among the 17 countries where import permits are required, only Bangladesh, Cameroon, Côte d'Ivoire, Ethiopia and the Philippines allow permits with no restrictions in terms of quantity or number of shipments, and the permits have a validity of 12 months. By comparison, Lao PDR and Myanmar require that importers apply for a permit for *each* tractor shipment and the permit validity is only three months, making it comparatively burdensome for tractor importers to introduce their products to the market.

The data also shows that many countries—almost all of them low-income or lower-middle-income countries—require private companies to register as tractor importers *in addition* to the general business license. Countries may have introduced this requirement to monitor trade flows and the quality of imported goods, but the process should be efficient and affordable to limit its impact on trade flows. In half of the countries where this procedure is required, the registration is indefinite and does not have to be repeated. But in 14 countries, the registration has to be renewed after a number of years or after half a year, as in the case of Colombia. While the registration renewal is automatic in four countries, tractor importers in six Sub-Saharan countries, and in Bangladesh, Colombia, Myanmar and Sri Lanka have to undergo the entire process of registration renewal each time.

Figure 4.2 | Countries with strong regulatory frameworks implement their laws more efficiently

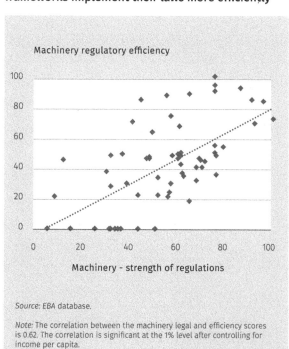

Source: EBA database.

Note: The correlation between the machinery legal and efficiency scores is 0.62. The correlation is significant at the 1% level after controlling for income per capita.

ENABLING THE BUSINESS OF AGRICULTURE 2017

Box 4.1 | What are the regulatory good practices for machinery?

	REGULATORY GOOD PRACTICES FOR MACHINERY	SOME COUNTRIES WHICH IMPLEMENT THE PRACTICE
TRACTOR IMPORTS	Businesses are not required to register as importers, beyond general business registration requirements. In countries where importer registration is required, the registration validity is indefinite or registration renewal is automatic.	**DENMARK, KOREA, REP., NIGERIA**
	Importers do not have to apply for an import permit each time they want to import. In countries where the import permit is required, it is a time-efficient, low-cost process. The permit is a blanket document (without any restrictions in terms of volume or number of shipments) with unlimited validity.	**COLOMBIA, ITALY, TANZANIA**
TRACTOR OPERATIONS	Tractor registration is required for on-the-road-use only, and the process is affordable and efficient	**BOSNIA AND HERZEGOVINA, MALAWI, POLAND**
	Regular inspections of in-use tractors are mandatory, affordable and undertaken in reasonable intervals (frequency of every two years).	**TURKEY, ZIMBABWE**
	Tractor dealers must provide after-market service and parts.	**JORDAN, MALAYSIA, ROMANIA**
TRACTOR TESTING AND STANDARDS	Countries have established national tractor performance and operator safety standards or follow established international standards.	**SERBIA, UKRAINE**
	Countries require tractors to be type approved before entering their market to ensure that the tractor conforms to the legal standards (such as safety, material, dimensional and performance standards) where it is being sold. Tractor type approvals and test reports issued by an authority in another country are recognized. If tractor tests are undertaken in a local testing center, the process is efficient and affordable.	**INDIA, MOROCCO**
	The tractor type approval is not time limited, provided that the specifications of the tractor remain unchanged.	**NIGERIA, RUSSIAN FEDERATION**

Source: EBA database.

Facilitate tractor durability by requiring roadworthiness inspections and tractor after-market service and parts

Most countries require vehicles to be maintained in safe, roadworthy condition for them to be used on their roads. Given that agricultural tractors are increasingly used to replace trucks in local transport activities and for commercial road haulage purposes, tractors in many countries are subject to roadworthiness inspections at regular intervals. The tests are conducted at an authorized test center and typically include testing of the brake and steering systems, vision features, noise pollution and other features. Of the 62 countries studied, about half make regular tractor roadworthiness testing mandatory. The data show that none of the countries in the Latin America and Caribbean region require inspections, with the exception of Chile and Haiti, while all four countries do in South Asia (Bangladesh, India, Nepal and Sri Lanka). European Union countries still have different requirements with regards to roadworthiness inspections of tractors. As of May 2018, however, the European Union will be harmonizing the minimum requirements for mandatory periodic roadworthiness tests for tractors with a maximum design speed exceeding 40km/h used for haulage on public roads.

Among those countries that require roadworthiness inspections, the period between required tests varies

Tractor. Aurangabad, India. Photo: Simone D. McCourtie / World Bank.

greatly. For example, in Burkina Faso, Malaysia and Uganda, the test is required every half-year. By contrast, in India the test is done only every five years. Experts suggest, however, that inspections should occur every two years.[16] Only five countries—Poland, Romania, Spain, Turkey and Zimbabwe—take this approach. The cost of inspections also varies across countries, ranging from 0.2% income per capita in OECD high-income countries, to 6.5% income per capita in Sub-Saharan African countries.

Countries that mandate roadworthiness inspections should logically also ensure that farmers have access to appropriate repair services and spare parts. All too often, tractor operators do not have any support if a machine breakdown occurs, and tractor "graveyards" can still be found in many countries.[17] Tractor dealers are not legally required to provide tractor maintenance and repair in the majority of countries studied for *EBA 2017*, with the exception of OECD high-income countries or those located in the Middle East and North Africa region.

Guarantee high-quality tractors by requiring type approval and testing of tractors in conformity with established standards

Agricultural tractors are imported from various countries. Although tractors are designed to satisfy a range of conditions, a machine produced in one country may or may not suit another country because of the prevailing edaphoclimatic conditions. The tractor design

and construction alone are not sufficient to judge and select a machine designed for a certain operation.[18] As such, a thorough testing and evaluation should be required of the tractor performance, quality, durability and safety.

Tractor tests are typically undertaken in conformity with established national or international standards.[19] Tractor performance and tractor operator safety standards ensure that only high-quality machines enter a country's supply chain and they provide unbiased information to manufacturers and consumers of tractors. Among the 62 countries studied, it is mostly countries in the Europe and Central Asia region and OECD high-income countries that have established national performance and safety standards or that enforce international tractor standards.

Tractor type approval is mandatory in about half the sample countries. All OECD high-income countries (with the exception of Chile) and European and Central Asian countries (with the exception of Georgia) have this requirement, along with India, Morocco, the Philippines, Vietnam and 10 countries in Sub-Saharan Africa. It should be noted that while the type approval is legally mandated in these countries, there appears to have been no such practice in Armenia, Kyrgyz Republic and Tajikistan.

The procedures involved in tractor type approval vary across countries, and the associated time and cost are consistently higher in countries where multiple

Figure 4.3 |Time and costs for tractor type approval vary across regions

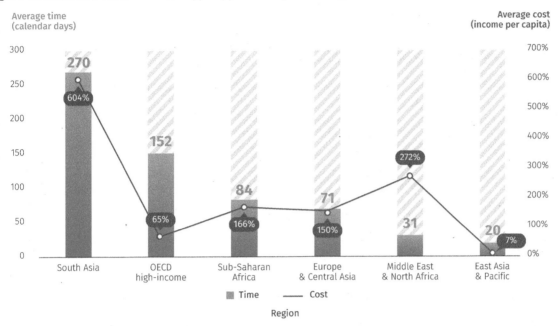

Average time
(calendar days)

Average cost
(income per capita)

■ Time ── Cost

Region

Source: EBA database.

Note: Latin America and Caribbean countries are excluded because tractor type approval is not mandatory in the countries studied in this region.

procedures are required (figure 4.3). While it is important that governments implement regulations in a time- and cost-efficient manner, a minimum number of steps should be involved to thoroughly test and evaluate a tractor and its performance. Tests should include laboratory testing and the issuance and publication of a test report. Many countries also test the tractor in the field, a procedure that is practiced in all OECD high-income countries (with the exception of Chile, where type approval is not required), as well as in Cameroon, India, Kazakhstan, Malawi, Nigeria, the Philippines, Romania, Russian Federation, Serbia, Sudan, Turkey and Ukraine.

Testing of agricultural tractors ensures the quality of tractors and their suitability for country conditions. Nonetheless, some of the main challenges traders face are costly and lengthy testing or certification of tractors, often duplicated across countries. Valuable business time and money could be saved if a tractor could be tested once and the results accepted in other markets for the tractor to be type approved.[20] The mutual recognition of conformity assessment results is strongly encouraged by the World Trade Organization (WTO) Agreement on Technical Barriers to Trade and is already operational in a number of existing networks in Europe and Asia and Pacific with regards to machinery testing.[21] Such a model could be applied in Africa.

The 22 countries in which tractor type approval is required—most of them OECD high-income countries and countries in Europe and Central Asia, but also in

Cameroon, Côte d'Ivoire, Ethiopia, Morocco, Uganda and Zimbabwe—recognize type approval certifications issued in other countries. In the European Union, a tractor that is tested by a designated testing facility and type approved by an authority in a member country is automatically recognized and accepted in other member countries without the need for further testing. The approval has unlimited validity and renewed testing is not required, provided that the specifications of the tractors are the same.

As outlined above, multiple testing or certification of agricultural tractors represents a burdensome endeavor for companies in many countries. In Kazakhstan, Kyrgyz Republic, the Philippines, Russian Federation and Ukraine, the tractor type approval process has to be repeated after five years and in India after three years.

Conclusion

An agricultural machinery procedural framework that balances control and efficiency requirements can help facilitate and ease the availability of tractors for agricultural production. Countries such as Poland, Serbia and Romania demonstrate that regulatory efficiency on the one hand—as defined by the time and cost involved in complying with target regulations—and tractor quality control regulations on the other, tend to be complementary and are important precursors for a well-functioning tractor market.

1   Mukherji 2013.

2   Reid 2011.

3   Sims and Kienzle 2006.

4   CEMA-European Agricultural Machinery 2014.

5   Food and Agriculture Data (FAOSTAT). FAO, Rome, http://faostat.fao.org/.

6   FAO and UNIDO 2008.

7   Houmy et al. 2013.

8   Clarke 2000.

9   Type approval (or "homologation") is the official recognition given by a national authority or agency that certifies that the tractor conforms to the prevailing regulatory, technical and safety requirements in the country. Before the tractor can be sold on the market and before reaching the farmer, the manufacturer (or an agency on behalf of the manufacturer) must complete its type approval and be certified by third-party verification that its design, construction and performance respect the country's regulations and standards.

10 UNESCAP/CSAM 2015.

11 Animaw et al. 2016.

12 The eight OECD high-income countries included in this year's report are Chile, Denmark, Greece, Italy, Korea, the Netherlands, Poland and Spain.

13 The 11 countries in the Europe and Central Asia region included in this year's report are as follows: Armenia, Bosnia and Herzegovina, Georgia, Kazakhstan, Kyrgyz Republic, Romania, Russian Federation, Serbia, Tajikistan, Turkey and Ukraine.

14 WTO Agreement on Import Licensing Procedures 1995.

15 UNCTAD 2012.

16 Council of the European Union 2014.

17 Houmy et al. 2013.

18 Tilakaratna 2005.

19 OECD 2012.

20 WTO 2016.

21 (1) The OECD Tractor Codes are a popular example of a standardization, testing and certification system under the umbrella of an intergovernmental organization; (2) the European Network for Testing of Agricultural Machines (ENTAM) is an agreement between different countries aimed at implementing standardized performance, safety and environmental tests of agricultural machinery and tools; and, (3) the Asian and Pacific Network for Testing of Agricultural Machinery (ANTAM), launched in 2013, aims at promoting "harmonization of testing codes and standards of agricultural machinery applied in the region that address quality, performance, occupational safety and environmental sustainability of agricultural machinery" (UN-CSAM 2016).

REFERENCES

Animaw, A. T., J. A. Mutegi Nkanya, J. M. Nyakiba and T. H. Woldemariam. 2016. "Agricultural Mechanization and South-South Knowledge Exchange: What Can Ethiopian and Kenyan Policymakers Learn from Bangladesh's Experience?" International Food Policy Research Institute (IFPRI), Washington, DC.

Clarke, L. J. 2000. "Agricultural Mechanization Strategy Formulation, Concepts and Methodology. Roles of the Private Sector and the Government." FAO, Rome.

Comité Européen des groupements de constructeurs du machinisme agricole (CEMA). 2014. "Advancing Agricultural Mechanization in Africa." CEMA, Brussels. http://cema-agri.org/publication/advancing-agricultural-mechanization-africa.

Council of the European Union. 2014. "Council Adopts the Roadworthiness Package." Council of the European Union, Brussels. http://www.consilium.europa.eu/uedocs/cms_data/docs/pressdata/en/trans/141818.pdf.

FAO (Food and Agriculture Organization) and UNIDO (United Nations Industrial Development Organization). 2008. "Agricultural Mechanization in Africa: Time for Action. Planning Investment for Enhanced Agricultural Productivity." Report of an Expert Group Meeting. FAO and UNIDO, Vienna.

Houmy, K., L. J. Clarke, J. E. Ashburner and J. Kienzle. 2013. "Agricultural Mechanization in Sub-Saharan Africa. Guidelines for Preparing a Strategy." FAO, Rome.

Mukherji, B. 2013. "India's Farmers Start to Mechanize Amid a Labor Shortage." *The Wall Street Journal*, New Delhi, India. http://www.wsj.com/articles/SB10001424052702304441404579121313326574626.

OECD (Organisation for Economic Co-operation and Development). 2012. "OECD Standard Code for the Official Testing of Agricultural and Forestry Tractor Performance." OECD, Paris. http://www.oecd.org/tad/code/Code%202%20-%20Final.pdf.

Reid, J. F. 2011. "The Impact of Mechanization on Agriculture." *The Bridge* Vol. 44. https://www.nae.edu/Publications/Bridge/52548/52645.aspx.

Sims, B. G. and J. Kienzle. 2006. "Farm Power and Mechanization for Small Farms in Sub-Saharan Africa; Agricultural and Food Engineering Technical Report." FAO, Rome.

Tilakaratna, H. M. 2005. "Country Report Sri Lanka. For the 1st Session of the Technical Committee." Asian Pacific Centre for Agricultural Engineering and Machinery, New Delhi.

UN (United Nations)-CSAM (Centre for Sustainable Agricultural Mechanization), Asian and Pacific Network for Testing of Agricultural Machinery (ANTAM). 2016. "About Us." CSAM, Beijing. http://www.antam-network.net/2016/about-us/.

UNCTAD (United Nations Conference on Trade and Development). 2012. "UNCTAD Coding System or Trade Control Measures." UNCTAD, Geneva. http://unctad.org/Sections/ditc_tab/docs/ditc_tab_Coding2012_en.pdf.

UNESCAP (United Nations Economic and Social Commission for Asia and the Pacific)/ CSAM (Centre for Sustainable Agricultural Mechanization). 2015. "ANTAM Standard Codes for Testing of Power Tillers." CSAM, Beijing.

WTO (World Trade Organization). 2016. "Technical Information on Technical Barriers to Trade." WTO, Geneva, Switzerland. https://www.wto.org/english/tratop_e/tbt_e/tbt_info_e.htm.

5 Finance

GADCO, a major rice processor in West Africa, buys rice from thousands of smallholder farmers. In the past, farmers had to travel, sometimes long distances, to the GADCO offices to receive payment in cash. However, in 2013, GADCO partnered with Tigo, a leading mobile operator in the region, to compensate farmers via mobile payments. Today farmers benefit from the convenience of accessing their money via agents who are available 24 hours a day, rather than waiting in line at a bank, and from the simplicity of buying mobile airtime directly with their Tigo-Cash virtual wallet, rather than having to buy and load airtime from a scratch card. Furthermore, because GADCO distributes monthly account statements, the program improves farmers' ability to monitor their accounts.[1]

Finance is a key element of agricultural development. Farmers require working capital, seasonal loans, and medium- to long-term credit to finance production, harvest, storage, transport and marketing. In addition to loans, farmers need access to payment services to expand operations. In this regard, reduction of rural poverty and increases of total per capita output can be achieved through enhancements in rural credit.[2] However, rural and agricultural finance are among the most challenging fields of financing. Agricultural production activities are seasonal, weather-dependent and spatially dispersed, making agricultural loans riskier and costlier than loans for business activities operated in urban locations. Formal financial institutions, especially commercial banks, have limited reach in rural areas.[3] Furthermore, farmers often have difficulty obtaining loans due to inadequate collateral. In developing countries, 78% of the capital stock of business is in the form of movable assets such as machinery, equipment or receivables, yet most financial institutions do not consider these assets as good sources of collateral.[4]

Innovation in the design and provision of financial services improves access to finance. Regulations need to be adapted to allow financial institutions, mobile operators and retailers to explore new services and partnership models, while protecting the integrity of transactions and the safety of customers' deposits.[5] Therefore, a strong legal framework is necessary to increase access to financial services. Laws and regulations should also provide farmers with the ability to use movable collateral to obtain a loan, while protecting lenders.

FINANCE

47

What do the EBA finance indicators measure?

EBA finance indicators measure laws and regulations that affect access to financial services for farmers and agribusinesses (table 5.1).

The indicators are organized as follows:

Non-bank lending institutions: This indicator measures the regulatory framework for deposit-taking microfinance institutions (MFIs) and financial cooperatives. MFIs and financial cooperatives are important providers of financial services to agribusinesses and farmers, especially those that cannot access financial services through commercial banks.[6]

Operation and prudential regulation of MFIs. This sub-indicator measures the requirements to establish an MFI and prudential regulations including minimum capital adequacy ratios and provisioning rules, as well as consumer protection requirements focusing on interest rate disclosure and enrollment in a deposit insurance system.

Operation and governance of financial cooperatives. This sub-indicator focuses on the regulatory framework for financial cooperatives including the minimum requirements for their establishment, prudential ratios, the ability to merge and consumer protection requirements similar to those measured for MFIs.

Branchless banking: Branchless banking, which consists of agent banking and e-money, can play an important role in providing financial services to clients who are traditionally excluded from formal financial services.[7] Strong regulations on branchless banking protect against the loss of customer funds,[8] fostering a positive customer experience that creates trust in the system.

Agent banking. This sub-indicator focuses on the regulations that allow third-party agents to provide financial services on behalf of financial institutions. It covers the minimum standards to qualify and operate as an agent, exclusivity of agent contracts, the range of financial services agents can provide and financial institution's liability for agent actions.

Table 5.1 | What do the EBA finance indicators measure?

NON-BANK LENDING INSTITUTIONS	***Operation and prudential regulation of MFIs*** • Prudential rules (capital adequacy ratio, minimum capital, loan loss provisioning) • Loan size limits • Consumer protection (effective interest rate disclosure, deposit insurance) ***Operation and governance of financial cooperatives*** • Prudential rules (minimum capital, prudential standards) • Consumer protection (effective interest rate disclosure, deposit insurance) • Ability to merge
BRANCHLESS BANKING	***Agent Banking*** • Minimum standards to operate as an agent and services offered by agents • Exclusivity of agent contracts • Financial institution liability for agent actions ***E-money*** • License requirements (interoperability, internal controls, consumer protection mechanisms) for non-financial institution e-money issuers • Safeguards for customer funds
MOVABLE COLLATERAL	***Warehouse receipts*** • Elements of a valid warehouse receipt • Performance guarantees • Receipt negotiability ***Legal rights and credit information*** • Security interest granted to movable assets and future assets • Collateral registry • Credit information from non-bank institutions

Sources: EBA database, Doing Business database.

E-money. This sub-indicator covers the regulations for the provision of e-money by non-financial institution issuers. It covers licensing and operational standards, as well as requirements on safeguarding customer funds and deposit insurance protection.

Movable collateral: The movable collateral indicator focuses on provisions relating to the use of collateral categories that are relevant to agricultural enterprises and smallholders. A warehouse receipts system creates the possibility for using agricultural products (such as crops) as collateral—farmers deposit products in a licensed warehouse in exchange for a warehouse receipt, which they can use to obtain a bank loan.

Warehouse receipts. This sub-indicator measures specific legal provisions governing the use of warehouse receipts as movable collateral. It covers the elements of a valid warehouse receipt, performance guarantees and receipt negotiability.

Legal rights and credit information. This sub-indicator takes some of the measures of legal rights of borrowers and lenders with respect to secured transactions and depth of credit information from the *Doing Business–*Getting Credit topic. It covers regulation on movable collateral, security rights on future and after-acquired assets, and the depth of credit information on small loans and availability of credit information from non-bank institutions.

How do countries perform on the finance indicators?

Countries from OECD high-income and the Latin America and the Caribbean regions perform the best on the finance topic, driven largely by the strength of regulations on MFIs and financial cooperatives, and a regulatory environment that enables branchless banking. Most OECD high-income countries have established a comprehensive regulatory environment for financial cooperatives and regulations that enable branchless banking, mainly for e-money. Meanwhile the Europe and Central Asia region earned the second highest score on the movable collateral indicator including the *Doing Business–*Getting Credit indicator and regulation of warehouse receipts. Although low-income countries score poorly on average, Tanzania emerged as one of the top five performers in the finance indicators (table 5.2). Tanzania earned high scores for its regulations on MFIs and financial cooperatives, as well as its warehouse receipt regulations, which describe the elements of a valid receipt and require the warehouse operator to provide multiple performance guarantees.

At the indicator level, countries' scores on non-bank lending institutions, branchless banking and movable collateral indicators do not correlate significantly

Table 5.2 | Where are finance regulations strongest according to the finance indicators?

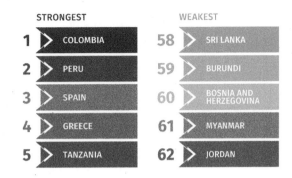

STRONGEST		WEAKEST	
1	COLOMBIA	58	SRI LANKA
2	PERU	59	BURUNDI
3	SPAIN	60	BOSNIA AND HERZEGOVINA
4	GREECE	61	MYANMAR
5	TANZANIA	62	JORDAN

Source: EBA database.

among themselves, suggesting that countries rarely score universally well on the indicators. For instance, Uganda has comprehensive legislations regulating the operation of warehouse receipts, but it lacks a regulatory framework for agent banking activities and does not allow non-financial institutions to issue e-money.

Between March 2015 and June 2016, a total of 16 countries conducted regulatory reforms to align with certain good practices (box 5.1) in areas that are measured by the finance indicators. E-money was the area with the highest number of reforms: nine countries in Sub-Saharan Africa (SSA) (Ghana, Tanzania, West African Monetary Union [WAMU] members,[9] and Zambia), and Myanmar reformed their e-money laws. Other reforms in the past year include Côte d'Ivoire, which adopted a new law regulating warehouse receipts; Ghana and Mozambique adopted new legal frameworks for agent banking; and Myanmar adopted a new banking regulation.

In addition to enacting legislative reforms and regulations to enable agriculture financing, countries also explored other policy measures such as state-sponsored Partial Credit Guarantees Schemes (PGCSs) and mandatory lending quotas to promote agricultural finance. There is strong evidence suggesting that the simple existence of a PCGS does not guarantee increased lending to the agriculture sector and that lending quotas for agriculture lead to low profitability for banks and high non-performing loans.[10] As country context and implementation details significantly affect the results of such policies, EBA did not score this data. Data collected show that 18 of the 62 countries studied have a PCGS specialized for agricultural loans lent by commercial banks. The SSA region has the highest number of countries (6 of 21) with PCGSs, followed by Latin America and the Caribbean (4). Only eight countries, mostly in SSA, allow MFIs to participate in the scheme. For lending quotas, only seven countries have policies requiring commercial banks to

Box 5.1 | What are the regulatory good practices for finance?

	REGULATORY GOOD PRACTICES FOR FINANCE	SOME COUNTRIES WHICH IMPLEMENT THE PRACTICE
NON-BANK LENDING INSTITUTIONS	MFIs can take deposits and maintain a capital adequacy ratio (CAR) that is equal to or slightly higher than the CAR for banks. MFIs also disclose the full cost of credit to loan applicants and participate in a deposit insurance system.	CAMBODIA, KENYA, PERU, TAJIKISTAN, TANZANIA
	Financial cooperatives disclose the full cost of credit to loan applicants, participate in a deposit insurance system and can merge to create a new financial cooperative.	BOLIVIA, COLOMBIA, MEXICO, POLAND
BRANCHLESS BANKING	Financial institutions can hire agents to provide services on their behalf. Regulations identify minimum standards to qualify and operate as an agent; allow agents to offer a wide range of services such as cash-in, cash-out, bill payment, transfers, account opening and "Know Your Customer" due diligence; and hold financial institutions liable for agent actions.	ETHIOPIA, INDIA, MEXICO, PERU
	Non-financial institutions can issue e-money. Regulations specify minimum licensing standards for non-financial institution e-money issuers (such as existence of internal control mechanisms that comply with anti-money laundering and combatting the financing of terrorism laws—Anti-Money Laundering and Combatting Financing of Terrorism (AML/CFT)—and consumer protection and recourse mechanisms) and require e-money issuers to safeguard customer funds in a prudentially regulated financial institution.	CÔTE D'IVOIRE, DENMARK, ROMANIA, SERBIA, SPAIN
MOVABLE COLLATERAL	A legal framework exists for a warehouse receipts system. Regulations require warehouse operators to obtain either insurance, pay into an indemnity fund or file a bond with the regulator to secure performance of obligations as an operator; define the elements of a valid warehouse receipt; and allow both paper and electronic receipts.	ROMANIA, TURKEY, UGANDA, UKRAINE, ZAMBIA
	A legal framework exists for secured transactions that grant security interest in movable and future assets. Credit information can be distributed by non-banking institutions such as retailers and borrowers can access their data through the credit bureau or credit registry.	COLOMBIA, MEXICO, RWANDA

Sources: EBA database , Doing Business database.

Figure 5.1 | Strong regulation for deposit-taking MFIs enables agribusiness activities

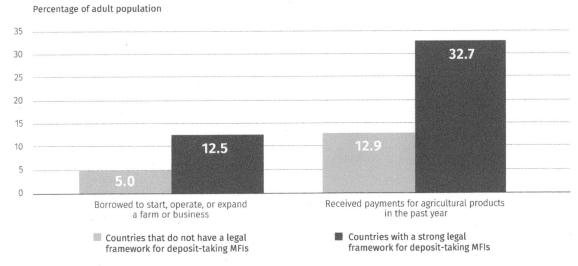

Percentage of adult population

Borrowed to start, operate, or expand a farm or business: Countries that do not have a legal framework for deposit-taking MFIs = 5.0; Countries with a strong legal framework for deposit-taking MFIs = 12.5

Received payments for agricultural products in the past year: Countries that do not have a legal framework for deposit-taking MFIs = 12.9; Countries with a strong legal framework for deposit-taking MFIs = 32.7

■ Countries that do not have a legal framework for deposit-taking MFIs

■ Countries with a strong legal framework for deposit-taking MFIs

Sources: EBA database; Findex database.

Note: Countries with a strong legal framework for deposit-taking microfinance institutions (MFIs) are those that have a score standing in the first quartile of the MFI scores. Countries classified with a high level of financial inclusion are not measured under the MFI and agent banking indicators. Countries that score 0.8 or higher, as measured by the average of the normalized value of the Findex variables "account at a financial institution (% of rural adult population)" and "account at a financial institution (% of adult population)," are classified as having a high degree of financial inclusion. Countries under this classification are as follows: Denmark, Greece, Italy, Korea, Rep., the Netherlands and Spain. Lao PDR, Liberia, Morocco and Mozambique are not included in the sample as data are missing from the Findex database.

lend a percentage of their portfolio for the purposes of promoting agricultural activities—namely, Bangladesh, Bolivia, India, Nepal, the Philippines, Sri Lanka and Zimbabwe. Bolivia is the only country that also requires MFIs to lend a percentage of total loans to the agricultural sector.

What are the regulatory good practices?

Box 5.1 highlights regulatory good practices and some countries that implement these practices.

Adopting a tiered approach for regulating deposit-taking financial institutions

The non-bank lending institution indicator measures consumer protection and prudential regulation for deposit-taking MFIs and financial cooperatives. Countries with a strong legal framework for deposit-taking MFIs in particular tend to have a higher share of the adult population that borrows to start, operate or expand a farm or business, or received payment related to agribusiness products (figure 5.1). This situation suggests that strengthening the legal framework for deposit-taking MFIs has great potential for enabling agribusiness activities.[11]

In establishing a regulatory framework for deposit-taking institutions, it is a good practice to adopt a tiered approach that corresponds with the financial institution's risk portfolio. Prudential regulation such as capital requirements, capital adequacy ratio (CAR) and loan loss provisioning are important components

of a legal framework that limits risk-taking of deposit-taking institutions. These regulations are risk management tools that ensure that financial institutions are well-capitalized in the event of a financial shock. Given their tendency to have riskier portfolios and higher operating costs,[12] a good practice for regulating deposit-taking MFIs is to establish capital adequacy requirements and provisioning rules that are equal to or slightly more aggressive than those of commercial banks.[13] Among the 33 countries with a legal framework for deposit-taking MFIs, nearly 90% include capital adequacy requirements for MFIs. In contrast, countries have adopted diverse risk management practices for regulating financial cooperatives. While 26 out of the 56 countries with a legal framework for financial cooperatives have established minimum capital adequacy requirements for financial cooperatives, the remaining 30 have adopted various other risk management practices, such as establishing a minimum liquidity requirement or a maximum credit exposure.

Increasing consumer protection through deposit-insurance scheme and transparency in pricing

Financial consumer protection ensures that customers receive clear information on products and services to allow them to make informed decisions, and increases trust in the banking system. Regulations can help improve consumer understanding of terms and products and increase market competition by requiring financial institutions to disclose the effective interest or full cost of credit to the customer. While 76% of countries studied require commercial banks to disclose the full cost of

Figure 5.2 | Countries that lack regulations that enable non-traditional financial service providers to perform branchless banking

Source: EBA database.

Note: Countries classified with a high level of financial inclusion are not measured under the agent banking indicator. If a country earns a score of 0.8 or higher, as measured by the average of the normalized value of the Findex variables "account at a financial institution (% of rural adult population)" and "account at a financial institution (% of adult population)," it is classified as having high degree of financial inclusion. Countries under this classification are Denmark, Greece, Italy, Korea, Rep., the Netherlands and Spain.

credit to customers, only 39% require MFIs to disclose this information (42% for financial cooperatives). These requirements are either embedded in the legal framework regulating the specific financial institution or can be found in the general consumer protection laws.

In addition, although a majority of countries (69%) require traditional banks to participate in a deposit insurance scheme, only 14 countries also require MFIs and only 11 countries require financial cooperatives[14] to participate in a deposit insurance system. Mexico is one of the countries that scores highest on the non-bank lending institutions indicator and it requires both MFIs and financial cooperatives to participate in a deposit insurance system.

Diversity of financial service providers in branchless banking operations

Strengthening regulation on branchless banking operations such as e-money and agent banking promotes greater financial inclusion. Countries with an enabling legal framework for branchless banking activities tend to have a higher share of adult population with an account at a financial institution.[15] E-money and agent banking benefit farmers by enabling them to receive payments through mobile phone-based accounts or via a local agent rather than having to travel to a financial institution or to a producer to obtain payment, which reduces transaction costs and the risks associated with holding cash.

Countries should adopt branchless banking frameworks that include a wide array of financial service providers, as this encourages competition and reduces

transaction costs for customers.[16] In the past year, 10 countries reformed their e-money regulations including Ghana, Tanzania and Zambia. Of the 56 countries that now have laws on e-money, only two-thirds allow non-financial institutions to issue e-money. In addition, only 15 of the 27 countries with laws on agent banking allow individuals, as well as businesses, to act as banking agents (figure 5.2).

Ghana scores well in branchless banking due to amendments to both its "Agent Guidelines" and its "Guidelines for E-money Issuers in Ghana, 2015." The new "Agent Guidelines" allow both individuals and businesses to operate as agents and increases the number of minimum standards required to qualify as a bank agent. The "Guidelines for E-money Issuers in Ghana, 2015" allow non-financial institutions to issue e-money and provide high standards such as a minimum capital requirement, existence of internal control mechanisms to comply with anti-money laundering and combatting of financing terrorism (AML/CFT) standards and consumer protection mechanisms to obtain a license. In addition, in 2015, WAMU countries strengthened their e-money regulations when they adopted a regulation governing the conditions and terms of e-money issuers' activities in WAMU. The regulation set new requirements for interoperability and consumer protection measures to obtain a license as an e-money issuer. Previously there were no such requirements. The regulation also strengthens consumer protection standards for e-money issuers by requiring 100% of consumers' funds to be safeguarded in a prudentially regulated financial institution.

Figure 5.3 | Most countries require at least one performance guarantee in a warehouse receipts system

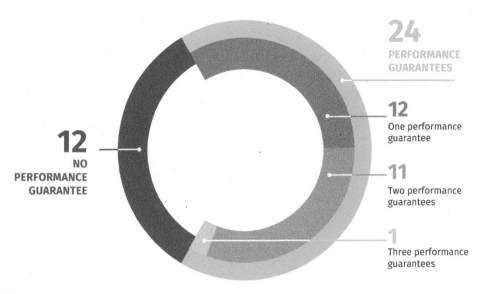

24
PERFORMANCE
GUARANTEES

12
One performance
guarantee

11
Two performance
guarantees

1
Three performance
guarantees

12
NO
PERFORMANCE
GUARANTEE

Source: EBA database.

Reducing risk through performance guarantees for warehouse receipts

A performance guarantee is a requirement placed on a warehouse operator to secure performance of obligations as an operator. Performance guarantees reduce both the depositor's risk in depositing goods in a warehouse and the bank's risk in lending against a warehouse receipt.[17] Therefore, a strong legal framework for warehouse receipts includes at least one performance guarantee. The finance topic measured the existence of the following three types of performance guarantees, namely: 1) filing a bond with the regulator; 2) paying into an indemnity fund; and 3) insuring the warehouse and stored goods against fire, theft and natural disasters. Among the 36 countries with a legal framework for warehouse receipts, 24 require at least one performance guarantee, among which 11 countries require two (figure 5.3). Requiring warehouse operators to insure the warehouse and stored goods against theft and natural disasters is the most common form of performance guarantee, with almost 60% of countries requiring insurance, including Colombia, Ethiopia and Romania. Filing a bond with the regulator is the second most common form of performance guarantee, with 28% of countries requiring this option.

Conclusion

Financial regulations are rarely established to serve certain sectors. Instead, a comprehensive financial regulatory environment can have beneficial effects for all sectors, including agriculture.

For example, regulations that are appropriate to the portfolio risks and operating characteristics of MFIs and financial cooperatives are essential to ensure their smooth operation serving generally across all sectors. Having these regulations in place is particularly important for agriculture because it enables these institutions to better provide credit and financial services to smallholder farmers and agribusinesses who are usually excluded from traditional banking credit or services. Kenya and Vietnam are among the countries that have established either the same or slightly more stringent requirements on the capital adequacy ratio and provisioning rules for MFIs, as compared with commercial banks. In response to the recent boom in branchless banking activities, regulations are needed to engender trust and transparency in such systems, promote innovation, as well as minimize risk, protect customers and ensure system stability. The majority of OECD high-income countries have established legislation regulating e-money activities, which helps to create a level playing field for financial institutions and non-financial institutions that are active in this area. With regards to movable collateral, comprehensive legal frameworks on secured transactions and warehouse receipts, such as in Rwanda, allow borrowers to use their agricultural assets to obtain essential credit.

NOTES

1   CTA 2015.

2   Burgess and Pande 2005.

3   Rabobank Nederland 2005.

4   Alvarez de la Campa 2011. "While in the developing world 78% of the capital stock of a business enterprise is typically movable assets such as machinery, equipment or receivables and only 22% immovable property, financial institutions are reluctant to accept movable property as collateral."

5   Alexandre, Mas and Radcliffe 2011.

6   CGAP 2012.

7   Mahmood and Sarker 2015.

8   Dias and McKee 2010.

9   *EBA17* covers the following 6 WAMU members: Benin, Burkina Faso, Côte d'Ivoire, Mali, Niger and Senegal.

10 Rani and Garg 2015.

11 The correlation is 0.55 between the *EBA17* finance indicator score of MFI and the FINDEX data on the percentage of adult population that have borrowed to start, operate or expand a farm or business. The correlation is 0.58 between the *EBA17* finance indicator score of MFI and the FINDEX data on the percentage of adult population that have received payment related to agribusiness products. Both correlations are significant at 1% level after controlling for GNI per capita.

12 CGAP 2012.

13 *Ibid.*

14 Countries classified with a high level of financial inclusion are not measured under the agent banking and MFI indicators. If a country earns a score of 0.8 or higher as measured by the average of the normalized value of the FINDEX variables "account at a financial institution (% of rural adult population)" and "account at a financial institution (% of adult population)," it is classified as having high degree of financial inclusion. Countries under this classification are Denmark, Greece, Italy, Korea, the Netherlands and Spain.

15 The correlation is 0.46 between *EBA17* finance-branchless banking score and the FINDEX data on the percentage of adult population having an account at a financial institution. The correlation is significant at 5% level after controlling for GNI per capita.

16 Tarazi and Breloff 2011.

17 Wehling and Garthwaite 2015.

REFERENCES

Alexandre, C., I. Mas and D. Radcliff. 2011. "Regulating New Banking Models to Bring Financial Services to All." *Challenge Magazine* 54 (3): 116–34.

Alvarez de la Campa, A. 2011. "Increasing Access to Credit through Reforming Secured Transactions in the MENA Region." Policy Research Working Paper 5613. World Bank, Washington, DC.

Burgess, R. and R. Pande. 2005. "Can Rural Banks Reduce Poverty? Evidence from the Indian Social Banking Experiment," *American Economic Review* 95 (3): 780–95.

CGAP (Consultative Group to assist the Poor). 2012. "A Guide to Regulation and Supervision of Microfinance: Consensus Guidelines." CGAP, Washington, DC.

CTA. 2015. "Mobile Payments: How Digital Finance Is Transforming Agriculture." Technical Centre for Agricultural and Rural Cooperation, Wageningen.

Dias, D. and K. McKee. 2010. "Protecting Branchless Banking Consumers: Policy Objectives and Regulatory Options." *CGAP Focus Note 64*, September. CGAP, Washington, DC.

Mahmood, R. and S. Sarker. 2015. "Inclusive Growth through Branchless Banking: A Review of Agent Banking and its Impact." *Journal of Economics and Sustainable Development* 6 (23).

Rabobank Nederland. 2005. "Access to Financial Services in Developing Countries." Economic Research Department, Rabobank Nederland, Netherlands.

Rani, S. and D. Garg. 2015. "Priority Sector Lending: Trends, Issues and Strategies." *International Journal of Management and Social Sciences Research* (IJMSSR) 4 (1), January.

Tarazi, M. and P. Breloff. 2011. "Regulating Banking Agents." *CGAP Focus Note 68*, March. CGAP, Washington, DC.

Wehling, P. and B. Garthwaite. 2015. "Designing Warehouse Receipt Legislation: Regulatory Options and Recent Trends." Prepared in collaboration with the Development Law Service of the FAO Legal Office. FAO, Rome.

6 Markets

COEXPHAL, founded by 17 agricultural cooperatives in 1977, is the Association of Fruit and Vegetable Producers of Almería in southeast Spain. Throughout the years, it has provided a wide range of services and helped its members implement innovative changes in production and processing activities. For example, to address food safety and plant health concerns, COEXPHAL established its own laboratory to perform quality testing and analysis for farmers and cooperatives, facilitating compliance with horticultural product standards in destination markets. It also led the implementation of integrated pest management strategies to encourage more sustainable production practices. As a result, COEXPHAL now has market access in 43 countries, represents 65% of exports and 70% of fruit and vegetable production in Almería, and can directly sell consumer-ready products to large buyers such as supermarket chains.[1]

Market accessibility is vital to the growth and prosperity of agribusiness, and the surrounding regulatory environment has a direct effect on the ability of farmers to bring their products to market and respond to growing global food demand. However, agricultural products, such as fruits and vegetables, cereals or commodities such as tea, coffee and cocoa beans, cannot be marketed until companies have satisfied relevant legal requirements, including registrations, licenses and memberships, and products have met safety and quality standards.[2]

Trade is facilitated where licensing requirements and export procedures are less burdensome, time-consuming and costly. Furthermore, commercially-oriented agricultural production requires strong plant protection regulations that ensure reliable pest management in the field and robust inspection and verification practices at the border.[3] Pest and disease outbreaks can lead to infested products, reduced yields or even crop failures, all of which compromise the ability of producers to achieve consistent production levels and meet phytosanitary standards in destination markets.[4] The 2015 outbreak of the bacterium *Xylella fastidiosa* in Italy's Salento region, for example, affected more than 1 of the 11 million olive trees there. Buffer and containment zones have been established to stop the bacteria from spreading, but Italian olive and olive oil production is projected to drop in the coming years.[5] Regulatory good practices include a clear mandate for national plant protection authorities to conduct pest surveillance and for farmers to report unusual pest occurrences, to promptly deal with any outbreaks and manage endemic pest populations.[6]

A fruit and vegetable stand in Kampala, Uganda.
Photo: Arne Hoel / World Bank.

Market access can also be enhanced when farmers participate in producer organizations, such as cooperatives and other forms of associations, which can aggregate production and facilitate compliance with regulatory requirements. In addition, producer organizations enable farmer members to achieve economies of scale that can, in turn, result in more profitable and stable market participation.[7] In Europe, producer organizations process and market 60% of agricultural commodities and about 50% of input supply.[8] In Brazil, cooperatives are responsible for 37% of agricultural GDP, and in Egypt, 4 million farmers earn their income through cooperative membership.[9]

What do the markets indicators measure?

EBA markets indicators measure laws and regulations that impact access to agricultural markets for producers and agribusinesses (table 6.1). The indicators are organized as follows:

Agricultural trade: Agricultural trade plays an important role in securing greater quantity, wider variety and better quality food at lower prices. Trade also creates economies of scale, establishes and strengthens product value chains, facilitates the transfer of technology and attracts foreign investment. This indicator measures regulatory requirements on trade in agricultural products, including price controls and auction requirements, mandatory trader-level licenses

and memberships to operate in the domestic and/or export market, phytosanitary certification procedures and the time and cost to obtain mandatory, agriculture-specific, per-shipment export documents.[10]

Plant protection: Strong plant protection frameworks protect crops from pests and diseases by regulating the processes and practices to which agricultural products may be subjected during production, processing and trade.[11] This indicator measures key aspects of phytosanitary legislation on the management and control of pests and diseases, including the existence and accessibility of pest lists and information, pest surveillance and reporting obligations, risk analysis and risk-based inspections on agricultural imports.

Producer organizations: Not only can producer organizations enable members to access inputs at lower costs, but they can also facilitate sales, negotiate long-term agricultural contracts and enter high-value, reliable value chains for the benefit of their members.[12] This indicator measures key issues relating to the establishment and operation of producer organizations, including capital and membership requirements, profit distribution, government involvement, nondiscrimination, measures to promote female participation and procedures to establish a producer organization.

Additional data on contract farming were collected but not scored and are presented in appendix D.

Table 6.1 | What do the markets indicators measure?

AGRICULTURAL TRADE	• Domestic price controls • Auctions and/or fixed market places • Licenses, memberships or registration requirements to trade in the domestic market and export • Per-shipment export documents (number, time and cost)
PLANT PROTECTION	• Existence of a designated agency to conduct pest surveillance on plants • List of regulated quarantine pests and pest databases • Legal obligation and penalties on land owners/users to report pest outbreaks • Existence of designated agency to conduct pest risk analysis (PRA) • Publicly available PRA reports (online) and risk-based phytosanitary import inspections
PRODUCER ORGANIZATIONS	• Registration process (statutory time for registration; reasons for rejection) • Minimum capital requirements to establish a producer organization • Rules on membership (legal and natural persons, nationality, government) and nonmember participation • Nondiscrimination requirements and gender-equality promotion • Distribution of profits and dividends

Source: EBA database.

Table 6.2 | Where are markets regulations strongest and most efficient?

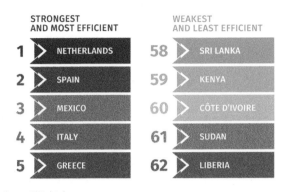

STRONGEST AND MOST EFFICIENT		WEAKEST AND LEAST EFFICIENT	
1	NETHERLANDS	58	SRI LANKA
2	SPAIN	59	KENYA
3	MEXICO	60	CÔTE D'IVOIRE
4	ITALY	61	SUDAN
5	GREECE	62	LIBERIA

Source: EBA database.

How do countries perform on the markets indicators?

Countries do not perform uniformly across the markets indicators (table 6.2). For example, the 2013 Cooperative Societies Act of Tanzania sets out a number of regulatory good practices that can facilitate the capitalization and growth of producer organizations, such as the provision of nonmember shares and dividends that can be freely established, which place the country's performance on the producer organizations indicator above the global average. However, to obtain the four documents required to export agricultural products from Tanzania, it takes 16 days and costs 4.3% income per capita, which is more cumbersome and costly than other Sub-Saharan African countries.

For OECD high-income countries such as Chile, even if they are among the top performers on average, there is potential for improvement in their rules governing producer organizations, such as the adoption of time-frames for the review of applications to establish a producer organization and potential for nonmembers to invest in producer groups.

Among the three indicators under the markets topic, country performance with respect to plant protection regulations varies the most. The phytosanitary legislation of the Netherlands, Poland and Spain showcases almost all the good practices covered by this indicator, whereas the laws of Haiti, Liberia and Myanmar do not include any. In Sub-Saharan Africa, the region that performs the worst on this indicator, 7 of the 21 countries do not have a clearly designated government agency to conduct pest surveillance and only Senegal and Tanzania have a publicly available database with information on plant pests and diseases. Nevertheless, last year more countries in Sub-Saharan Africa adopted regulatory reforms in the area of plant protection than countries in other regions. The Government of Rwanda introduced a new plant protection law, which creates obligations on citizens to report pest outbreaks. In

Uganda, the new 2015 Plant Protection and Health Act provides that phytosanitary import inspections can now be carried out on a risk-management basis. Finally, the list of regulated quarantine pests for the Government of Sudan is now available on the International Plant Protection Convention (IPPC) website, as is the case for Nicaragua, which is the only country outside of Sub-Saharan Africa that improved on the plant protection indicator this year.

Regarding the total time and cost to obtain per-shipment documents to export agricultural products, OECD high-income countries have the most streamlined process—on average, it costs 0.0% income per capita and takes 0.4 days (figure 6.1). For example, due to regional integration in the European Union (EU), companies do not have to obtain any additional agriculture-specific documents when trading products between EU member states. In East Asia and Pacific, South Asia and Sub-Saharan Africa, however, at least two documents are required for each shipment. It is most time-consuming to complete the process in Sub-Saharan African countries, taking 6.0 days on average, and the documents are most expensive in South Asia and Sub-Saharan Africa, costing 2.5% income per capita on average. That said, the Government of Kenya has taken steps to reform and improve the export process. Not only did the Government of Kenya reduce the official fees for the phytosanitary certificate, but it also abolished the requirement to obtain an export release order and pay a special tea levy to the Tea Directorate, which was previously imposed on a per-shipment basis.

At the commodity level, the process to obtain the mandatory documents to export perishable products (for example, fruits and vegetables) is on average more efficient and less costly than that for exports of cereals and cash crop products such as coffee, cocoa and tea, which are more often subject to specific export permits and additional safety and quality control procedures.

What are the regulatory good practices?

Box 6.1 highlights regulatory good practices for markets and some countries that implement such practices.

Streamlining phytosanitary certification procedures

The sanitary and phytosanitary rules, technical standards and product regulations that importing countries apply to agricultural products often lead to lengthy and costly export processes, including complex phytosanitary inspection and certification procedures in the exporting country.[13] Improving the efficiency of these processes can reduce the burden on the export businesses and potentially encourage larger volumes of trade.

Figure 6.1 | The cost to obtain per-shipment export documents for agricultural products is highest in South Asia and Sub-Saharan Africa

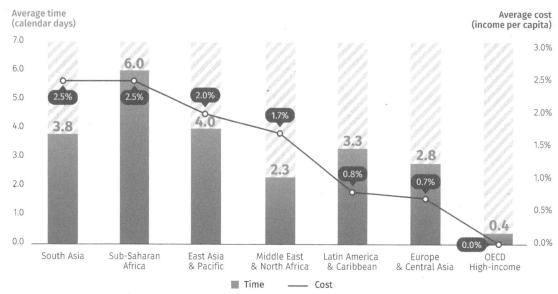

Average time (calendar days)

Average cost (income per capita)

	South Asia	Sub-Saharan Africa	East Asia & Pacific	Middle East & North Africa	Latin America & Caribbean	Europe & Central Asia	OECD High-income
Time	3.8	6.0	4.0	2.3	3.3	2.8	0.4
Cost	2.5%	2.5%	2.0%	1.7%	0.8%	0.7%	0.0%

■ Time ——— Cost

Source: EBA database.

Note: Data on time to obtain per-shipment export documents are not available for Ghana, Haiti, Malaysia and Zimbabwe. Data on cost to obtain per-shipment export documents are not available for Liberia. These cases were excluded from the calculation of the averages by region.

Phytosanitary certification procedures, in particular, are subject to duplicative, costly and inefficient processes due to the need for product inspection and, at times, sampling and laboratory testing. To increase efficiency in a phytosanitary certification system, having an electronic means to initiate the phytosanitary certification process and allowing for on-site inspection and issuance of the certificate, would allow products to be packed and sealed in the same place as the inspection and certificate issuance are carried out. This process would reduce associated transport and logistics costs, and allow for immediate shipment for export. In countries that have electronic systems and allow on-site inspection and issuance of phytosanitary certificates, the time and cost to obtain a phytosanitary certificate are lower than in those that still only allow for paper-based applications and offsite inspection and certificate issuance (figure 6.2).

Of the 62 countries studied, 19 provide for an electronic means to initiate the phytosanitary certification process, which includes either email or the use of an online portal. In 33 countries, applications continue to be submitted in hard copy form to the nearest plant protection office or electronic systems are not currently working.[14] The ability of plant protection officers to conduct inspections and issue phytosanitary certificates on-site where products are produced, processed, packaged and/or stored is possible in only 19 countries.

Chile, Kenya, Korea, and the Netherlands also have the capacity to generate, issue and send phytosanitary certificates in electronic form (ePhyto); these certificates can be sent electronically to destination countries that have ePhyto systems in place. The ePhyto mechanism allows for the exchange of phytosanitary certificates between governments based on bilateral agreements; it can increase the security and efficiency of government certification processes and, in turn, facilitate trade. In Chile, for example, electronic phytosanitary certificates are used for agricultural exports to China. The system was initially tested with grapes and, due to its success, was later rolled out to all fruit and vegetable products. However, this was only made possible through sustained bilateral efforts to standardize the electronic exchange of information and ensure that software interfaces could communicate directly with one another in a secure and timely manner.[15] In an effort to facilitate the expansion of ePhyto globally, the IPPC Secretariat recently launched the Global ePhyto Solution project to develop a standardized approach to the security and method of exchange of certificates, to ensure that all of their contracting parties are able to easily use ePhyto processes.[16]

Open agricultural markets

Government regulation on a tradeable commodity is likely to have some impact on trade and particularly on costs, risk and barriers to competition.[17] Policy and regulatory factors that are important to agricultural trade

Box 6.1 | Regulatory good practices for markets

	REGULATORY GOOD PRACTICES FOR MARKETS	SOME COUNTRIES WHICH IMPLEMENT THE PRACTICE
AGRICULTURAL TRADE	Price controls are not imposed on agricultural products and agricultural products do not have to be sold at an auction or in a specific marketplace.	BANGLADESH, PHILIPPINES
	Applications for phytosanitary certificates may be submitted electronically or an ePhyto system is in place.	CHILE, KENYA
	The official fee schedule for the phytosanitary certificate is published online or in the law.	COLOMBIA, KAZAKHSTAN
	It is efficient and affordable to obtain the mandatory per-shipment documents to export agricultural products.	GUATEMALA, JORDAN
PLANT PROTECTION	The list of regulated quarantine pests and information on pests and disease are available online.	MEXICO, TURKEY
	Owners and occupiers of land and/or crop owners are required to report any pests occurring on their land.	KYRGYZ REPUBLIC, MOZAMBIQUE
	A specific government agency or unit is designated to conduct pest surveillance.	BOLIVIA, ROMANIA
	A specific government agency or unit is designated to conduct pest risk analysis and the results are made available online.	KOREA, REP., VIETNAM
	Phytosanitary import inspections may be conducted on a risk-management basis.	MOROCCO, NICARAGUA
PRODUCER ORGANIZATIONS	Minimum capital requirements, if any, are low relative to a country's income per capita.	CAMEROON, MALAWI
	Decisions to register producer organizations must be issued within a timeframe specified in the law and rejections are explained to the applicants.	CAMBODIA, COLOMBIA
	The rate of dividends that can be paid to member or nonmember shares is not capped, and profits or surpluses may be distributed to members in the form of shares.	URUGUAY, ZAMBIA
	Membership is available to both domestic and foreign, natural and legal persons, although government membership is prohibited.	ARMENIA, KAZAKHSTAN
	Limitations on membership that disparately impact women do not exist and measures are in place to promote women's participation.	GREECE, KENYA
	The principles of open membership and nondiscrimination apply.	BURKINA FASO, MALI

Source: EBA database.

Figure 6.2 | It is cheaper and faster to obtain a phytosanitary certificate in countries that have electronic processes in place and that can conduct inspections and issue certificates on-site

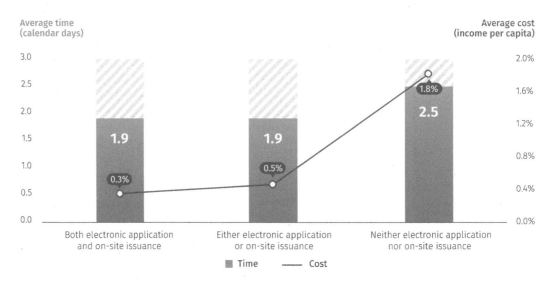

Notes: Data on electronic application of phytosanitary certificates are not available for Egypt, Arab Rep., Senegal, Serbia, Spain, Sudan, Tajikistan, Turkey, Uganda, Ukraine and Uruguay. Data on on-site issuance of phytosanitary certificates are not available for Ghana and Sudan. These cases were excluded from the calculation of the averages.

include unpredictable and/or discretionary policies, price controls, and non-tariff barriers such as complex licensing systems.[18]

Price volatility, particularly in essential commodities such as grains or high-value exports such as cocoa, coffee or tea, is a traditional driving force behind government regulation, particularly price controls, with the ultimate goal being to keep food prices low or to ensure farmers receive a minimum guaranteed price for their outputs. Price controls have been a common policy choice due to the social stigma surrounding other assistance mechanisms, such as direct payments. However, a broad evidence base now exists to show that price controls can artificially increase production, distort the land market, raise prices for consumers and disrupt international trade. Indeed, both mandatory and recommended prices are considered to have market distorting effects.[19] Although the majority of countries do not have any explicit price controls in place, 14 operate some form of mandatory price control mechanism on fruits, cereals or other traditional cash-crop commodities such as cocoa, coffee and tea, and 9 of those countries are located in Sub-Saharan Africa (figure 6.3).

In some cases, regulations prescribe the mode and location for agricultural trade, for example, via auction and/or at a fixed physical marketplace. Auction requirements apply in 6 of the 62 countries. In addition, in India, the majority of state governments operate a strict "mandi" system, which involves mandatory, fixed physical markets where farmers are required to sell

their products often via auction and/or using commission agents. Around 7,500 mandis currently exist, each being regulated by different state-level laws and covering various agricultural products.[20] Although licenses do not apply to farmers or other sellers of agricultural products, buyers have to obtain various licenses depending on their particular activity, and traditionally each license is attached to a physical unit or space in the market. Thus, when all units are occupied, no new licenses can be issued. Of the four Indian states studied in *EBA 2017*, only Bihar has abolished the mandi system (in 2006) in an effort to open up the market and reduce the role of middlemen. In Maharashtra, although the mandi system is still in place, a 2006 legal reform allowed for direct marketing contracts between agribusinesses and farmers, as well as for new private market areas to be established by individual businesses.

Facilitating the establishment of producer organizations

Producer organizations can be a useful vehicle to achieve market integration for their members. At the outset, ease of establishment can be a major obstacle to the development of producer organizations in the rural economy. Governments may establish minimum capital requirements to address undercapitalization issues, which are especially prevalent among agricultural cooperatives. However, minimum capital requirements directly hinder entrepreneurship and business growth, and capital formation is a major challenge for smallholder farmers. Where a minimum amount of

Figure 6.3 | Almost one-quarter of the countries studied impose agriculture-specific price controls, primarily on cereals and cash crops

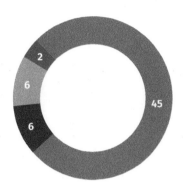

- ■ Countries that do not have price controls
- ■ Countries that have price controls on fruits
- ■ Countries that have price controls on cash crops
- ■ Countries that have price controls on cereals

Source: EBA database.

Notes: Data on price controls are not available for Haiti, Malaysia and Zimbabwe.

Figure 6.4 | The majority of countries do not impose minimum capital requirements

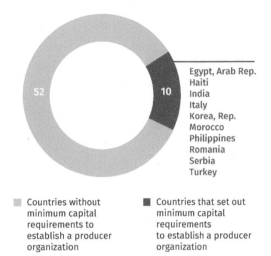

Egypt, Arab Rep.
Haiti
India
Italy
Korea, Rep.
Morocco
Philippines
Romania
Serbia
Turkey

- ■ Countries without minimum capital requirements to establish a producer organization
- ■ Countries that set out minimum capital requirements to establish a producer organization

Source: EBA database.

capital is required, it should be relatively low so that farmers can still afford to consolidate.[21] Within the sample of 62 countries, 10 impose minimum capital requirements on producer organizations, ranging from 0.1% income per capita in Egypt, to 1,616.9% income per capita in Korea (figure 6.4). Only two of these countries are OECD high-income countries, and there is no regional or income-based trend among the others (Egypt, Haiti, India, Italy, Korea, Morocco, Philippines, Romania, Serbia and Turkey). In 2016, Greece abolished the previous minimum capital requirement of 10,000 Euros.

In Korea the minimum capital requirement to establish a producer organization is significantly higher than in other countries, which operates as a severe barrier to the establishment of new agricultural cooperatives. Historically, the Korean agricultural cooperative sector developed largely under government guidance and direction, and through the network of the National Agricultural Cooperative Federation.[22] More than 2 million farmers are currently members of the 1,134 cooperatives in Korea, comprising the majority of the country's farming population.[23]

In Denmark, no minimum capital requirements apply. No specific legislation on cooperatives or other producer groups exists, and such entities are subject to the same laws as other commercial entities. As a result, the regulatory framework leaves producer organizations to adopt statutes that best fit their activity and establish their own principles of cooperative governance.[24] Notwithstanding the absence of a

special legal framework, however, cooperatives and other types of agricultural entities are thriving, with a high market share of around 65% in the agricultural sector, and cooperatives are altogether responsible for around 10% of GDP.[25] A similar situation exists in the Netherlands, where the regulation of cooperatives is also minimal.

Conclusion

Open markets that are unencumbered by unnecessary, overly complex or costly regulatory requirements are an important component of a dynamic agricultural sector. Government policies and regulations that impose burdensome marketing requirements on traders or exporters, as seen in India, or compromise pest management and control, can reduce farmers' income. Furthermore, they inhibit agribusinesses from developing efficient value chains that can meet the food demands of large, urbanizing populations, both domestically and overseas. Producer organizations can help farmers to consolidate and play a more powerful role in the marketplace; where such organizations are underdeveloped, governments may wish to consider adopting or amending relevant laws to enable their establishment and operation as commercial entities protected from government involvement.

NOTES

1 http://ica.coop/en/media/co-operative-stories/
coexphal-uniting-farmers-moving-forward.

2 In the context of the markets indicator, membership requirements refer to the obligation, for exporters, to be members of a specific association or organization to obtain the right to export the selected product or agricultural products more generally.

3 International Plant Protection Convention (IPPC) 2012; World Bank 2012.

4 Murina and Nicita 2014.

5 The bacterium slowly kills trees by restricting the supply of water from the roots of a tree to its branches and leaves. http://www.nytimes.com/2015/05/12/world/europe/fear-of-ruin-as-disease-takes-hold-of-italys-olive-trees.html.

6 International Plant Protection Convention (IPPC) 2012.

7 IFAD 2012.

8 Cogeca 2010.

9 Aal 2008; http://www.fao.org/news/story/en/item/93816/icode/.

10 Brookings 2012. Agricultural products are defined and grouped as cash crops, cereals, fruits and vegetables according to the Harmonized Commodity Description and Coding System 1996 version (HS 96). All data are sourced from the UN Comtrade Database, using the export data from 2009–13. For each country, the combination of the product and the partner country which represents the highest five-year average export value (in U.S. dollars) is selected. In addition, for countries where cash crops are selected as the export product, the HS 4-digit product within the category that is exported the most to the partner country is used for studying the legal and regulatory requirements. For example, coffee exports to the United States is selected for Colombia since coffee is the top product in the cash crop category and the USA is Colombia's main trading partner.

11 Prévost 2010.

12 Moïsé et al. 2013; Arias et al. 2013.

13 ITC 2015.

14 No data were received for 10 countries (Egypt, Senegal, Serbia, Spain, Sudan, Tajikistan, Turkey, Uganda, Ukraine and Uruguay).

15 Since 2005, the year before the Chile-China FTA entered into force, exports of agricultural goods recorded an average annual growth of 73% from 2005 to 2014, reaching a record US$739 million in 2014 (Ministerio de Relaciones Exteriores de Chile 2015).

16 The IPPC will develop both a Global ePhyto Hub that receives and transfers certificates from National Plant Protection Organizations and a generic web-based ePhyto system that will allow countries with limited IT capacity to access the Hub and participate in ePhyto exchanges. The initial pilot phase to test the Hub and generic web-based system involves 15 countries and will be carried out in 2017 (IPPC 2016).

17 Tothova 2009; Divanbaegi and Saliola (forthcoming).

18 Chapoto and Jayne 2009.

19 World Bank 2007; http://www.econlib.org/library/Enc1/AgriculturalPriceSupports.html#; OECD 2015.

20 Kapur and Krishnamurthy 2014.

21 Dreher and Gassebner 2013; Van Stel, Storey and Thurik 2007.

22 Kim 2013.

23 National Agricultural Cooperative Federation Annual Report 2015.

24 Pyykkönen, Bäckman and Kauriinoja 2012.

25 Groeneveld 2016; http://www.agricultureandfood.dk/~/media/lf/tal-og-analyser/aarsstatistikker/facts-and-figures/facts-and-figures-2016/facts-and-figures-rev2.pdf.

REFERENCES

Aal, M. H. A. 2008. "The Egyptian Cooperative Movement: Between State and Market." In *Cooperating Out of Poverty: The Renaissance of the African Cooperative Movement*, edited by P. Develtere, I. Pollet and F. Wanyama. 241–63. Geneva: ILO.

Arias, P., D. Hallam, E. Krivonos and J. Morrison. 2013. "Smallholder Integration in Changing Food Markets." FAO, Rome.

Brookings Africa Growth Initiative. 2012. "Accelerating Growth through Improved Intra-African Trade." Brookings Institution, Washington, DC.

Chapoto, A. and T. S. Jayne 2009. "The Impacts of Trade Barriers and Market Interventions on Maize Price Predictability: Evidence from Eastern and Southern Africa." Draft Working Paper 102. Department of Agricultural, Food, and Resource Economics Department of Economics Michigan State University.

Cogeca. 2010. *Agricultural Cooperatives in Europe: Main Issues and Trends*. Brussels: Cogeca.

Divanbeigi, R. and F. Saliola. Forthcoming. "Regulation and the Transformation of Agriculture." Working Paper presented at FAO Conference on Rural Transformation, Agricultural and Food System Transition.

Dreher, A. and M. Gassebner. 2013. "Greasing the Wheels? The Impact of Regulations and Corruption on Firm Entry." *Public Choice* 155: 413–32.

Groeneveld, H. 2016. "Doing Co-operative Business Report Methodology and Exploratory Application for 33 Countries." Tilburg University and International Co-operative Alliance. https://ica.coop/en/media/library/publications/doing-co-operative-business-report.

IFAD (International Fund for Agricultural Development). 2012. *The International Year on Cooperatives 2012*. Rome: IFAD.

International Plant Protection Convention (IPPC). 1997. "Guidelines for Surveillance." International Standards for Phytosanitary Measures 6. IPPC, Rome.

——. 2012. "IPPC Strategic Framework 2012–2019: Celebrating 60 Years of Protecting Plant Resources from Pests." IPPC, Rome.

——. 2016. "The Global ePhyto Solution." IPPC ePhyto Steering Group, v1.0. IPPC, Rome.

International Trade Center (ITC). 2015. "The Invisible Barriers to Trade: How Businesses Experience Non-Tariff Measures." ITC, Geneva.

Jouanjean, M.-A. 2013. "Targeting Infrastructure Development to Foster Agricultural Trade and Market Integration in Developing Countries: An Analytical Review." Overseas Development Institute, London.

Kapur, D. and M. Krishnamurthy. "Understanding Mandis: Market Towns and the Dynamics of India's Rural and Urban Transformations." CASI Working Paper Series, Number 14-02, 10/2014. Center for the Advanced Study of India, University of Pennsylvania, Philadelphia.

Kim, S. 2013. "The Cooperative Movement in Korea." *Journal of Global Business Research* 25 (2). Hankuk University of Foreign Studies, Seoul.

Ministerio de Relaciones Exteriores de Chile. 2015. "Analisis de las relaciones comerciales entre Chile y China en el marco del Tratado de Libre Comercio." https://www.direcon.gob.cl/wp-content/uploads/2015/08/AN--LISIS-RELACIONES-COMERCIALES-CHILE-CHINA.pdf.

Moisé, E. et al. 2013. "Estimating the Constraints to Agricultural Trade of Developing Countries." OECD Trade Policy Paper 142. OECD, Paris.

Murina, M. and A. Nicita. 2014. "Trading with Conditions: The Effect of Sanitary and Phytosanitary Measures on Lower Income Countries' Agricultural Exports." Policy Issues in International Trade and Commodities Research Study Series No. 68. UNCTAD, Geneva.

National Agricultural Cooperative Federation (NACF). 2015. "Annual Report." NACF, Seoul, Korea.

OECD. 2003. *Multifunctionality: The Policy Implications*. Paris: OECD.

——. 2015. *Agricultural Policy Monitoring and Evaluation 2015 – Highlighted*. Paris: OECD.

Prévost, D. 2010. "Sanitary, Phytosanitary and Technical Barriers to Trade in the Economic Partnership Agreements between the European Union and the ACP Countries." International Centre for Trade and Sustainable Development (ICTSD), Geneva.

Pyykkönen, P., S. Bäckman and H. Kauriinoja. 2012. "Support for Farmers' Cooperatives; Country Report Denmark." Wageningen UR, Wageningen.

Tothova, M. 2009. "The Trade and Trade Policy Implications of Different Policy Responses to Societal Concerns." OECD Food, Agriculture and Fisheries Working Papers, No. 20. Paris: OECD.

van Stel, A., D. J. Storey and A. R. Thurik. 2007. "The Effect of Business Regulations on Nascent and Young Business Entrepreneurship." *Small Business Economics* 28: 171.

World Bank. 2007. *World Development Report 2008: Agriculture for Development*. Washington, DC: World Bank.

——. 2012. "Africa Can Help Feed Africa: Removing Barriers to Regional Trade in Food Staples." World Bank, Washington, DC.

7 Transport

Small trucking companies in Java, Indonesia offer relatively cheap services but at the expense of service reliability and often with the resulting late delivery of goods. Strengthening the legal framework by establishing a road transport licensing system that imposes certain minimum quality standards, including professional certification for drivers and regular vehicle technical inspections, can reduce overall road transport costs by 7%, according to a recent empirical study. Indonesian road transport is responsible for more than 90% of all freight and is the largest contributor to high logistic costs in the country. Such high costs cause remote areas to experience more volatile food prices.[1]

Reliable and affordable food transport logistics services are essential to enable agricultural producers to reach consumers in growing urban areas. As such, transport can be considered a critical factor for urban food availability. Good transportation systems are required to minimize the time lag between harvest, processing and retail,[2] and provide adequate temperature control to preserve the quality and shelf life of perishable products as they are transported to markets.[3] Food losses during transport are frequently due to mechanical injury, spillage or leakage, which typically go unrecorded.[4] In addition, transport inefficiencies may decrease the food supply to local markets and reduce farmer profits.[5]

Access to efficient transport logistics as part of modern supply chains has been found to increase farmer income by 10 to 100%.[6] Transport costs can account for one-third of the price of agriculture inputs in some Sub-Saharan African countries,[7] which can lead to higher food prices. High marketing costs discourage farmers from commercializing their production[8] and can be traced back to poor road quality, isolation from markets, lack of vehicles and inefficient trucking logistics. Transportation services are also critical in mature economies like the United States, where the majority of domestic agricultural freight is still transported by road and agriculture is the largest user of freight transportation.[9] For instance, trucks transport food supplies for more than 80% of US cities and communities.[10]

What do the transport indicators measure?

EBA transport indicators measure the legal and regulatory framework that affects the provision of commercial road transportation services for agricultural products, including licenses, quality of trucking operations and cross-border transportation (table 7.1).

The indicators are organized as follows:

Trucking licenses and operations: Competition among truck service providers is key to curbing transport prices, increasing service quality and mitigating road transport inefficiencies.[11] This indicator assesses the extent to which regulations provide for a clear, transparent and efficient system for accessing and operating in the domestic transport sector. Strong legal systems reconcile the ease of accessing the market with minimum quality criteria to ensure food safety and environmental protection. This indicator covers the following:

Licensing regimes for transport operators. Excessive or cumbersome regulation for market entry can lower firm productivity[12] and promote concentration.[13] Thus, easing the process to obtain licenses for transport vehicles and operations is considered to be among the most important ways to improve trade and transport. The data cover the different licensing regimes, their time and cost requirements, and the existence of online platforms for submitting a license application.

Nontechnical requirements to obtain a truck license. Unjustified license requirements can artificially limit competition among transport providers and ultimately lead to higher transport prices and lower service quality. The data examine the existence of potentially discriminatory or unnecessary requirements relating to nationality, company size, operational capacity, professional affiliation or gender, among others.

Special regulations applicable to the transport of agri-food products. Given the potential impact of transport conditions on food safety and hygiene, transport regulations should include rules applicable to agriculture and food products. The data cover aspects such as vehicle refrigeration, insulation, co-mingling prohibitions and mandatory cleaning protocols, among others.

Transport documents. Road transport documents facilitate and standardize transactions, and have the capacity to increase trade and reduce risks and informality. A strong legal framework will institute written documents defining the conditions of carriage and a description of goods transported.

Pricing and freight allocation mechanisms. Price-setting or quantitative mandatory guidelines distort the market and restrain competition. The data focus on the presence of legally-binding queueing systems or mandatory road transport prices.

Cross-border transportation: Allowing foreign trucks to transport third-country cargo is one means of improving trade and transport.[14] Increasing the exposure of domestic truck operators to wider regional competition has also been cited as a determinant in lowering transport prices in Southern Africa.[15] The cross-border transportation indicator measures the following:

Cross-border licensing. The data cover the legal and regulatory framework governing cross-border transport between each country and its largest trading partner, including transport rights granted to foreign companies and cross-border licenses applicable to foreign trucks.

Limitations to foreign competitors. Despite regional and international efforts to liberalize trucking sectors, quantitative and operational restrictions to foreign competition still exist. These data identify potential

Table 7.1 | What do the transport indicators measure?

TRUCKING LICENSES AND OPERATIONS	• Type of license required to offer third-party trucking services domestically and ease of application process • Nontechnical requirements and total time (calendar days) and cost (in % of income per capita) to obtain a domestic license • Transport regulations specific to agriculture and food products
CROSS-BORDER TRANSPORTATION	• Foreign operator transport rights and operational limitations on foreign truck operations • Cross-border licensing and total time (calendar days) and cost (in % of income per capita) to obtain a cross-border license

Source: EBA database.

Figure 7.1 | Better performance on EBA transport's market access indicators is associated with higher logistic capacity

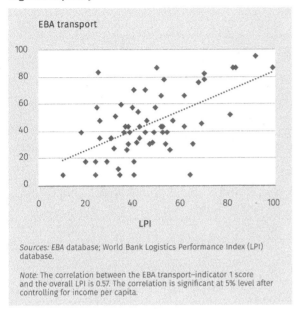

Sources: EBA database; World Bank Logistics Performance Index (LPI) database.

Note: The correlation between the EBA transport–indicator 1 score and the overall LPI is 0.57. The correlation is significant at 5% level after controlling for income per capita.

limitations such as quotas on the number of cross-border licenses that can be issued and mandatory corridors through which foreign trucks must operate.

Additional data on quality control for truck operations were collected but not scored, and are presented in appendix D.

How do countries perform on the transport indicators?

Countries that perform well on the trucking licenses and operations indicator also tend to have greater logistics capacity, according to the Logistics Performance Index (LPI)[16] (figure 7.1). As the most common type of transportation in developing countries, road transport is an essential precursor for effective general transportation. Country performance for trucking licenses and operations follows a distribution pattern similar to the LPI, thus implying an underlying relationship between the quality of road transport market access regulations and the overall quality of trade logistics infrastructure. Both indicators exhibit similar trends by income levels.

High-income OECD countries perform better on the transport indicators due to an efficient regulatory framework for truck licenses and domestic operations, a comprehensive system for ensuring the quality of truck operations and a high degree of openness to foreign competition. Particularly, Spain, Romania, Denmark and Italy display the strongest performance on the regulations measured, driven by a strong body

of harmonized regulations (table 7.2). Egypt, Ghana, Haiti, the Kyrgyz Republic and Liberia perform poorly on the transport indicators due to their domestic and cross-border trucking regulations; they do not require a license at the company level, they do not establish norms for the transport of perishable products and they do not have any rules on cross-border transport.

Regarding the time to obtain licenses, it generally takes longer to obtain a license in high-income OECD countries where company-level licenses are used, as compared with low-income countries where individual truck-level licensing is predominant (figure 7.2). Truck-level licenses can generally be issued faster because fewer quality standards apply. However, the average cost in countries with company-level licenses is almost five times lower than that of low-income countries. In Poland, for example, domestic company-level licenses take 90 days and cost 1.8% of income per capita on average to be processed, while in Uganda it takes only one day but almost 6% of income per capita to obtain a domestic truck-level license. In addition, even though shorter times are recorded for truck-level licenses, countries with company-level licenses tend to compensate operators with longer license validities; for example, five years is the average validity across the 21 countries operating a company-level system, as compared with one year for truck-level licenses. In certain cases, company–level licenses may also be unlimited (Colombia, Mexico, Serbia or Spain).

Table 7.2 | Where are transport regulations strongest and least burdensome, and where are they not?

Source: EBA database.

Figure 7.2 | Stricter licensing requirements in high-income countries drive up the time required to obtain a license, but licenses are less costly

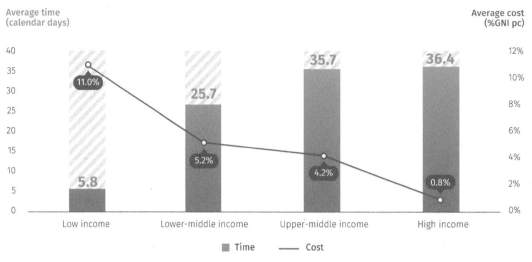

Source: EBA database.

Note: 49 of the 62 countries require a company-level license, a truck-level license, or both. The remaining 13 countries do not have any licensing requirements. Income-level grouping by country includes the following: low-income countries—Benin, Burkina Faso, Burundi, Ethiopia, Malawi, Mali, Mozambique, Nepal, Niger, Rwanda, Senegal, Tanzania, Uganda and Zimbabwe; lower-middle-income countries—Bangladesh, Bolivia, Cambodia, Cameroon, Côte d'Ivoire, India, Kenya, Lao PDR, Morocco, Myanmar, Nicaragua, Nigeria, Philippines, Sri Lanka, Tajikistan, Vietnam and Zambia; upper-middle-income countries—Bosnia and Herzegovina, Colombia, Jordan, Malaysia, Mexico, Peru, Romania, Serbia and Thailand; and high-income countries—Denmark, Greece, Italy, Korea, Rep., Netherlands, Poland, Spain and Uruguay. Turkey was excluded from its income grouping (upper-middle income) for graphing purposes given its extreme values for cost required.

What are the regulatory good practices?

Box 7.1 highlights regulatory good practices and some countries that implement these practices.

Company-level licenses promote stronger quality standards

Company- and truck-level licensing regimes differ with respect to the number of vehicles allowed under each license, license validity, the obligation for operators to register and often the requirement that operators and managers are certified. Acknowledging that the best licensing systems may be tailored to local circumstances, company-level licenses are generally regarded as stronger systems to promote both market entry and quality-based standards in the transport sector.[17] For example, while operators in Colombia benefit from the flexibility of a company-level license system that allows for whatever fleet size may be commercially desirable, truck operators in Tanzania must obtain individual truck licenses for each vehicle they want to operate.

Company-level licenses establish stricter quality standards on operators than truck-level or deregulated systems (see EU example in box 7.2). Across the 62 countries studied, company-level licenses require, on average, over six out of nine good practice quality criteria, a substantially higher number than the requirements that exist for truck-level licenses, which have four quality criteria in place, or countries with

no licensing schemes, which have none. While vehicle-specific requirements such as vehicle registration, technical inspections and third-party insurance are common to all licensing types, operator requirements such as minimum financial capacity, good repute, permanent establishment and professional competence for managers and drivers are predominant in company-level license regimes.

Only one-third of the countries that *EBA* surveyed require a company-level license for truck operators. Bosnia and Herzegovina, Korea, Morocco, Rwanda, Tajikistan, Turkey and Vietnam adopted company-level licensing regimes during the past 15 years. Burkina Faso,[18] Côte d'Ivoire[19] and Serbia[20] have recently reformed their laws to move to a company-level system.

Improving cross-border transport and foreign competition

High transport prices and low service quality have been attributed to the lack of competition in the domestic market in Africa.[21] In landlocked countries in the Western, Southern and Central African region, transport costs can contribute as much as 26% to import costs,[22] which is more than three times the amount in developed economies.[23] Increasing foreign participation in trucking and logistics services can help to increase competition, reduce prices and improve the quality of such services in the agriculture sector.[24] In Lao PDR, for example, eliminating the domestic trucking cartel and abolishing restrictions on backhauling

Box 7.1 | What are the regulatory good practices for transport?

	REGULATORY GOOD PRACTICES FOR TRANSPORT	SOME COUNTRIES WHICH IMPLEMENT THE PRACTICE
TRUCKING LICENSES AND OPERATIONS	Operating licenses are applied for at the company level and the process of obtaining a domestic license is efficient and affordable.	ETHIOPIA, TURKEY
	Licensing requirements do not discriminate on the basis of nationality, gender, professional affiliation or operational capacity.	ITALY, ROMANIA
	Truck operating requirements and necessary procedures are public and available online, and electronic platforms for submitting license applications and processing online payments are available.	COLOMBIA, SRI LANKA
	Written road transport documents are required in transport transactions.	CÔTE D'IVOIRE, KOREA, REP.
	Agriculture and food products are subject to special road transport regulations.	NICARAGUA
	Truck service prices and freight allocation are freely determined by the contracting parties.	NIGERIA, ZAMBIA
	Vehicles must complete periodic and mandatory technical and emissions inspections.	GEORGIA, INDIA
	Third-party liability insurance policy and vehicle registration certificates are mandatory and must accompany all trucks.	BOSNIA AND HERZEGOVINA, POLAND
CROSS-BORDER TRANSPORTATION	Foreign truck operators are granted transport rights similar to domestic operators and are not limited by quotas or mandatory routes when operating in the domestic market.	NETHERLANDS, SERBIA
	Truck operators are required to have a license when performing cross-border transport and the process of obtaining a cross-border license is efficient and affordable.	PERU, RUSSIAN FEDERATION

Source: EBA database.

Box 7.2 | The EU example

Through Regulation (EC) 1071/2009 and 1072/2009, the EU adopted a harmonized, company-level license system based on a common set of quality conditions with which all EU truck operators must comply permanently. The criteria include sound financial capacity, good repute and professional competence for managers and permanent establishment. This approach, which grants unrestricted market access to any EU Member State, constitutes a source of inspiration for other countries in the Europe and Central Asia (ECA), Middle East and North Africa (MENA) and Sub-Saharan Africa (SSA) regions, which still rely predominantly on truck-level or no license regimes. Some countries such as Burkina Faso or Côte d'Ivoire are in the process reforming their truck-level licensing schemes accordingly.

by foreign trucking companies led to a 20% reduction in road transport prices.[25] However, cross-border competition is typically hampered by restrictions on cabotage operations[26] or on services from third countries not covered by a bilateral agreement.

Openness to foreign competition can be measured by the number of rights granted to foreign truck operators. While more than 92% of countries allow certain basic transport rights (transport and backhaul), others, such as triangular[27] and cabotage rights, are allowed in only 68% and 13%—of the countries surveyed, respectively (figure 7.3). Across the EBA sample, only Korea, Malaysia, Myanmar, Sri Lanka and Thailand do not allow trucks registered in their largest trading partner to enter their territory at all. Cabotage rights, the most permissive regime for foreign operators, are observed in only eight countries, namely: Denmark, Greece, Italy, the Netherlands, Poland, Romania, Serbia and Spain.[28] Even in these countries, cabotage rights are subject to certain limitations such as the maximum number of cabotage operations and specific time limits.

Regional trade integration dynamics can also stimulate cross-border transport by harmonizing market access criteria and establishing most-favored nation clauses. The data show that countries regulating cross-border transport through regional transport agreements record a higher number of good practices than countries doing so bilaterally. While 90% of countries with a regional agreement in place require a cross-border license, only 65% do so when regulated bilaterally. Similarly, the average number of transport rights granted to trading partners under regional agreements is 20% higher than its bilateral equivalent. Moreover, quotas to the number of cross-border licenses issued and the existence of specific transit corridors are all limitations that are less frequent under regional agreements than under bilateral ones (20% and 14% lower, respectively). The East African Community (EAC)[29] is a good example of a regional trade agreement that harmonizes truck licensing requirements; the agreement guarantees four of five transport rights and removes quantitative or qualitative limitations on the number of trucks licensed in any of the five EAC member countries that can operate in the domestic market of another member.

Strong transport regulations promote food safety and reduce food waste

In developing countries, 40% of food losses occur at the post-harvest and handling stages of the value chain, including degradation and spillage from poor transportation conditions.[30] Strong legal frameworks for agricultural transport include specific provisions for the transport of agri-food products. These provisions include rules such as mandatory refrigeration standards, special insulation and roofing conditions, cleaning protocols, special labelling requirements and a prohibition on comingling of certain items, all of which seek to prevent foodborne diseases and contamination, avoid spillage and ensure the quality of the products being transported. Countries with stronger regulations pertaining to food products have a much lower incidence of food waste.[31]

Figure 7.3 | Higher income countries tend to be more open to foreign truck competition

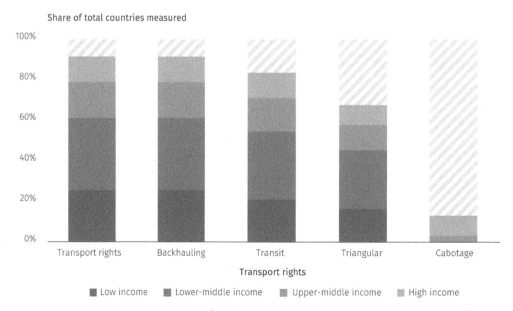

Share of total countries measured

Source: EBA database.

Figure 7.4 | A vast majority of low-income countries have not adopted any agri-food transport regulations while most high-income countries have done so

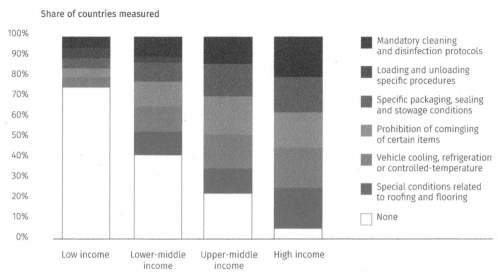

Share of countries measured

Source: EBA database.

Only 38% of the economies studied have implemented specific regulations that seek to ensure food safety during transportation. The prevalence of agri-food transport regulations is predominant in high- and upper-middle-income economies (figure 7.4). A very small number of countries in the low- and lower-middle-income tiers, including Cameroon, Guatemala, India, Kazakhstan, Nicaragua, Senegal and Tajikistan, have such rules in place. For example, since 2010 Nicaragua has imposed specific requirements for safe transport including vehicle refrigeration specifications, cleaning protocols, loading and unloading procedures and mandatory documentation requirements.[32]
Other low- and middle-income countries limit such regulations to one or two particularly relevant commodities for that country, rather than the agri-food sector more broadly. For instance, Cameroon recently issued a regulation dealing with the safe transport of cocoa and the Russian Federation has specific regulations on wheat safety.

Conclusion

Strong and efficient truck licensing frameworks that are nondiscriminatory, transparent and conditional on minimum quality standards, can play an important role in leveling the playing field for transport service providers and ultimately contribute to better access to such services in rural areas. As suggested by the EU example, opening up truck service markets to foreign competition is another important regulatory component that can reduce fragmentation, stimulate the adoption of improved standards and reduce overall transport costs.

NOTES

1 Meeuws 2014.

2 Bourne 1977.

3 Jedermann et al. 2014.

4 Tefera 2012.

5 Lundqvist et al. 2008.

6 World Bank 2008.

7 *Ibid.*

8 Gebremedhin et al. 2012.

9 Casavant et al. 2010.

10 *Ibid.*

11 Teravaninthorn et al. 2009.

12 Barseghyan 2008.

13 Fisman et al. 2004.

14 World Bank 2010.

15 Raballand et al. 2008.

16 LPI is a World Bank knowledge product measuring logistic "friendliness" perceptions as reported by freight forwarders and express carriers. The 2016 edition provides data on 160 countries, 60 of which are also part of EBA.

17 The transport topic categorizes licenses based on level: company, truck, both company and truck or the absence of a license.

18 Burkina Faso recently established a company-level licensing system, in force since October 2016. The new license will comprise quality criteria to access the market and have a validity of five years. With the new regulation, each truck operator will be able to have an unlimited number of trucks under the license.

19 In 2015, Côte d'Ivoire introduced a company-level-based operator licensing system with clear quality criteria to access the profession. The decree also establishes strategic plans containing an estimation of the demand for transport services, a registry of licensed operators and their fleets, and user satisfaction rates, among others. As a result of this reform, Côte d'Ivoire is now the best performer in the "trucking licenses and operations" sub-indicator of the ECOWAS region.

20 Serbia will fully harmonize its licensing system to EU requirements by February 2017. The new company-level license will establish quality criteria including good repute, Certificate of Professional Competence (CPC) for drivers and managers, financial capacity standards and a more generous validity, and will remove the limitation to the number of trucks.

21 Teravaninthorn et al. 2009.

22 MacKellar et al. 2000.

23 Raballand et al. 2008.

24 *Ibid.*

25 Record et al. 2014.

26 By definition, cabotage rights are defined as follows: a truck registered in country A is able to pick up agricultural goods in country B and deliver them to a different point in country B.

27 By definition, triangular rights are defined as follows: a truck registered in country A is able to pick up agricultural goods in country B and transport them to be delivered into country C (assuming foreign country B is the final destination of the foreign truck).

28 Cabotage rights in EU countries are granted on the basis of Council Regulation (EC) No. 1072, 2009. In the case of Serbia, instead, cabotage rights are granted on the basis of a specific permit issued by the Ministry following the "Act on the Transport of Goods by Road."

29 The East African Community is a regional intergovernmental organization with headquarters in Arusha, Tanzania and it currently comprises the following countries: Burundi, Kenya, Rwanda, Tanzania and Uganda.

30 FAO 2011.

31 Food losses in European countries where food safety transport regulations are extended are 9% for tubers, 0.5% for milk, 5% for fruits and vegetables and 1% for oilseeds and pulses; compared to 18%, 11%, 9% and 8% for Sub-Saharan Africa; 14%, 6%, 10% and 3% for Latin America; and 19%, 6%, 9% and 12% for South and South-East Asia, respectively (FAO 2011).

32 "Norma técnica obligatoria nicaragüense de requisitos para el transporte de productos alimenticios," NTON 03 079-08, enacted in 2008 and in force since 2011.

REFERENCES

Barseghyan, L. 2008. "Entry Costs and Cross-Country Differences in Productivity and Output." *Journal of Economic Growth* 13: 145–67.

Bourne, M. C. 1977. "Post Harvest Food Losses – The Neglected Dimension in Increasing the World Food Supply." New York State College of Agriculture and Life Sciences, Cornell University, New York.

Casavant, K. et al. 2010. "Study of Rural Transportation Issues." US Department of Agriculture, Washington, DC.

FAO (Food and Agriculture Organization of the United Nations). 2011. "Global Food Losses and Food Waste – Extent, Causes and Prevention." FAO, Rome.

Fisman, R. and V. Sarria-Allende. 2004. "Regulation of Entry and the Distortion of Industrial Organization." NBER Working Paper 10929. National Bureau of Economic Research Cambridge, MA.

Gebremedhin, B. and M. Jaleta. 2012. "Market Orientation and Market Participation of Smallholders in Ethiopia: Implications for Commercial Transformation." Paper presented at the International Association of Agricultural Economists (IAAE), August 18–24.

Jedermann, R., M. Nicometo, I. Uysal and W. Lang. 2014. "Reducing Food Losses by Intelligent Food Logistics." *Phil. Trans. R. Soc. A.* 372 (2017): 1–20.

Lundqvist, J., C. de Fraiture and D. Molden. 2008. "Saving Water: From Field to Fork – Curbing Losses and Wastage in the Food Chain." SIWI Policy Brief. SIWI, Stockholm.

MacKellar, L., A. Wörgötter and J. Wörzand. 2000. "Economic Development. Problems of Landlocked Countries." Working Paper 14. Institut für Höhere Studien (IHS), Vienna.

Meeuws, R. 2014. "How the Road Freight Transport Sector Can Contribute to the Reduction of Logistics Costs in Indonesia." Report commissioned by the Government of Indonesia for the World Bank. World Bank, Washington, DC.

Raballand, G., C. Kunaka and B. Giersing. 2008. "The Impact of Regional Liberalization and Harmonization in Road Transport Services: A Focus on Zambia and Lessons for Landlocked Countries." Policy Research Working Paper 4482. World Bank, Washington, DC.

Record, R. et al. 2014. "Lao PDR – Trade and Transport Facilitation Assessment." World Bank, Washington, DC.

Tefera, T. 2012. "Post-harvest Losses in African Maize in the Face of Increasing Food Shortage." Springer Science & Business Media B.V. and International Society for Plant Pathology, *Food Sec.* 4 (2): 267–77.

Teravaninthorn, S. and G. Raballand. 2009. *Transport Prices and Costs in Africa: A Review of the Main International Corridors.* Washington, DC: World Bank.

World Bank Group. 2008. *Agriculture for Development. World Development Report.* Washington, DC: World Bank.

———. 2010. *Trade and Transport Facilitation Assessment: A Practical Toolkit for Country Implementation.* Washington, DC: World Bank.

8 Water

For the past nine years, Caroline has been growing rice on a four-hectare plot of land in a sprawling area of rice production near the banks of a river. Until recently, irrigation water pumped from the river allowed her to add an extra season of rice production per year, almost doubling her prior annual income. However, this year, the water level is significantly lower than average, and Caroline doesn't think she can grow anything this season. Some neighboring farmers believe that upstream users are extracting more than their allocated share of the river's water. Caroline agrees and notes that several large farms and industrial plants have appeared upstream in the past few years, but when she complained to the local river basin office tasked with allocation decisions, an official told her that they don't have information on those users—they "just sell water." She is now concerned that her water permit is useless.[1]

Water is an essential input for crop production and vital to the task of increasing yields and feeding the world's growing population. Farmers must have access to sufficient quantities of water, at an adequate quality level and at the appropriate time and location, for crop production to be commercially viable. The availability of water for crop production depends on many factors: water scarcity, pollution, climate variability and increased demand for alternative uses. These factors necessitate improvements in water management.

At the farm level, although rain-fed agriculture remains predominant in many climates across the world,[2] increased crop production in developing countries is expected to be achieved predominantly through irrigation. Irrigated land can be as much as twice as productive as nearby rain-fed land, and in developing countries irrigated agriculture already provides for approximately half of crop production, while comprising only 20% of all arable land.[3] However, the availability of water for irrigation is constrained both by climatic conditions and the effectiveness of public water management. Moreover, any increase in the use of water for irrigation has important consequences for the overall water balance and the broader environment. It is also important to recognize that farmers' access to water for irrigation is also impacted by legal frameworks that extend beyond the direct relationship between regulators and water users to include measures affecting the resource itself as well as the infrastructure used to deliver water to the place of use at the time needed.[4]

What do the water indicators measure?

The water indicators measure key elements within the legal and regulatory frameworks that impact farmers' access to sufficient quantities of water, at an adequate quality level and at the time and location needed for crop production (table 8.1). The indicators are organized as follows:

Integrated water resources management: Water scarcity and degradation present significant practical constraints to both irrigation and agricultural development.[5] In addition, while irrigation poses a variety of benefits for agricultural growth such as increased crop production, it can also heavily impact the availability of water resources. To this end, integrated water resources management (IWRM) promotes a view towards managing water in conjunction with land and other interconnected resources to achieve equitable and sustainable use.[6] This indicator measures the regulatory framework applicable to water management in each country, including the establishment of institutions at the basin level, water planning, the development of information systems and water resource protection.[7]

Individual water use for irrigation: Systems for water use permits are critical tools for managing and allocating water resources, including water for agriculture.[8] Effective water use permit systems provide secure rights to water users and allow resource managers to review existing water uses and make meaningful allocation decisions in pursuit of broader planning and management goals.[9] This indicator measures requirements for water use permits, as well as the quality of these permit requirements by examining public notice requirements, transfers, water use charges and enforcement measures.

How do countries perform on the water indicators?

Countries that have developed a strong legal framework for IWRM also tend to have a strong legal framework for individual water use for irrigation, with top- and middle-scoring countries only displaying minor deficiencies across the range of features covered by the water indicators. In these countries, the most common gaps include the absence of mandates to periodically update plans and information systems, limited promotion of water conservation and efficiency, and the absence of water use permit trading. In contrast, countries with weaker frameworks tend to have one or more concentrated areas of weakness impacting their frameworks, rather than across-the-board weakness. For example, Nepal's legal framework for broader water resources management is largely absent with no planning or information systems in place, but it is relatively more comprehensive in supporting individual water use for irrigation; in contrast, the opposite is true in Bangladesh and Mali where water use permit requirements for medium-size farms are currently absent, but their water resource management frameworks are relatively stronger.

Spain's legal framework represents the most comprehensive enabling framework for water management and use. Overall it provides for strong legal mechanisms that drive integrated water resources management (such as institutional frameworks, water inventorying and monitoring activities). In addition, it provides for a dynamic permit system for water use activities that facilitates transfer of water permits and other mechanisms that allow the system to adapt in response to changed circumstances (table 8.2).

Table 8.1 | What do the water indicators measure?

INTEGRATED WATER RESOURCES MANAGEMENT	• Institutional mandates to manage water at basin levels • Water planning at the national and basin levels • Information systems on water resources and water use to support management decisions • Resource protection mechanisms in cases of depletion or pollution
INDIVIDUAL WATER USE FOR IRRIGATION	• Abstraction and use permit requirements for medium-size farms (2–10 hectares) • Transfers of active permits separate from land transactions • Charging for the abstraction and use of water resources • Enforcement of permit-related obligations

Source: EBA database.

Figure 8.1 Countries with more variable water availability tend to have stronger legal frameworks

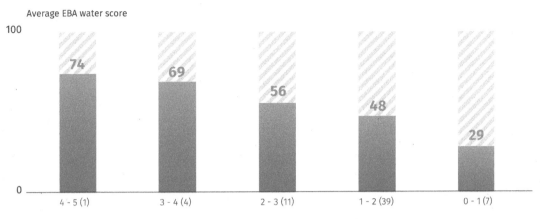

Average EBA water score

Interannual Variability Index (FAO/WRI)

Sources: EBA database; FAO Aquastat/WRI 2016.

Note: Sample size in parentheses. A normalized indicator of the variation in water supply between years, created by WRI, ranges from 0–5, where 0 is lowest and 5 is highest (most variable). Correlation coefficient is 0.335, significant at 1% level after controlling for gross national income per capita.

Context-specific concerns that may impact a country's regulatory priorities include inter-annual water variability and water stress issues related to population growth and/or water scarcity. Countries with higher water variability tend to have developed stronger legal frameworks for water management and use in response (figure 8.1). Both Kenya and Mexico, for example, perform well on the water indicators, which illustrates how challenges identified in a country's water resources situation can be a driver to adopt a strong legal framework for water management and use. Recognizing its water variability challenges, Kenya began a series of legal and regulatory reforms in 2002 with the introduction of a new Water Act (Cap. 372) and supporting regulations that upgraded and repealed

outdated colonial-era legislation. In response to rapidly growing demand and overexploitation, Mexico has developed comprehensive legislation anchored by the 1992 National Water Law.[10] In contrast to both Kenya and Mexico, Denmark's relative abundance of stable, high-quality water resources and the absence of acute water stress issues[11] may be one factor to explain why their legal framework for water management and use is currently less comprehensive than that of either Kenya or Mexico.

What are the regulatory good practices?

Box 8.1 highlights regulatory good practices and some countries that implement these practices.

Informed institutions and planned water management

Institutional entities that manage water at the level of basins and aquifers are a critical component of IWRM and the starting point for improved planning, management and allocation of water among different water users.[12] Across the countries studied, many have created institutional entities that manage water at the level of basins and aquifers, but fewer have taken steps toward the planning and information systems necessary to sufficiently inform those institutions and water users.

Approximately three-quarters of the countries studied have enacted legal provisions that require the

Table 8.2 | Where are water regulations strongest?

STRONGEST		WEAKEST	
1	SPAIN	58	GUATEMALA
2	MEXICO	59	SUDAN
3	COLOMBIA	60	THAILAND
4	KENYA	61	LIBERIA
5	ARMENIA	62	MYANMAR

Source: EBA database.

Box 8.1 | What are the regulatory good practices for water?

	REGULATORY GOOD PRACTICES FOR WATER	SOME COUNTRIES WHICH IMPLEMENT THE PRACTICE
INTEGRATED WATER RESOURCES MANAGEMENT	Institutions exist with an adequate legal mandate to manage water at the appropriate geographical scale.	GREECE, KENYA
	Water planning is carried out at the national and basin levels and involves public consultation, periodic updating and monitoring planning.	NETHERLANDS, SERBIA
	Systems, such as an inventory of water resources and a water user registry, are publicly available, providing information on water availability, location, and use and any changes over time.	DENMARK, KOREA, REP.
	Quality standards exist for irrigation water, and the government can restrict water use in cases of depletion and pollution.	MEXICO, SPAIN
	Legally mandated quotas are in place to ensure the participation and involvement of water users and women in water management.	RWANDA, TANZANIA
INDIVIDUAL WATER USE FOR IRRIGATION	A mandatory permit system applies to water abstraction and use by medium-size and larger farms (larger than 2 hectares). Laws and regulations should set out the application procedure, permit duration and public notice requirements for new applications.	ITALY, TANZANIA
	Water permits are transferable—separate from land—and the procedural rules are clearly stated in the law. Certain limitations, such as notification requirements, also apply to avoid subverting the water allocation and planning process.	ARMENIA, CHILE
	Water users pay for the quantity of water resources used, and governments are obligated to set and collect fees for the use of water resources.	PERU, RUSSIAN FEDERATION
	Individuals keep records, and the government is given powers to conduct inspections for permit compliance.	MEXICO, PHILIPPINES
	Noncompliance with core water management and/or use obligations is an offense.	KAZAKHSTAN, MALAWI

Source: EBA database.

Figure 8.2 | Basin planning and water information systems

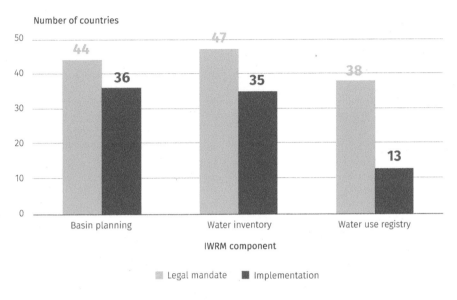

Source: EBA database.

Note: Availability of plan, inventory or registry information online is taken as verifiable proxy indicator for implementation. IWRM = integrated water resources management.

establishment of institutions to manage water at the river basin level. Of those countries, 87% have actually established at least one of these institutions. Those countries that have a legal mandate but have not yet created any basin institutions tend to have relatively recent legislative or regulatory enactments, such as Cambodia (2015), Malawi (2013), Rwanda (2013) and Turkey (2012). Overall, 77% of all countries studied have at least one basin-level water management institution in place, taking into account those that have such entities without a legal mandate. Of those countries that do not have a legal mandate to establish basin institutions, 47% have them in practice, including Cameroon, Ghana, Senegal and Uganda. However, without a clear anchor in the legal framework, the role and impact of these institutions are typically restricted to consensus building, rather than exercising the necessary functions for planning and allocation of water resources.

Effective water planning and information systems guide water allocation decisions and thereby benefit farmers by helping to reduce the likelihood of situations where resources are over-allocated and irrigation needs go unmet.[13] Of the countries studied, 44 require water planning at the basin level and 36 have actually completed at least one basin plan to date. To make good water planning decisions, water managers must have sufficient information about the current state of available resources, as well as the future demand from existing and potential water users. Furthermore, making information about water resources and water users available online helps to inform on-farm

decisions to invest in irrigation development. But, whereas approximately 76% of the countries studied mandate the completion of an inventory of available water resources, only 56% currently have any inventory information made publicly available online (see figure 8.2). Similarly, although 61% of the countries studied require the creation and maintenance of a registry of water users, only 21% currently make any registry-related information publicly available online. For example, although more than half of low-income countries currently require a registry of water users, none of them currently makes any registry information available online.

The shared nature of water resources makes farmers dependent on institutions to monitor the ongoing status of water resources and to take actions to protect water resources from water depletion and pollution. These regulatory activities are critical because once resources have become degraded, recovery is complex and expensive, and at times impossible.[14] Of the countries studied, 66% mandate monitoring of both water availability and water quality. However, far fewer of these countries require the government to actively publicize monitoring information. Overall, only 40% of the countries studied require water monitoring results to be made publicly available. In conjunction with inventory and registry information, publication of monitoring results helps to inform farmers about where it is reasonable to invest in irrigation and has important broader implications for the long-term ability to track protection of water-related ecosystems.

Protecting farmer investments through transparent permit systems

Strong water use permit systems benefit farmers by helping to ensure access to water in the face of potentially competing demands and strained resources. Moreover, at the broader level, as agriculture accounts for approximately 70% of water withdrawals globally and up to 90% in some country contexts,[15] water use permit systems are a critical tool for managing and allocating water resources, including water for agriculture.[16] Accordingly, an overwhelming majority of countries—82%—have put in place water use permit systems that are applicable to irrigation water use on medium-size farms[17] (figure 8.3). Of the remaining 11 countries that do not require permits, four (Benin, Burkina Faso, Côte d'Ivoire and India) have instituted a partial system that requires these users to declare their water use, but offering no allocation control to water resource managers. The final seven countries (Bangladesh, Guatemala, Kyrgyz Republic, Liberia, Myanmar, Thailand and Turkey) do not have either requirement for individual water use for irrigation.

Significant variations are observed with respect to the quality of permit systems used to manage water withdrawals and those features that directly impact investment security for water users. For example, permit systems should require public notice of a new permit application before a decision is made, which promotes transparency and seeks to protect the rights of existing water users. Thus, for example, Armenia's 2002 Water Code requires the agency issuing water permits to publish notice of pending water applications to allow for comments for 30 days prior to making a final decision. Only 27 of the countries studied have this legal requirement and only 21 of those set a mandatory minimum length for public notice. Recordkeeping requirements for water users are an additional transparency feature intended to facilitate water management and support water managers as they try to ensure sustainable water withdrawals. Romania provides an example of this good practice, as its water law requires water users to meter the quantity of water abstracted and keep records to be periodically submitted to the overseeing agency, which in turn must compile and make that information publicly available. Only 45% of countries studied have set a recordkeeping requirement in their legal framework.

Promoting efficiency and conservation through resource pricing

In response to water scarcity concerns and increasing demand, many countries are establishing the legal foundation necessary to charge user fees for the individual abstraction of water resources. An appropriate fee structure is one tool for water managers to promote efficient water use and water conservation, but, to this end, it is especially important to tailor any proposed legal approach to the specific country context, as defined by socioeconomic factors, the needs of smallholders and the most vulnerable water users, and the general profile of water users and farm sizes in the country.[18] Nonetheless, when tailored to each country's context, managing water as an economic good can

Figure 8.3 | Widespread adoption of permit systems for sustainable management of water withdrawals

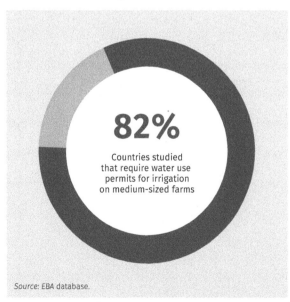

82%

Countries studied that require water use permits for irrigation on medium-sized farms

Source: EBA database.

Figure 8.4 | Legal foundation to calculate water pricing

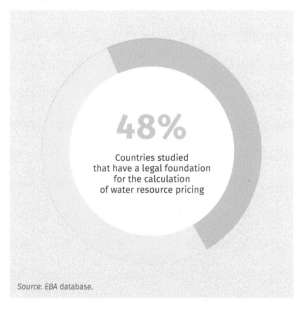

48%

Countries studied that have a legal foundation for the calculation of water resource pricing

Source: EBA database.

Terraced rice paddies near a Red Zao village, northern Vietnam. Photo: Tran Thi Hoa / World Bank.

lead to efficient and equitable use, as well as promote water conservation.[19] Morocco's legal framework demonstrates good practices in this field by placing both an obligation on the user to pay charges and an obligation on the agency to collect charges, as well as by clearly defining how charges are calculated. In 40 of the countries studied, the legal framework requires medium- and large-size farms to pay a charge for water resources abstraction, but in only 29 of those countries does the legal framework specify the method for calculating the charge due (figure 8.4).

Conclusion

Water-related challenges vary widely between countries. One of the most important qualities of a country's regulation for water management is the ability to meet the specific needs presented by the relevant country (and even basin) context. Nevertheless, while allowing for adequate tailoring, comprehensive laws and effective institutions generally contain a common range of tools and systems that allow for resilience in the face of challenging and/or changing conditions, such as water scarcity, fluctuations in availability or growing demand. Comprehensive regulation also supports the long-term durability of core practices for water management and use, which in the absence of a legal mandate may be compromised by future challenges related to available funding and/or political will.

NOTES

1   Adapted from Mdee et al. 2014.

2   IWMI 2007.

3   FAO 2011.

4   OECD 2010.

5   IFAD – UNEP 2013; HLPE 2015.

6   Integrated water resources management can be defined as "a process which promotes the coordinated development and management of water, land and related resources in order to maximize economic and social welfare in an equitable manner without compromising the sustainability of vital ecosystems." (GWP 2010).

7   Vapnek et al. 2009.

8   Permits can also be referred to as licenses, concessions, or authorizations, all of which convey a "water right"—that is, a right to use water, subject to the terms and conditions of the grant. (See Burchi and D'Andrea [2003], chapter 1 [1]).

9   Cap-Net 2008.

10 Grey and Sadoff 2006.

11 Danish Ministry of Foreign Affairs 2012; OECD 2015.

12 Vapnek et al. 2009.

13 Pegram et al. 2013.

14 Vapnek et al. 2009.

15 HLPE 2015.

16 Burchi and D'Andrea 2003.

17 "Medium-size farms" are defined as being between 2 and 10 hectares in area in the case study assumptions used for data collection.

18 Johansson et al. 2002.

19 Tsur 2004; Rogers et al. 1998.

REFERENCES

Burchi, S. and A. D'Andrea. 2003. "Preparing National Regulations for Water Resources Management: Principles and Practice." Legislative Study 80. FAO, Rome.

Cap-Net. 2008. "Integrated Water Resources Management for River Basin Organizations." UNDP, Pretoria.

Danish Ministry of Foreign Affairs. 2012. "A Land Enriched by Water." http://denmark.dk/en/green-living/sustainable-projects/a-land-enriched-by-water.

FAO (Food and Agriculture Organization). 2011. "State of the World's Land and Water Resources for Food and Agriculture: Managing Systems at Risk." FAO/Earthscan, Rome.

——. 2013. "Aquastat: Mexico." http://www.fao.org/nr/water/aquastat/countries_regions/MEX/index.stm.

——. 2015. "Aquastat: Kenya." http://www.fao.org/nr/water/aquastat/countries_regions/ken/index.stm.

Grey, D. and C. W. Sadoff. 2006. "Water for Growth and Development." In Thematic Documents of the IV World Water Forum. Comision Nacional del Agua, Mexico City.

GWP (Global Water Partnership). 2010. "What Is IWRM?" http://www.gwp.org/The-Challenge/What-is-IWRM/.

High Level Panel on Water. 2016. "Action Plan." https://sustainabledevelopment.un.org/content/documents/11280HLPW_Action_Plan_DEF_11-1.pdf.

HLPE (High Level Panel of Experts on Food Security and Nutrition). 2015. "Water for Food Security and Nutrition: A Report by the High Level Panel of Experts on Food Security and Nutrition of the Committee on World Food Security." FAO, Rome.

IFAD (International Fund for Agricultural Development). 2012. "Water and Food Security." IFAD, Rome.

IFAD – UNEP (United Nations Environment Programme). 2013. "Smallholders, Food Security and the Environment." IFAD, Rome.

IWMI (International Water Management Institute). 2007. "Water for Food, Water for Life: A Comprehensive Assessment of Water Management in Agriculture." IWMI/Earthscan, Colombo/London.

Johansson, R. C., Y. Tsur, T. L. Roe, R. Doukkali and A. Dinar. 2002. "Pricing Irrigation Water: A Review of Theory and Practice." *Water Policy* 4: 173–99.

Mdee, A., E. Harrison, C. Mdee, E. Mdee and E. Bahati. 2014. "The Politics of Small-Scale Irrigation in Tanzania: Making Sense of Failed Expectations." Future Agricultures Working Paper 107. http://www.future-agricultures.org/publications/research-and-analysis/1915-the-politics-of-small-scale-irrigation-in-tanzania-making-sense-of-failed-expectations/file.

OECD. 2010. "Sustainable Management of Water Resources in Agriculture." OECD, Paris.

———. 2015. "Water Resources Allocation. Denmark." https://www.oecd.org/denmark/Water-Resources-Allocation-Denmark.pdf.

Pegram, G., L. Yuanyuan, T. Le Quesne, R. Speed, L. Jianqiang and S. Fuxin. 2013. "River Basin Planning: Principles, Procedures and Approaches for Strategic Basin Planning." UNESCO, Paris.

Rogers, P., R. Bhatia and A. Huber. 1998. "Water as a Social and Economic Good: How to Put the Principle into Practice." Global Water Partnership/Swedish International Development Cooperation Agency, Stockholm.

Tsur, Y. 2004. "Economic Aspects of Irrigation Water Pricing." *Canadian Water Resources Journal* 30 (1): 31–46. http://www.tandfonline.com/doi/pdf/10.4296/cwrj300131.

UNEP. "Kenya Water Profile." http://www.unep.org/dewa/Portals/67/pdf/Kenya.pdf.

Vapnek, J., B. Aylward, C. Popp and J. Bartram. 2009. "Law for Water Management: A Guide to Concepts and Effective Approaches." Legislative Study 101. FAO, Rome.

9

Information and Communication Technology

In Kerala, a state in western India, 72% of adults eat fish at least once a day. Further, over one million people are directly employed in the fisheries sector. Between 1997 and 2001, mobile phone service was introduced throughout Kerala. In a short period of time, the adoption of mobile phones by fishermen and wholesalers was associated with a dramatic reduction in price dispersion and the complete elimination of waste. In particular, variation of prices across fish markets declined from 60–70 to 15% or less. Waste, averaging 5–8% of daily catch before mobile phones, was completely eliminated. As a result, fishermen's profits increased on average by 8%.[1]

Almost half of the global population lives in rural areas, where access to communications can be significantly more difficult. Mobile-broadband networks (3G or above) reach 84% of the global population, but only 67% of the rural population worldwide; in Africa, only about 25% of the population is using the internet.[2] In Nepal, Cambodia, Lao PDR, Bangladesh and Myanmar less than 20% of the population is benefiting from the use of mobile internet.[3]

The ability to connect to the internet in remote areas using mobile devices can make a significant difference to farmers in terms of their food security and commercial viability. It can provide them with a wide range of opportunities—from obtaining real-time data on market and transport prices, to information on seed varieties, pests and farming techniques, as well as basic information on the weather and analytical and management tools for production and marketing processes.[4] Ultimately, the use of mobile applications and other information and communication technology-(ICT-) enabled services can stimulate access to markets and increase the income of smallholder farmers by improving agricultural productivity, reducing costs for input suppliers and enhancing traceability and quality standards.[5] For example, Indian farmers using the Reuters Market Light (RML) mobile information service, which reports on market prices, have benefited from an average increase in income of 5–15%.[6]

Telecommunications in Cambodia.
Photo: Chhor Sokunthea / World Bank.

The most significant impediment for smallholder farmers to fully exploit the benefits of ICT in agriculture is the network coverage gap due to a lack of infrastructure and underdeveloped mobile networks. Policies and regulations should aim at closing this gap. One strategy to address these gaps is to establish a universal access fund, which is a multi-source financing mechanism to support ICT infrastructure development in rural areas. In addition, reducing regulatory burdens can encourage private sector investment. Cumbersome regulatory frameworks, such as two-layer licensing requirements, can hinder competition and inhibit the creation of innovative solutions that are responsive to users' needs. This situation can prevent price reductions and the wider use of new, efficient technologies. Transparency creates greater predictability for mobile operators that have to take decisions on huge infrastructure investments and thereby encourages the expansion of networks to remote areas in a more sustainable manner.

What does the ICT indicator measure?

The ICT indicator measures laws, regulations and policies that promote an enabling environment for the provision and use of ICT services, particularly in rural areas. Given the significant capital investments required to provide ICT access in underserved areas,[7] mobile operators often have no incentive to invest in network rollouts to remote areas without regulatory stimuli. As a result, network coverage gaps continue to affect predominantly rural areas where populations, income levels and potential profit margins are relatively low. The ICT indicator measures regulatory good practices that can provide some of these incentives (table 9.1). It focuses on the licensing framework and assesses the type of licensing regime used in a country, the validity of the operating license, the public availability of operating license costs, spectrum allocation strategies and the predictability of renewal conditions for operating and spectrum licenses. Additional data on universal access funds were not scored and are presented in the appendix D.

How do countries perform on the ICT indicator?

The higher quality of the licensing and regulation is associated with higher mobile internet market penetration (figure 9.1).[8] Low-income countries in Sub-Saharan Africa display mobile internet market penetration levels below 20%, as compared to mobile internet market penetration levels above 60% for OECD high-income countries. Due to high capital investments required to expand mobile networks, higher income countries achieve faster universal access to ICT services.

Countries with stronger ICT regulations under the EBA ICT indicator (table 9.2) tend also to perform well on the GSMA's Mobile Connectivity Index,[9] which measures the strength of key enabling factors in a country (infrastructure, affordability, consumer readiness, content) to support universal adoption of the mobile internet (figure 9.2).

This result suggests that an enabling regulatory environment can contribute to better access to ICT services. European Union countries are among the top performers on both the ICT indicator and Mobile Connectivity Index, reflecting the significant harmonization efforts undertaken as part of the Digital Single Market Strategy initiative. The EU policy framework has been directed towards the creation of sound regulatory systems for electronic communications with simplified and inclusive rules that promote competition.[10] The EU member states have transposed the provisions of the Authorization Directive 2002/20/EC into their national laws and regulations.

In contrast, countries that have implemented few regulatory good practices perform relatively poorly on the ICT indicator. For example, Ethiopia's low performance is explained by the absence of technology and service neutrality, and the lack of liberalization in the market, among other factors. The Herfindahl-Hirschman Index, measuring market concentration on a scale of 0 (evenly distributed competition) to 10,000 (no competition), for Ethiopia is 10,000,[11] reflecting the absence of

Table 9.1 | What does the ICT indicator measure?

INFORMATION AND COMMUNICATION TECHNOLOGY	• Type of licensing regime • Technology and service neutrality • Validity of operating license • Public availability of operating license costs • Predictability of renewal conditions for operating and spectrum licenses • Allocation of low frequency spectrum and digital dividend • Voluntary spectrum trading • Infrastructure sharing

Source: EBA database.

Figure 9.1 | Countries with high mobile internet market penetration also perform better on the ICT indicator

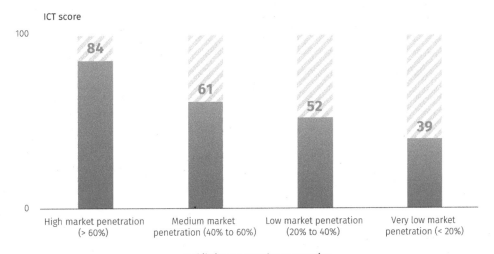

ICT score

Mobile internet market penetration

Sources: EBA database; GSMA.

Note: Total unique mobile internet subscribers is expressed as a percentage share of the total market population. The correlation between the mobile internet market penetration and the ICT score is 0.66. The correlation is significant at 1% level after controlling for income per capita.

Figure 9.2 | Countries performing well on the Mobile Connectivity Index have stronger ICT regulations

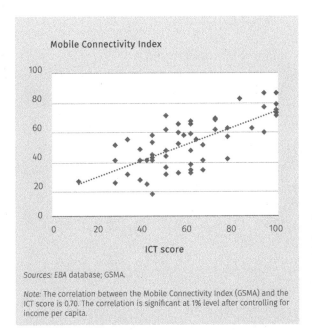

Mobile Connectivity Index

ICT score

Sources: EBA database; GSMA.

Note: The correlation between the Mobile Connectivity Index (GSMA) and the ICT score is 0.70. The correlation is significant at 1% level after controlling for income per capita.

Table 9.2 | Where are ICT regulations strongest?

STRONGEST		WEAKEST	
1	GREECE	57	EGYPT, ARAB REP. AND SUDAN
1	NETHERLANDS	59	BURKINA FASO
1	POLAND	59	LAO PDR
1	ROMANIA	59	SRI LANKA
1	SPAIN	62	ETHIOPIA

Source: EBA database.

Note: Greece, the Netherlands, Poland, Romania, and Spain all perform the same and are thus tied at the 1st position. Burkina Faso, Lao PDR and Sri Lanka all receive the same score.

market competition in the telecommunications sector. In fact, the Ethiopian Telecommunications Corporation has the monopoly on telecommunications services in Ethiopia and there is little incentive to improve connectivity. This situation is reflected in the relatively low number of mobile cellular subscriptions in the country (42.76 per 100 people).[12]

What are the regulatory good practices?

Box 9.1 highlights regulatory good practices and some countries that implement these practices.

General authorization regimes foster competition

Traditionally, a licensing regime has been applied to authorize mobile operators to provide telecommunication services. Due to rapid technological development and the convergence of networks and services, a more open authorization framework is considered to be a good practice (box 9.1). General authorization regimes allow any telecommunication provider to offer electronic communications services, subject to general conditions applicable to all providers in the sector. They take the form of either open, license-exempt entry or simple notification requirements[13] to start a telecommunications business. As a result, general authorization regimes increase competition by reducing barriers to entry and simplifying the regulatory process, and reduce administrative costs for regulators.

Only 10 countries out of the sample studied implement a general authorization regime (Colombia, Denmark, Georgia, Guatemala, Greece, Italy, Netherlands, Poland, Romania and Spain). In all 10 countries, administrative charges associated with general authorization regimes are publicly available. Furthermore, in most cases (Italy being an exception),[14] the validity of general authorization is indefinite, which eliminates any uncertainty surrounding license renewal. In contrast, individual licenses are prone to regulatory uncertainty and ambiguity over licensing fees, renewal conditions and/or universal access obligations. Twenty-one of the 52 countries that impose individual licenses do not publish online the exact fees associated with obtaining an operating license. In 12 countries the renewal conditions of the operating licenses are also not clearly articulated in the existing regulations, and in 10 countries the validity of the individual operating license is less than 15 years. Such uncertainties regarding fees, renewal conditions and relatively short license terms make infrastructure investments riskier for mobile operators and thus deter investments into rural areas that are more challenging in terms of their commercial viability.

Box 9.1 | What are the regulatory good practices for ICT?

REGULATORY GOOD PRACTICES FOR ICT	SOME COUNTRIES WHICH IMPLEMENT THE PRACTICE
A general authorization regime is in place.	COLOMBIA, DENMARK
A technology and service neutrality principle is applied.	THE NETHERLANDS, SERBIA
The validity of the operating license is more than 15 years.	CAMBODIA, MEXICO
Operating license costs are transparent.	BOSNIA AND HERZEGOVINA, KENYA
Renewal conditions for operating and spectrum licenses are predictable.	TANZANIA, THAILAND
Low frequency spectrum is allocated to mobile operators.	KOREA, REP., VIETNAM
Digital dividend bands are licensed to mobile operators.	ROMANIA
Voluntary spectrum trading is allowed.	CHILE, INDIA
Passive and active infrastructure sharing are allowed.	MALAYSIA, POLAND

Source: EBA database.

Figure 9.3 | Digital dividend promotes greater coverage for rural areas

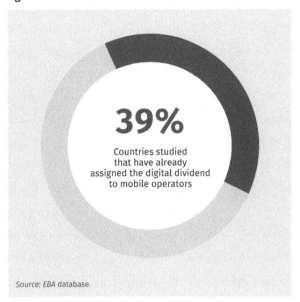

39%

Countries studied that have already assigned the digital dividend to mobile operators

Source: EBA database.

Figure 9.4 | Voluntary spectrum trading facilitates better allocation and more efficient use of resources

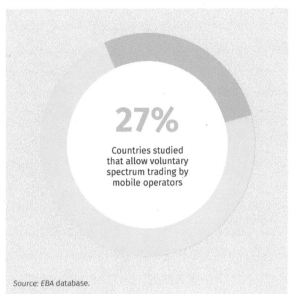

27%

Countries studied that allow voluntary spectrum trading by mobile operators

Source: EBA database.

Promote greater coverage for rural areas through efficient spectrum management

To provide mobile services, telecommunication network providers have to obtain permission from the government to use radio frequencies or electromagnetic spectrum waves to operate within a network. Efficient spectrum management by the government incentivizes private sector investments to rollout networks to rural and remote areas. If mobile operators are permitted to use digital dividend bands, deployment costs are reduced, as fewer base stations are needed to cover the same geographic area. As such, good spectrum management that allows for a digital dividend to be licensed to mobile operators is useful for rural areas where population density is low and rollout costs are high.[15] Among the 62 countries studied, only 24 have licensed the digital dividend spectrum to mobile operators (figure 9.3). No countries studied in the East Asia and Pacific or the Sub-Saharan Africa regions have licensed the digital dividend to mobile operators. In contrast, all OECD high-income countries have licensed a digital dividend to mobile operators.

In addition to digital dividend use, good spectrum management also allows for voluntary spectrum trading, "a mechanism whereby rights and any associated obligations to use spectrum can be transferred from one party to another in the market." This process can facilitate more efficient allocation and use of scarce spectrum resources, and foster innovation and the introduction of new services. The countries studied have various regulatory approaches towards spectrum trading, although generally voluntary spectrum trading is associated with higher levels of development. Only 17 of the 62 countries allow the practice, including all 8 OECD high-income countries (figure 9.4). No low-income countries and no countries located in the Sub-Saharan Africa region have implemented voluntarily spectrum trading. The countries that do not allow voluntarily spectrum trading are operating in less open telecommunication markets and in many cases do not implement the principle of technology and service neutrality that allows any service to be provided and any technology to be deployed within suggested frequency bands.

Conclusion

The type of licensing framework and efficiency of spectrum allocation can play important parts in encouraging the private sector to invest and rollout mobile networks in remote areas. The experience of EU countries suggests that greater liberalization of the telecommunications sector, including the introduction of general authorization regimes, supports ubiquitous connectivity. Efficient spectrum management is another regulatory stimulus than can provide benefits to mobile network operators through lower deployment costs and innovation opportunities, and to the end user in terms of greater access to ICT services.

NOTES

1   Jensen 2007.

2   ITU 2016.

3   GSMA 2015.

4   World Bank 2016.

5   World Bank 2012.

6   Vodafone Foundation 2015.

7   Kendal and Singh 2012.

8   GSMA Intelligence Database 2016. https://www.gs-maintelligence.com/. Mobile internet market penetration=total unique mobile internet subscribers expressed as a percentage share of the total market population. Mobile internet means any activity that consumes mobile data (for example, mobile applications for farmers).

9   There is a strong positive correlation between Mobile Connectivity Index (GSMA) and the EBA ICT score (0.70). The correlation is significant at 1% level after controlling for income per capita.

10 See European Commission (2016), *Telecoms*, https://ec.europa.eu/digital-single-market/en/telecoms.

11 See GSMA Intelligence Database (2016), https://www.gsmaintelligence.com/.

12 See World Bank Open Data (2015), http://data.worldbank.org/.

13 In a simple notification system, "[s]ervice providers are required only to provide the regulator with notification of the start and termination of the provision of services or the operation of a network" (InfoDev and ITU 2016).

14 The validity of simple notification in Italy is 20 years.

15 Picot et al. 2009.

REFERENCES

GSMA. 2015. *Mobile Internet Usage Challenges in Asia—Awareness, Literacy and Local Content.* London: GSMA.

———. 2016. *Unlocking Rural Coverage: Enablers for Commercially Sustainable Mobile Network Expansion.* London: GSMA.

Hawthorne, R. 2015. "Economic Regulation and Regulatory Performance in the Electronic Communications Sector: Key Themes for African Regulators." *The African Journal of Information and Communication* 14: 3–8.

InfoDev and ITU (International Telecommunication Union). 2016. *ICT Regulation Toolkit.* http://www.ictregulationtoolkit.org/en/home.

ITU. 2008. "Spectrum Sharing." Discussion Paper GSR 2008. ITU, Geneva.

———. 2016. *ITU Facts and Figures 2016.* Geneva: ITU.

Jensen, Robert. 2007. "The Digital Provide: Information (Technology), Market Performance and Welfare in the South Indian Fisheries Sector." *Quarterly Journal of Economics*, 122(3): 879–924.

Kendall, Jake and Nirvikar Singh. 2012. "Internet Kiosks in Rural India: Gender, Caste and Location." *Review of Market Integration*, 4(1): 1–43.

Picot, A., N. Grove, F. K. Jondral and J. Elsner. 2009. "Why the Digital Dividend Will Not Close the Digital Divide." *InterMedia* 39: 32–37.

United Nations, Department of Economic and Social Affairs, Population Division. 2014. *World Urbanization Prospects: The 2014 Revision.* CD-ROM Edition. http://esa.un.org/Unpd/Wup/CD-ROM/Default.aspx.

Vodafone Foundation. 2015. "Connected Farming in India. How Mobile Can Support Farmers' Livelihoods." Vodafone Group, Newbury, U.K.

World Bank. 2012. *Agricultural Innovation Systems – An Investment Sourcebook.* Washington, DC: World Bank.

———. 2016. *World Development Report 2016: Digital Dividends.* Washington, DC: World Bank.

INFORMATION AND COMMUNICATION TECHNOLOGY

Environmental Sustainability

Tar spot complex (TSC), a disease affecting maize crops, has decimated the yields of farmers in the high valleys in Mexico. Most of the maize varieties planted in Mexico are susceptible to it, which means that farmers' have to pay for fungicides throughout the year to protect their crops. Developing a variety that is resistant to TSC is an environmentally and economically sustainable alternative. Testing carried out from 2011 to 2014 successfully identified two local varieties with outstanding genetic disease resistance and scientists are now using them to develop germplasms with a view to make them available to breeders by 2017. This process will help produce new varieties that combine the higher yields of elite lines with local varieties' resistance to TSC, to reduce fungicide use and improve farmer's productivity.[1]

Agriculture uses a range of natural resources that include water, soil and plant genetic resources. The quality and availability of these resources are fundamental to sustain production and respond to increasing global food demand. However, farming can also contribute to the depletion of natural resources including the loss of biodiversity, pollution of soil and water resources, and accelerated rates of soil erosion.

Despite its dependence on diverse genetic resources, modern farming can pose a challenge for the preservation of biodiversity. The increased use of improved seed varieties over local varieties, together with environmental degradation, urbanization and land clearing have contributed to genetic erosion. It is estimated that during the last century nearly 75% of plant genetic diversity has been lost, as farmers have replaced their genetically richer local varieties with genetically uniform, high-yielding varieties.[2]

As the largest user of water resources globally, the agricultural sector consumes approximately 69% of all water withdrawn[3] and accounts for 36% of the land surface that is suitable for crop production.[4] For example, chemical pesticides can pollute surface and groundwater through leaching and run off, causing negative effects in aquatic ecosystems and human health. Furthermore, deforestation and poor agricultural practices such as over cultivation and excessive grazing and water use can contribute to land degradation and desertification.[5] A study conducted in Brazil shows that pasture and agricultural expansions have been the main causes of deforestation in the Amazon between 2000 and 2006.[6]

Mitigating the impact of farming on the environment is an important challenge to guarantee the long-term sustainability of agricultural production.

Landscape of fields and homes, Indonesia.
Photo: Curt Carnemark / World Bank.

What do the EBA environmental sustainability indicators measure?

The EBA environmental sustainability indicators measure the legal and regulatory framework applicable to the management and sustainable use of natural resources that are vital for agricultural production. The data cover the following areas:

Conservation of plant genetic resources: The conservation of a diverse pool of genetic resources supports future crop production, since the development of adapted and improved seed varieties relies on the use of genetic variability, mainly found in local varieties and crop wild relatives.[7] Data in this area cover the laws, regulations and policies that address the conservation of plant genetic resources in national genebanks.[8] It also includes alternative conservation mechanisms at the farm and local level, such as community seed banks, diversity fairs or participatory plant breeding. These alternatives allow farmers to participate in the conservation, breeding and circulation of diverse seed.

Access and sustainable use of plant genetic resources: Farmers will preserve diverse genetic resources depending on the commercial value such resources can command in the market. Regulations and policies that facilitate the commercialization of seeds of local varieties through registries[9] or simplified registration requirements are important ways to increase the availability of these genetically rich varieties in markets. Data cover laws and regulations that facilitate the circulation of seed in the informal sector, by recognizing farmer's rights to reuse seed from their own harvests, and establish clear rules for accessing plant genetic resources.

Water quality management: Agriculture is a major cause of the degradation of surface and groundwater resources. Erosion and chemical runoff, such as nitrate pollution from excessive use of fertilizers and intensive livestock rearing,[10] affect water quality. Data cover the institutional framework and regulations aimed at minimizing the contamination of water bodies from agricultural activities, such as buffer zones and setbacks, and regulations on hazardous and obsolete pesticides.

Soil health management: Land use plans allow governments to assess all current and potential uses in a territory and adopt the land use structure that best meets users' needs[11] while safeguarding valuable resources for future generations. Soil quality indicators are useful to better understand and monitor the impact of soil management practices.[12] Data are collected on the legal and institutional frameworks applicable to land use planning and soil monitoring.

Some insights emerging from the data

Plant genetic resources

Improved seed varieties can provide significant benefits to farmers such as higher yields, resistance to certain diseases and more stable production. The development of these modern varieties relies on the use of genetic variability. National genebanks play a critical role in the preservation of genetic diversity, performing important functions such as the provision of genetic material to researchers, breeders and farmers for the development of new plant varieties or rebuilding agricultural production after conflicts or natural disasters. Among the 62 countries studied, 32 countries have established a national genebank.

Figure 10.1 | A limited number of countries have adopted laws that specifically regulate the commercialization of local varieties

16
Countries **that have adopted** laws that specifically regulate the commercialization of local varieties

46
Countries **that have not adopted** laws that specifically regulate the commercialization of local varieties

Source: EBA database.

Figure 10.2 | Land use planning mandates are less frequent in the Middle East and North Africa, Europe and Central Asia, and South Asia

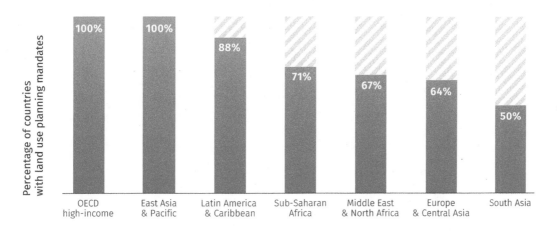

Source: EBA database.

In addition to conserving plant genetic resources, genebanks also publish information associated with the plant material conserved to facilitate its use by potential users.[13] Among the 32 countries that have established a national genebank, 16 publish information associated with their activities online. Although most of these countries are OECD high-income and upper-middle-income countries, Bolivia—a lower-middle-income country that recently joined the International Treaty on Plant Genetic Resources for Food and Agriculture —has a national genebank holding 18,434 collections of significant value to agricultural biodiversity, detailed information on which is available online.[14]

The commercialization of local varieties has been recognized as a pathway to enhance the utilization and conservation of diverse genetic resources.[15] Registries[16] or simplified registration requirements can facilitate the commercialization of seed of local varieties. Registering local varieties in order to integrate them into formal channels can result in increased availability of diverse seed in the market.

To be registered and accepted for commercialization, most countries require a new variety to pass tests that evaluate distinctiveness, uniformity, and stability (DUS) and value of cultivation and use (VCU). However, as these tests are not appropriate for local varieties, which are genetically heterogeneous and adapted to local conditions, laws should provide for certain exceptions.[17] Only one-quarter of the countries studied explicitly support this practice (figure 10.1). Of these, Denmark, Greece, Italy, the Netherlands, Poland, Romania and Spain, and as European Union (EU) members, have implemented EU Directive 2008/62/EC establishing certain exceptions for the acceptance and

marketing of certain crop varieties that are adapted to local conditions and threatened by genetic erosion. Other countries with similar exceptions include Bangladesh, India, Nepal, Peru, Thailand and Uruguay. In Uruguay, for example, the range of genetic heterogeneity allowed for local varieties during testing is higher than for conventional varieties and VCU tests are not required.

Water quality management

As stated above, agricultural production is a principal cause of surface and groundwater resources degradation. Forest buffers, a type of restrictions on land use, can address pollution caused by pesticides and excess fertilizers by functioning as filters that trap sediment, excess nutrients, pesticides and other chemical contaminants that would otherwise reach water sources.[18] These practices are infrequently adopted by the countries studied; only 26 countries have regulations that provide for buffer zones or setbacks adjacent to water bodies, most of which are high-income and upper-middle-income countries. In Rwanda, for example, the law on environmental protection specifically restricts agricultural activities within 10 meters of streams and rivers, and 50 meters of lakes; instead, these areas have been reserved for protection and conservation activities.

Pesticides should also be controlled to guard against water and soil pollution. Because their ingredients are toxic and have the potential to harm human and ecosystem health,[19] governments should establish legal frameworks that regulate their distribution and use, especially in the case of hazardous pesticides.[20] Fifty-seven of the countries studied (92%) have

Sifting grain. India. Photo: Ray Witlin / World Bank.

regulations that restrict the distribution and manage-ment of hazardous pesticide products. A large majority of high-income and upper-middle-income countries also impose specific rules to deal with obsolete or unwanted pesticides, which remain hazardous to the environment if improperly stored or disposed of. The adoption of this practice is less common in regions such as Sub-Saharan Africa, where only 12 of the 21 countries studied have regulations addressing obso-lete pesticides, and South Asia, where only one of the four countries studied has such regulations in place. Regulations on this issue vary, from an obligation to include disposal methods on the pesticide label in Tanzania, to specialized facilities or collection services to safely collect and dispose of pesticides in Denmark and India.

Soil health management

Land use plans allow governments to assess all cur-rent and potential uses in a territory and adopt the land use structure that best meets users' needs,[21] while safeguarding valuable resources for future gen-erations. Soil quality data provide useful information that governments, farmers and other stakeholders can use to monitor the impact of agricultural activities and inform land management decisions and farming practices.[22]

Forty-eight of the countries studied have regula-tions mandating the development of land use plans, and 50 countries have an authority that monitors

agricultural soil. While land use planning is mandated in all high-income OECD countries and East Asian and Pacific countries, it is less common in other regions such as South Asia, where only Nepal and India have such regulations (figure 10.2). In India, where land use planning is regulated by state-level governments, two of the studied states, Odisha and Maharashtra, man-date the development of land use plans, while Bihar and Uttar Pradesh do not make it a requirement. India is also implementing a soil monitoring program at the national level that aims to provide farmers with rele-vant data on soil health.

Conclusion

Agriculture depends on the availability of certain nat-ural resources that are essential production inputs. In this context, the preservation of soil, water and plant genetic resources must remain a policy priority for governments and form part of their broader efforts to increase agricultural productivity. In particular, reg-ulations that protect soil and water quality from the negative effects of fertilizers, pesticides and intensive livestock rearing are necessary to maintain vital eco-systems and guarantee the availability and utility of these resources for future generations. Institutions and regulations that safeguard diverse plant genetic resources are also crucial to ensure that the agricul-tural sector can respond to increased food demand and changing environmental conditions.

NOTES

1   Johnson et al. 2016.

2   FAO 1999.

3   http://www.fao.org/nr/water/aquastat/tables/
    WorldData-Withdrawal_eng.pdf.

4   Bruinsma 2003.

5   Horrigan et al. 2002.

6   Barona et al. 2010.

7   Ford-Lloyd et al. 2011.

8   Genebanks are repositories where genetic material of
    plants is stored and preserved in forms such as seeds
    or cuttings.

9   Spataro and Negri 2013.

10 Morris et al. 2003.

11 Van Lier and De Wrachien 2002.

12 Arshad and Martin 2002.

13 FAO 2014.

14 FAO 2016.

15 Gautam and Pant 2011.

16 Spataro and Negri 2013.

17 Paavilainen 2009.

18 Aguiar et al. 2015.

19 Horrigan et al. 2002.

20 FAO and WHO 2016.

21 Van Lier and De Wrachien 2002.

22 Arshad and Martin 2002.

REFERENCES

Aguiar, T. R. Jr. et al. 2015. "Nutrient Removal Effectiveness
    by Riparian Buffer Zones in Rural Temperate
    Watersheds: The Impact of No-Till Crops Practices."
    Agricultural Water Management 149: 74–80.

Arshad, M. A. and S. Martin. 2002. "Identifying Critical
    Limits for Soil Quality Indicators in Agro-Ecosystems."
    Agriculture, Ecosystems and Environment 88: 153–60.

Barona, E., N. Ramankutty, G. Hyman and O. Coomes. 2010.
    "The Role of Pasture and Soybean in Deforestation
    of the Brazilian Amazon." *Environmental Research
    Letters* 5 (2): 1–9.

Bruinsma, J., ed. 2003. *World Agriculture: Towards
    2015/2030. An FAO Perspective*. London, UK: Earthscan
    Publications.

FAO (Food and Agriculture Organization of the United
    Nations). 1999. "Women: The Key to Food Security."
    Rome: FAO.

—— 2014. "Genebank Standards for Plant Genetic
    Resources for Food and Agriculture." FAO, Rome.

—— 2016. "Bolivia Joins the International Treaty on
    Plant Genetic Resources for Food and Agriculture."
    FAO, Rome. http://www.fao.org/plant-treaty/news/
    detail-events/en/c/448725/.

—— and WHO (World Health Organization). 2016.
    "International Code of Conduct on Pesticide
    Management. Guidelines on Highly Hazardous
    Pesticides." FAO and WHO, Rome.

Ford-Lloyd, Brian V. et al. 2011. "Crop Wild Relatives—
    Undervalued, Underutilized and Under Threat?"
    BioScience 61 (7): 559–65.

Gautam, J. C. and K. Pant. 2011. "Commercialization and
    Market Linkages for Promoting the Use of Local Rice
    Varieties: A Nepalese Case Study." In *The Economics
    of Managing Crop Diversity On-farm*, edited by E.
    Wale, A. G. Drucker and K. K. Zander, 111–21. London:
    Earthscan.

Horrigan, L., R. S. Lawrence, and P. Walker. 2002.
    "How Sustainable Agriculture Can Address the
    Environmental and Human Health Harms of Industrial
    Agriculture." *Environmental Health Perspectives* 110
    (5): 445–56.

Johnson, J., T. Molnar and M. Willcox 2016. "Ancient Maize
    Varieties Provide Modern Solution to Tar Spot
    Complex." Retrieved from http://maize.org/ancient-
    maize-varieties-provide-modern-solution-to-tar-
    spot-complex/

Morris, B. L. et al. 2003. "Groundwater and its Susceptibility
    to Degradation: A Global Assessment of the Problem
    and Options for Management." Early Warning and
    Assessment Report Series, RS. 03-3. United Nations
    Environment Programme, Nairobi.

Paavilainen, K. 2009. "National Policies and Support
    Systems for Landrace Cultivation in Finland."
    In *European Landraces: On-Farm Conservation,
    Management and Use*. Bioversity Technical Bulletin
    No. 15. Bioversity International, Rome.

Spataro, G. and V. Negri. 2013. "The European Seed
    Legislation on Conservation Varieties: Focus,
    Implementation, Present and Future Impact on
    Landrace on Farm Conservation." *Genetic Resources
    and Crop Evolution* 60: 2421–430.

Van Lier, H. N. and D. De Wrachien. 2002. "Land Use
    Planning: A Key to Sustainable Development." Paper
    presented at the XXX International Symposium Actual
    Tasks on Agricultural Engineering. Opatija, Croatia,
    March 12–15.

Livinesi Mateche has always depended on farming as the main source of income in her home, located in the Mchinji district of Malawi. As she sought to improve her farming techniques, she joined the National Smallholder Farmers' Alliance of Malawi (NASFAM), the largest independent smallholder-owned membership organization in the country. During the next planting season, she benefited from NASFAM's farmer-to-farmer training program and learned good agricultural practices to improve crop quality and yields. Her membership benefits went beyond increased productivity. Thanks to NASFAM's capacity to procure in bulk the members' produce and transport them to points of sale domestically and abroad, Livinesi found more profitable commercial outlets for her production and her earnings increased substantially. Through her membership, Livinesi was able to improve her farming operation's production and marketing prospects.[1]

Identifying and analyzing the direct and indirect regulatory barriers to women's full participation in the agricultural sector are essential to increasing productivity among women. Underlying constraints include unequal access to finance, land and agricultural inputs such as improved seeds, fertilizer and machinery. In addition, traditional norms may impact the utility of agricultural resources for women. The private sector has a role to play in addressing some of those constraints, and examples abound of agricultural and agribusiness companies that have designed creative initiatives to lift certain obstacles (box 11.1). In addition to those private sector-led efforts, regulatory initiatives are needed to secure land tenure for women, provide financial inclusion and market access, and increase women's access to crucial agricultural inputs.[2]

In Sub-Saharan Africa, for example, although women make up around 40% of the agricultural labor force, their agricultural productivity lags far behind.[3] Controlling for plot size and geographic factors, the gender productivity gap is estimated to be 66% in Niger and 23% in Tanzania.[4] Not only does the gender productivity gap carry direct social and economic consequences for women farmers, but it also has a significant impact on the economy. In Malawi and Tanzania, for example, lower female productivity is estimated to cause annual losses of $100 million and $105 million, respectively. For those same countries, experts also estimate that closing the gender productivity gap could increase crop output up to 8.1% and 3.9%, respectively.[5] Research conducted in Burkina Faso further suggests that, at the household level, reallocating some agricultural inputs, and notably fertilizers, from the plots farmed by men to those farmed by women could lead to a 6% increase in output.[6] Finally, closing the gender gap in agricultural productivity could lift tens of thousands of people out of poverty.[7]

Wheat harvest in central India.
Photo: Scott Wallace / World Bank.

Box 11.1 | How can the private sector support gender equality and increase women's role in agribusinesses?

A 2015 report indicated that $12 trillion could be added to global income by 2025 by advancing women's equality through the public, private and social sectors acting to close the gender gap. Correspondingly, agribusinesses have been engaged in numerous projects targeting women, including their role and influence in agriculture. For example, one project aims to help women overcome barriers in cocoa farming communities in Côte d'Ivoire, where only 4% of the cocoa farmers are women. The project provides female-only training to farmers to help them improve their agriculture and business skills, as well as offering gender-sensitive trainings for rural development agents. In Zambia, another project runs a training program for female tractor drivers in the coffee estates. In Mali there is a program that seeks to address women's participation in agricultural leadership roles, by offering women's producer organizations farming tools and additional training free of charge.[a]

Food conglomerates and other food companies are increasingly demanding that the raw materials they purchase are produced sustainably and in a gender-sensitive manner. For example, one project reviewed women's role in the cocoa value chain in Côte d'Ivoire and Ghana. The project was based on the recognition that women's leadership at all levels is required to achieve transformative change in the sector.[b]

a. Woetzel et al. 2015; http://www.cargill.com/connections/empowering-women-cocoa-farmers-in-Cote-dIvoire/index.jsp; http://olamgroup.com/sustainability/gender-hub/agri-employment-women/just-jobs-boys/; http://www.louisdreyfusfoundation.org/en/what-we-do/micro-farming-initiatives-africa/program-support-female-smallholders-their-daily-farming-providing-them-training-and-equipment/.
b. http://insights.careinternational.org.uk/publications/women-s-leadership-in-cocoa-life-communities.

How can the EBA indicators help female farmers?

Although not all EBA indicators are specifically designed to capture differences in legal and regulatory treatments between men and women, they all measure aspects of the business environment that matter for all participants along agricultural value chains, regardless of gender. The EBA indicators measure the business environment for farmers and agribusinesses in the context of inputs (seed, fertilizer and machinery), finance, markets, transport, information and communication technology (ICT), water and land, and are relevant to the economic and social advancement of those involved in those sectors. Among them, women can benefit from an improved business environment as measured by EBA indicators, through at least four channels, namely: 1) streamlined procedural and operational requirements for businesses; 2) member-based rural institutions; 3) innovation for financial inclusion; and 4) land use and ownership.

Streamlined procedural and operational requirements for businesses

Streamlining the agribusiness environment, lifting cumbersome procedures and minimizing procedural costs and delays can benefit farmers. Nevertheless, the benefits that could accrue to women are particularly significant due to their proportionately higher numbers in the agricultural sector, and the low-quality capital, information and time resources to which they typically have access.[8] EBA markets indicators, for example, measure some of the transaction costs for exporting agricultural goods. Women who wish to export

agricultural products will benefit from streamlined procedures to obtain all the necessary documents, such as phytosanitary and quality certificates, in less time and at a lower cost. Minimizing entry requirements such as export licensing and mandatory memberships will also facilitate women's access to export opportunities. Furthermore, EBA indicators on inputs measure the regulatory constraints for registering new seed varieties, fertilizer products and agricultural tractors. Regulations that ease the burden on importers and dealers can make such inputs more readily available and affordable in remote regions, and thus more accessible to women farmers.

Member-based rural organizations

Rural women can also benefit from and be empowered through member-based organizations such as producer organizations (measured by the markets topic), financial cooperatives (measured by the finance topic) and water users' associations (measured by the water topic), all of which help their members overcome obstacles relating to access to productive capital (seed, fertilizer, machinery and water), access to markets or access to finance. For example, where laws and regulations facilitate the establishment, operations and capitalization of agricultural sales cooperatives, women can benefit from a regulatory environment that enables them to create, join and take leadership positions in such entities.[9]

Innovation for financial inclusion

Several studies suggest that low financial inclusion rates for women not only constrain agricultural productivity but also reduce food security, nutrition and education investments.[10] Accessing appropriate finance continues to be a significant challenge for women. For example, in Uganda, although 38% of all registered companies are owned by women, only 9% of credit is accessible to them; and in Kenya, where women own 48% of micro and small enterprises, only 7% of credit is accessible to them.[11] Women generally face legal impediments, discriminatory bank practices and male-favored cultural assumptions that limit their access to suitable financial services.[12] The fact that women usually do not possess assets that could serve as collateral also reduces access to finance, as does the lack of formal credit institutions in rural areas.[13] Microfinance institutions (MFIs) are a crucial alternative to traditional credit providers and banks, and the majority of MFI clients in many regions of the world are women.[14] Financial cooperatives can also provide an alternative to commercial banks. EBA finance indicators encourage the creation of a regulatory environment for MFIs and financial cooperatives, and they analyze the range of assets that banks accept as collateral.

Land use and ownership

Land is one of the most essential elements for agriculture, and therefore any limitations on land use or ownership by women also restrict the economic autonomy of women and compromise agricultural productivity.[15] Less than 20% of agricultural landholders worldwide are women.[16] Insecure land tenure for women discourages financial and physical investments to improve the quality of land for production, and compromises the ability of women to pledge land as collateral to obtain financing.[17] EBA land data measure leasing of land, public land management, procedural safeguards in case of expropriation, gender disaggregation of land records and relevance of land records—implementing good policies and regulatory practices in these indicators can help improve women's use and access of agricultural land.

What gender-relevant data were collected this year?

The following areas of research were chosen for coverage in EBA 2017: availability of gender-disaggregated data, restrictions on women's employment and activity, women's participation and leadership in collective groups and nondiscrimination legal provisions. These questions build on findings from the *Women, Business and the Law* dataset, which already identifies many relevant constraints.[18]

Availability of gender-disaggregated data

Regulation can ensure banks and MFIs collect gender-disaggregated data by including such requirements in their reporting obligations. In only 6 of the 62 countries studied, however, are commercial banks required to disaggregate their loan portfolio information by gender. The same obligation applies to deposit-taking MFIs in 14 of the 33 countries where MFIs are allowed to take deposits (figure 11.1).

The land topic provides information on the availability of gender-disaggregated data on land ownership across 38 countries. In 18 of those countries, land registries gather gender-disaggregated data for individually and jointly-registered land.

Restrictions to women's employment and activity

Regulations restricting women's participation in certain professions actually deny income-generating opportunities to women and shrink the pool of workers that firms can employ. Identifying employment restrictions in the agricultural and agribusiness sector can complement the sectors already identified by the *Women, Business and the Law* dataset, including construction, factory work, metalworking and mining. EBA collected data on employment restrictions in the context of handling pesticides or fertilizers, driving trucks and using agricultural tractors.

Among the countries surveyed, Kyrgyz Republic and Vietnam both prohibit women from handling fertilizers and operating tractors. Egypt, and the Russian Federation also impose restrictions on handling fertilizer and tractor use, respectively.

Figure 11.1 | Are commercial banks and MFIs required to collect gender-disaggregated data?

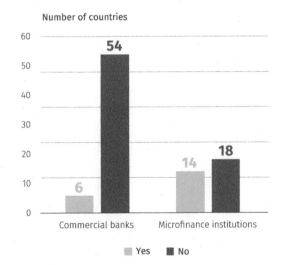

Number of countries

Source: EBA database.

Figure 11.2 | Do quotas or other mechanisms exist to promote women's leadership in member-based institutions?

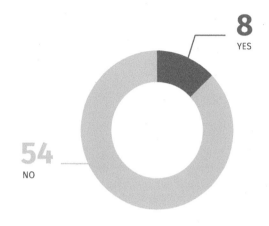

8
YES

54
NO

Source: EBA database.

Note: Member-based institutions cover producer organizations, financial co-operatives, and water user organizations. All of the 62 countries covered have enacted specific legislation to govern producer organization or have at least some mention of producer organization in their broader legal framework, 56 have done so for financial cooperatives, and 44 have done so for water user organizations. In addition to quotas, other mechanisms to promote women's leadership include general mentions of gender balance for board selection and composition. A country is considered to have such quota or other mechanism in place if any of those applies to at least one of the three member-based institutions under consideration.

Women's membership and participation in producer organizations

Limitations on the ability of women to become members of organizations such as agricultural cooperatives compromise their ability to capitalize and commercialize their produce, and turn smallholdings into profitable agribusinesses.

Strong laws and regulations stipulate mandatory membership criteria that cooperatives apply to all member applicants, to avoid the development of bylaws that may restrict women's participation. Membership criteria requiring land ownership or full-time farm employment, or restricting membership to heads of household or to one member per household, have a tendency to limit women's access to member-based institutions on a *de facto* basis.[19] Of the 62 countries surveyed, only 4 countries (India, Russian Federation, Rwanda and Serbia) require that producer organization membership be limited to one member per household. In Nigeria, cooperative members must have legal ownership over land. On the other hand, a new agricultural cooperative law adopted in Greece in April 2016, now allows women-only cooperatives to be established with only 5 female founding members, compared to regular cooperatives where 20 members are required.

Encouraging women to hold leadership positions in local organizations also plays an important role in

Women create terrace, Rwanda. Photo: A'Melody Lee / World Bank.

Figure 11.3 | Do producer organizations have to comply with the principle of nondiscrimination?

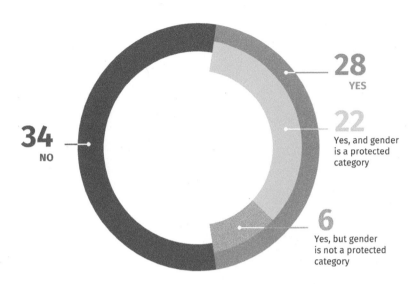

28
YES

22
Yes, and gender is a protected category

6
Yes, but gender is not a protected category

34
NO

Source: EBA database.

promoting gender equality. Quotas can establish the necessary critical mass of women as members and leaders to engender change in policy and the institutional culture and lead to more productive, profitable organizations. Eight of the 62 countries surveyed (Greece, India, Kenya, Korea, Nepal, Nicaragua, Rwanda, and Spain) have proactive policies to promote women's participation in the leadership of such groups (figure 11.2). In most cases, a quota is used and set out in applicable legislation. This is the case in India, where most state cooperative laws have a legally mandated minimum requirement regarding the number of women to be included in cooperative managing committees. Similarly, in Kenya, the 2010 Constitution mandates that no more than two-thirds of the members of elective or appointive bodies, including cooperatives boards, shall be of the same gender.

Nondiscrimination

EBA also collected data on whether specific laws on producer organizations, financial cooperatives and water user organizations require them to adhere to principles of nondiscrimination and if gender is specified as a protected category.[20]

In the laws directly applicable to producer organizations, legal protection against discrimination is provided in 28 of the countries studied. Among those, 22 specifically provide that gender-based discrimination is prohibited (figure 11.3). For example, Mexico's Law on Cooperatives provides that cooperatives must guarantee equality in rights and duties among members and equality for women. Similarly, Nicaraguan and Bolivian laws establish the principle of gender equality as applicable to cooperative operations. Nicaragua requires cooperatives

to promote the integration of women in cooperatives through specific programs and campaigns.

In other countries the constitution contains a nondiscrimination clause. According to the *Women, Business and the Law* database, 42 countries from the EBA sample have legal protection against discrimination, 28 of which mention gender as a protected category.[21]

Conclusion

As they assess the overall business environment for agriculture and agribusiness, EBA indicators cover a range of regulatory and procedural aspects that have a direct impact on women working as producers and at other levels of the agricultural value chain. New data were collected this year to highlight some areas where regulations can have a more direct impact on women's productivity and opportunities for advancement. Those areas include the availability of sex-disaggregated data with regard to banking and land transactions, the existence of legal restrictions to women's employment in agriculture-related activities and the existence of legal obstacles to women's participation in membership-based organizations such as producer organizations, financial cooperatives and water users' associations. Progress on these areas as well as across EBA indicators in general can improve women's prospects and participation in agricultural value chains and ensure that women are on an equal footing with men. It is hoped that through a mix of existing agricultural policies becoming more gender-inclusive, and the designing of new policies that are gender-targeted, constraints will be lifted and the particular needs of women in agriculture will be better met.

NOTES

1   http://www.wfo-oma.com/women-in-agriculture/case-studies/the-story-of-livinesi-mateche.html.

2   UN Women 2016.

3   Palacios-Lopez, Christiaensen and Kilic 2015.

4   O'Sullivan et al. 2014.

5   FAO 2011.

6   Duflo 2012; Udry 1996.

7   World Bank 2015.

8   Simavi, Manuel and Blackden 2010.

9   http://www.fao.org/gender/gender-home/gender-insight/gender-insightdet/en/c/164572/; Clugston 2014.

10 World Bank 2015; African Development Bank Group 2015.

11 African Development Bank Group 2015.

12 OECD 2016.

13 World Bank 2009.

14 Almodovar-Reteguis, Kushnir and Meilland 2011.

15 OECD 2014.

16 UN Women 2016.

17 OECD 2016; African Development Bank Group 2015.

18 *The Women, Business and the Law* indicator, using property, is extremely useful in determining some constraints women face related to land use and ownership. For example, according to this dataset, in about 20% of the EBA sample countries, the law does not give men and women equal inheritance rights.

19 Prakash 2003.

20 A nondiscrimination provision is based on the principle of fairness and equality under the law. It prohibits discrimination in the treatment of members in regardless of gender, profession, income and so on. For instance, it may include language requiring fair terms for women and men when joining as a member or applying for a loan.

21 See wbl.worldbank.org.

REFERENCES

African Development Bank Group. 2015. *Africa Gender Equality Index 2015.* Abidjan: African Development Bank.

Almodovar-Reteguis, N., K. Kushnir and T. Meilland. 2011. "Mapping the Legal Gender Gap in Using Property and Building Credit." http://wbl.worldbank.org/~/media/WBG/WBL/Documents/Notes/Legal-Gender-Gap-in-Using-Property-and-Building-Credit.pdf.

Clugston, C. 2014. "The Business Case for Women's Participation in Agricultural Cooperatives." http://hungercenter.wpengine.netdna-cdn.com/wp-content/uploads/2015/08/ACDI-VOCA-Leland-CDP-Paraguay-Business-Case-for-Women-Participation-Agricultural-Cooperatives.pdf.

Duflo, Esther. 2012. "Women Empowerment and Economic Development." *Journal of Economic Literature* 50 (4): 1051-1079.

Food and Agriculture Organization (FAO). 2011. *The State of Food and Agriculture 2011. Women in Agriculture: Closing the Gender Gap for Development.* Rome: FAO.

IFAD (International Fund for Agricultural). 2010. "Promoting the Leadership of Women in Producers' Organizations." Special Session of the Third Global Meeting of the Farmers' Forum. IFAD, Rome.

Kenney, N. and A. de la o Campos. 2016. "Developing Gender-Equitable Legal Frameworks for Land Tenure." FAO Legal Papers No. 98. FAO, Rome.

OECD. 2014. "Social Institutions & Gender Index 2014 Synthesis Report." OECD, Paris.

——— 2016. "Women's Roles in the West African Food System: Implications and Prospects for Food Security and Resilience." West African Papers, No. 3. OECD Publishing, Paris.

O'Sullivan, M., A Rao, R. Banerjsee, K. Gulati, and M.Vinez 2014. "Levelling the Field: Improving Opportunities for Women Farmers in Africa." World Bank Group, Washington, DC.

Palacios-Lopez, A., L. Christiaensen and T. Kilic. 2015. "How Much of the Labor in African Agriculture Is Provided by Women?" Policy Research Working Paper, No. WPS 7282. World Bank Group, Washington, DC.

Prakash, D. 2003. "Rural Women, Food Security and Agricultural Cooperatives." Rural Development and Management Centre, New Delhi.

Simavi, S., C. Manuel and M. Blackden. 2010. *Gender Dimensions of Investment Climate Reform: A Guide for Policy Makers and Practitioners*. Washington, DC: World Bank.

Udry, C. 1996. "Gender, Agricultural Production, and the Theory of the Household." *Journal of Political Economy*, 104 (5): 1010-1046.

UN Women. 2016. "Women's Empowerment Through Climate-Smart Agriculture." UN Women, New York.

Woetzel, J. et al. 2015. "How Advancing Women's Equality Can Add $12 trillion to Global Growth." McKinsey Global Institute Report, September.

World Bank. 2009. *Gender in Agriculture Sourcebook*. Washington, DC: World Bank.

——. 2015. "The Cost of the Gender Gap in Agricultural Productivity in Malawi, Tanzania, and Uganda." Working Paper. World Bank Group, Washington, DC.

12 Land

Profits per hectare on maize-cassava farms vary widely across similar plots cultivated by different families in the Akwapim region of southern Ghana. Most of the land cultivated by farmers in these villages is under the ultimate control of a paramount chief and is allocated locally through the matrilineage leadership. Insecure land tenure is associated with greatly reduced investment in land fertility. Individuals who are not central to the networks of social and political power that permeate these villages are much more likely to have their land expropriated when it is fallow. As a consequence, farm productivity for these individuals is correspondingly reduced. Women are rarely in positions of sufficient political power to be confident of their rights to land. So women fallow their plots less than their husbands and achieve 30% lower yields.[1]

Secure tenure provides incentives for land-attached investments to enhance productivity of land use and discourage unsustainable practices (such as soil mining) that generate negative effects. The definition of land rights and avenues to access it affect equality of opportunity, women's bargaining power, households' ability to bear risk and their sense of identity. If land can be transferred and markets are sufficiently liquid and their functioning not impeded by other market imperfections, it is ideal collateral that can allow those previously excluded to access financial markets. However, impediments to land market functioning can undermine the ability to use land as collateral in financial markets and make it more difficult for entrepreneurs, small or large, to access land to develop entrepreneurial activities.[2]

By allowing the productive use of land by individuals moving out of the agricultural sector, land rentals or sales can contribute to structural transformation. Land records are also indispensable to effectively manage public land in rural areas and to plan and finance urban expansion in a way that is associated with higher density rather than sprawl. Moreover, without well-defined land rights, it is difficult to provide incentives for production of environmental amenities.

Klaus Deininger authored this chapter. Constructive input and comments from steering committee members Julio Berdegue (RIMISP), Dave Bledsoe (Landesa), Theo de Jager (Pan-African Farmers Association), Elshad Khanalibayli (UN-ECA Working Party on Land Administration), Steve Lawry (CIFOR), Father Francis Lucas (Asian NGO Coalition) and Peter Veit (World Resources Institute) throughout the process are gratefully acknowledged.

LAND

The village of Ait Sidi Hsain, near Meknes, Morocco.
Photo: Arne Hoel / World Bank.

What do the land indicators measure?

EBA land indicators measure laws and regulations that impact access to land markets for producers and agribusinesses (table 12.1). The indicators are organized as follows:

Coverage, relevance, and currency of land records: This indicator measures the extent to which relevant and up to date documentation of land rights is available for all. A key purpose of land records is to ensure land owners are confident enough about their rights being protected to make long-term investments in agriculture and transfer them to others, if they decide to take up nonagricultural opportunities.

Coverage and ease of use. This sub-indicator measures if land records provide information on ownership and location of land in an integrated fashion. Broad coverage is essential for land records to support access to finance and transferability, and to protect existing rights from an equity point of view. Moreover, to prevent disputes over boundaries or overlaps, and allow use of records for planning, land rights documentation needs to include a clear reproducible description of boundaries together with the written record that is updated in case of transfer or subdivision.

Visibility of restrictions on land records. This sub-indicator assesses the extent to which restrictions relating to a land parcel are evident on the record. Ensuring that all relevant restrictions are visible on the record is key to ensure that, before entering into contractual relationships involving a parcel of land, interested third parties need not conduct time-consuming and costly searches and inquiries. Complete records also reduce conflict and speed up dispute resolution.

State land management: The indicator measures how state-owned land, such as forests, parks, road reserves and other public spaces are identified and thus can be protected against encroachment.[3] The issue is particularly acute in low-income settings where laws stipulate that all land not explicitly registered or occupied by private parties—which are often farmlands—belongs to the state.

Record information on state-managed land. This sub-indicator measures whether state land is identified and mapped, and whether a field-based process is put in place before any land is transferred. Failure to have them may render large parts of the population vulnerable to dispossession and affect willingness to invest in the land.

Transfer of state land for commercial use. This sub-indicator measures if regulations governing the transfer of state land for commercial use ensure a transparent process. To ensure that state land is put to its best use, any transfer of state land for commercial purposes (excluding social concerns) should be via public auction. If applicable, development conditions, means of verification, or sanctions for noncompliance should be clearly stipulated with key contractual provisions public and open to independent third-party monitoring.

Equity and fairness: This indicator measures the extent to which gender aspects of land are considered in policy-making, land can be accessed via rental or sales markets, and land rights are protected against expropriation without fair compensation. As a basic asset, equal treatment for different types of land owners or users is important, whether by gender or type of documentation.

Gender-differentiated recording and reporting. This sub-indicator measures regulations on monitoring the gender dimension of land rights to lay out the foundation for identifying the magnitude of this gap and assess if measures to close it are having any effect. Even if gender equality is guaranteed constitutionally, the extent to which such principles are translated into practice may be lagging.

Freedom of leasing. This sub-indicator focuses on regulations and restrictions on leasing. While the fact that land also provides an important social safety net may lead communities to restrict the ability to permanently transfer land,[4] leasing is critical for structural transformation and restrictions on its use may not only drive many efficiency-enhancing land transactions underground, enhancing insecurity for lessors (often single women), but also restricting the scope for more effective land use.

Procedural safeguards in case of expropriation. This sub-indicator measures regulations to ensure that expropriation is limited to public purpose, implemented transparently and with effective appeals mechanisms.[5] While provision of infrastructure and reallocation of agricultural land for industry and urban expansion can provide significant social benefits, having to fear land being expropriated without adequate compensation or due process can undermine investment incentives, lead to over-acquisition of land from a social point of view, and precipitate conflict. Often, expropriation threats imply that peri-urban land is not used for high value crops as in China[6] or Nigeria.

How do countries perform on the land indicators?

Overall scores for the 38 countries in the EBA land sample point towards wide variation in performance across countries (figure 12.1). OECD countries rank highest, followed by Europe and Central Asia where large sums were invested in land administration

Table 12.1 | What do the land indicators measure?

COVERAGE, RELEVANCE AND CURRENCY OF RECORDS FOR PRIVATE LAND	*Coverage and ease of use* • Type of system for archiving information on land ownership • Type of system for archiving maps • Link between property ownership registry and mapping system • How immovable property is identified *Visibility of restrictions on land records* • Online linkage to bans for registering mortgages • Online linkage to enter public encumbrances • Online linkage for the judiciary to record civil disputes pertaining to a parcel
STATE LAND MANAGEMENT	*Record information on state-managed land* • State land is registered • State land is mapped • Field-based process *Transfer of state land for commercial use* • Public tender mechanism • Transparency and monitoring of contractual obligations
EQUITY AND FAIRNESS	*Gender dimension of land records* • Gender information kept at the registry • Regular reporting on gender-disaggregated statistics *Freedom of leasing* • Standardized lease contracts • Negotiation on rental rates • Legal restrictions on minimum duration on the leases *Procedural safeguards in case of expropriation* • Eligibility of compensation • Out-of-court arbitration process • Market value compensation (land, improvements, standing crops) • Appeal process • Safeguard on compensation

Source: EBA database.

Figure 12.1 | Values of EBA land scores at the country level

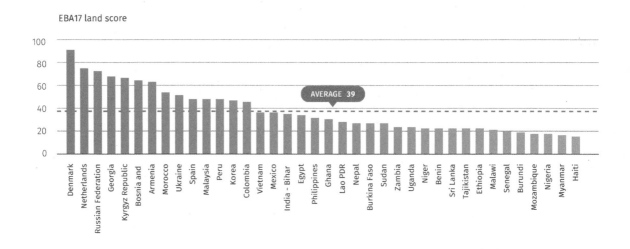

EBA17 land score

AVERAGE 39

Source: EBA database.

infrastructure over the last decade. Although scores are lowest for Sub-Saharan Africa, strengthening the regulatory environment for land governance can lead to considerable gains also in other regions such as South and East Asia or Latin America.

Figure 12.2 displays the scores for the three land sub-indicators by income group. With the possible exception of upper-middle-income countries, scores are lowest for management of state land, suggesting that, in the short term, improved mapping and demarcation together with processes for transferring state land for commercial use that are more transparent and rely on independent monitoring offer opportunities for significant gains. Given the increased scrutiny of supply chain governance by private sector institutions, especially financiers, such measures could provide opportunities to attract investment into the sector.

While low-income countries score reasonably well on equity and inclusion, they differ markedly from the rest in terms of coverage, quality and relevance of records. Recent technological improvements in IT and earth observation provide a basis for rapid improvement and leapfrogging in this area, ideally followed by state land registration.

Coverage, relevance and currency of records for private land

Data from the *Doing Business* land administration quality indicator point towards a considerable

difference in coverage of land records, which is lowest for agricultural land in most countries. Figure 12.3 shows that, conditional on coverage, digitization of textual and spatial records can have high returns, especially for low-income countries. Less than 20% of sample countries in the low-income category have textual and spatial records digitized, limiting the scope for land data integration.

In many of the countries where coverage with digital records is low, paper records may either be outdated or overlap with each other, in which case they may provide little tenure security. In high-potential agricultural areas or urban settings, record digitization should be prioritized and combined with rigorous quality checking and, in case there are issues, a participatory low-cost process of systematic registration to update records and expand coverage, following the example of Rwanda. In rural areas with lower levels of agricultural potential, limited market activity and communal governance structures that are still functional, registration of individual plots may be neither desirable nor cost effective. Recording of community boundaries together with clarifying internal management structures and modalities for recording of land rights and transfers, may bring social and economic benefits by securing rights, providing the basis for negotiation with outsiders and allowing a transition towards more sophisticated systems as and when the need arises.

All the top performing countries have digitized and integrated textual records and cadastral maps as well as

Figure 12.2 | Values of EBA land sub-indicators by countries' income group

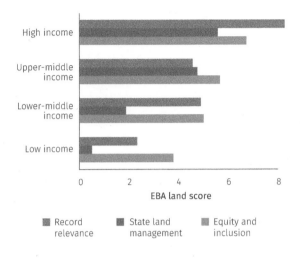

EBA land score

- Record relevance
- State land management
- Equity and inclusion

Source: EBA database.

Figure 12.3 | EBA sub-scores for relevance of land records by countries' income group

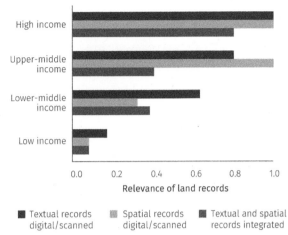

Relevance of land records

- Textual records digital/scanned
- Spatial records digital/scanned
- Textual and spatial records integrated

Source: EBA database.

mechanisms to ensure that material changes in rights are recorded, be it transfer of ownership via sale or inheritance or creation of a link to ensure that mortgages or a civil dispute involving a specific land parcel is automatically reflected in the registry. Alerting third parties of such changes minimizes the potential for fraud and obviates the need for costly and socially wasteful examination of rights by each party.

State land management

Key indicators of the state land management quality (figure 12.4) point towards a considerable gap between high- and upper-middle-income countries and the rest in terms of the share of state land that is registered and mapped and the extent to which such records are publicly available. While all of the former have most of their state land mapped and most of them have such rights registered and maps publicly available, this is the case only for less than 20% of the lower-middle and low-income countries in the sample.

Similarly, stark differences emerge for the extent to which state land transfers are by public tender, key contract provisions are publicly available and compliance is monitored. Differences along these dimensions are likely to not only reduce prices received by the public but also land use efficiency on land subject to such transfers. It may also jeopardize countries' ability to attract investment by investors whose supply chains are subject to scrutiny either from customers or financiers.

Equity and inclusion

Figure 12.5 displays information on values for three key sub-scores under the equity and fairness sub-indicator, namely: (i) if there is gender-differentiated monitoring of land rights; (ii) whether registered and unregistered land are compensated equally (or all land is registered so that the question does not arise); and (iii) the expropriation process and, in particular, associated valuations can be contested.

Data suggest that in the low-income countries in the *EBA 2017* sample, the scope of receiving compensation for unregistered land that is equal to what would be received for registered land is much lower, despite the fact that in such countries most land remains unregistered, the scope for market-based transfers for land acquisition is more limited and regulations often require expropriation of land to transfer it to investors.[7] Although a higher share of low- and lower-middle-income countries allows appeals against valuations, there is little administrative support for such appeals to be successful.

With economic development and expansion of opportunities for nonagricultural employment, opportunities for (long-term) land leasing will be important to ensure that rural areas allow (young) farmers with higher skills to expand and invest in more capital-intensive production methods. Leasing is also an important way for women to access land. Regulatory barriers to leasing or the high cost of entering into/registering

Figure 12.4 | EBA sub-scores for quality of state land management by countries' income group

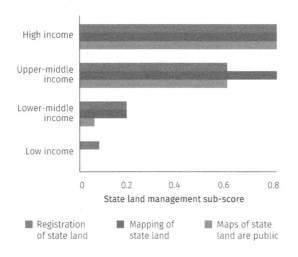

Source: *EBA* database.

Figure 12.5 | EBA sub-scores for equity by countries' income group

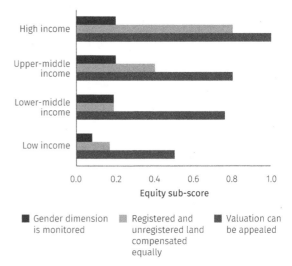

Source: *EBA* database.

such transfers may prevent these transactions from happening. The incidence of leasing restrictions has been reduced and many countries report availability of standard leases to reduce the transaction cost of engaging in such transactions. Still, some changes go in the other direction; for example, Ukraine imposed a seven-year minimum duration for any lease to be registered. The ensuing immediate and massive drop in the number of registered leases, from more than 140,000 to some 30,000 per month, illustrates that regulation can set important repercussions.

What are the regulatory good practices?

Good practice examples for each of the main areas of emphasis are provided in box 12.1 and some cases are described in more detail below.

Registration of land rights and computerization of land registry information

Land tenure regularization in Rwanda illustrates the scope for combining modern technology and participatory processes and the multiple benefits form land registries. Following passage of the 2004/5 land policy and organic land law, a three-year pilot in 2007-10 on some 15,000 parcels helped design locally implementable low cost and participatory processes. This helped double the rate of investment in soil conservation while tripling it for female-headed households who suffered from higher insecurity. Land rights by legally married women improved, although those without marriage certificate were negatively affected,

an issue corrected before the national roll-out.[8] The refined process led to demarcation and registration of the country's 11.5 million parcels in less than three years at US$ 6 per parcel,[9] improving investments in land and tree planting, females' tenure security and functioning of land rental markets.[10] The registry can be accessed online by Banks or local staff (via mobile phones) and viewed by investors; potential increments in urban residential land tax revenue due to having a complete register alone are more than sufficient to recoup the program cost in less than a decade.[11]

Focusing on communities allowed Mexico to regularize more than 60 mn. hectares in slightly more than a decade. A first step involved recognizing communities' legal personality and establishing mechanisms for internal self-governance (general assembly, executive, and an oversight committee). Once approved by the assembly, land registration then involved officials working with members to identify plot owners, resolving pending disputes in specifically created courts, and creating a map with boundaries of individual or communal plots for approval by the assembly that triggered issuance of certificates to all rights-holders. It enhanced productivity,[12] investment, economic and migration opportunities, especially for those with weak rights or lower endowments.[13]

Sequential computerization of land registration in the Indian state of Andhra Pradesh helped to make information on land rights accessible and thus increased mortgages by 18% and credit volume by 10.5%.[14]

Box 12.1 | Good Practices for Land

	REGULATORY GOOD PRACTICES FOR LAND	SOME COUNTRIES WHICH IMPLEMENT THE PRACTICE
COVERAGE, RELEVANCE, AND CURRENCY OF RECORDS FOR PRIVATE LAND	Private land rights are registered and mapped for land owned individually or by groups.	MEXICO, RWANDA
	Textual and spatial records are maintained digitally and integrated, and can be easily accessed by all interested parties.	GEORGIA
	Mortgages and disputes pertaining to a land parcel are visible on the record and can be entered online by banks or the courts.	INDIA
PUBLIC LAND MANAGEMENT	State land is fully mapped and registered.	KOREA, REP., NETHERLANDS
	Encroachment is monitored regularly and actively.	DENMARK
	State land transfers for commercial use are by transparent public tender, and a field-based process is used to ascertain absence of competing land claims and obtain occupants' informed consent.	BRAZIL
	A list of state land transfers as well as key contractual provisions (for example, prices, expected use and land development plans) are public and independently monitored.	PERU
EQUITY AND FAIRNESS	Land ownership information is recorded by gender and regularly monitored.	VIETNAM
	Standardized contracts for land leasing are available and there are no specific restrictions on land leasing.	INDIA
	If not all land is registered, three is no difference in the compensation paid in case of acquisition between registered and unregistered land.	PERU

Source: EBA database.

Public land management in Peru and Brazil

Peru shows that transparent public state land auctions can enhance transparency and efficiency of land use. Once the auction is initiated, the intention to divest the land and the terms of the bidding are published for at least 90 days. Bidders must prequalify by posting a bond of at least 60% of the minimum bid price plus intended investment. Auctions of 235,500 hectares brought almost $50 million in investment to Peru's coastal regions over the last 15 years, generating large numbers of jobs and underpinning the country's emergence as a major force in high-value agro-exports.

To limit deforestation due to area expansion, Brazil's Forest code long required that, in environmentally sensitive areas, a certain share of each property be kept under forest, though impact remained limited to weak enforcement. A shift to satellite-based monitoring of land use changes together with local enforcement in 2004 was, in 2008, complemented with a decision to make preferential credit access conditional on demonstrated compliance with environmental norms. In 2005-09, this is estimated to have helped avoid 73,000 km^2 of deforestation.[15] In Brazil's Para state, use of such information by the private sector drove adoption of the environmental cadaster[16] and further reductions in deforestation.[17] As a result, a tripling of the Amazon's cattle herd and a six-fold increase of area planted to soy since 1990 was associated with a decline in deforestation to about one third of the 1990 level, effectively decoupling soy and beef production and deforestation.[18]

Equity and inclusion through gender recording standard leases and regulations on expropriation

While Vietnam's 1993 Land Law made rights more secure by introducing Certificates to allow farmers to trade, transfer, rent, bequeath or mortgage land use rights with positive economic impact,[19] women were often left out partly because the nature of the forms. Regulation requiring two spaces implied that, by 2015, more than 70% of certificates were issued jointly, overcoming gender discrimination[20] and improving women's bargaining power and educational attainment of their children.[21]

Many Indian states historically imposed rent ceilings or outlawed leasing. But instead of benefit them as intended, this is driving tenants—often poor women—underground, making them more vulnerable, reducing productivity[22] and investment[23] and causing owners to leave large tracts of land idle. To address this, Government drafted model legislation and contracts that are being considered for implementation in several Indian states.[24]

Widespread past abuses of expropriation for political purposes led Peru to impose constitutional rules to limit expropriation to tightly defined public purpose. New regulations introduced to implement the rules require Congressional authorization for any expropriation and voiding it if the state is not the direct beneficiary or if land has not been transferred to the intended use within 24 months so that land reverts back to the original owner.[25]

What are other areas of research?

Group rights: As a cost-effective way to cover large areas, group rights have long played a role to protect right to indigenous areas and significantly contribute to conserving natural resources.[26] Pilots all over the world to demarcate communal rights in a comprehensive participatory way are currently underway and the main issue is the extent to which results from such initiatives enjoy legal recognition. In fact, if regulations and laws are fashioned appropriately, there is scope for expanding such approaches to support comprehensive and cost-effective demarcation of the outer boundary of villages. If linked to adoption of clear approaches to within-group governance, this could be linked to mechanisms for internal management of rights to individual agricultural or house plots and avenues for greater formalization if and when the need arises. A highly policy relevant approach would be to identify the cost, in terms of time and motion, of acquiring a document to certify group rights on a demand-driven basis.

Cost of conducting a survey: High survey standards and anachronistic requirements open the door to discretion and increase the cost of conducting surveys, and constrains the scope for registry expansion and currency as it drives transactions underground. To address this, professionals have long recommended a "fit for purpose" approach to surveying as a measure that could provide enormous benefits, to improve coverage and reduce informality.[27] Working with professional associations to establish benchmarks that can then be pilot tested in a range of countries would have a high return and allow to address a key bottleneck.

Linking to national parameters: All the three indicator groups include elements that relate to national systems and are easy to assess. Doing so through the *Doing Business* registering property indicator, to be complemented with more specific assessment of aspects related to the agricultural sector, will greatly strengthen the ability to use EBA results for global comparison and in relevant policy dialogues.

Factory workers producing fresh fruit in Nsawan District, Ghana. Photo: Dominic Chavez/World Bank.

Conclusion

The above discussion suggests that ways to make quick improvements differs somewhat between countries in the high- and low-income groups. The former can score quick wins by ensuring integration of textual and spatial elements of land records, making these available to economic actors and other government departments, ensuring that an appropriate regulatory framework allows different actors to harness benefits from this infrastructure, and closely monitor elements of its expansion, including the gender dimension.

By comparison, for most low- and lower-middle-income countries, enormous short-term advances can be made by improving the regulatory framework and associated records for managing public land, ensuring equal treatment of women as well as owners of registered and non-registered land, and from moving existing land records to a digital platform to identify issues that need to be addressed to ensure transparency and explore opportunities for expansion in high potential areas to protect existing right holders, allow them to transfer their land to higher uses as appropriate, and provide investment incentives. Based on digitization of existing records and review of the regulatory framework, approaches to enhance coverage in a participatory and low-cost way can then be identified and carefully piloted, with the scope for larger roll-out in the medium term.

NOTES

1 Goldstein and Udry 2008.

2 The difficulty of accessing land for enterprise development has emerged as one of the main complaints by private sector operators in a large number of enterprise surveys in African countries.

3 Kaganova and McKelar 2006.

4 Andolfatto 2002.

5 Tagliarino 2016.

6 Deininger and Xia 2016.

7 Deininger and Byerlee 2011.

8 Ali et al. 2014.

9 Nkurunziza 2015.

10 Ali et al. 2015.

11 Ali et al. 2016.

12 de Janvry et al. 2015.

13 Valsecchi 2014.

14 Deininger and Goyal 2012.

15 Assuncao et al. 2015.

16 Gibbs et al. 2016.

17 L'Roe et al. 2016.

18 Pacheco 2016.

19 Do and Iyer 2008.

20 Newman et al. 2015.

21 Menon et al. 2014.

22 Deininger et al. 2008.

23 Deininger et al. 2013.

24 Haque 2016.

25 Deininger et al. 2011.

26 Miranda et al. 2016.

27 Enemark et al. 2014.

REFERENCES

Ali, D. A., K. Deininger and M. Goldstein. 2014. "Environmental and Gender Impacts of Land Tenure Regularization in Africa: Pilot Evidence from Rwanda." *Journal of Development Economics.* 110 (0): 262–75.

Ali, D. A., K. Deininger, M. Goldstein and E. La Ferrara. 2015. "Investment and Market Impacts of Land Tenure Regularization in Rwanda." World Bank Policy Research Paper. Washington, DC.

Ali, D. A., K. W. Deininger and M. Duponchel. 2016. "Using Administrative Data to Assess the Impact and Sustainability of Rwanda's Land Tenure Regularization." Policy Research Working Paper 7705. World Bank. Washington, DC.

Andolfatto, D. 2002. "A Theory of Inalienable Property Rights." *Journal of Political Economy* 110 (2): 382–93.

Assuncao, J., C. Gandour and R. Rocha. 2015. "Deforestation Slowdown in the Brazilian Amazon: Prices or Policies?" *Environment and Development Economics* 20 (6): 697–722.

de Janvry, A., K. Emerick, M. Gonzalez-Navarro and E. Sadoulet. 2015. "Delinking Land Rights from Land Use: Certification and Migration in Mexico." *American Economic Review* 105 (10): 3125–149.

Deininger, K., S. Jin and H. K. Nagarajan. 2008. "Efficiency and Equity Impacts of Rural Land Market Restrictions: Evidence from India." *European Economic Review* 52 (5): 892–918.

Deininger, K. and D. Byerlee. 2011. *Rising Global Interest in Farmland: Can It Yield Sustainable and Equitable Benefits?* Washington, DC: World Bank.

Deininger, K., H. Selod and A. Burns. 2011. *Improving Governance of Land and Associated Natural Resources: The Land Governance Assessment Framework.* Washington, DC: World Bank.

Deininger, K. and A. Goyal. 2012. "Going Digital: Credit Effects of Land Registry Computerization in India." *Journal of Development Economics* 99 (2): 236–43.

Deininger, K., J. Songqing and V. Yadav. 2013. "Does Sharecropping Affect Long-Term Investment? Evidence from West Bengal's Tenancy Reforms." *American Journal of Agricultural Economics* 95 (3): 772–90.

Deininger, K. and F. Xia. 2016. "Gender-Differentiated Impacts of Tenure Insecurity on Agricultural Productivity in Malawi's Customary Tenure System." World Bank Policy Research Working Paper. World Bank, Washington, DC.

Do, Q. T. and L. Iyer. 2008. "Land Titling and Rural Transition in Vietnam." *Economic Development and Cultural Change* 56 (3): 531–79.

Enemark, S., K. C. Bell, C. Lemmen and R. McLaren. 2014. "Fit for Purpose Land Administration." A joint publication of the International Federation of Surveyors and the World Bank, Frederiksberg, DK.

Gibbs, H. K. et al. 2016. "Did Ranchers and Slughterhouses Respond to Zero-Deforestation Agreements in the Brazilian Amazon?" *Conservation Letters* 9 (1): 32–42.

Goldstein, Markus and Christopher Udry. 2008. "The Profits of Power: Land Rights and Agricultural Investment in Ghana." *Journal of Political Economy*, 116(6): 981-1022.

Haque, T. 2016. "Report of the Expert Committee on Land Leasing." Niti Aayog, New Delhi.

Kaganova, O. and J. McKelar. 2006. "Managing Government Property Assets: International Experiences." Urban Institute Press, Washington, DC.

L'Roe, J., L. Rausch, J. Munger and H. K. Gibbs. 2016. "Mapping Properties to Monitor Forests: Landholder Response to a Large Environmental Registration Program in the Brazilian Amazon." *Land Use Policy* 57: 193–203.

Menon, N., Y. van der Meulen Rodgers and H. Nguyen. 2014. "Women's Land Rights and Children's Human Capital in Vietnam." *World Development* 54: 18–31.

Miranda, J. J. et al. 2016. "Effects of Protected Areas on Forest Cover Change and Local Communities: Evidence from the Peruvian Amazon." *World Development* 78: 288–307.

Newman, C., F. Tarp and K. van den Broeck. 2015. "Property Rights and Productivity: The Case of Joint Land Titling in Vietnam." 91 (1): 91–105.

Nkurunziza, E. 2015. "Implementing and Sustaining Land Tenure Regularization in Rwanda." In *How Innovations in Land Administration Reform Improve on Doing Business,* edited by T. Hilhorst and F. Meunier, 10–19. Washington, DC: World Bank.

Pacheco, P. 2016. "Public and Private Actions for Shifting Towards Sustainable Production of Beef and Palm Oil." Paper presented at the 17th Annual World Bank Conference on Land and Poverty, Washington, DC.

Tagliarino, N. K. 2016. "Encroaching on Land and Livelihoods: How National Expropriation Laws Measure Up against International Standards." World Resources Institute, Washington, DC.

Valsecchi, M. 2014. "Land Property Rights and International Migration: Evidence from Mexico." *Journal of Development Economics* 110: 276–90.

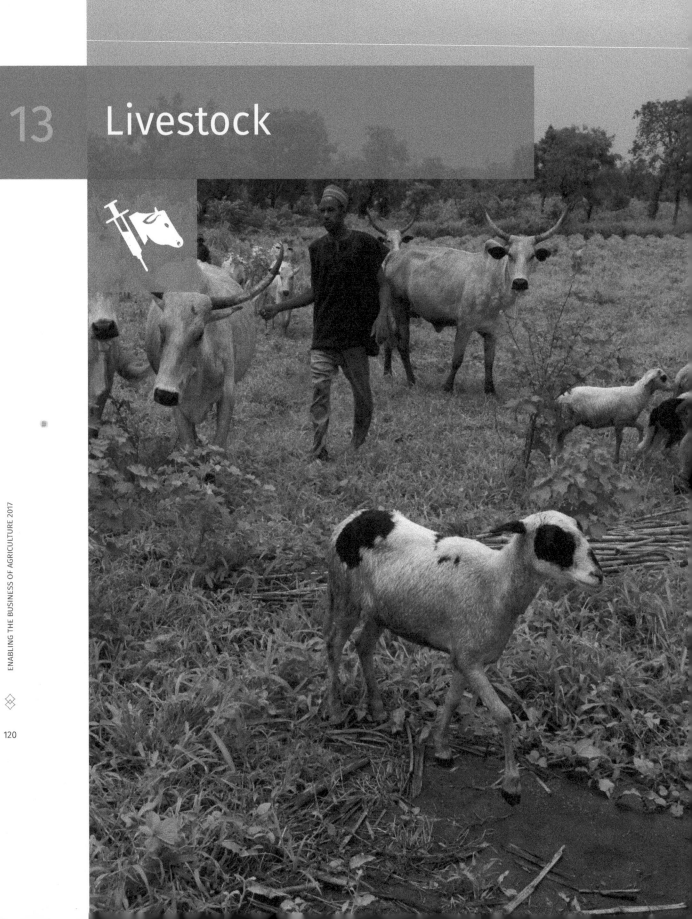

13 Livestock

Today Johnson is a successful cattle farmer in Garissa in northeastern Kenya. He started his business in 2006, but it almost did not make it. In 2006 Kenya and its neighbors, Somalia and Tanzania, experienced an outbreak of the Rift Valley Fever disease—an infectious animal disease that can also be transferred to humans. Johnson lost a significant number of his cattle herd. He was not alone in experiencing the destructive impact of the disease outbreak. By the end of the outbreak in 2007, the economic loss in Kenya was estimated to have been greater than US$9.3 million, due to the ban on livestock trade and the forced quarantine of animals.[1] Thankfully, the disease was contained within a year; Johnson purchased more cattle and was able to continue with his business.

Livestock is one of the fastest-growing agricultural sub-sectors in the world, accounting for around 40% of agricultural output in the developing world.[2] The term of livestock is used in this report to refer to domestic or domesticated animals that are raised mainly for agriculture purposes and includes, for example, large ruminants such as cattle, small ruminants such as goats, as well as pigs and poultry.[3] Aquaculture is not considered by the livestock topic.

Livestock is a main source of income for one in five people across the globe.[4] Livestock infectious diseases, therefore, pose a significant risk to that contribution if left unchecked. Estimates suggest that these diseases are responsible for more than 20% of livestock production losses globally.[5] Furthermore, approximately 70% of all new human diseases are zoonotic, transferring between animals and humans, and mostly originating from animals.[6]

Maintaining animal health is thus central to the global food system's stability and safety. Readily available preventative and curative veterinary medicinal products (VMPs) can minimize the negative economic impact of diseases and safeguard the livelihoods of millions of farmers around the world.[7] However, VMPs (biologicals and pharmaceuticals) have to be used in the correct circumstances and in accordance with prescribed conditions and dosages if they are to be truly effective. If not, for example, their use can lead to increased drug resistance and illness in humans due to drug residues in consumed animal foods.[8] Further, open borders, inadequate legal frameworks and poor law enforcement can lead to counterfeit and substandard VMPs in the market.[9]

Cattle grazing in Ta Kuti village, Nigeria.
Photo: Arne Hoel / World Bank.

Comprehensive regulations on the manufacture, registration, import, distribution, sale and/or administration of livestock medicinal products can contribute to establishing a reliable market supply of effective and safe VMPs.[10] Since research and development in the veterinary medicine sector is expensive, specialized and time consuming, most manufacturing facilities are established and owned by large companies located in specific regions of the world.[11] While large companies represent the bigger market share of VMP manufacturing, a diversified mix of private sector entities supply the market—large companies, small and medium enterprises (SMEs), breeders' organizations, and veterinarians. Given this dominant role of private sector in the development, manufacturing and market supply of VMPs, it is important that regulations are streamlined and efficient in order not to discourage them from entering and operating in markets.[12]

Access to effective and safe VMPs is just one critical input into livestock production. Other key production inputs are feed resources, productive animal breeds and veterinary services. While the focus of the livestock topic in *EBA17* is on VMPs, the topic will be further developed in the coming years to assess the impact of regulations on other relevant issues in livestock production. Once a more comprehensive data set is established, an adequate livestock scoring methodology will be developed and implemented.

What does the veterinary medicinal products topic cover?

The data collected cover regulations impacting the private sector's ability to supply the market with effective and safe VMPs. Data assess regulatory requirements for registration, importation and marketing of VMPs:

Registration of VMPs: Registration, or marketing authorization, is a critical step in a country's control system for VMPs. Most countries require VMP registration before it can be manufactured, imported, distributed and sold.[13] Data were collected on:

Institutional structure. Literature suggests that a country's ability to provide effective regulatory institutions is an important determinant of how well markets function.[14] Having multiple government institutions involved in the registration process can create a burden for the private sector, especially when roles and responsibilities are not clearly defined and the applicants are required to interact with multiple different institutions.

Registration process. Data points assess the existence of obstacles and good practices during the registration process. Unclear and irrelevant registration requirements often lead to delays in the registration process

and create severe registration backlogs of products awaiting marketing authorization.[15] In addition, the private sector's knowledge of and trust in the registration process influence the decision to supply markets with VMPs and whether to participate in the legally mandated registration process.[16]

Registration output. The registration system can produce a registry of authorized VMPs and temporarily protect proprietary data submitted during the registration process for newly developed products. The registry's existence has legal consequences, given that most countries require that products must be registered prior to market entry and circulation.[17] Time-bound proprietary data provides incentives for innovation and research and development.[18] Unlike human medicinal products, the financial return for VMPs can be significantly less, given the lower sales prices and potentially smaller market size, especially for the market for small animals.[19]

Authorization of importers: In many countries, the main supply of VMPs comes from outside the country and import licenses are a useful way to impose minimum safety and qualification requirements on the companies inolved. The data collected cover import restrictions such as types of entities allowed to import VMPs and whether importers are required to employ specialized staff.

Marketing of VMPs: Labeling requirements on marketed VMPs are critical to ensuring their proper handling and administration. In addition, knowing what diseases are present in a country, their geographic location and the size of the livestock populations threatened are all key factors in determining resource mobilization of VMPs.[20] In particular, data assess:

Labeling of marketed VMPs. VMPs are often administered by veterinarians and farmers; as such, adequate labeling is of paramount importance. [21]

Information availability on animal diseases. The private sector can use information in a national disease database, beyond data available on transboundary diseases and zoonosis (diseases transferable from animals to humans) found in World Organization for Animal Health (OIE) and regional databases, to make distribution and sales decisions and to explore new market niches.

Some good practice examples are showcased in box 13.1.

Box 13.1 | Good practices for veterinary medicinal products (VMPs)

	REGULATORY GOOD PRACTICES FOR VMPS	SOME COUNTRIES WHICH IMPLEMENT THE PRACTICE
REGISTRATION OF VMPS	There is both a regulatory framework and an institution actively registering VMPs.	ALL EBA COUNTRIES EXCEPT: BURUNDI, HAITI, LAO PDR, MOZAMBIQUE AND RWANDA
	Dossiers are required to be checked for completeness prior to the start of an evaluation to ensure all required documents are included.	DENMARK, MEXICO, NIGERIA, POLAND, RUSSIA, SPAIN AND TURKEY
	Applicants are provided with information on the number of days within which a VMP will be registered and expectations are adhered to.	BOSNIA AND HERZEGOVINA, GEORGIA AND GHANA
	Information on registration requirements and the registry of VMPs are easily accessible to the public.	COLOMBIA, ITALY, MOROCCO AND ZIMBABWE
MARKETING OF MEDICINAL PRODUCTS	Labeling requirements are comprehensive and provide distinction between what information is required to be on the outer and immediate package.[a]	MALAYSIA, NICARAGUA, PERU AND SERBIA
	Withdrawal periods are required on VMP labels to protect consumers of animal products.	DENMARK, ITALY AND NICARAGUA

Source: EBA database.

[a] Outer packaging is the packaging into which the immediate packaging is placed (for example, the box), while immediate packaging is the container or any other form of packaging that is in direct contact with the medicinal product (for example, the vial or bottle).

Some insights emerging from the data

Ensuring the predictability of registration systems for VMPs

The VMP registration system's predictability influences private sector decisions to supply a market with VMPs using the legally mandated process.[22] Ease in accessing information on registration requirements and the VMP registry, confidence that all necessary documentation are included in the application package (dossier) and awareness of the timeframe by which the registration is intended be completed, are all factors that can contribute to the predictability of the registration process.

It is vital that applicants are aware of all the registration requirements and are able to easily obtain such information. Of the 59 countries legally requiring VMP registration, 5 countries do not provide information on dossier requirements on the website of the authority mandated to register VMPs (Haiti, Malawi, Rwanda, Sri Lanka and Tajikistan). In Rwanda, the registration process is yet to start. In Haiti (currently not registering products), Sri Lanka and Tajikistan, documentation specifying dossier requirements is not on the website

of the relevant authority. In Malawi, there is no functioning publicly accessible website. The three EBA countries not requiring VMP registration do not have a legal framework and are either in the process of developing a framework or are yet to commence the process (Burundi, Lao PDR and Mozambique).

Given the requirement to register products prior to market introduction and circulation, it is also important that an applicant is able to easily access information on products already authorized for market circulation in a country. Of the 57 countries actively registering VMPs, a registry is available online in 37 countries, 21 of which are high-income or upper-middle-income countries. Only 12 lower-middle-income countries and 4 low-income countries provide a registry on the registering authority's website.

In most countries, during the dossier evaluation process, each time the regulatory authority requires additional information from an applicant, the registration process is put on a hold. To limit this outcome, the application package (dossier) can be checked for completeness prior to the start of evaluation. Sixteen EBA sample countries indicate either in a legally-binding

Chicken farm near Santander, Colombia. Photo: Charlotte Kesl / World Bank.

document or in a non-legally binding guideline, that dossiers will be checked for completeness. In Mexico, for example, the 2012 Regulation of the Federal Law on Animal Health (a legally binding document) explicitly addresses issues concerning the checking of dossiers for completeness. Another example is Armenia, which does not directly state such requirement in a legal document, but rather indicates the checking for completeness in non-legally binding registration guidelines from the authority. In addition, these countries also provide timeframes within which the applicant can be contacted for missing documents prior to the start of evaluation. These timeframes range from 3 days in the Kyrgyz Republic to 60 days in Bosnia and Herzegovina.

The awareness of how long the registration process can take allows the private sector to plan the market introduction of products accordingly. The expected registration times are an estimation by regulatory authorities of how long the process can take based upon the registration process adopted in a country. Some countries implement a detailed registration complete with the testing of products, while others may rely on the use of reference countries and other parameters, thus sometimes explaining the shorter expected registration time. Thirty-eight countries currently provide a time limit for the registration process in a legally binding document or a non-legally binding guideline. The time limit ranges from 30 days (Cambodia) to 365 days (Jordan and Kenya) for biologicals and pharmaceuticals.

Adhering to the expected registration time limit can be challenging in some countries. In comparing the timeframe between the expected and actual registration time, regulators could potentially use the difference to assess the efficiency and quality of the registration process. In addition, the difference could be used by applicants to hold the regulatory authority accountable.

Safeguarding animal and human health by comprehensively labeling VMPs sold

Labeling requirements help to ensure that drugs are properly used. The legal requirement can provide information on the characteristics of the product, such as the list of active substances per dosage or weight, the proper handling and storage conditions for the product, the proper use of the product and route of administration and information to ensure consumer protection such as the withdrawal period. The withdrawal period is the time between the last administration of medicine to the animal and the production and marketing of animal foods for consumption.[23] Following appropriate withdrawal periods for VMPs reduces the risks to human health associated with drug residues in products such as meat, milk, eggs and honey.[24] Only 27 out of the 60 countries studied require that withdrawal periods are included on the labeling of VMPs (figure 13.1). This number includes all high-income countries and the majority of upper-middle-income countries. Only 2 out of 16 low-income countries, or 13% of this income group, have this requirement.

Figure 13.1 | Few countries require withdrawal periods on veterinary medicinal product labels

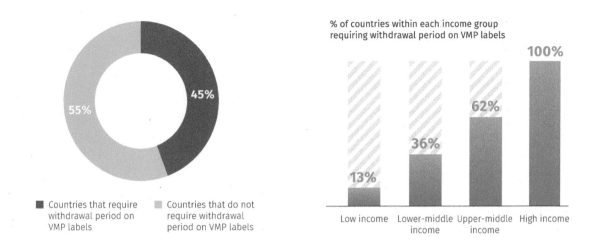

% of countries within each income group requiring withdrawal period on VMP labels

45%

55%

■ Countries that require withdrawal period on VMP labels

■ Countries that do not require withdrawal period on VMP labels

13% — Low income
36% — Lower-middle income
62% — Upper-middle income
100% — High income

Source: EBA database.

Note: No data were received for Egypt and Tajkistan on the requirements of withdrawal periods on VMP labels. The total sample is distributed as follows: high-income (9), upper-middle-income (13), lower-middle-income (22), and low-income (16) countries. VMP=veterinary medicinal product

Facilitating the market distribution of VMPs using national animal disease information systems

The outbreak of animal diseases directly impacts animal and human health. Therefore, it is important for countries to have a functioning animal disease surveillance and information system in place to mitigate the risk of disease outbreaks. One important dimension of such a system is the existence of national databases that can be used to monitor and track local outbreaks.[25] Sophisticated systems follow not only those diseases that are required to be notified to the World Organization for Animal Health (principally diseases that impact trade and are transboundary),[26] but also diseases that may be endemic to a local livestock population. National disease databases can be provided and maintained by national veterinary authorities and include information on when a disease was identified, its geographic distribution and spread. The private sector can then use such databases to make distribution decisions and understand the potential size of the market for a VMP.

EBA data suggest that lower-middle and low-income countries have serious gaps in terms of animal disease information systems that are publicly accessible online. At the regional level, Sub-Saharan Africa has the fewest countries with animal disease databases publically available on the responsible authority's website. None of the 21 Sub-Saharan African countries studied have an animal disease database available online.

The situation is also similar in South Asia, where only Nepal has an electronically accessible database.

Conclusion

The level of transparency, predictability and efficiency of relevant regulatory systems is critical to private sector decisions to supply a market with VMPs, and thus can affect the availability of effective and safe VMPs in the market. While capacity and systems to control VMPs may vary in countries, it is vital that information needed to adhere to regulatory requirements is readily available and that the processes do not delay nor discourage market supply. It is also equally important that there is adequate infrastructure to assess the effectiveness and safety of VMPs, and effective mechanisms to ensure both animal and human safety in the context of VMP use.

NOTES

1 Muga et al. 2015.

2 Livestock Global Alliance 2016.

3 FAO 2010.

4 Livestock Global Alliance 2016.

5 OIE nd (a).

6 Wang et al. 2014.

7 Roth 2011.

8 Beyene 2015.

9 Kinglsey 2015; Luseba 2015.

10 OIE 2016; Fingleton 2004.

11 HealthforAnimals 2012.

12 Fingleton 2004.

13 *Ibid.*

14 Julilian et al. 2007.

15 Smith 2013; European Commission 2011.

16 HealthforAnimals 2005.

17 Fingleton 2004.

18 European Commission 2011.

19 Roth 2011.

20 FAO 1999.

21 Fingleton 2004.

22 HealthforAnimals 2005.

23 The World Organization for Animal Health (OIE) has developed guidelines to estimate the necessary withdrawal period for specific veterinary drugs in order to avoid excess residues in animal foods (OIE 2013).

24 Beyene 2015.

25 FAO 1999; OIE nd (b).

26 http://www.oie.int/en animal-health-in-the-world/ oie-listed-diseases-2016/.

REFERENCES

Beyene, T. 2015. "Veterinary Drug Residues in Food-Animal Products: Its Risk Factors and Potential Effects on Public Health." *Veterinary Science and Technology* (2016) 7:1.

European Commission. 2011. "Better Regulation of Veterinary Pharmaceuticals: How to Put in Place a Simpler Legal Framework, Safeguarding Public and Animal Health While Increasing the Competitiveness of Companies." Report on the European Commission's Public Online, Brussels.

FAO (Food and Agriculture Organization). 1999. "Manual on Livestock Disease Surveillance and Information Systems." FAO, Rome.

———. 2010. "World Programme for the Census of Agriculture 2010." FAO Statistical Development Series No. 11. FAO, Rome.

Fingleton, J. 2004. "Legislation for Veterinary Drugs Control." FAO legal papers 38: 17–18.

HealthforAnimals. 2005. "The Marketing Authorization Process for Veterinary Medicinal Products in Europe." Originally published under International Federation for Animal Health (IFAH), Brussels.

———. 2012. "The Protection of Registration Data for Existing and New Veterinary Medicinal Products." http://healthforanimals.org/resources-and-events/resources/papers/132-the-protection-of-registration-data-for-existing-and-new-veterinary-medicinal-products.html.

Jones, K. E. et al. 2008. "Global Trends in Emerging Infectious Diseases." *Nature* 451: 990–93.

Julilian, H., C. Kirkpatrick, and D. Parker. 2007. "The Impact of Regulation on Economic Growth in Developing Countries: A Cross-Country Analysis." *World Development* 35 (1): 87–103.

Kingsley, P. 2015. "How Fake Animal Medicines Threaten African Livestock." World Economic Forum, https://www.weforum.org/agenda/2015/02/how-fake-animal-medicines-threaten-african-livestock/.

Livestock Global Alliance. 2016. "Livestock for Sustainable Development in the 21st Century." http://www.livestockdialogue.org/fileadmin/templates/res_livestock/docs/2016/LGA-Brochure-revMay13th.pdf.

Luseba, D. 2015. "Review of the Policy, Regulatory and Administrative Framework for Delivery of Livestock Health Products and Services in West and Central Africa." GALVmed, http://www.galvmed. org/wp-content/uploads/2015/09/East-Africa-Review-of-Policy-Regulatory-and-Administrative-Framework-for-Delivery-of-Livestock-Health-Products-and-Services-March-2015.pdf.

Muga, G. et al. 2015. "Review Article: Sociocultural and Economic Dimensions of Rift Valley Fever." *Am. J. Trop. Med. Hyg.* 92 (4): 730–38.

OIE (World Organization for Animal Health). 2016. "Terrestrial Animal Health Code: Volume 1." OIE, Paris.

———. 2013. "Estimation of the Withdrawal Period in Edible Tissues." OIE, Paris.

———. nd (a). "Feeding the World Better by Controlling Animal Diseases." http://www.oie.int/for-the-media/ editorials/detail/article/feeding-the-world-better-by-controlling-animal-diseases/.

———. nd (b). "Veterinary Medicinal Products and Vaccines: Indispensable Tools for any Effective Animal Health and Welfare Policy." OIE, Paris, http:// www.oie.int/en/for-the-media/editorials/detail/ article/veterinary-medicinal-products-and-vac-cines-indispensable-tools-for-any-effective-ani-mal-health-and/.

Roth, J. 2011. "Veterinary Vaccines and their Importance to Animal Health and Public Health." *Procedia in Vaccinology* 5: 127–36.

Smith, M. 2013. "The Role of Veterinary Medicine Regulatory Agencies." *Rev. Sci. Tech. Off. int. Epiz.* 32 (2): 393–408.

Wang, L. and G. Crameri. 2014. "Emerging Zoonotic Viral Diseases." *Rev. sci. tech. Off. int. Epiz.* 33 (2): 569–81.

APPENDIX A

Methodology

Enabling the Business of Agriculture 2017 (EBA 2017) presents indicators and data that measure regulations that affect the business in and around agriculture. In the project's third year, the team collected data in 62 countries in the following 12 topic areas: seed, fertilizer, machinery, finance, markets, transport, water, information and communication technology (ICT), land, environmental sustainability, gender, and livestock. Eight of the topics were scored this year and are presented below. The other four will be expanded, refined and potentially scored in future years.

EBA Methodology

EBA 2017 data are collected in a standardized way. The team designs questionnaires for each topic area and administers them to experts in each country. The questionnaires use a hypothetical, standardized case scenario to ensure comparability across countries. The standard business case with assumptions about the legal form of the business, its size, its location and the nature of its operations for each topic applied for all countries. Assumptions guiding respondents through their completion of the survey questionnaires vary by topic and are presented in more detail in appendix B. In addition, in the interest of comparability, the values in the assumptions are not fixed values but proportional to the country's gross national income (GNI) per capita.

Once the data are collected and analyzed, several follow-up rounds address and resolve any discrepancies in the answers the respondents provide, including through conference calls, written correspondence and country visits. For the *EBA 2017* data collection, the team traveled to 14 countries to verify data and recruit respondents. The data in this report are current as of June 30, 2016.

Legal indicators

Legal indicators emerge from a reading of the laws and regulations. In a few instances, the data also include some elements which are not in the text of the law but relate to implementing a good regulatory practice—for example, the online availability of a fertilizer catalogue. The team identified good regulatory practices for each topic area. The individual questions or regulatory dimension are assigned numerical scores ranging from 0 to 1 (see topic data notes, below, for details). The scores of the different indicators within one topic are also averaged into a topic score.

Efficiency indicators

Efficiency indicators reflect the efficiency of the regulatory system—for example, the number of procedures and the time and cost to complete a process such as certifying seed for sale in the domestic market. Data of this type are built on legal requirements, and the cost measures are backed by official fee schedules, when available. Time estimates often involve an element of judgment by respondents who routinely administer the relevant regulations or undertake the relevant transactions. To construct the time estimates for a particular regulatory process, such as completing the requirements to import fertilizer, the process is broken down into clearly defined steps and procedures. The time to complete these steps is verified with expert

Country assumptions and characteristics

Region and income group
EBA 2017 uses the World Bank regional and income group classifications, available at http://data.worldbank.org/about/country-and-lending-groups. While the World Bank does not assign regional classifications to high-income countries, regional averages presented in figures and tables in the report include countries from all income groups. For the report, high-income Organisation for Economic Co-operation and Development (OECD) countries are assigned the "regional" classification as *OECD high income.*

Gross national Income (GNI) per capita
EBA 2017 uses 2015 income per capita as published in the World Bank's *World Development Indicators 2016.* Income is calculated using the Atlas method (current U.S. dollars). For cost indicators expressed as percentage of income per capita, 2014 GNI in U.S. dollars us used as the denominator.

respondents—through conference calls, written correspondence and visits by the team—until there is convergence on a final answer. The specific rules followed by each topic on defining procedures, time and cost estimates are described below.

Distance-to-Frontier and Topic Rankings

About distance-to-frontier score

EBA 2017 presents two aggregate measures per topic: (i) the distance-to-frontier scores and (ii) the topic rankings that results from ordering distance-to-frontier scores.

The distance-to-frontier score benchmarks economies with respect to regulatory best practice in each topic, showing the absolute distance to the best performance on each EBA indicator.

The distance-to-frontier score captures the gap between a country's performance and a measure of best practice across the entire sample of 27 indicators for eight EBA topics (land, environmental sustainability, livestock and gender indicators are excluded). For transport, for example, the Russian Federation has the shortest time (1 day) to obtain a cross-border license required for domestic trucks in the partner country; Denmark has the highest number of regulatory good practices in terms of trucking licenses and operations (10.8 out of 11).

The complete list of indicators is presented in table A.1, below. EBA indicators are divided into legal and efficiency indicators. In efficiency indicators, the time, cost and documents required to conduct a specific administrative procedure (such as the registration of a new fertilizer product) are combined to build a single indicator.

Calculation of the topic distance-to-frontier score

Calculating the topic's distance-to-frontier score for each country involves two main steps. In the first step individual component indicators are normalized to a common unit where each of the 27 component indicators is rescaled using the linear transformation (worst–y)/(worst–frontier). In this formulation the frontier represents the best performance on the indicator across all countries. The best performance and the worst performance are established based on the data collected as of June 2016. For legal indicators such as branchless banking indicator in the finance topic, or the plant protection indicator in the markets topic, the frontier score is set at the highest possible value and the worst performance corresponds to the worst possible score. For efficiency indicators, a score of 0 is assigned in cases of "No practice" and "N/A" (see topic data notes).

To mitigate the effects of extreme outliers in the distributions of the rescaled data for efficiency indicators (for example, very few economies need more than 954 days to complete the procedures to register a fertilizer product), the worst performance is calculated after the removal of outliers. The definition of outliers is based on the distribution for each component indicator. To simplify the process two rules were defined: the 95th percentile is used for the indicators with the most dispersed distributions (including the time and cost indicators), and the 99th percentile is used for the number of documents (for example, the number of documents required to export agricultural products). No outlier is removed for legal indicators scores (such as seed quality control and assurance, tractor testing and standards, or producer organizations).

In the second step for calculating the distance-to-frontier score, the scores obtained for individual indicators for each country are aggregated through simple averaging into one distance-to-frontier score for each topic: fertilizer, seed, machinery, finance, markets, transport, water, and ICT. *EBA 2017* uses the simplest method: it gives equal weight to each of the topic components or indicators. The only exception are efficiency indicators, where the distances to frontier associated with the time, cost and documents are combined and averaged to build a single efficiency indicator. In the area of registration of a new seed variety, the team has made sure that countries are not penalized by their geographical conditions, and different distance-to-frontier scores are established for countries with one or two cropping seasons.

If no data could be obtained for a specific data point, such data point was excluded from the corresponding DTF indicator score in that country. If more than half of the data points could not be obtained for a particular legal or efficiency indicator, that indicator was excluded from the calculation of the DTF topic score in that country.

A country's distance-to-frontier score is indicated on a scale from 0 to 100, where 0 represents the worst performance and 100 the frontier. The difference between a country's distance-to-frontier score in 2016 and future score will illustrate the extent to which the country has closed the gap to the regulatory frontier over time. And in any given year the score measures how far a country is from the best performance at that time.

Table A.1 | What is the frontier in regulatory practice?

	INDICATORS	FRONTIER	WORST PERFORMANCE
SEED	Plant breeding index (0–10)	10	0
	Variety registration index (0–8)	8	0
	Seed quality control index (0–12)	12	0
	Time to register new varieties (days)	298[a]; 166[b]	860[a]; 716[b]
	Cost to register new varieties (% income per capita)	0.0	969.7[a]; 268.3[b]
FERTILIZER	Fertilizer registration index (0–7)	7	0
	Quality control of fertilizer index (0–7)	7	0
	Importing and distributing fertilizer index (0–7)	7	0
	Time to register a new fertilizer product (days)	11	954
	Cost to register a new fertilizer product (% income per capita)	0.0	845.8
MACHINERY	Tractor operation index (0–5)	5	0
	Time to register a tractor (days)	1	27
	Cost to register a tractor (% income per capita)	0.0	37.0
	Tractor testing and standards (0–8)	8	0
	Time to obtain type approval (days)	4	279
	Cost to obtain type approval (% income per capita)	0.5	560.9
	Tractor import (0–5)	5	0
FINANCE	**Branchless banking**		
	Agent banking index (0-5)	5	0
	E-money index (0-4)	4	0
	Movable collateral		
	Warehouse receipts index (0-5)	5	0
	Doing Business getting credit index (0-8)	8	0
	Non-bank lending institutions		
	Microfinance institutions index (0-7)	7	0
	Financial cooperatives index (0-7)	7	0
MARKETS	Producer organizations index (0–13)	13	0
	Plant protection index (0–8)	8	0
	Agricultural trade index (0–9)	9	0
	Documents to export agricultural goods (number)	0	4
	Time to export agricultural goods (days)	0	11
	Cost to export agricultural goods (% income per capita)	0.0	5.2
TRANSPORT	Trucking licenses and operations index (0–11)	11	0
	Time to obtain trucking licenses (days)	1	80
	Cost to obtain trucking licenses (% income per capita)	0.0	31.8
	Cross-border transportation index (0–9)	9	0
	Time to obtain cross-border licenses (days)	1	60
	Cost to obtain cross-border licenses (% income per capita)	0.0	60.3
WATER	Integrated water resource management index (0–29)	29	0
	Individual water use for irrigation index (0–20)	20	0
ICT	Information and communication technology index (0–9)	9	0

Note: a. For countries with one cropping season. b. For countries with two cropping seasons.

The report team welcomes feedback on the methodology. All the data and sources are publicly available at http://eba.worldbank.org.

APPENDIX B
Topic data notes

Seed

The seed indicators aim to identify obstacles affecting the timely release and production of high-quality seed by the formal seed supply system, by examining the regulatory environment for plant breeding, registration of new varieties and seed quality control.

Three indicators have been developed:
1. Plant breeding.
2. Variety registration.
3. Seed quality control.

The seed topic has four types of respondents: (i) seed producers and seed companies; (ii) national and regional seed associations; (iii) government authorities (for example, the Ministry of Agriculture); and (iv) academics. The data are collected through surveys sent to contributors from Washington, DC, and completed with calls, emails and interviews that are conducted with respondents during country visits. Responses from contributors are crosschecked by reviewing the applicable laws and regulations. Desk research and literature review are also performed to verify certain data points.

To make the data comparable across countries, several assumptions about the new variety to be registered are used. Furthermore, only certain procedures are captured by EBA data, and specific rules are used to calculate time and cost. More detail on each issue, including the scoring methodology for each data point (table B.1) and specific terms, is set out below.

Assumptions about the variety
The variety:
- Is a maize variety developed by the private sector.
- Is being registered for the first time in the entire country.
- Has not been registered in any other country.

Note: In exceptional cases when maize varieties are not being developed by the private sector in the country, we consider imported maize variety, which may have been previously registered elsewhere.

Procedures
A procedure is defined as any interaction of the seed company's owner, manager or employees with external parties, including any relevant government agencies, lawyers, committees, public and private inspectors and technical experts. All procedures are counted that are legally or in practice required for the seed company to release a new variety of seed. Procedures are consecutive but can be simultaneous.

Time
Time is recorded in calendar days and captures the median duration of each procedure. The time span for each procedure starts with the first filing of the application or demand, and ends once the last procedure required to release a new seed variety on the market has been fulfilled, such as the listing in the national catalog or gazette. Any tests performed by the seed company prior to filling an application are not counted. The minimum time for each procedure is one day. The calendar days for distinctiveness, uniformity and stability (DUS) and value for cultivation and use (VCU) tests are determined based on the number of testing seasons required by the authority and the number of cropping seasons existing in the country, as follows:

Countries with two cropping seasons per year:
- If one season is required by law to perform the tests, 135 days are counted for the testing procedure.
- If two seasons are required by law to perform the tests, 275 days are counted for the testing procedure. This accounts for the two seasons of 135 days each and 5 days to account for the time needed to plow and prepare the land before the next cropping season (135+5+135 = 275 days).

Countries with one cropping season per year:
- If one season is required by law to perform the tests, 182 days are counted for the testing procedure.
- If two seasons are required by law to perform the tests, 547 days are counted for the testing procedure. This accounts for the full calendar year including one season (365 days) and an additional testing season (182 days).

Cost
Only official costs are recorded, including fees and taxes. In the absence of fee schedules, a government officer's estimate is taken as an official source. In the absence of government officer's estimate, estimates by seed companies are used. If several seed companies provide different estimates, the median reported value is applied. Professional fees (for example, notary fees)

131

are only included if the company is required to use such services. All costs are recorded as a percentage of the country's income per capita.

Specific terms

Basic/foundation seed has been produced under the responsibility of the maintainer according to the generally accepted practices for the maintenance of the variety and is intended for the production of certified seed. Basic or foundation seed must conform to the appropriate conditions set by regulations, and the fulfillment of these conditions must be confirmed by an official examination.

Breeder/pre-basic seed is directly controlled by the originating or sponsor plant breeding institution, firm or individual, and is the source for the production of seed of certified classes.

Distinctiveness, Uniformity and Stability (DUS) testing is performed to compare candidate varieties for registration with varieties already listed in seed register, on these qualities:

- *Distinctness* (UPOV definition): A variety shall be deemed distinct if it is clearly distinguishable in at least one character from any other variety whose existence is a matter of common knowledge at the time of filing the application for registration.

- *Uniformity* (UPOV definition): A variety shall be deemed to be uniform if, subject to the variation that may be expected from the particular features of its propagation, it is sufficiently uniform in its relevant characteristics.

- *Stability* (UPOV definition): A variety shall be deemed stable if its relevant characteristics remain unchanged after repeated propagation by the method that is normally used for the particular variety.

Post-control tests are performed to ensure that the variety is true to its varietal identity and that the plants must conform to the characteristics of the variety listed by the national catalog at the time of its registration.

Seed certification (Organisation for Economic Co-operation and Development [OECD] definition) is the quality assurance process during which seed intended for domestic or international markets is controlled and inspected by official sources to guarantee consistent high quality for consumers.

Traceability is the ability to document the history of the origin, production, participants and handling steps involved in the seed production.

UPOV is the International Union for the Protection of New Varieties of Plants, an intergovernmental organization based in Geneva, Switzerland. Its mission is to provide and promote an effective system of plant variety protection, with the aim of encouraging the development of new varieties of plants for the benefit of society. To be a member, the law of a country must conform to the standards of the 1991 Act of the UPOV Convention. The country can also have an observer status after having officially expressed an interest in becoming a UPOV member and in participating to the sessions of the Council. To date, 74 states have member status and 57 states have observer status.

Value for Cultivation and Use (VCU) testing is performed to assess whether a variety has characteristics and properties that affect improvement in the cultivation or in the utilization of the harvest or its products in comparison to the existing listed varieties.

Variety (UPOV definition) is a plant grouping within a single botanical taxon of the lowest known rank, which, irrespective of whether the conditions for the grant of a breeder's right are fully met, can be:

- Defined by the expression of the characteristics resulting from a given genotype or combination of genotypes;
- Distinguished from any other plant grouping by the expression of at least one of the said characteristics; and
- Considered as a unit with regard to its suitability for being propagated unchanged.

Variety catalog is a list of varieties that have been registered and released by a national authority and can be produced and marketed in a country or region as certified seed.

Variety release committee (VRC) decides whether a new variety can be registered and introduced on the domestic market.

Note: In addition to the initial consultations with seed experts, the team received technical support from Joseph Cortes and Adelaida Harries. The World Seed Project, which is a combined effort from the OECD Seed Scheme, the Food and Agriculture Organization (FAO), International Seed Testing Association (ISTA), ISF (International Seed Federation) and UPOV, also provided technical expertise for the development of the indicator methodology.

Fertilizer

The fertilizer indicators measure regulatory bottlenecks limiting access to fertilizer. The indicators also focus on operational and economic constraints, as well as the implementation of legislation affecting the fertilizer industry.

Three indicators have been developed, as follows:
1. Fertilizer registration.
2. Importing and distributing fertilizer.
3. Quality control of fertilizer.

The fertilizer topic area has three main types of respondents: i) fertilizer companies, ii) relevant government authorities (for example, the ministry of agriculture), and iii) agricultural input dealer associations. The questionnaire targets all three groups of respondents, whereby the time and motion component is typically answered by the private sector. Data was collected through face-to-face, by phone, or email interviews with respondents.

To make the data comparable across countries, several assumptions about the company and the fertilizer product are used. Furthermore, only certain procedures are captured by EBA data, and specific rules are used to calculate time and cost. More detail on each issue, including the scoring methodology for each data point (table B.2) and specific terms, is set out below.

Assumptions about the fertilizer company
The fertilizer company:
- Is a private entity (company, a nongovernmental organization [NGO] and/or a farmer organization or cooperative);
- Is registered in the country;
- Imports fertilizer to sell in the country;
- Has registered at least one new fertilizer product in the country.

Assumptions about the registered fertilizer
The fertilizer:
- Is a new chemical fertilizer product—a fertilizer product is any product containing nitrogen, phosphorus, potassium or any recognized plant nutrient element or compound that is used for its plant nutrient content.
- Is produced in a foreign country.
- Is being registered for marketing purposes.

Procedures
A procedure is defined as any interaction of the company's owners, managers or employees with external parties, for example, government agencies, lawyers, auditors, notaries and customs or border authorities. It includes all procedures that are officially required for the business to legally perform its described activities, such as registering and importing fertilizer. Interactions among owners, managers and employees are not counted as procedures.

Time
Time is recorded in calendar days and captures the median duration of each procedure. The time span for each procedure starts with the first filing of the application or demand, and ends once the company has received the final document, such as the fertilizer registration certificate. It is assumed that the company's owners, managers or employees have had no prior contact with any of the officials.

Cost
The cost captures official fees and taxes associated with the relevant licenses, permits and certificates, along with their required documents. All costs are recorded as a percentage of the country's income per capita.

Specific terms
Fertilizer registration is the process of registering a fertilizer product or blend with the public sector, during which fertilizer intended for markets is controlled and inspected by official sources to guarantee consistent high quality and safety for consumers.

Fertilizer product is any product containing nitrogen, phosphorus, potassium, or any recognized plant nutrient element or compound that is used for its plant nutrient content.

Importer registration is a government-issued license authorizing a company to import. The import registration is not to be confused with a sales license, which authorizes the company to sell fertilizer.

Import permit is a document issued by a government agency authorizing the importation of fertilizer products into its territory. An import permit can either be a blank permit with no restrictions, or impose volume, shipment or time limits.

Machinery

The machinery indicators measure regulatory barriers and associated practices limiting access and use of agricultural tractors by farmers. In particular, the indicators capture the requirements for tractor import, registration and inspection, tractor testing, the prevailing approval process, as well as tractor performance and operator safety standards.

The following three indicators were developed:
1. Tractor imports.
2. Tractor operation.
3. Tractor testing and standards.

The machinery topic area has five types of respondents, namely: i) tractor companies (tractor manufacturers, local dealers and distributors); ii) industry associations; iii) tractor testing centers; iv) government authorities, such as the ministry of agriculture or the ministry of transport; and, v) national agricultural research institutes. Data were collected through interviews with respondents.

To make the data comparable across countries, several assumptions about the machinery company and the machinery product are used. Furthermore, only certain procedures are captured by EBA data, and specific rules are used to calculate time and cost. More detail on each issue, including the score assigned to each data point (table B.3) and specific terms, is set out below.

Assumptions about the importing business
The business:
- Is a private sector company (manufacturer, dealer or distributor of agricultural machinery).
- Is registered as a business in the country.
- Does not operate in an export processing zone or in an industrial estate with special import or export privileges.
- Uses the most-used seaport for importation of tractors in the country. If the country is land-locked, it is assumed that the most-used border posts are used.

Assumptions about the machinery product:
The machinery product:
- Is a two-axle or four-wheel drive agricultural tractor.
- Has more than 20 engine horsepower.
- Is designed to furnish the power to pull, carry, propel or drive implements.
- All self-propelled implements are excluded.

A tractor is used as a proxy to assess the enabling regulatory framework and the practices impacting access and use of agricultural tractors for farm mechanization.

Procedures
Procedures capture any required company interaction with external parties, such as ministries, government agencies, testing centers, accredited labs and so on to obtain a tractor type approval/homologation. Internal interactions among owners, managers and employees within the company do not count as procedures.

Time
Time is recorded in calendar days and captures the average duration of the company interaction with relevant agencies to obtain the tractor type approval or to obtain required licenses, permits and certificates.

Cost
Cost captures official fees and taxes associated with the tractor type approval/homologation or the licenses, permits and certificates, along with their required documents. All costs are recorded as a percentage of the country's income per capita.

Specific terms
Falling-object protective structures (FOPS) are a system attached to the tractor to protect the operator from falling objects such as branches, rocks, and other falling objects.

Roll-over protection structures (ROPS) are attached to the tractor frame and come as either two-post fixed or foldable, four post, or as an integral part of a ROPS cab. They generally will limit a side overturn to ninety degrees (90°) and will provide an important safety zone for the operator provided the operator is wearing a seat belt. Seat belts should not be used when a foldable ROPS is down or when a fixed ROPS is removed.

Type approval (also called *homologation*) is the official recognition given by a national authority or agency that certifies that the tractor conforms to the country's prevailing regulatory, technical and safety requirements. Before the tractor can be sold on the market and before reaching the hands of the farmer, the manufacturer (or an agency on behalf of the manufacturer) must complete its type approval/homologation procedure and be certified by third-party verification that its design, construction and performance respect the country's regulations and standards.

Finance

The finance indicators measure laws and regulations that promote access to a range of financial services, with a focus on areas that are particularly relevant for potential customers in rural areas. These customers are partially or fully excluded from traditional financial services due to factors such as their geographical location or available type of collateral.

Three indicators have been developed:
1. Non-bank lending institutions.
   - Operation and prudential regulations of microfinance institutions (MFIs).
   - Operation and governance of financial cooperatives.
2. Branchless banking.
   - Agent banking.
   - Electronic money (e-money).
3. Movable collateral.
   - Warehouse receipts.
   - *Doing Business*–Getting Credit.

Data for the finance indicators are obtained from three main types of respondents: financial sector supervisory authorities, financial lawyers, and legal officers of financial institutions. Data collections include interviews conducted during country visits directly with respondents, followed by rounds of follow-up communication via email and conference calls with respondents as well as with third parties. Data are also verified through analyses of laws and regulations, including a review of public information sources on banking law, warehouse receipt law, financial institutions law and others. More detail on each indicator, including the scoring methodology for each data point (table B.4) and specific terms, is set out below.

1. Non-bank lending institutions

This indicator measures regulations relevant to deposit-taking MFIs and financial cooperatives. Countries with a high level of financial inclusion will be scored only based on data on financial cooperatives, while the rest of the countries will be scored based on data on both MFIs and financial cooperatives. Finance indicators are designed to measure laws and regulations that promote access to financial services for potential customers that are partially or fully excluded from traditional financial services. In particular, the MFI and agent banking indicators focus on supporting the provision and proliferation of financial services to those who are excluded from traditional banking system. These indicators are not applicable to countries with a high level of financial inclusion where agribusinesses and smallholder farmers have few obstacles accessing the formal financial sector. Therefore, those countries are not measured under these indicators and the corresponding data for those countries are shown as "N/A" (not applicable).

The threshold used to establish what countries fall under those with a high level of financial inclusion has been determined as the average of the normalized values (0–1) of two variables, namely: "account at a financial institution (% of rural adult population)," and "account at a financial institution (% of adult population) based on the World Bank Findex database. Following this approach, those countries with a number higher than 0.8 on the average of normalized values of the above-mentioned two variables will be identified as countries with high level of financial inclusion. Countries under this classification are Denmark, Greece, Italy, Korea, the Netherlands and Spain.

To make the data comparable across countries, several assumptions about the financial institutions are used, as follows:

Assumptions about the financial institutions
Microfinance institutions (MFIs): MFIs are financial institutions that specialize in the provision of small-volume financial services (such as credit, deposits and loans) to low-income clients. MFIs can take deposits, lend, and provide other financial services to the public and are licensed to operate and are supervised by a public authority.

Financial cooperatives: Financial cooperatives are member-owned, not-for-profit, cooperatives that provide savings, credit, and other financial services to their members. There are typically two types of financial cooperatives, namely: i) small financial cooperatives that provide services only to their members; are typically supervised by either the central bank, the department of cooperatives, or the ministry of finance; and are referred to as savings and credit cooperatives

(SACCOs) in some countries; and, ii) cooperative banks that take deposits from and lend to the public, and are regulated under the main financial institution laws and supervised by the central bank. The financial cooperative indicator does not measure cooperative banks but only small financial cooperatives to be consistent with the topic's emphasis on small-scale lending and financial inclusion.

2. Branchless banking

The second indicator includes aggregated data related to agent banking and e-money. In this case, countries with a high level of financial inclusion will be scored only based on data on e-money, whereas the rest of the countries will be scored based on both agent banking and e-money.

3. Movable collateral

For the third indicator all countries will be scored on data on warehouse receipts. Data points from the *Doing Business*-Getting Credit indicator, including data on security interest granted to movable assets and future assets, collateral registry, and credit information from non-bank institutions, will be added to this indicator.

Specific terms
Agent banking is the delivery of financial services through a partnership with a retail agent (or correspondent) to extend financial services to locations where bank branches would be uneconomical.

Capital adequacy ratio (CAR) is a measure of the amount of a bank's total capital expressed as a percentage of its risk-weighted assets.

Effective interest rate is the annual interest rate plus all fees associated with the administration of the loan to the client. It is a symbol of the total cost of the loan to the client. Proxies for the effective interest rate are the annual percentage rate or the amortization table/schedule for the loan.

E-money refers to money that is stored and exchanged through an electronic device. E-money is regulated and does not necessarily need to be associated with a deposit account at any financial institution. Examples include electronic funds transfers and payments processed through mobile phones or prepaid cards.

Deposit-taking MFIs are financial institutions specializing in the provision of small-volume financial services (for example, credit, deposits and loans) to low-income clients, which can take deposits, lend and provide other financial services to the public and are licensed to operate and supervised by a public authority.

Negotiable receipt allows the transfer of ownership without having to physically deliver the commodity.

Non-financial institution businesses are those that do not hold a financial institution license, including telecoms, post offices, or other businesses licensed by the central bank/financial supervisory authority to issue e-money.

Provisioning rules determine how much money banks must set aside as an allowance for bad loans in their portfolios. The share of a loan that must be covered by provisioning can either be the full loan amount or the part that is not secured by collateral (unsecured share).

Ratios to ensure financial stability can include the liquidity ratio, capital adequacy ratio, solvency ratio, credit to deposit ratio, assets to liabilities ratio, stable funding ratio, net loan receivables to total assets, and others. Countries address the issue of stability of financial cooperatives using different criteria, therefore all the above ratios can be included in this measure.

Warehouse receipts are documents issued by warehouse operators as evidence that specified commodities are of a stated quantity and quality, deposited or stored at particular locations by named depositors and owned by the beneficiary of the receipt issued. Where supported by an appropriate legal framework, warehouse receipts can serve as a form of collateral to obtain a loan from financial institutions and facilitate future sales.

Markets

The markets indicators monitor and analyze laws and regulations that can impact smallholder producers and agribusinesses when accessing domestic and foreign agricultural markets for their products.

Three indicators have been developed:
1. Agricultural trade.
2. Plant protection.
3. Producer organizations.

Markets indicators have five main types of respondents: (i) government agencies responsible for agricultural trade, plant protection and cash crops; (ii) private-sector agribusinesses producing and trading agricultural products in domestic and/or international markets, and related trade/export associations; (iii) farmers' organizations, including unions, federations, cooperatives and other similar entities; (iv) chambers of commerce; and (v) lawyers. Data were collected from these respondents using three different surveys: one for the public sector and two for the private sector. Data were collected through interviews conducted during country visits directly with respondents and by email and teleconference calls from Washington, DC.

Details on the methodology for each indicator, including the score assigned to each data point (table B.5) and specific terms, are set out below.

1. Agricultural trade

To make the data on agricultural trade more comparable across countries, several assumptions about the business, the agricultural products, trading partner and shipment are used. Furthermore, only certain requirements are captured by EBA data, and specific rules are used to calculate time and cost.

Assumptions about the business
The business:
· Performs general agricultural trading activities.
· Does not directly engage in agricultural production, processing or retail activities.
· Does not operate in a special export processing zone.

Assumptions about the traded product and trading partner
A theoretical product and trading partner are selected for each country based on official export statistics in accordance with the following rules:
· The traded products are defined and grouped as cash crops, cereals, fruits and vegetables according to the Harmonized Commodity Description and Coding System 1996 version (HS 96).
· All data are sourced from the UN Comtrade Database, using the export data from 2009–13.
· For each country, the combination of the product and the partner country selected represents the highest five-year average export value (in US dollars). For example, cereal exports to Zimbabwe is selected for Zambia. In addition, the HS 4-digit product within the category that is exported the most to the partner country is used for studying the specific legal and regulatory requirements. For example, coffee exports (the top product within the cash crop category) to the United States is selected for Colombia.

Assumptions about the shipment
The shipment:
· Is transported via a 20-foot full container-load.
· Weighs 10 metric tons or costs US $10,000, whichever is most appropriate.
· All packing material that requires fumigation (such as wood pallets) is assumed to be treated and marked with an approved international mark certifying that treatment.

Requirements to trade
A "requirement" for purposes of the study is any legally required qualification or document that must be obtained by the business to buy or sell the selected

product in the domestic market or export the product to the trading partner. These requirements may apply to the trader (for example, a selling/buying license, periodic export registration, mandatory memberships, and so on) or to the export consignment on a per shipment basis (for example, phytosanitary certificate, quality certificate, and so on). These requirements involve interactions with external parties, including government agencies, inspectors and other relevant institutions. Buyer-driven requirements such as private laboratory tests are not considered for purposes of the study.

The following principles apply to the requirements recorded:

- Only requirements specific to the product group (or the top exported sub-product within that group) and agricultural products more generally are captured. Customs, commercial and shipping documents that are not specific in this way are not measured (for example, certificate of origin, export declaration, bill of lading, letter of credit, and so on).
- Mandatory membership of a public or private entity is included if it is required to obtain and exercise the right to export the selected product or agricultural products more generally.
- Trader-level licenses include any document or action that is required to obtain and exercise the right to buy or sell the product in the domestic market or export overseas, including registration or accreditation requirements and traditional licenses.
- Documents are collected on a per shipment basis, and one document includes both application and completion of the process (for example, obtain a phytosanitary certificate or obtain a quality certificate).

  > Where multiple documents are obtained simultaneously, they are recorded as separate documents but time is adjusted to reflect their simultaneity.
  > The mandatory documents required by both the country studied and the selected trading partner are included.
  > Both public and private fumigation certificates are excluded if they are not required by the laws of either the country studied or the selected trading partner. Only fumigation that is required for the product itself is captured, and separate fumigation for packaging prior to its purchase/use is not included.

Time

Time is recorded in calendar days and captures the median duration to obtain each mandatory document to export on a per shipment basis. Time to complete membership requirements or to obtain trader-level licenses is not captured. The time span for each document starts with the first filing of the application or demand, and ends once the company has received the final document, such as the phytosanitary certificate.

If time is obtained only in working days, the data are converted to calendar days based on the assumption that there are five working days per week and the procedure starts on a Monday. It is assumed that the company's owners, managers or employees have had no prior contact with any of the officials and that the company completes each procedure to obtain the document without delay on its side.

The following principles apply to how time to obtain documents is measured:

- It is assumed that the minimum time required for each document is one day, except for documents that can be fully obtained online, for which the time required is recorded as half a day.
- Although multiple documents may be obtained (and related processes completed) simultaneously, the process to obtain each document cannot start on the same day (that is, simultaneous processes start on consecutive days).
- If the process to obtain a document can be accelerated for an additional cost and is available to all types of companies, the fastest legal process is chosen and the related costs are recorded. Fast-track options applying only to firms located in an export processing zone or to certain accredited firms under authorized economic operator programs are not taken into account.

Cost

The cost includes all official fees and fees for legal or professional services if such services are required by law to complete the qualification requirement or obtain a document. Service fees (for example, those charged by fumigation companies) are only included if the company is required by law to use such services. Traditional (scheduled) border taxes/tariffs are not captured. Other special charges or taxes that apply to the export product or sub-product, or the export of agricultural products generally, are included only where they result in the issuance of a stand-alone mandatory document to export or are conditional to obtain another mandatory document to export.

Where possible, laws, regulations and fee schedules are used as sources for calculating costs. In the absence of fee schedules, estimates by the public/private sector respondents are used. If several respondents provide different estimates, the median reported value is applied. In all cases the cost excludes bribes. All costs are recorded as a percentage of the country's income per capita.

2. Plant protection

Plant protection encompasses regulations, policies and institutional frameworks that affect plant health in a country, including domestic pest management measures as well as phytosanitary controls at the border. In cases where relevant regulations are specific to a product or product group, those applicable to the selected traded product are used.

3. Producer organizations

Producer organizations are also known as agricultural cooperatives, farmers' cooperatives, farmers' organizations or producer associations. A producer organization is defined as a formal, voluntary, jointly-owned and democratically controlled organization established for the economic benefit of agricultural producers by providing members with services that support farming activities, such as bargaining with customers or providing inputs, technical assistance, or processing and marketing services.

To render data on producer organizations comparable across countries, the following case study is used to select the most appropriate legal form in each country:

Several agricultural producers wish to pool their production within a producer organization to sell it on the spot market or through long-term sales contracts with buyers ("the transaction"). The principal function of the organization is to pool and sell the members' production, and the organization takes ownership of the produce in question.

The following principles also apply:
· Voluntary and open membership;
· Democratic member control ("one member, one vote");
· Joint-ownership by members; and,
· Created to support and promote the economic interests of its members through joint economic activity.

If different forms of producer organizations exist in a country's laws, the one which obtains the highest aggregated score under the producer organizations indicator is selected for inclusion in the dataset.

Specific terms
Definitions below are adapted from the International Plant Protection Convention (IPPC) website (http:www.ippc.int) and the International Standards for Phytosanitary Measures No. 5 *Glossary of Phytosanitary Terms*, adopted by the IPPC.

Electronic phytosanitary certificate (ePhyto) is the electronic version of a phytosanitary certificate in XML format. All the information contained in a paper phytosanitary certificate is also in the ePhyto. ePhytos can be exchanged electronically between countries or the data can be printed out on paper.

Pest risk analysis (PRA) is defined as "[t]he process of evaluating biological or other scientific and economic evidence to determine whether a pest should be regulated and the strength of any phytosanitary measures

to be taken against it." It consists of three stages: initiating the process for analyzing risk; assessing pest risk; and managing pest risk.

Phytosanitary measures include "[a]ny legislation, regulation or official procedure having the purpose to prevent the introduction and/or spread of quarantine pests, or to limit the economic impact of regulated non-quarantine pests."

Regulated quarantine pest refers to "[a] pest of potential economic importance to the area endangered thereby and not yet present there, or present but not widely distributed and being officially controlled."

Transport

The transport indicators measure regulatory and administrative constraints affecting the provision of reliable and sustainable commercial road transport services.

The following two sub-indicators have been developed:

1. Truck licensing.
2. Cross-border transportation.

Data were collected through interviews conducted during country visits directly with respondents, by email and teleconference calls from Washington, DC, and by local staff in the different target countries. The topic mainly targeted private sector respondents including trucking associations, trucking companies and lawyers; and to a lesser extent, public sector respondents including ministries of transport, road transport regulatory authorities and ministries of infrastructure. Even though the questionnaire targeted both groups of respondents, time and cost information was typically answered by the private sector.

To make the data comparable across countries, several assumptions about the trucking company, its environment and scope of cross-border operations are used Furthermore, only certain procedures are captured by EBA data, and specific rules are used to calculate time and cost. More detail on each issue, including the scoring methodology for each indicator (table B.6) and specific terms, is set out below.

Assumptions about the business
The business:
· Is a private entity or natural person whose core business is transporting goods by road for commercial purposes;
· Has met all formal requirements to start a business and perform general industrial or commercial activities;
· Is located in the country's largest business city;

- Has a maximum of five trucks; each truck has two axles and a maximum loading capacity of 15 MT (metric tons);
- Transports agricultural products within the country, including perishable products, and it does not transport fertilizers, pesticides, hazardous products or passengers;
- The trucks were first registered in the largest business city less than six months ago; the "trucks" comprise a tractor unit and a trailer;
- All employed drivers have the domestically required driver's license to drive a 15 MT vehicle; and,
- Carries out cross-border transport services with its largest agricultural border-adjacent trading partner.

Assumptions about the "reference" product

The "relevant" product selection was based on UN Comtrade's 2009–13, five-year average export value of major plant product groups, and mirror data in cases where data were not sufficient. For example, cereals constitute the reference-product for Bolivia and tomatoes are the ones for Morocco. A list of each country's reference product is available in the Country Data tables.

Assumptions about the cross border trading partner

This partner selection was based on UN Comtrade's 2009–13, five-year average trade value of major plant product groups (and mirror data when needed), as well as on a border-adjacent criterion. The partner selection methodology was used as a proxy for defining the largest trading partner by truck, in the absence of transport data disaggregated by mode of transport (sea, air, rail or road). It is also assumed the agricultural products being shipped to and from the largest trading partner were produced locally, not imported. For instance, the largest trading partner of Burundi is Tanzania. A list of each country's largest trading partner is available in Country Data tables.

Time

Time was recorded in calendar days and captures the median duration of obtaining the required company or truck license, excluding preparation time. The timespan starts once all required documents have been submitted to the relevant authority and ends once the company has received the final document. It is assumed that the company's owners, managers or employees have had no prior contact with any of the officials.

Cost

Costs capture only official costs required by law, including fees and taxes. Fee schedules in transport laws and regulations have been used as legal basis when available, and an estimation from qualified contributors in the alternative scenario. It is assumed that all documents have been submitted in the timely and correct form. All costs are recorded as a percentage of the country's income per capita.

Validity

Validity is measured for domestic and cross-border truck licenses. Validity is expressed in years.

Specific terms

Backhauling rights: For example, when a truck registered in country A is able to transport agricultural goods into country B for sale, load other goods in country B and carry them back to country A.

Bourse de fret: A platform in which freight supply and demand are made publicly available for the purposes of freight access and allocation, often in the form of online service offered by a private company.

Certificate of good repute or equivalent: An official document issued by a competent judicial or administrative authority certifying that the trucking company was not convicted for a serious criminal offence or had not incurred in a penalty for a serious infringement of rules relating to road transport.

Cabotage rights: For example, when a truck registered in country A is able to pick up agricultural goods in country B and deliver them to a different point in country B.

Company-level license or permit: A special authorization required for established companies or individuals to legally transport goods (different from general business registration). It allows the company to operate several trucks under the same license.

Consignment note: A transport document attesting the nature and quantity of the goods transported when taken into charge by the carrier and attesting the delivery to the consignee.

Government registry or notification certificate, or equivalent: An official document issued by a competent administrative authority certifying registration in a road transport body.

Queuing system: A practice by which freight is sequentially allocated by trucking associations/unions or the government.

Transit rights: For example, when a truck registered in country A is able to travel through country B to deliver agricultural goods into country C (assuming foreign country B is the final destination of the foreign truck).

Transport/Import rights: For example, when a truck registered in country A is able to transport agricultural goods produced in its country into country B for sale.

Triangular rights: For example, when a truck registered in country A is able to pick up agricultural goods in country B and transport them to be delivered into country C (assuming foreign country B is the final destination of the foreign truck).

Truck-level license or permit: This is a special authorization required for a truck to legally transport goods (different from vehicle registration or technical inspection certificates). A truck-level license regime requires an individual transport license or permit for each truck.

Water

The water indicators measure laws and regulations that promote sustainable, inclusive and efficient governance of water resources, with a particular focus on the use of water for irrigation.

Two indicators have been developed:
1. Integrated water resources management.
2. Individual water use for irrigation.

Water indicators have three main types of target respondents: (i) lawyers specialized in water law and environmental law, both from private practice and the public sector; (ii) technical specialists in the field of water resources management, typically from the public sector; and (iii) academic experts. The questionnaire targets all three groups of respondents, whereby the legal questions are typically answered by lawyer respondents, and implementation questions are typically answered by technical specialists and academic experts. Data collection includes interviews conducted directly with respondents during country visits, followed by rounds of follow-up communication via email and conference calls with respondents, as well as with third parties. Data are also verified through analysis of laws and regulations and a review of publicly-available sources of information on water management and permits.

To make data for the *individual water use for irrigation* indicator comparable across countries, several assumptions about the water user and water source are used. More detail, as well as the score assigned to each data point (table B.7) and specific terms, is set out below.

Assumptions about the water user
The water user:
- Is a farm that grows crops.
- Is a medium-sized farm for the country, with land area that falls between 2 and 10 hectares.
- Uses mechanical means to individually abstract water for irrigation.
- Is not located in a broader irrigation scheme.

If medium-sized farms in the country, as prescribed in any official farm-size classification system, deviate significantly from this given range, it is assumed that the case study farm does not qualify for any exemption from permit requirements that may otherwise apply to small farms (such as exemptions for smallholders or subsistence farmers).

Assumptions about the water source
The water source:
- Is a river located 300 meters away from the farm; or
- Is a groundwater well located on the farm.

The choice between surface water and groundwater as a source for irrigation water is made based on the predominant irrigation water source for the country, determined using Food and Agriculture Organization (FAO) 2016 AQUASTAT data. The majority of EBA countries predominantly use surface water for irrigation; those with predominant groundwater use for irrigation are: Bangladesh, Denmark, India, Jordan, Nicaragua and the Netherlands.

Specific terms
Abstraction and use permit refers to the right to abstract and use a certain defined quantity of water resources. Depending upon the country context, permits may alternatively be referred to as authorization, license, right, concession and so on. For consistency, the term "permit" shall be used here.

Basin institutions are specialized entities that deal with the water resource management issues in a particular river basin, lake basin, or aquifer.[1]

Charges refers to a fee or tax to abstract a certain volume of water as a natural resource, rather than a service charge for provided water or a one-time administrative application fee.

Water conservation refers to preservation and maintenance of the quantity and quality of water (surface and/or groundwater).

Water efficiency means to minimize water wastage in order to use the minimum amount of water required to perform a specific function.

Water stress "occurs when the demand for water exceeds the available amount during a certain period or when poor quality restricts its use."[2]

Transfer refers to when holders of water abstraction and use permits may sell, assign, trade, lease or otherwise transfer to a third party their permit.

ICT

The information and communication technology (ICT) indicator measures laws, regulations and policies that promote an enabling environment for the provision and use of ICT services, with a particular focus on rural areas. The ICT indicator focuses on the regulations and policies to improve access to ICT services.

The ICT topic area has three main types of respondents, as follows: i) mobile operators; ii) ICT and/or telecommunication regulatory authorities; and iii) telecommunication lawyers. The questionnaire targets all three groups of respondents. Data were collected through interviews conducted during country visits directly with respondents and also by email and teleconference calls from Kuala Lumpur, Malaysia and Washington, DC.

The data points below (table B.8) measure the legal requirements to operate as a mobile service provider that offers core mobile services which include voice, SMS (Short Message Service) and/or data.

Specific terms

Active infrastructure sharing requires operators to share elements of the active network layer including, for example, radio access nodes and transmission.

Digital dividend is the amount of spectrum made available by the transition of terrestrial television broadcasting from analog to digital.

Operating license is a license that authorizes the provision of telecommunications services.

Passive infrastructure sharing is the sharing of space or physical supporting infrastructure which does not require active operational coordination between network operators.

Service neutral is any service that can be offered in the used frequency band.

Technology neutral is any available technology to date that can be employed to provide a certain service in the used frequency band.

Voluntary spectrum trading is a mechanism whereby rights and any associated obligations to use spectrum can be transferred from one party to another by way of a market-based exchange for a certain price.

1 See for example, Global Water Partnership. 2013. River basin organizations. http://www.gwp.org/en/ToolBox/TOOLS/INSTITUTIONAL-ROLES/ Creating-an-Organisational-Framework/River-basin-organisations/.
2 European Environment Agency. Water Stress. http://www.eea.europa.eu/ themes/water/wise-help-centre/glossary-definitions/water-stress.

Table B.1 | Scoring methodology for seed indicators

INDICATOR	DESCRIPTION	WHAT IS MEASURED	HOW IT IS SCORED
PLANT BREEDING	This indicator measures the regulatory good practices identified as supporting the plant breeding process.	1. There is a regulation governing plant breeders' rights	**A score of 1** if yes **A score of 0** if no
		2. The duration (in years) of the plant breeders' rights (PBR)	**A score of 1** if the protection lasts at least 20 years **A score of 0** if the protection lasts less than 20 years
		3. Conditions to benefit from plant breeders' rights do not differ between national and foreign applicants	**A score of 1** if conditions do not differ **A score of 0** if conditions differ
		4. A list of protected varieties is publicly available	**A score of 1** if yes **A score of 0** if no
		5. Companies are legally allowed to produce breeder/pre-basic seed of local public varieties for use in the domestic market	**A score of 1** if yes **A score of 0** if no
		6. Companies are legally allowed to produce foundation/basic seed of local public varieties for use in the domestic market	**A score of 1** if yes **A score of 0** if no
		7. Companies are obtaining access to germplasm preserved in publically managed gene banks	**A score of 1** if yes **A score of 0** if no
		8. Plant breeding rights can be licensed to another party for production and sale of the variety	**A score of 1** if yes **A score of 0** if no
		9. There are public research institutes in the country that license public varieties to companies for production and sale in the domestic market	**A score of 1** if yes **A score of 0** if no
		10. Companies importing germplasm for the development of new varieties are required to undergo government testing (other than phytosanitary tests)	**A score of 1** if government testing is not required **A score of 0** if yes, government testing is required
VARIETY REGISTRATION	This indicator measures the regulatory good practices identified as supporting the efficient registration and release of a locally developed new seed variety into the domestic market. It also measures the efficiency of the registration process through case studies.	1. DUS testing data from other countries' authorities are accepted as official data for the purpose of registration	**A score of 1** if yes **A score of 0** if no
		2. The law establishes a variety release committee (VRC) in the country	**A score of 1** if yes **A score of 0** if no
		3. The composition of the legally mandated VRC includes the private sector	**A score of 1** if governmental and nongovernmental representatives (that is, seed associations, seed companies) constitute one-half or more of the VRC **A score of 0.5** if nongovernmental representatives are included in the committee but constitute less than one-half **A score of 0** if nongovernmental representatives are not included in the VRC or the VRC does not exist
		4. The frequency of VRC meetings	**A score of 1** if the VRC meets on demand or at least once per cropping season **A score of 0** if the VRC meets less than once per cropping season, or if the VRC does not meet at all
		5. A variety can be commercialized immediately after the decision of the VRC	**A score of 1** if yes **A score of 0** if no
		6. A catalog listing new registered varieties is publicly available online	**A score of 1** if yes **A score of 0.5** if the variety catalog is not available online **A score of 0** if the variety catalog does not exist
		7. The variety catalog specifies agro-ecological zones suitable for the variety.	**A score of 1** if yes **A score of 0** if no
		8. The frequency with which the variety catalog is updated	**A score of 1** if the catalog is updated each cropping season **A score of 0** if the catalog is updated less than once a year
		9. Time to register a new maize variety	**Total time** required for all legally mandated procedures is aggregated and presented in calendar days. **A score of 0** if there is no requirement to register or if the registration is not done in practice
		10. Cost required to register a new maize variety	**Total cost** for all legally mandated procedures is aggregated and presented in % of income per capita. **A score of 0** if there is no requirement to register or if the registration is not done in practice

(continued)

INDICATOR	DESCRIPTION	WHAT IS MEASURED	HOW IT IS SCORED
SEED QUALITY CONTROL	This indicator measures legally mandated processes and practices of seed certification.	1. There is an official fee schedule for seed certification activities performed by the competent public authority	**A score of 1** if yes **A score of 0** if no
		2. Plant breeders are required to ensure the traceability of the plant reproductive material used	**A score of 1** if the plant breeder is required to retain: (i) records of the plant reproductive material or (ii) both records of the plant reproductive material and of their suppliers **A score of 0.5** if the plant breeder is required to retain records of their suppliers **A score of 0** if neither are required
		3. Time in years during which plant breeders are legally obliged to keep the traceability records	**A score of 1** if more or equal to two years **A score of 0.5** if less than two years **A score of 0** if no obligation
		4. There is a legal framework for the accreditation of private seed companies and/or third parties for the performance of certification activities	**A score of 1** if yes **A score of 0** if no
		5. Private seed companies and/or third parties (non-governmental institutions) are accredited in practice for the performance of certification activities	**A score of 1** if yes **A score of 0** if no
		6. The following seed certification activities can be performed by an accredited seed company/third party: a. Field inspection b. Sampling c. Lab testing d. Labelling	**A score of 0.25** for each of the listed activities
		7. The competent public authority is required to perform post-control tests on certified seed	**A score of 1** if both laboratory and field post-control tests are required or if only field post-control tests are required **A score of 0.5** if only laboratory post-control tests are required **A score of 0** if neither are required
		8. A minimum percentage of certified seed must be subject to post-control tests	**A score of 1** if yes **A score of 0** if no
		9. The competent public authority is required to take measures in the case of noncompliance with the varietal purity standards	**A score of 1** if the law imposes the withdrawal of the seed and a formal request to comply with applicable standards, or if the law only provides for a formal request to comply with applicable standards **A score of 0.5** if the law imposes the withdrawal of the seed **A score of 0** if none are required
		10. Seed containers must be labeled	**A score of 1** if yes **A score of 0** if no
		11. Seed container labels must provide the following information: a. Name and address of seed producer b. Crop species c. Class of seed d. Net weight e. Lot number f. Certificate number g. Germination (minimum %) h. Purity (minimum %) i. Year of production j. Repacking or relabeling k. Chemical treatment on the seed	**A score of 1** if 8 or more if the label requirements must be included in the label: **A score of 0** if less than 8
		12. There is a penalty for the fraudulent sale of mislabeled seed bags	**A score of 1** if yes **A score of 0** if no

Table B.2 | Scoring methodology for fertilizer indicators

INDICATOR	SUB-INDICATOR	DESCRIPTION	WHAT IS MEASURED	HOW IT IS SCORED
FERTILIZER REGISTRATION	Fertilizer registration (legal)	This indicator measures the legal requirements to register a fertilizer and the extent to which public information on registered products is available through fertilizer catalogues.	1. Private entities are required to register new fertilizer products to sell them in the country	**A score of 1** if yes **A score of 0** if no
			2. The following type(s) of fertilizer products must be registered: a. Chemical or mineral fertilizer products b. Organic fertilizer products	**A score of 0.5** for each category that must be registered
			3. Field testing is not required to register a fertilizer product	**A score of 1** if field testing is not required **A score of 0** if field testing is required
			4. A lab sample analysis is required to register a fertilizer product	**A score of 1** if yes **A score of 0** if no
			5. The validity of the chemical fertilizer product registration is not time-limited	**A score of 1** if yes **A score of 0.8** if time-limited and validity is equal to or greater than 10 years **A score of 0.4** if time-limited and validity is less than 10 years **A score of 0** if fertilizer products are not required to be registered by law or if the private sector is not allowed to register fertilizer products
			6. An official catalogue listing all registered fertilizer products in the country is publicly available online	**A score of 1** if yes
			7. Re-registration of a fertilizer product is not required in the country if it has already previously been registered in another country that is part of an agreement or approved in the regional catalogue	**A score of 1** if re-registration is not required
	Fertilizer registration in practice (efficiency)	Building up on legal requirements to register fertilizer, this indicator captures the time and cost needed to comply with the legal requirements to register a fertilizer.	1. Total time to register a fertilizer product	**Total time required** for all legally mandated procedures is aggregated and presented in calendar days **A score of 0** if there is no requirement to register or if the registration is not done in practice
			2. Total cost to register a fertilizer product	**Total cost required** for all legally mandated procedures is aggregated and presented in % of income per capita **A score of 0** if there is no requirement to register or if the registration is not done in practice
IMPORTING AND DISTRIBUTING FERTILIZER		As fertilizer production is concentrated in only a few countries, requiring most others to rely on imports, these data focus on the private sector's role and the requirements for importing and distributing fertilizer.	1. Private entities are allowed to import fertilizer products into the country to sell them	**A score of 0** if any of the restrictions apply
			2. Private entities are required to register as importers to import fertilizer products but the registration is not time-limited	**A score of 1** if yes, or the time limit is greater or equal to 10 years **A score of 0.5** if importer registration is time-limited and the time is greater or equal to 5 years **A score of 0** if the company doesn't have to register as an importer or if the company has to register and registration is time-limited to less than five years
			3. Private entities are not required to obtain an import permit to import fertilizer products. If an import permit is required, the permit is a blank import permit without a volume restriction	**A score of 1** if no permit is required **A score of 0.5** if a blank permit is required **A score of 0** if a permit is required with per shipment or volume restrictions
			4. If an import permit is required, the time validity of the import permit is at least 12 months	**A score of 1** if no permit is required **A score of 0.5** if validity is equal or greater than 12 months **A score of 0** if validity is less than 12 months

(continued)

INDICATOR	SUB-INDICATOR	DESCRIPTION	WHAT IS MEASURED	HOW IT IS SCORED
			5. The official cost to obtain an import permit is equal or less than 50% income per capita	**A score of 1** if no permit is required **A score of 0.5** if the cost is equal or less than 50% of income per capita **A score of 0** if the cost is more than 50% of income per capita
			6. The time it takes to obtain the import permit is less or equal to 14 calendar days	**A score of 1** if no permit is required **A score of 0.5** if less or equal to 14 calendar days **A score of 0** if more than 14 calendar days
			7. Private entities are allowed to distribute fertilizer products in the country	**A score of 1** if yes
QUALITY CONTROL OF FERTILIZER		These indicators focus on labeling requirements, legislation on the sale of mislabeled and open fertilizer containers, and practices in monitoring fertilizer quality.	1. The law requires labeling of fertilizer containers	**A score of 1** if yes
			2. The law requires that labeling must be in at least one of the country's official languages	**A score of 1** if yes
			3. The law establishes that the label must provide the following: a. brand name b. net weight or volume c. content description d. name of the manufacturer e. contact information of the manufacturer f. country of origin g. name of the importer h. contact information of importer i. manufacturing date j. expiration date k. safety instructions l. storage instructions m. registration number	**A score of 1** if 10 or more label requirements are included in the label **A score of 0.5** if between 5 and 9 label requirements are included in the label **A score of 0** if less than 5 label requirements are included in the label or if no label is required
			4. If the fertilizer law prohibits the sale of mislabeled fertilizer bags	**A score of 1** if yes
			5. If the law establishes a penalty for the sale of mislabeled fertilizer	**A score of 1** if yes
			6. If the fertilizer law prohibits the sale of fertilizer products from opened bags or containers	**A score of 1** if yes
			7. If the law establishes a penalty for the sale of fertilizer products from opened bags or containers	**A score of 1** if yes

Table B.3 | Scoring methodology for machinery indicators

INDICATOR	SUB-INDICATOR	DESCRIPTION	WHAT IS MEASURED	HOW IT IS SCORED
TRACTOR IMPORTS	Tractor imports	This indicator examines the private machinery sector's ability to import agricultural tractors, importer registration and renewal requirements, and import permit requirements.	1. Companies are not required to register as importers of agricultural tractors. If the registration is required, the validity is indefinite or greater than 10 years	**A score of 1** if companies are not required to register as importers **A score of 0.5** if the registration is required but the validity is indefinite or greater than or equal to 10 years **A score of 0** if the registration is required and the validity is less than 10 years
			2. If registration is required and limited to a certain number of years, the registration is automatically renewed	**A score of 1** if the registration is not required or the registration is automatically renewed **A score of 0** if registration renewal is required
			3. An import permit is not required to import agricultural tractors. If a permit is required, the cost is less than 25% of income per capita	**A score of 1** if import permit is not required **A score of 0.5** if the import permit is required and the cost is smaller or equal to 25% of income per capita **A score of 0** if the import permit is required and the cost is greater than 25% of income per capita
			4. If an import permit is required, it is a blank import permit without volume or other restrictions	**A score of 1** if the permit is a blank permit, or if the import permit is not required **A score of 0** if the import permit is required for each tractor shipment or the permit is limited to a certain number of tractors annually
			5. If an import permit is required, it is valid for a period of at least 12 months	**A score of 1** if the import permit has unlimited validity or if the import permit is not required **A score of 0.5** if the permit has a validity of 12 months or longer **A score of 0** if the permit has a validity of less than 12 months
TRACTOR OPERATIONS	Tractor operations (legal)	This indicator evaluates the requirement of tractor registration, roadworthiness inspections of in-use tractors, and provision of after-market parts and services.	1. According to the law, tractors must be registered once imported if they will be used on public roads	**A score of 1** if registration is required for use on public roads only **A score of 0.5** if registration is required for all usage **A score of 0** if registration is not required
			2. According to the law, in-use tractors have to be inspected for roadworthiness/road-fitness and if the cost of inspection is affordable	**A score of 1** if the roadworthiness inspection is required and the cost is less than or equal to 2% of income per capita **A score of 0.5** if the roadworthiness-inspection is required and the cost is greater than 2% of income per capita **A score of 0** if the roadworthiness-inspection is not required or it is not done in practice
			3. The roadworthiness inspection is required for all types of tractors	**A score of 1** if inspection is required for all types of tractors **A score of 0.5** if inspection is required for specific types of tractors **A score of 0** if no inspection is required
			4. If the roadworthiness inspection is required, the results are valid for more than two years but less than four years	**A score of 1** if yes **A score of 0.5** if renewal is required and the period between roadworthiness tests is less than two years or greater than four years **A score of 0** if renewal is not required
			5. Tractor dealers must provide tractor after-market service and parts	**A score of 1** if both tractor after-market service and parts must be provided **A score of 0.5** if either tractor after-market service or parts must be provided **A score 0** if neither tractor after-market nor parts must be provided
	Tractor registration in practice (efficiency)	Building on the legal indicator with regards to tractor registration, this indicator measures the time and the cost required to register a tractor.	1. Total time to register a tractor	**Total time required** for all legally mandated procedures is aggregated and presented in calendar days **A score of 0** if there is no requirement to register or if the registration is not done in practice
			2. Total cost to register a tractor	**Total cost** for all legally mandated procedures is aggregated and presented in % of income per capita **A score of 0** if there is no requirement to register or if the registration is not done in practice

INDICATOR	SUB-INDICATOR	DESCRIPTION	WHAT IS MEASURED	HOW IT IS SCORED
TRACTOR TESTING AND STANDARDS	Tractor testing and standards (legal)	This indicator examines national and international tractor standards, the legal framework applicable to testing and the type of approval of tractors, and safety standards.	1. National and/or international tractor standards are used in the country	**A score of 1** if international standards are used **A score of 0.5** if national standards are used **A score of 0** if no standards are used
			2. If national and/or international tractor standards are used in the country, the following standards are included: > operator safety standards > tractor performance standards > engine emission standards	**A score of 0.33** is assigned to each of the standards that is included. **A score of 0** if none of the three standards are used or there are not national and/or international standards used in the country
			3. Tractors are required to obtain the type approval before they can be marketed in the country	**A score of 1** if yes **A score of 0** if no
			4. To obtain the type approval, the following procedures are required: > tractor testing in a test laboratory > the issuance of the test report > the publication of the test report	**A score of 0.33** is assigned to each requirement **A score of 0** if the type approval is not required or it is not done in practice
			5. The country recognizes the tractor type approvals issued by authorities in other countries	**A score of 1** if yes **A score of 0** if no
			6. The country recognizes tractor test reports by the tractor manufacturer for the issuance of the type approval	**A score of 1** if yes **A score of 0** if no
			7. The type approval has unlimited validity provided that the specifications of the tractor do not change	**A score of 1** if yes **A score of 0.5** if limited to five or more years **A score of 0** if less than five years or the type approval is not required
			8. The national regulations/standards require tractors to be equipped with protective structures, such as roll-over protection (ROPS) structures or falling object protection (FOPS) structures, and seatbelts	**A score of 1** if ROPS or FOPS are required in combination with seatbelts **A score of 0.33** if neither ROPS or FOPS nor seatbelts are required **A score of 0** if ROPS or FOPS are required and seatbelts are not required **A score of 0** if seatbelts are required and ROPS or FOPS are not required
	Tractor testing in practice (efficiency)	Building on the legal indicator with regards to tractor testing and the type approval, this indicator measures the time and the cost required to test an agricultural tractor and obtain a tractor type approval.	1. Time to obtain the tractor type approval	**Total time** for all legally mandated procedures to obtain the type approval is aggregated and presented in calendar days **A score of 0** if there is no requirement to obtain type approval or if the tractor type approval is not done in practice
			2. Cost to obtain the tractor type approval	**Total cost** for all legally mandated procedures to obtain the type approval in % of income per capita **A score of 0** if there is no requirement to obtain type approval or if the tractor type approval is not done in practice

Table B.4 | Scoring methodology for finance indicators

INDICATOR	SUB-INDICATOR	DESCRIPTION	WHAT IS MEASURED	HOW IT IS SCORED
NON-BANK LENDING INSTITUTIONS	Operation and prudential regulation of MFIs (operations)[a]	This indicator measures the regulatory framework for deposit-taking MFIs.	1. The country allows and regulates deposit-taking MFIs 2. There is a minimum capital requirement to establish an MFI 3. The regulated minimum capital adequacy ratio for MFIs is at least equal to, or no more than 2 percentage points higher, than the capital adequacy ratio for commercial banks[b] 4. Loan sizes of MFIs are: not limited to a specific amount; or are greater than 10 times the gross national income (GNI) per capita if there is a specific amount; or are a percentage of capital, equity or deposits[c] 5. MFIs must disclose the effective interest rate or a proxy to loan applicants 6. MFIs are required to fully provision a delinquent, unsecured loan after the same number of days required for commercial banks, or within half the number of days required for commercial banks 7. MFIs are required to subscribe to a deposit insurance system	**A score of 1** if yes for each question
	Operation and governance of financial cooperatives (operations)	This indicator measures the regulatory framework for financial cooperatives.	1. There is a law regulating financial cooperatives, or there is a specific section of a general cooperatives law that regulates the governance and operation of financial cooperatives 2. There is a minimum capital requirement to establish a financial cooperative 3. A minimum number of members is required to establish a financial cooperative 4. Ratios are defined in the law to ensure the financial stability of financial cooperatives 5. Financial cooperatives must disclose the effective interest rate or a proxy to loan applicants 6. Financial cooperatives must subscribe to a mandatory deposit insurance system 7. Two or more financial cooperatives may merge or amalgamate into a new financial cooperative	**A score of 1** if yes for each question
BRANCHLESS BANKING	Agent banking (operations)[d]	This indicator measures the entry and operational requirements for agent banking.	1. There exists a legal framework to regulate agent banking activities	**A score of 1** if yes
			2. Whether there are minimum standards to qualify and operate as an agent in the following areas: 1) can either be an operating/established business or an individual; 2) has to have financial soundness; 3) has no criminal record; 4) has to have real-time connectivity to a commercial bank; and 5) location	**A score of 0.2** for each standard
			3. Agents can enter into both exclusive and non-exclusive contracts with financial institutions	**A score of 1** if yes **A score of 0.5** if only non-exclusive contracts are allowed **A score of 0** is assigned if only exclusive contracts are allowed
			4. The types of services that agents can offer on behalf of a bank includes: a. cash deposits; b. cash withdrawals; c. transfer of funds to other customers' accounts; d. bill payments; e. balance inquiry; f. opening a deposit account; g. collection/processing of loan application documents; h. know your customer (KYC) and customer due diligence (CDD) procedures	**A score of 0.125** for each service that can be offered
			5. Commercial banks are liable for the acts of commission and omission of agents providing financial services on their behalf	**A score of 1** if yes

(continued)

INDICATOR	SUB-INDICATOR	DESCRIPTION	WHAT IS MEASURED	HOW IT IS SCORED
	Electronic money (e-money) (operations)	This indicator measures the legal framework for e-money, in particular, the entry and operational requirements for non-financial institution e-money issuers.	1. E-money is defined and regulated 2. Non-financial institution businesses are allowed to issue e-money 3. Non-financial institution e-money issuers are required to keep customer's funds safeguarded and deposited in a trust at a fully prudentially regulated financial institution under which funds are held on behalf of clients	**A score of 1** if yes for each question
			4. There are four requirements for non-financial institution businesses to receive a license to issue e-money: a. an initial capital requirement; for the initial capital requirement, countries are divided into four groups (1, 2/3, 1/3 and 0) based on the country's capital requirement as a multiple of its income per capita	**A score of "1*1/4"** if the capital requirement is less than 101 times the GNI per capita, but greater than 0 **A score of "2/3*1/4"** if the minimum capital is equal to or greater than 101 times the income per capita, but less than 501 **A score of "1/3*1/4"** if the minimum capital is equal to or greater than 501 times the income per capita, but less than 901 **A score of 0** if the minimum capital requirement is equal to or greater than 901 times the income per capita or if there are no provisions on the minimum capital requirement
			b. interoperability with other existing electronic money payment/transfer systems c. existence of internal control mechanisms to comply with Anti-Money Laundering and Combatting Financing of Terrorism (AML/CFT) laws, standards and measures d. consumer protection measures such as consumer recourse mechanisms, consumer awareness programs, and so on	**A score of 1/4** if the law states the requirement and 0 if it does not

(continued)

a Countries with a high level of financial inclusion are not measured under the operation and prudential regulation for MFIs sub-indicator.

b The methodology adopts the Basel Committee recommendation in "Microfinance activities and the Core Principles for Effective Banking Supervision" and the International Development Bank's Jansson et al. (2004) "Principles and Practices for Regulating and Supervising Microfinance" report in establishing a CAR that falls within 2-3 percentage point of commercial banks or in the range of 10% to 15%.

c In some countries, the maximum loan an MFI can extend is limited to a percentage of deposits or a percentage of core capital. This language is included in risk management regulations, intended to limit the exposure of the institution to a single borrower. For countries with this type of loan limitation, *EBA 2017* considers it "no limit" because the currency value corresponding to that percentage is so high as to present no effective limit to borrowers.

d Countries with high level of financial inclusion are not measured under the agent banking sub-indicator.

INDICATOR	SUB-INDICATOR	DESCRIPTION	WHAT IS MEASURED	HOW IT IS SCORED
MOVABLE COLLATERAL	Warehouse receipts (operations)	This indicator measures the regulatory framework facilitating the use of agricultural commodities as collateral.	1. There is a law regulating the operation of warehouse receipts or the regulation of warehouse receipts is included in other general legislation 2. Warehouse operators are required to file a bond with the regulator, pay into an indemnity fund to secure performance by him of his obligations as a warehouse operator, or are required to insure the warehouse or the stored goods against fire, earthquakes, theft, burglary or other damage 3. Warehouse receipts are negotiable	**A score of 1** if yes for each question
			4. The types of warehouse receipts that are legally valid: paper-based, electronic or both	**A score of 1** is assigned if the law allows both paper-based and electronic warehouse receipts, and if electronic warehouse receipts are explicitly mentioned in the regulation **A score of 0.5** is assigned if the law allows only paper-based receipts **A score of 0** is assigned if warehouse receipt is not recognized or used
			5. Information that must be listed on a warehouse receipt for it to be valid. There are four details measured, namely: > date of issuance or serial number > location of storage > description of goods in storage, (for example, type, quality and harvest) > information on security interest over the goods (for example, a certificate of pledge)	**A score of 0.25** for each piece of information that needs to be listed
	Doing Business– Getting Credit (operations)[e]	This indicator measures the legal rights of borrowers and lenders with respect to secured transactions and the reporting of credit information. A total of eight data points from the indicator's sub-indices (five data points from the strength of legal rights sub-index and three data points from the credit information sub-index) are included.	1. There is a legal framework for secured transactions that grant security interest in movable assets 2. The law allows businesses to grant a non-possessory security right in a single category of movable assets without requiring a specific description of collateral 3. The law allows businesses to grant a non-possessory security right in substantially all of its assets, without requiring a specific description of collateral 4. Security rights are granted to future or after-acquired assets, and they extend automatically to the products, proceeds or replacements of the original assets 5. Existence of a collateral registry for movable assets in operation for both incorporated and non-incorporated entities, that is unified geographically and by asset type, with an electronic database indexed by debtor's name 6. The credit information is distributed from retailers or utility companies—in addition to data from banks and financial institutions 7. Credit information includes data on loan amounts below 1% of income per capita 8. There is a legal framework that allows borrowers to access their data in the credit bureau or credit registry	**A score of 1** if yes for each question

e   *Doing Business*–Getting Credit data are used as secondary data.

Table B.5 | Scoring methodology for markets indicators

INDICATOR	SUB-INDICATOR	DESCRIPTION	WHAT IS MEASURED	HOW IT IS SCORED
AGRICULTURAL TRADE	Agricultural trade (legal)	This indicator measures regulatory requirements applicable to the domestic trade and export of agricultural products.	1. There are no price controls in the sector of the selected product (explicit price control regulations are considered, including those that apply only to government purchases. Recommended prices are not included)	**A score of 1** if price controls do not exist **A score of 0** if price controls exist
			2. Sales and purchases of the selected product do not have to occur at an auction or a fixed (electronic or physical) marketplace	**A score of 1** if sales and purchases do not have to occur at an auction or a fixed market **A score of 0** if sales and purchases have to occur at an auction or a fixed market
			3. Traders do not have to obtain a trader-level license to buy/sell the selected product or agricultural products more generally in the domestic market	**A score of 1** if the license is not required **A score of 0** if the license is required
			4. Exporters do not have to be a member of a specific association or organization to obtain the right to export the selected product or agricultural products more generally	**A score of 1** if membership is not required **A score of 0** if the membership is required
			5. Exporters do not have to obtain a trader-level export license to export the selected product or agricultural products more generally to the selected trading partner	**A score of 1** if the license is not required **A score of 0** if the license is required
			6. Phytosanitary certificate applications may be submitted electronically	**A score of 1** if yes
			7. Phytosanitary certificates may be generated, issued and sent in an electronic form (for example, an ePhyto system is in place)	**A score of 1** if yes
			8. Phytosanitary certificates may be issued on-site where the selected product is produced, processed, packaged, stored and so on	**A score of 1** if yes
			9. The official fee schedule for the phytosanitary certificate is publicly available	**A score of 0.5** is assigned to each of the following: > The official fee schedule is available on a government website. > The official fee schedule is available in legislation.
	Agricultural trade (time and motion)	This indicator measures the number, time and cost of agriculture- and product-specific documents to export agricultural products.	10. Total number of mandatory documents required to export the selected product to the selected trading partner	**Total number** of mandatory, agriculture-specific documents is aggregated and presented in number form
			11. Total time to obtain the mandatory documents required to export the selected product to the selected trading partner	**Total time** required to obtain the mandatory, agriculture-specific documents is aggregated and presented in calendar days
			12. Total cost to obtain the mandatory documents required to export the selected product to the selected trading partner	**Total cost** required to obtain the mandatory, agriculture-specific documents is aggregated and presented in % income per capita

(continued)

INDICATOR	SUB-INDICATOR	DESCRIPTION	WHAT IS MEASURED	HOW IT IS SCORED
PLANT PROTECTION		This indicator examines the strength of the domestic plant protection framework by considering the legal obligations applicable to domestic pest management.	1. A specific government agency or unit is designated by law to conduct pest surveillance on plants	**A score of 1** if yes
			2. The government or national plant protection agency maintains a list of regulated quarantine pests	**A score of 1** if yes
			3. The list of regulated quarantine pests is publicly available on a relevant government website and uploaded to the IPPC website	**A score of 0.5** is assigned to each of the following: > The list of regulated quarantine pests is uploaded to the IPPC website. > The list of regulated quarantine pests is made available on a relevant government website.
			4. A pest database that contains details on the pests present in the country is available on a government website and contains the following features: a. pictures b. host information c. current status d. potential treatment methods	**A score of 0.25** is assigned to each of the features available in the pest database
			5. Land owners/users are obligated to report pest outbreaks to the government, and penalties are in place for non-compliance	**A score of 1** if yes **A score of 0.5** if land owners/users are obligated to report pest outbreaks to the government, but there are no penalties for noncompliance **A score of 0** if land owners/users are not obligated to report pest outbreaks to the government
			6. A specific government agency or unit is designated by law to conduct pest risk analysis (PRA) for imports of plant products	**A score of 1** if yes
			7. The PRA reports are publicly available online	**A score of 1** if yes
			8. Phytosanitary inspections on imports of plant products may be carried out on a risk basis	**A score of 1** if yes

(continued)

ENABLING THE BUSINESS OF AGRICULTURE 2017

INDICATOR	SUB-INDICATOR	DESCRIPTION	WHAT IS MEASURED	HOW IT IS SCORED
PRODUCER ORGANIZATIONS		This indicator measures the laws applicable to the creation of producer organizations, their growth, efficiency and inclusiveness.	1. There is no minimum capital requirement to establish a producer organization	**A score of 1** if there is no minimum capital requirement **A score of 0.5** if the minimum capital requirement is equal to or less than 1 time the income per capita **A score of 0** if the minimum capital requirement is greater than 1 time the income per capita
			2. Foreign natural persons may be members of a producer organization	**A score of 1** if foreign natural persons are explicitly allowed to be members or if there is no prohibition on their membership (for example, the law is silent)
			3. Domestic and foreign legal persons may be members of a producer organization	**A score of 1** if both domestic and foreign legal persons may be members **A score of 0.8** if all domestic legal persons are allowed to be members but foreign legal persons are prohibited **A score of 0.6** if only certain domestic legal persons are allowed to be members and foreign legal persons are not prohibited **A score of 0.4** if only certain domestic legal persons are allowed to be members and foreign legal persons are prohibited **A score of 0** if legal persons are not allowed to be members
			4. The government may not own shares in a producer organization	**A score of 1** if government shares in a producer organization is prohibited
			5. There is no cap on the dividends paid on member shares	**A score of 1** if there is no cap on dividends
			6. Profits may be distributed in the form of shares	**A score of 1** if yes.
			7. Nonmembers may own shares in a producer organization and there is no cap on dividends	**A score of 1** if nonmember shares are allowed and there is no cap on dividends **A score of 0.8** if nonmember shares are allowed and there is a cap on dividends **A score of 0** if nonmember shares are not allowed or if the law is silent on the issue of nonmember participation
			8. An application to register a producer organization must be reviewed and decided upon within an explicit time limit set out in the law	**A score of 1** if there is a time limit and it is equal to or less than 10 days **A score of 0.75** if there is a time limit and it is equal to or less than 30 days **A score of 0.5** if there is a time limit and it is equal to or less than 60 days **A score of 0.25** if there is a time limit and it is more than 60 days **A score of 0** if there is no time limit
			9. The designated regulating authority must explain its reasons for rejecting an application to establish a producer organization	**A score of 1** if yes
			10. The open membership principle applies to producer organizations	**A score of 1** if yes

(continued)

INDICATOR	SUB-INDICATOR	DESCRIPTION	WHAT IS MEASURED	HOW IT IS SCORED
PRODUCER ORGANIZATIONS *(continued)*			11. Women's membership in a producer organization is not restricted by any additional requirements, such as: a. legal ownership over land b. only one member per household c. a married woman has to receive her husband's authorization before joining a producer organization d. other legal restrictions that might apply to female members and limit their participation in producer organizations	**A score of 1** if none of the listed restrictions exist **A score of 0** if any of the listed restrictions exist
			12. A quota or other mechanism is established by law to promote women in producer organizations, such as: a. a gender quota for the board of directors of producer organizations b. a gender quota for the supervisory committee of producer organizations c. other gender-related quotas or mechanisms applicable to producer organizations	**A score of 1** if any of the listed quotas exist
			13. The constitution and the law on producer organizations contain provisions on nondiscrimination and both mention gender as a specifically protected category[f]	This question is scored in two parts: *For the constitution:* **A score of 0.5** if the constitution contains a clause on nondiscrimination and it mentions gender **A score of 0.3** if the constitution contains a clause on nondiscrimination, but it does not mention gender **A score of 0** if the constitution does not contain a clause on nondiscrimination *For the law on producer organizations:* **A score of 0.5** if the law requires producer organizations to comply with the principle of nondiscrimination and it mentions gender **A score of 0.3** if the law requires producer organizations to comply with the principle of nondiscrimination, but it does not mention gender **A score of 0** if the law does not require producer organizations to comply with the principle of nondiscrimination

f   The 2016 data of Women, Business and the Law – Accessing Institutions are used as secondary data. The specific data points included: (1) whether the constitution contains a clause on nondiscrimination or not; and (2) if it exists in the constitution, whether the nondiscrimination clause mentions gender or not.

Table B.6 | Scoring methodology for transport indicators

INDICATOR	SUB-INDICATOR	DESCRIPTION	WHAT IS MEASURED	HOW IT IS SCORED

TRUCK LICENSING	Truck licensing (legal)	This indicator measures the regulatory and normative framework and associated efficiency to access and operate domestically within the road freight transport service market. Overall, the indicators determine the extent to which legal foundations provide for a clear, transparent and efficient system for accessing the market, guarantee a level playing field for competition, and dedicate special legal provisions for transporting agriculture and food products.	1. Type of license legally required to transport goods commercially in the domestic market:
			
			  a. License at the company level
			
			  b. License at the truck level
			
			  c. Both at the company and truck level licenses
			
			  d. No license required
				A score of 1 if only the company-level license is required
				
				A score of 0.5 if both company-level and truck-level licenses are required or only the truck license is required
				
				A score of 0 if no license is required

			2. Validity of the relevant domestic license(s) is at least five years *Note:* If the country does not require a domestic license, the score of this question will read "N/A" (not applicable)	**A score of 1** if yes **A score of 0** if the validity is less than five years or N/A *Note:* If a country has "both" licenses, a score of 1 if both licenses have a validity of at least five years, and a score of zero if otherwise
			3. Citizenship requirements do not apply to obtain a license (foreign nationals or businesses are allowed to obtain the relevant licenses) *Note:* If the country does not require a domestic license, the score of this question will read "N/A"	**A score of 1** if yes **A score of 0** if no or N/A

			4. The law does not establish any of the following additional requirements to obtain a license:
			
			  a. Maximum number of trucks covered under the license
			
			  b. Maximum transported tonnage
			
			  c. Geographical operational limitations
			
			  d. Minimum number of trucks under the license
			
			  e. Licenses are only issued to members of a truckers' association or professional body
			
			  f. Licenses cannot be issued to women
			
			  g. Obtain government registry or notification certificate
			
			Note: If the country does not require a domestic license, the score of this question will read "N/A."
				A score of 1 if no additional requirements
				
				A score of 0 if any additional requirement or "N/A"

			5. Documents required by law when transporting goods by road domestically include:
			
			  a. Written contract describing the conditions of carriage, including carrier's liability for loss, damage or delay
			
			  b. Consignment note, packing list, bill of lading, waybill, commercial invoice or any other official document describing the goods shipped, their origin and destination
				A score of 1 if documents listed under both (a) and (b) are required
				
				A score of 0.5 if yes only to either (a) or (b)
				
				A score of 0 if no documents are required by law when transporting

			6. The law establishes specific regulations related to the transport of perishable agriculture products or foodstuffs, or related to the reference product	**A score of 1** if yes **A score of 0** if no

			7. The law considers the following aspects as part of regulations for the transport of agri-food products:
			
			  a. Special conditions related to covering/roofing and flooring/insulation to protect loads from external and internal contaminants
			
			  b. Vehicle cooling, refrigeration or controlled-temperature aspects
			
			  c. Prohibition of co-mingling of certain items
			
			  d. Specific packaging, sealing and stowage conditions for the goods transported
			
			  e. Loading and unloading specific procedures
			
			  f. Mandatory cleaning and disinfection protocols and routines of truck container
			
			Note: If the country has no specific regulations for agricultural or food products, the score of this question will read "N/A"
				A score of 0.166 for each aspect regulated
				
				A score of 0 for each aspect not regulated
				
				A score of 0 if "N/A"

(continued)

INDICATOR	SUB-INDICATOR	DESCRIPTION	WHAT IS MEASURED	HOW IT IS SCORED
TRUCK LICENSING *(continued)*			8. There is a public registry of licensed transport operators *Note:* If the country does not require a domestic license, the score of this question will read "N/A"	**A score of 1** if the registry is available online or by other means (official gazette, phone, certified agent, billboards at public authority, and so on) **A score of 0** if no or "N/A"
			9. Public availability of requirements that companies must fulfill to obtain or renew a road transport license *Note:* If the country does not require a domestic license, the score of this question will read "N/A"	**A score of 1** if the requirements are published on a government website or available by other means (official gazette, phone, certified agent, billboards at public authority, and so on) **A score of 0** if no or "N/A"
			10. The application or renewal for a license can be submitted electronically *Note:* If the country does not require a domestic license, the score of this question will read "N/A"	**A score of 1** if yes **A score of 0** if no or "N/A"
			11. Freight is allocated through direct contracting between a producer or trader and a trucking service provider	**A score of 1** if yes
	Truck licensing (time and cost)	This indicator measures the procedural efficiency (time and cost required) of the licensing systems in place in a country, as perceived by the relevant road transport operators.	12. Total time required to obtain a domestic license	**Total time** required to obtain the relevant license is presented in calendar days **A score of 0** if there is no license required *Note:* If "both" licenses are required, their times and costs are aggregated.
			13. Total cost required to obtain a domestic license *Note:* If the country does not require a domestic license, the score of this question will read "N/A"	**Total cost** to obtain the relevant license is presented in % of income per capita **A score of 0** if there is no license required *Note:* If "both" licenses are required, their times and costs are aggregated.

ENABLING THE BUSINESS OF AGRICULTURE 2017

156

INDICATOR	SUB-INDICATOR	DESCRIPTION	WHAT IS MEASURED	HOW IT IS SCORED
CROSS-BORDER TRANSPORTA-TION	Cross-border transport license (legal)	This indicator measures the completeness of the legal and regulatory framework governing cross-border transport between a given country and its largest trading partner. Overall the indicators aim to assess whether a country's national regulatory environment encourages cross-border transport.	1. Transport rights are granted to foreign transport companies or trucks registered in the trading partner	**A score of 1** if yes **A score of 0** if no
			2. Backhauling rights are granted to foreign transport companies or trucks registered in the trading partner	**A score of 1** if yes **A score of 0** if no
			3. Triangular rights are granted to foreign transport companies or trucks registered in the trading partner	**A score of 1** if yes **A score of 0** if no
			4. Transit rights are granted to foreign transport companies or trucks registered in the trading partner	**A score of 1** if yes **A score of 0** if no
			5. Cabotage rights are granted to foreign transport companies or trucks registered in the trading partner	**A score of 1** if yes **A score of 0** if no
			6. Transport rights are not specific to certain transit routes or corridors.	**A score of 1** if transit rights are not specific **A score of 0** if transit rights are specific
			7. A cross-border license is required for foreign trucks to operate in your country.	**A score of 1** if yes **A score of 0** if no
			8. The validity of the cross-border license required when operating in trading partner is at least five years. *Note:* If the country does not require a cross border license, the score of this question will read "N/A."	**A score of 1** if yes **A score of 0** if the validity is less than five years, N/A, or if the license constitute a "single-entry" permit
			9. The law does not establish an official limit or quota on the number of cross-border licenses granted. *Note:* If the country does not require a cross-border license, the score of this question will read "N/A."	**A score of 1** if yes **A score of 0** if no or "N/A"
	Cross-border licensing (time and cost)	This indicator measures the procedural efficiency (time and cost required) of the licensing systems in place in a country, as perceived by the relevant road transport operators. This license refers to trucks going from the home country to the largest trading partner.	10. Total time required to obtain a cross-border license	**Total time** required to obtain the cross border license is presented in calendar days **A score of 0** if there is no license required or if licensing does not apply in practice *Note:* If the country is considered an "island country",[a] this question is not taken into account for the final score.
			11. Total cost required to obtain the cross-border license in income per capita	**Total cost** required to obtain the cross-border license is presented in % of income per capita **A score of 0** if there is no license required or if the licensing is not applied in practice *Note:* If the country is considered an "island country",[a] this question is not taken into account for the final score.

Note: The truck licensing indicator refers exclusively to domestic operations. In contrast, the cross-border transport indicator refers to transport operations undertaken between a given country and its largest neighboring agricultural trading partner.

a "Island countries" include Korea, the Philippines and Sri Lanka.

Table B.7 | Scoring methodology for water indicators

INDICATOR	DESCRIPTION	WHAT IS MEASURED?	HOW IT IS SCORED
INTEGRATED WATER RESOURCES MANAGEMENT	This indicator measures legal mandates to undertake the core activities and features that comprise modern water management, including the establishment of basin-level institutions, water planning, the development of information systems, and source protection.	1. The establishment of basin institutions is provided for in the law.	**A score of 1** if yes
		2. Number of basin institutions existing	**A score of 1** if at least one basin institution exists
		3. A specific government agency or unit is designated by law to manage groundwater	**A score of 1** if yes
		4. Basin institutions have the following remits: a. special purpose government b. advisory c. stakeholder consensus	**A score of 1** if the law provides for all of the listed remits **A score of 0.5** if the law provides for at least one of the listed remits **A score of 0** if the law provides for none of the listed remits
		5. The internal organizational structure for basin institutions is set out in the law 6. Water users must be represented in basin institutions 7. A national water plan is required 8. Individual basin plans are required	**A score of 1** if yes
		9. The following specific components must be included in basin plans: a. resource description and categorization b. uses c. pollution sources d. protected areas e. drought/ flood plan f. economic analysis g. long-term objectives	**A score of 1** if the legal framework requires all of the listed components **A score of 0.5** if at least three of the listed components are required **A score of 0** if none of the listed components are required
		10. Water users must be consulted during the development of basin plans 11. Basin plans must be periodically updated in accordance with a mandatory timeline provided for in the law	**A score of 1** if yes
		12. Number of basin plans completed	**A score of 1** if at least one plan has been completed
		13. An order of priority for water allocation between different types of users is required	**A score of 1** if yes
		14. A water resources monitoring plan is required, including the following components: a. criteria for monitoring locations b. criteria for monitoring frequency c. monitoring objectives d. reference test/ measurement methods	**A score of 1** if the legal framework requires the development of a water resources monitoring plan and provides for each of the listed components: **A score of 0.5** if the legal framework requires the development of a water resources monitoring plan and provides two of the listed components **A score of 0** if the legal framework does not require the development of a water resources monitoring plan
		15. Monitoring plans must be periodically updated in accordance with a mandatory timeline provided for in the law	**A score of 1** if yes
		16. Public monitoring of water resources quantity and quality is required	**A score of 1** if the legal framework requires monitoring both water resources quantity and quality **A score of 0.5** if the legal framework requires monitoring of only one aspect or the other (quality or quantity) **A score of 0** if the legal framework does not require monitoring of water resources

(continued)

WHAT IS MEASURED?	HOW IT IS SCORED
17. There is a legal obligation to make monitoring results publicly available	
18. Monitoring results are publicly available in practice (online)	
19. There is a legal obligation to create an inventory of water resources	
20. The inventory of water resources must be periodically updated in accordance with a mandatory timeline provided for in the law	
21. There is a legal obligation to make water inventory data publicly available	**A score of 1** if yes for each question
22. Water inventory data are publicly available in practice (online)	
23. There is a legal obligation to create a registry of water users	
24. There is a legal obligation to make the water users registry publicly available	
25. The water users registry is publicly available in practice (online)	
26. Special measures may be imposed in cases of water stress	

27. The following special measures may be imposed in cases of water stress:
  a. restricted issuance of new water use permits
  b. curtailment of existing water use permits
  c. restricted issuance of new construction / activity permits with impacts on water resources
	A score of 1 if all of the listed measures may be imposed by the government
	
	A score of 0.5 if at least one of the listed measures may be imposed by the government
	
	A score of 0 if none of the listed measures may be imposed by the government

28. Water conservation and efficiency are promoted through the following features in the law:
  a. mandate for the government to promote conservation and efficiency
  b. incentives
  c. obligation to adopt improved water use practices
  d. promotion of less water-intensive crops
  e. obligation to implement a mechanism to quantify efficiency
	A score of 1 if the legal framework promotes water conservation and efficiency and provides all of the features listed.
	
	A score of 0.5 if the legal framework provides at least two of the listed features
	
	A score of 0 if the legal framework does not promote water conservation and efficiency

29. Water quality standards for use in irrigation are set out in the law and include the following parameters:
  a. coliforms
  b. salinity
  c. nitrates
  d. phosphates
	A score of 1 if the legal framework prescribes all the listed water standards for use in irrigation
	
	A score of 0.5 if the legal framework includes at least two of the listed parameters
	
	A score of 0 if the legal framework does not prescribe water quality standards for use in irrigation

(continued)

INDICATOR	DESCRIPTION	WHAT IS MEASURED?	HOW IT IS SCORED
INDIVIDUAL WATER USE FOR IRRIGATION	This indicator measures legal requirements for water abstraction and use permits, as well as the depth and quality of these permit requirements by examining public notice requirements, transfers, water use charges, and obligations and enforcement.	30. A permit or declaration before abstracting and using water for irrigation is required	**A score of 1** if a permit is requiredw **A score of 0.5** if only a declaration is required **A score of 0** if neither are required
		31. Permit issuance must comply with an applicable basin plan 32. Detailed procedures to acquire a new abstraction and use permit are set out in the law 33. There is a public notice obligation for new permit applications 34. A minimum time length applies to public notice 35. Public notice for new permit applications must be via a specific medium (for example, a newspaper, government website, billboard and so on) 36. Water abstraction and use permits are subject to a maximum time duration set out in the law 37. Legal framework specifies streamlined renewal procedures 38. Legal framework allows permit transfer	**A score of 1** if yes for each question
		39. Notification or approval by the government is required before a permit can be transferred	**A score of 1** if notification is required **A score of 0.5** if approval is required **A score of 0** if neither notification nor approval is required
		40. Detailed procedures for permit transfer are set out in the law 41. Charges apply based on the amount of water resources abstracted for irrigation 42. A specific government agency or unit is designated by law to set charges for water abstraction 43. A method for calculating the water abstraction charge is provided in the law 44. A specific government agency or unit is designated by law to collect charges for water abstraction	**A score of 1** if yes

		45. Standard permit conditions include the following:
		
		  a. volume/rate of withdrawal
		  b. place of abstraction
		  c. place of use
		  d. purpose of use
		  e. return flows
		  f. quality of returned water
			A score of 1 if the legal framework specifies all of the listed conditions.
			
			A score of 0.5 if only three of the listed conditions are specified
			
			A score of 0 if none of the listed conditions are specified

		46. Record keeping on the quantity of water abstracted is required	**A score of 1** if yes

		47. The government has certain inspection powers to ensure permit compliance, including:
		
		  a. demand users to produce relevant documentation
		  b. enter premises
		  c. take measurements
			A score of 1 if the government has all listed inspection powers
			
			A score of 0.5 if the government has only general inspection powers or two of the listed specific inspection powers
			
			A score of 0 if the government has neither general nor specific inspection powers

		48. Specific offenses in violation of permit-related obligations are prescribed in the law, including:
		
		  a. using water without a required permit or declaration
		  b. failure to comply with permit conditions
		  c. misrepresenting or omitting information to regulators
		  d. hindering investigators or disabling monitoring equipment
		  e. constructing water abstraction points without permission
			A score of 1 if the law prescribes specific offences and includes all the listed specific offenses.
			
			A score of 0.5 if the law declares that any water-related violation will be considered an offense or prescribes only two of the specific offenses listed
			
			A score of 0 if neither general nor specific offenses are prescribed in the law

		49. Before it can curtail permits, the government is required to make a formal declaration of drought or emergency	**A score of 1** if yes

Table B.8 | Scoring methodology for ICT indicator

INDICATOR	DESCRIPTION	WHAT IS MEASURED	HOW IT IS SCORED
ICT	These data measure countries' ICT licensing framework, validity and transparency of associated costs. The data also cover spectrum management and infrastructure sharing.	1. Operators offering core mobile services do not require a license to operate or a simple notification to the regulatory agency is allowed	**A score of 1** if a simple notification is required or an operating license is not required **A score of 0** if an individual license is necessary to operate
		2. The licensing framework for mobile operators offering core mobile services is technology and service neutral	**A score of 1** if yes **A score of 0.5** if technology or service neutral **A score of 0** if neither technology nor service neutral
		3. The validity (in years) of the operating license for mobile operators offering core mobile services is equal to or greater than 15 years	**A score of 1** if yes **A score of 0** if no
		4. The operating license costs, including first-time fee and/or annual fees, if applicable, are publicly available	**A score of 1** if available online or if license not required **A score of 0.5** if available in hard copy **A score of 0.25** if available upon individual written request **A score of 0** if not publicly available
		5. The renewal conditions for operating and spectrum licenses for mobile operators offering core mobile services are stated in laws and/or regulations	**A score of 1** if yes, for both operating and spectrum licenses **A score of 0.5** if yes, for operating or spectrum licenses **A score of 0** if neither operating nor spectrum licenses
		6. Digital dividend has been licensed in practice to mobile operators	**A score of 1** if yes **A score of 0** if no
		7. Low frequency spectrum (below 1 GHz [gigahertz]) has been licensed in practice to mobile operators	**A score of 1** if yes **A score of 0** if no
		8. Voluntary spectrum trading among operators is allowed by law	**A score of 1** if yes **A score of 0** if no
		9. Infrastructure sharing between mobile operators is legally allowed	**A score of 1** if both passive and active infrastructure sharing **A score of 0.75** if active infrastructure sharing **A score of 0.5** if passive infrastructure sharing **A score of 0** if neither passive nor active infrastructure sharing

APPENDIX C

Additional ways of presenting the data

This appendix highlights two additional ways of presenting certain components of the EBA dataset.

Good practices related to nondiscriminatory measures and access to information are included in EBA topic scores. For example, the private sector's eligibility to import fertilizer products is included in both the nondiscriminatory measures and the fertilizer topic score. Similarly, the existence of an online seed variety catalog is captured by both the access to information and the score of the seed topic.

Nondiscriminatory measures

The data on nondiscriminatory measures were collected across six EBA topics (table C.1). The total score of the 29 questions reflects the number of good practices related to nondiscrimination. These questions are also part of the corresponding topic and are scored based on the same methodology detailed in the data notes.

Access to information

The data on access to information were collected across seven EBA topics (table C.2). The total score of the 21 questions reflects the number of good practices related to access to information. These questions are also part of the corresponding topic and are scored based on the same methodology detailed in the data notes.

Table C.1 | Data on nondiscriminatory measures by topic

GOOD PRACTICES BY TOPIC

SEED	Conditions to benefit from plant breeders' rights do not differ between national and foreign applicants
	Companies are legally allowed to produce breeder/pre-basic seed of local public varieties for use in the domestic market
	Companies are legally allowed to produce foundation/basic seed of local public varieties for use in the domestic market
	Companies are obtaining access to germplasm preserved in publically managed genebanks
	There are public research institutes in the country that license public varieties to companies for production and sale in the domestic market
	The composition of the legally mandated variety release committee (VRC) includes the private sector
	Private seed companies and/or third parties (nongovernmental institutions) are accredited in practice for the performance of certification activities
	The following seed certification activities can be performed by an accredited seed company/third party: (a) field inspection; (b) sampling; (c) lab testing; (d) labelling
FERTILIZER	Private entities are required to register new fertilizer products to sell them in the country
	Private entities are allowed to import fertilizer products into the country to sell them
	Private entities are allowed to distribute fertilizer products in the country
FINANCE	A minimum number of members is required to establish a financial cooperative
	There is a minimum capital requirement to establish a financial cooperative
	Nonfinancial institution businesses are allowed to issue e-money
MARKETS	There is no minimum capital requirement to establish a producer organization
	Foreign natural persons may be members of a producer organization
	Domestic and foreign legal persons may be members of a producer organization
	The open membership principle applies to producer organizations
	Women's membership in a producer organization is not restricted by any additional requirements
	A quota or other mechanism is established by law to promote women in producer organizations
	The constitution and the law on producer organizations contain provisions on nondiscrimination and both mention gender as a specifically protected category
TRANSPORT	Citizenship requirements do not apply to obtain a license (foreign nationals or businesses are allowed to obtain the relevant licenses)
	The law does not establish requirements regarding minimum number of trucks or gender to obtain a license
	Transport rights are granted to foreign transport companies or trucks registered in the trading partner
	Backhauling rights are granted to foreign transport companies or trucks registered in the trading partner
	Triangular rights are granted to foreign transport companies or trucks registered in the trading partner
	Transit rights are granted to foreign transport companies or trucks registered in the trading partner
	Cabotage rights are granted to foreign transport companies or trucks registered in the trading partner
WATER	Water users must be represented in basin institutions

Table C.2 | Data on access to information by topic

GOOD PRACTICES BY TOPIC

SEED	A list of protected varieties is publicly available
	A catalog listing new registered varieties is publicly available online
	There is an official fee schedule for seed certification activities performed by the competent public authority
FERTILIZER	An official catalogue listing all registered fertilizer products in the country is publicly available online
FINANCE	Financial cooperatives must disclose the effective interest rate or a proxy to loan applicants
MARKETS	Phytosanitary certificate applications may be submitted electronically
	Phytosanitary certificates may be generated, issued and sent in an electronic form (for example, an ePhyto system is in place)
	The official fee schedule for the phytosanitary certificate is publicly available
	The list of regulated quarantine pests is publicly available on a relevant government website and uploaded to the IPPC website
	A pest database that contains details on the pests present in the country is available on a government website and contains features including pictures, host information, current status and potential treatment methods
	The pest risk analysis (PRA) reports are publicly available online
	The designated regulating authority must explain its reasons for rejecting an application to establish a producer organization
TRANSPORT	There is a public registry of licensed transport operators
	The application or renewal for a license can be submitted electronically
WATER	Water users must be consulted during the development of basin plans
	Monitoring results are publicly available in practice (online)
	Water inventory data are publicly available in practice (online)
	The water users registry is publicly available in practice (online)
	Public notice for new permit applications must be via a specific medium (for example, a newspaper, government website, billboard and so on)
	A method for calculating the water abstraction charge is provided in the law
ICT	The operating license costs, including first-time fee and/or annual fees (if applicable), are publicly available

APPENDIX D

Other research

Fertilizer

The fertilizer topic collected data on additional areas including competition, import and sale restrictions, subsidies and extension services. These areas were not scored since the evidence was anecdotal or no best practices could be identified to generate scores and trends at the global level.

Several questions were asked on competition issues, particularly if entities other than private companies are allowed or required to follow the same procedures as private companies to register, distribute or import fertilizer products. Evidence showed that in most instances the required procedures were uniform across countries for the private sector and other entities such as nongovernmental organizations (NGOs) and producer organizations/cooperatives. Different requirements existed only under special circumstances, most notably under subsidy programs, or where producer organizations were owned by the government and thus enjoyed the same privileges as the public sector.

Information on import and sale restrictions was also collected, including import bans on specific fertilizer types or products and country of origin. In addition, EBA looked at temporal import restrictions, company-level import quotas, restrictions on sales based on the type of products and geographical restrictions. In terms of specific fertilizer types or product restrictions, EBA found that most restrictions were based on health hazards that could be related to organic or bacterial content in the fertilizer product. EBA also found that some countries restrict fertilizers based on the country of origin and that subsidy programs often included specific conditions on imports. In general, no other restrictions were found in terms of products, geography or time of import.

Data were collected on subsidies, including the existence of subsidy schemes, subsidy targets (such as crops, products, farmer type or gender), subsidy administration models (reduced prices or vouchers) and timely duration of implementation (exit strategy). Although the data were not scored since there is no established best practice, EBA aims to contribute to

Figure D.1 | The majority of subsidy schemes are targeted and located in Sub-Saharan Africa

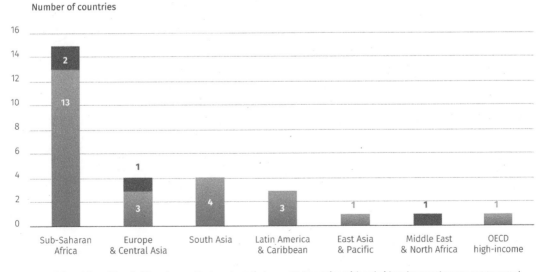

Number of countries

- ■ Countries with subsidy schemes that are targeted
- ■ Countries with subsidy schemes that are not targeted

Source: EBA database.

Produce market in Guatemala. Photo: Maria Fleischmann / World Bank.

the overall policy discourse by disseminating the information collected thus far.

Twenty-eight out of 62 countries surveyed have a subsidy scheme in place, among which half are in Sub-Saharan Africa (figure D.1) The concentration of subsidy schemes in Sub-Saharan Africa is undoubtedly linked to the fact that countries in the region are among the lowest consumers of fertilizer overall.[1] As part of the debate on the effectiveness of subsidies, some countries are moving towards "smart" subsidies that have clear goals and targets.[2] Targeted fertilizer subsidy schemes often include more than one type of target. Of the 15 Sub-Saharan African countries, 12 target subsidies by crop and 11 target by specific type of fertilizer product. Ten of the countries also target the schemes based on the type of farmers, and four target based on the region. For example, in Malawi, subsidies target beneficiaries such as maize and tobacco farmers, and there is an exclusive poverty reduction objective through a program that focuses on smallholder farmers with food security issues. In Senegal, subsidies target small-scale family production of rice, maize, sorghum, millet, fonio, groundnuts, sesame, onion, tomato and watermelon.[3]

Machinery

Data were collected on additional areas that are critical to the machinery sector but that were ultimately not included in the topic scoring either because only anecdotal evidence was found, international best practices for these areas are not fully developed or government regulation is not always of direct relevance. Tractor hire and rental services, financing, taxes and duties on tractors and spare parts were all investigated, but not included in the final score.

Tractor hiring and rental services are crucial aspects of agricultural mechanization, given that not all farmers have the resources to invest in agricultural machinery, nor the need given the small size of their plots. Renting and hiring services therefore become the most realistic option for many farmers. In the majority of cases, these services are provided by private machinery owners and public hiring services have been largely unsuccessful.[4] The data collected show that most of the countries studied have some form of tractor hiring or rental services available, either offered by public operators, private companies or individual tractor owners. The services offered typically include plowing, harrowing, planting and harvesting, with plowing being the service that is available in most countries. Given that tractor hiring and renting is generally not regulated by government, this aspect of agricultural mechanization was excluded from the topic scoring.

Access to finance is another major impediment to improving agricultural productivity in developing countries. Most farmers cannot afford to buy a tractor without financial assistance and many banks are reluctant to finance agricultural businesses due to associated risks. EBA findings on available tractor financing mechanisms are largely perception based and therefore have not been included in the scored indicators for this year's machinery topic. However, the data collected indicate that of the three categories of financial assistance considered—(i) banks (private or public); (ii) leasing companies; and (iii) supplier credit—supplier credit stands out as the most restricted across regions. According to respondents, access to credit from banks and leasing companies is also a major impediment in East Asia and Pacific and Sub-Saharan Africa regions, and respondents in other regions indicated moderate availability of these financing mechanisms.

Taxes and import duties imposed on agricultural machinery and spare parts have a direct bearing on the cost of tractors and create an unproductive financial burden on tractor maintenance. The data show that about one-fourth of countries studied levy low or no import duties on agricultural tractors, but high duties on replacement parts. This process has an adverse effect on the maintenance and repair of tractors because it increases operational costs and, in turn, hinders tractor utilization among farmers. The data collected also indicate that the prevailing tax regulations often lead to ambiguity and confusion over which tractor parts are tax exempted, as some parts are also used in the automotive industry, which typically attracts higher import duties.

Finance

This year the finance topic collected data on additional areas that are critical to agricultural finance, but for which international best practices are not fully developed. Partial credit guarantee systems (PCGSs) and agricultural lending quotas are two areas the finance topic studied, but did not score.

PCGSs can be a powerful tool to increase credit to agriculture. They reduce the risk that financial institutions take when lending to farmers and agribusinesses by acting as a collateral substitute, wherein "if the borrower fails to repay, the lender can resort to partial repayment from the guarantor."[5] However, the simple existence of a PCGS does not guarantee increased agriculture sector lending; rather, PCGS design and implementation have direct effects on program sustainability and effectiveness. Because there is no "one-size-fits-all" design for PCGSs, the team chose not to score this data. The data collected show that 18 of the 62 countries studied have a PCGS specific to agricultural loans issued by commercial banks. Only two high-income countries (Italy and Korea) have PCGSs. Sub-Saharan Africa is the region with the highest number of countries (6) with PCGSs, followed by Latin America and the Caribbean (4). Among the 18 countries with PCGSs for loans issued by commercial banks, only 8, most of which are located in Sub-Saharan Africa, also allow microfinance institutions (MFIs) to participate in the credit guarantee system—namely Bolivia, Colombia, Ethiopia, Mali, Mexico, Niger, Nigeria, and Rwanda.

The finance topic also collected data on the implementation of mandatory quotas to encourage credit in the agricultural sector. There is strong evidence that suggest lending quotas for agriculture lead to low profitability for banks and high nonperforming loans, as well as misallocation of credit and distorted market dynamics.[6] Nevertheless, some countries employ such interventions to support agri-finance. Data collected show that seven countries have policies requiring commercial banks to lend a percentage of their portfolio for the purpose of promoting agricultural activities—namely, Bangladesh, Bolivia, India, Nepal, the Philippines, Sri Lanka and Zimbabwe. The required percentage ranges from 2.5% of a bank's total loans each year in Bangladesh, to 25% of total loans per year in Bolivia and the Philippines. Bolivia is the only country that also requires MFIs to lend a percentage of all loans to agriculture.

Transport

The transport topic collected data on other areas of relevance to the transport sector, including exclusions from licensing, electronic platforms, and quality criteria to address social and environmental concerns, although these areas could not be scored due to the absence of global best practices or low variance among countries.

Countries often allow for various exceptions to transport licensing requirements, such as in cases where vehicles have a loading capacity less than 3.5 tons and where operators are transporting goods less than 10 kilometers or on their own account.[7] Too many licensing requirements may generate high compliance costs for operators and lead to increased informality. Data show that out of 39 countries having at least one exception to regular licensing requirements, 20 exempt operators who transport goods on their own account, 15 exempt certain vehicles based on loading capacity and 7 exempt transporting goods over short distances. Because the need for these exceptions depends significantly on the specific country context, the data were not scored.

Electronic platforms can streamline processes and facilitate the authorization of transport licenses, particularly cross-border licenses, by allowing transport operators to apply for licenses and process payments remotely. Such systems can also reduce transport costs and contribute to transparency. Only two countries, Denmark and Spain, have electronic platforms in place for processing cross-border licenses.

The use of certain quality and safety criteria to obtain a trucking license and access the market may also be used by governments to counteract market failures and address negative externalities for society and the environment. The International Road Transport Union (IRU) states that "quality criteria of the access to the profession should always remain the core of any relevant legislation."[8] Such requirements can include the obligation for managers and drivers to obtain specialized training, demonstrate financial standing or possess a certificate of good repute. Good vehicle standards include valid vehicle technical or emissions inspections certificates, third-party liability insurance and a vehicle registration certificate.

Bosnia and Herzegovina, Morocco and Thailand have strong legal frameworks that establish conditions to qualify for a truck license and operate a truck in public roads, including regular technical and emissions inspections, professional standards for truck owners or mandatory third-party insurance. While some countries such as Burkina Faso, Côte d'Ivoire and Serbia have embarked on a series of reforms to improve the qualifications of their truck operators and thereby the quality of trucking services, others such as Sudan or Zimbabwe do not have trucking regulations that ensure certain minimum standards are met to guarantee the formality or professionalism of operators. Countries with comprehensive licensing systems tend to have better quality control mechanisms for operators, suggesting that countries can promote market entry while improving standards in the sector. Countries such as Guatemala, Kyrgyzstan and Tajikistan do not have a minimum set of basic requirements such as third-party liability insurance or technical inspections. Guatemala is the only country in which technical inspections are not mandatory for heavy trucks, while Georgia established them in early 2016, bringing its regulatory framework in line with other countries in the Eastern Europe and Central Asia region.

Technical inspections are an important component of transport operations since they ensure safety and roadworthiness, and reduce negative externalities particularly related to the environment. If technical inspection certificates are valid only for a short period of time, however, this can increase costs for truck operators and may amount to rent-seeking in a country. Across the 61 countries mandating periodic vehicle technical inspections, 43 require inspections to be repeated annually, 13 require every 6 months, and the remaining six have various other validity periods. Given the different standards and procedures involved in each country's vehicle inspections, there is no internationally accepted best practice in terms of the validity of technical inspection certificates. For example, some countries may impose a relatively low maximum age requirement for the truck at the time of applying for a license, and in such cases the validity of the technical inspections tends to be longer than in countries where trucks are generally older and require more frequent checking.

Markets

This year the markets topic continued to collect data on regulations impacting contract farming arrangements, but determined not to assign any scores due to methodological constraints and the lack of recognized regulatory best practices.

The concept of contract farming covers many different types of arrangements. Typically, a farmer or a group of farmers commits to provide, at a future date, an agreed quantity of a specific product that meets certain quality standards. In turn, the buyer commits to buy the product and, usually, to support production through the supply of farm inputs, the provision of credit, land preparation and/or the provision of technical advice.[9]

Evidence suggests that contract farming has been in use since at least the 19th century across various countries and sectors. Over time, contract farming has become more widespread and several studies indicate that it now governs more than one-third of agricultural production in the United States, three-quarters of Brazil's poultry production and 40% of Vietnam's rice sales; it has also emerged as a growing practice in China, India, Latin America and several African countries.[10] The global spread of contract farming stems from a range of factors, but particularly from changes in consumer preferences and needs prompted by rising incomes and increased urbanization. This trend has led agricultural buyers to demand more from producers in terms of supply regularity, as well as safety and quality standards. Contract farming serves as a coordination model whereby the supply of agricultural products is timely, in sufficient quantity and of sufficient quality, and farmers can secure an outlet for their products and receive the inputs, credit and technical assistance necessary to meet buyer requirements.[11] From a development perspective, contract farming has sparked the interest of donors, multilateral organizations and governments of developing countries as a way to link small-scale farmers to domestic and foreign markets, thereby contributing to poverty reduction.[12]

The main challenge involved in developing a global indicator on contract farming relates to the lack of consensus on regulatory best practices, and this stems from the diverse and complex nature of contract farming arrangements in each country context. For example, Morocco's law on *contrats d'agrégation agricole* provides for highly formalized contract farming arrangements concluded between a contractor ("agrégateur") and several producers ("agrégés") around a value-addition unit ("unité de valorisation") for designated products.[13] By contrast, in Cambodia, individual producers and buyers can conclude agricultural production contracts for any type of crop or animal product, and those contracts may take the form of market-specifications contracts, production-management contracts or resource-providing contracts.[14] These contract farming laws differ in scope as they pursue policy goals that are context-specific, such as the focus on value-addition investments in the case of Morocco.

Local fruit stand, Armenia Photo: Flore de Préneuf / The World Bank.

Furthermore, only a minority of countries has adopted laws and regulations that specifically address contract farming arrangements: 9 of the 62 countries analyzed this year have such rules, while the remaining 53 rely solely on general contract law and default rules that fill contractual gaps.[15] There is no evidence to indicate that contract farming arrangements do better or worse depending on whether specific regulations exist. Proponents of the general contract law approach argue that the parties themselves are best-placed to define the contractual terms in their business relationships.[16] In this context, soft law instruments, such as recommendations or codes of practices, may be more suitable than government regulations to promote fair and efficient contractual practices between producers and buyers of agricultural products.[17] However, comparing and assessing those types of private sector- or civil society-led soft law instruments go beyond the scope of EBA's focus on regulatory indicators.

Among the nine countries that have adopted contract farming regulations, certain "better" practices were identified. For example, all countries but Zimbabwe explicitly require contracts to be in writing, although in Zimbabwe the obligation on buyers to submit detailed schedules of their contractual agreements to the Agricultural Marketing Authority could serve the same purpose as written contracts.[18] By contrast, of the 53 countries where contract farming arrangements are governed by general contract law, only 8 require that the agricultural production contract be made in writing and 6 have the same requirement for contracts above a certain amount. Written contracts can improve the clarity, completeness, and enforceability of the parties' rights and obligations, and they serve an important evidentiary purpose in the context of any related court proceedings.[19]

Another key issue in the contract farming context relates to contract duration. Because agricultural production contracts may require significant investments and the crop production cycle may require a long-term relationship, a legal obligation to comply with a minimum duration can make up for a lack of or unclear contractual agreement on the timeframe to carry out certain performance obligations.[20] Only 3 of 62 countries studied in *EBA17* establish a minimum duration for agricultural production contracts and all of them have adopted laws that specifically address contract farming arrangements. In Morocco,[21] for example, aggregation contracts must be concluded for a duration of at least five years, with the possibility to terminate them, while in India (Maharashtra),[22] the mandatory minimum duration is set at one cropping season, without the possibility to terminate.

Four of the nine countries with specific contract farming rules have also established special commodity- or sector-specific institutions that offer alternative dispute resolution mechanisms to enforce agricultural contracts. Such tailored mechanisms can be particularly beneficial due to the sector-specific knowledge and expertise developed by the institution.[23] In Cambodia, for example, the Contract-based Agricultural Production Committee, which is composed mostly of public sector representatives, is mandated to help solve any conflict or problem in the implementation of agricultural production contracts.[24] In Zimbabwe, the Grain and Oilseeds Technical Committee, in which private sector stakeholders are largely represented, determines any disputes arising from grain and oilseeds contracts, and its decisions can be appealed to the Agricultural Marketing Authority Board.[25]

Figure D.2 | Strongest regulation of water user organizations (WUOs) evident in lower-middle-income countries

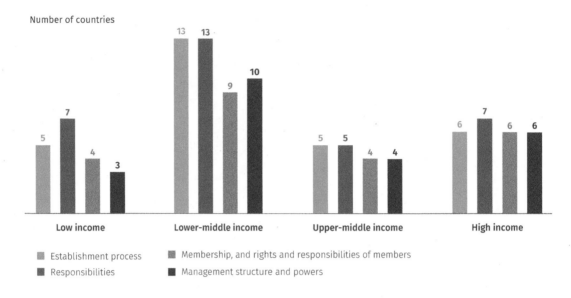

Number of countries

Low income: 5, 7, 4, 3
Lower-middle income: 13, 13, 9, 10
Upper-middle income: 5, 5, 4, 4
High income: 6, 7, 6, 6

- Establishment process
- Responsibilities
- Membership, and rights and responsibilities of members
- Management structure and powers

Source: EBA database.

Water

This year, the EBA water topic collected exploratory data on collective water use in irrigation schemes and, although it will not be scored this year, this information will inform the future development of a collective water use indicator, to mirror the current individual water use indicator. Across countries, many farms rely on large-scale, publicly provided irrigation schemes to supply water, and one trend in this realm is the development of water user organizations (WUOs). Alternatively known as irrigation associations, user associations, or water user associations, WUOs may be defined as "non-governmental organizations that farmers and other water users form to manage an irrigation system at the local or regional level."[26] Among the countries studied, 14 have enacted specific independent legislation to govern WUOs and another 31 have at least some mention of WUOs in their broader legal frameworks. Further information was collected on the establishment process, responsibilities, powers and membership requirements for decentralized management of irrigation infrastructure (figure D.2).

Moving forward, the water topic aims to further explore issues related to transboundary waters that span national borders and the interface between customary practices and legislative requirements for water management and use by smallholders. As a starting point, this year the water topic collected data on exemptions from permit requirements for smallholders. This area will be explored for possible expansion in coming years.

ICT

This year the information and communication technology (ICT) topic collected data on additional areas that impact access to ICT in rural areas, but ultimately these areas were not scored due to the importance of country context or because government regulation is not always of direct relevance. Universal access or service funds, programs aimed at reducing the cost of smartphone devices, and tariff plans to address the usage needs of rural subscribers were some areas that the ICT topic investigated.

The "last mile" of telecommunication infrastructure in rural areas is typically provided at a very high cost, which, in some cases, may not be commercially justifiable based on projected use and potential economic impact.[27] Mobile and broadband service providers in rural areas often face high capital requirements and operating expenses, and have few incentives to invest given the relatively low rate of return as compared with more densely populated areas. One of the key challenges for governments, therefore, is to put in place appropriate financing mechanisms to support ICT development in rural areas.

Universal access/service funds are one of the most popular mechanisms for generating funds from multiple sources, including contributions from mobile operators, international organizations and government budgets. Mobile operators contribute to the universal access/service funds as part of their mandatory universal service obligations. In most countries, universal

Figure D.3 | Universal Access/Service Fund exists in 36 countries

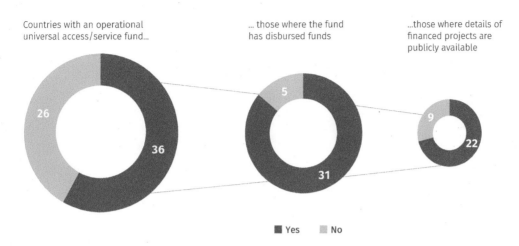

Countries with an operational universal access/service fund...

26 / 36

... those where the fund has disbursed funds

5 / 31

...those where details of financed projects are publicly available

9 / 22

■ Yes   ■ No

Source: EBA database.

access/service funds are created for ICT development projects that differ from country-to-country, depending on overarching policy goals.

Well-managed universal access/service funds help to expand ICT coverage in otherwise commercially unviable areas, but it is critical that the funds collected through the universal access/service funds are directed towards the development of ICT projects.[28] Failures to disburse money point to weak governance and accountability structures in fund management and resource allocation.[29] Efficient management of universal access/service funds is demonstrated by disbursing the money collected in a meaningful and transparent manner.[30] Similar to this, details on a universal access/service fund's projects and procedures should be provided to the public. Of the 62 countries studied, 36 have established a fund. Among these, five countries (Bangladesh, Burkina Faso, Cameroon, Egypt, and Niger) have operational funds that have never disbursed money for ICT development projects (figure D.3). Nine of the 36 countries with such funds (Guatemala, Mali, Morocco, Mozambique, Nepal, Sri Lanka, Sudan, Turkey and Zambia) do not make any information on projects financed by the fund public.[31]

Affordability greatly impacts the uptake of ICT technologies in the agriculture sector. The high costs of ICT solutions, including the costs of mobile devices (particularly smartphone devices) and mobile service charges, can be prohibitive for smallholder farmers,[32] reducing their ability to capitalize on the benefits of mobile agriculture. Although countries differ in their needs and approaches to tackle affordability gaps, targeted interventions to alleviate costs can be critical in expanding farmers' access to ICT.[33] This is particularly the case in countries with large rural populations and high poverty levels.[34]

Although governments often take the lead in initiatives to stimulate ICT access for undeserved communities, the private sector can also play a significant role. In Malaysia, for example, to accelerate the uptake of mobile broadband services, the Malaysian Communications and Multimedia Commission introduced the "Smart Device with Internet Package" initiative in 2014. The program aims at offering smartphones for subscribers in rural areas at a lower-than-retail price along with a mobile data subscription for one year.[35] In India, the private sector has taken a greater role in expanding coverage to rural areas. Given the high proportion of the population living in rural areas and the proportionately low mobile internet market penetration, mobile operators have an incentive to unlock a high potential subscribers' market. In a recent effort to increase coverage in remote areas, in 2008 Bharti Airtel Limited and the Indian Farmers Fertilizer Cooperative Limited (IFFCO) launched a joint venture that offers daily services tailored to farmers, including unique value-added services (for example, mobile applications) on commodity prices, farming techniques, weather forecasts, dairy farming, animal husbandry, rural health initiatives and fertilizer availability. Within the framework of this venture, Bharti Airtel provides lowered calling rates for calls between IFFCO members.[36] As a result an estimated 200,000 new rural connections are activated per month.[37] Similarly, in 2015 telecommunications operator BSNL Maharashtra developed the Maha Krishi Sanchar plan—a specifically designed, prepaid mobile tariff plan covering all farmers and employees of the State Department of Agriculture.

NOTES

1 FAOSTAT database.

2 Minde et al. 2008.

3 Druilhe and Barreiro-Hurlé 2012.

4 Kienzle et al. 2013.

5 Zander, Miller and Mhlanga 2013.

6 Rani and Garg 2015.

7 "Own account" designates a company transporting its own goods and using its own means to do so, as opposed to offering the service commercially to third parties.

8 International Road Transport Union 2007.

9 UNIDROIT, FAO and IFAD 2015.

10 Da Silva 2005.

11 UNIDROIT, FAO and IFAD 2015.

12 FAO 2013.

13 Dahir n°1-12-15 du 25 chaabane 1433 (17 juillet 2012) portant promulgation de la loi n°04-12 relative à l'agrégation agricole; Arrêté conjoint du ministre de l'agriculture et de la pêche maritime, du ministre de l'intérieur et du ministre de l'économie et des finance n°3073-14 du 12 kaada 1435 (8 septembre 2014) fixant les formes et les modalités d'approbation des projets d'agrégation agricole et de délivrance des attestations d'agrégation agricole.

14 Sub-Decree on Contract Farming, No. 36 of 24 February 2011; A "market-specification contract" specifies marketing information about demand, quality, timing, and price, a "production-management contract" covers those specifications and also specifies the cultivation practices necessary to achieve quality, timing, and price, and a "resource-providing contract" covers those specifications and also includes the provision of credit, inputs and/or extension services (FAO 2013).

15 UNIDROIT, FAO and IFAD 2015.

16 World Bank 2014.

17 UNIDROIT, FAO and IFAD 2015.

18 Agricultural Marketing Authority (Grain, Oilseed and Products) By-laws, 2013 (Statutory Instrument 140 of 2013), Art. 9(2)b.

19 UNIDROIT, FAO and IFAD 2015.

20 *Ibid.*

21 Arrêté n°3073-14 du 8 septembre 2014 fixant les formes et les modalités d'approbation des projets d'agrégation agricole et de délivrance des attestations d'agrégation agricole.

22 Maharashtra Agricultural Produce Marketing Act (1963) (as amended).

23 UNIDROIT, FAO and IFAD 2015; World Bank 2014.

24 Sub-Decree on Contract Farming, No. 36 of 24 February 2011.

25 Agricultural Marketing Authority (Grain, Oilseed and Products) By-laws, 2013 (Statutory Instrument 140 of 2013).

26 Vapnek et al. 2009.

27 World Bank 2011.

28 ITU 2013.

29 Williams 2016.

30 GSMA 2013.

31 Magiera 2009.

32 GSMA 2015a.

33 FAO and ITU 2016.

34 GSMA 2015b.

35 EBA data, http://www.skmm.gov.my/Sectors/Universal-Service-Provision/Distribution-of-all-projects-by-State.aspx.

36 EBA data, http://www.airtel.in/about-bharti/media-centre/bharti-airtel-news/corporate/pg_iffco+and+bharti+airtel+-join+hands+to+usher+in+the+second+green+revolution+to+benefit+millions+of+rural+consumers.

37 GSMA 2016a.

REFERENCES

Da Silva, C. 2005. "The Growing Role of Contract Farming in Agri-food Systems Development: Drivers, Theory and Practice." FAO (Food and Agriculture Organization), Rome.

Druilhe, Z. and J. Barreiro-Hurlé. 2012. "Fertilizer Subsidies in Sub-Saharan Africa." ESA Working Paper No. 12-04. FAO, Rome.

FAO (Food and Agriculture Organization). 2013. "Contract Farming for Inclusive Market Access." FAO, Rome.

FAO and ITU (International Telecommunication Union). 2016. *E-agriculture Strategy Guide. Piloted in Asia Pacific Countries.* Bangkok: FAO and ITU.

GSMA. 2013. "Universal Service Fund Study." GSMA, London.

———. 2015a. "Agricultural Value-added Services (Agri VAS): Market Opportunity and Emerging Business Models." GSMA, London.

———. 2015b. "The Mobile Economy. Sub-Saharan Africa 2015." GSMA, London.

———. 2016. "Case Study. IFFCO Kisan Agriculture App. Evolution to Data Driven Services in Agriculture." GSMA, London.

International Road Transport Union. 2007. "IRU Position on Access to the Profession of Road Passenger and Goods Transport Operator – Approved by the IRU General Assembly in Geneva on 13 April 2007." Informal document N°1 for the 101st session, Geneva.

ITU (International Telecommunication Union). 2013. *Universal Service Fund and Digital Inclusion for All.* Geneva: ITU.

Kienzle, J., J. Ashburner and B. G. Sims. 2013. "Mechanization for Rural Development: A Review of Patterns and Progress from Around the World." Rome, FAO.

Magiera, S. 2009. "Managing Universal Service Funds for Telecommunications. An ASEAN Manual for Output-Based Aid." United States Agency for International Development (USAID).

Minde, I., T. S. Jayne, E. Crawford, J. Ariga, and J. Govereh. 2008. "Promoting Fertilizer Use in Africa: Current Issues and Empirical Evidence from Malawi, Zambia, and Kenya." ReSAKSS Working Paper 13. International Crops Research Institute for the Semiarid Tropics (ICRISAT), International Food Policy Research Institute (IFPRI) and International Water Management Institute (IWMI), Pretoria, South Africa.

Rani, S., and D. Garg. 2015. "Priority Sector Lending: Trends, Issues and Strategies." *International Journal of Management and Social Sciences Research* (IJMSSR) 4: (1), January.

UNIDROIT, FAO, and IFAD. 2015. "UNIDROIT/FAO/IFAD Legal Guide on Contract Farming." UNIDROIT, FAO and IFAD, Rome.

Vapnek, J., B. Aylward, C. Popp and J. Bartram. 2009. "Law for Water Management: A Guide to Concepts and Effective Approaches." Legislative Study 101. FAO, Rome.

Williams, I. 2016. "Co-Financing of Bottom-Up Approaches towards Broadband Infrastructure Development: A New Opportunity for Universal Service Funding." *Journal of NBICT* 1: 39–64.

World Bank. 2011. *ICT in Agriculture, Connecting Smallholders to Knowledge, Networks, and Institutions.* e-Sourcebook. Report 64605. Washington, DC: World Bank.

———. 2014. *An Analytical Toolkit for Support to Contract Farming.*" Washington, DC: World Bank.

Zander, R., C. Miller and N. Mhlanga. 2013. "Credit Guarantee Systems for Agriculture and Rural Enterprise Development." FAO, Rome.

Country Tables

| Country Code | Country Name | General | | Water | Transport |
		Region	Income Group	Predominant Water Source for Irrigation (FAO Aquastat)	Reference product
ARM	Armenia	Europe & Central Asia	Lower middle income	Surface Water	Fruits (e.g. apricots)
BDI	Burundi	Sub-Saharan Africa	Low income	Surface Water	Coffee
BEN	Benin	Sub-Saharan Africa	Low income	Surface Water	Cashew nuts
BFA	Burkina Faso	Sub-Saharan Africa	Low income	Surface Water	Cashew nuts
BGD	Bangladesh	South Asia	Lower middle income	Groundwater	Nuts
BIH	Bosnia and Herzegovina	Europe & Central Asia	Upper middle income	Surface Water	Vegetables (e.g. cucumbers)
BOL	Bolivia	Latin America & Caribbean	Lower middle income	Surface Water	Cereals (e.g. buckwheat)
CHL	Chile	High income: OECD	High income	Surface Water	Fruits (e.g. grapes)
CIV	Côte d'Ivoire	Sub-Saharan Africa	Lower middle income	Surface Water	Cocoa beans
CMR	Cameroon	Sub-Saharan Africa	Lower middle income	Surface Water	Cocoa Beans
COL	Colombia	Latin America & Caribbean	Upper middle income	Surface Water	Coffee
DNK	Denmark	High income: OECD	High income	Groundwater	Cereals (e.g. barley)
EGY	Egypt, Arab Rep.	Middle East & North Africa	Lower middle income	Surface Water	Fruit (e.g. grapefruit)
ESP	Spain	High income: OECD	High income	Surface Water	Fruits (e.g. mandarins)
ETH	Ethiopia	Sub-Saharan Africa	Low income	Surface Water	Coffee
GEO	Georgia	Europe & Central Asia	Upper middle income	Surface Water	Cereals (e.g. wheat)
GHA	Ghana	Sub-Saharan Africa	Lower middle income	Surface Water	Cocoa beans
GRC	Greece	High income: OECD	High income	Surface Water	Fruits (e.g. grapes)
GTM	Guatemala	Latin America & Caribbean	Lower middle income	Surface Water	Fruits (e.g. bananas)
HTI	Haiti	Latin America & Caribbean	Low income	Surface Water	Fruits
IND	India	South Asia	Lower middle income	Groundwater	Cereals (e.g. rice)
ITA	Italy	High income: OECD	High income	Surface Water	Fruits (e.g. apples)
JOR	Jordan	Middle East & North Africa	Upper middle income	Groundwater	Vegetables (e.g. tomatoes)
KAZ	Kazakhstan	Europe & Central Asia	Upper middle income	Surface Water	Cereals
KEN	Kenya	Sub-Saharan Africa	Lower middle income	Surface Water	Tea
KGZ	Kyrgyz Republic	Europe & Central Asia	Lower middle income	Surface Water	Beans
KHM	Cambodia	East Asia & Pacific	Lower middle income	Surface Water	Cereals (e.g. rice)
KOR	Korea, Rep.	High income: OECD	High income	Surface Water	Vegetables (e.g. pepper)
LAO	Lao PDR	East Asia & Pacific	Lower middle income	Surface Water	Coffee
LBR	Liberia	Sub-Saharan Africa	Low income	Surface Water	Cocoa beans
LKA	Sri Lanka	South Asia	Lower middle income	Surface Water	Tea
MAR	Morocco	Middle East & North Africa	Lower middle income	Surface Water	Vegetables (e.g. tomatoes)
MEX	Mexico	Latin America & Caribbean	Upper middle income	Surface Water	Vegetables (e.g. tomatoes)
MLI	Mali	Sub-Saharan Africa	Low income	Surface Water	Fruits (e.g. mangoes)
MMR	Myanmar	East Asia & Pacific	Lower middle income	Surface Water	Beans
MOZ	Mozambique	Sub-Saharan Africa	Low income	Surface Water	Fruits (e.g. bananas)
MWI	Malawi	Sub-Saharan Africa	Low income	Surface Water	Tea
MYS	Malaysia	East Asia & Pacific	Upper middle income	Surface Water	Vegetables
NER	Niger	Sub-Saharan Africa	Low income	Surface Water	Vegetables (e.g. onions)
NGA	Nigeria	Sub-Saharan Africa	Lower middle income	Surface Water	Cocoa beans
NIC	Nicaragua	Latin America & Caribbean	Lower middle income	Groundwater	Coffee
NLD	Netherlands	High income: OECD	High income	Groundwater	Vegetables (e.g. tomatoes)
NPL	Nepal	South Asia	Low income	Surface Water	Cardamoms
PER	Peru	Latin America & Caribbean	Upper middle income	Surface Water	Coffee
PHL	Philippines	East Asia & Pacific	Lower middle income	Surface Water	Fruits (e.g. bananas)
POL	Poland	High income: OECD	High income	Surface Water	Cereals (e.g. wheat)
ROM	Romania	Europe & Central Asia	Upper middle income	Surface Water	Cereals (e.g. wheat)
RUS	Russian Federation	Europe & Central Asia	Upper middle income	Surface Water	Cereals (e.g. wheat)
RWA	Rwanda	Sub-Saharan Africa	Low income	Surface Water	Tea
SDN	Sudan	Sub-Saharan Africa	Lower middle income	Surface Water	Carob gum
SEN	Senegal	Sub-Saharan Africa	Low income	Surface Water	Cereals (e.g. rice)
SRB	Serbia	Europe & Central Asia	Upper middle income	Surface Water	Cereals (e.g. maize)
THA	Thailand	East Asia & Pacific	Upper middle income	Surface Water	Vegetables (e.g. cassava)
TJK	Tajikistan	Europe & Central Asia	Lower middle income	Surface Water	Fruits (e.g. dried apricots)
TUR	Turkey	Europe & Central Asia	Upper middle income	Surface Water	Fruits (e.g. mandarins)
TZA	Tanzania	Sub-Saharan Africa	Low income	Surface Water	Cashew nuts
UGA	Uganda	Sub-Saharan Africa	Low income	Surface Water	Coffee
UKR	Ukraine	Europe & Central Asia	Lower middle income	Surface Water	Cereals (e.g. maize)
URY	Uruguay	Latin America & Caribbean	High income	Surface Water	Soya beans
VNM	Vietnam	East Asia & Pacific	Lower middle income	Surface Water	Cereals (e.g. rice)
ZMB	Zambia	Sub-Saharan Africa	Lower middle income	Surface Water	Cereals (e.g. maize)
ZWE	Zimbabwe	Sub-Saharan Africa	Low income	Surface Water	Tea

Trading partner	Markets Product group	HS 4-digit Product	Trading Partner
Georgia	Fruit	Stone fruit, fresh (apricot, cherry, plum, peach, etc.)	Russian Federation
Tanzania	Cash crop	Coffee, coffee husks and skins and coffee substitutes	Switzerland
Nigeria	Fruit	Coconuts, Brazil nuts and cashew nuts, fresh or dried	India
Côte d'Ivoire	Fruit	Coconuts, Brazil nuts and cashew nuts, fresh or dried	Singapore
India	Fruit	Nuts except coconut, Brazil and cashew, fresh or dried	India
Serbia	Vegetable	Cucumbers and gherkins, fresh or chilled	Croatia
Argentina	Cereal	Buckwheat, millet and canary seed, other cereals	United States
Argentina	Fruit	Grapes, fresh or dried	United States
Ghana	Cash crop	Cocoa beans, whole or broken, raw or roasted	Netherlands
Congo, Rep.	Cash crop	Cocoa beans, whole or broken, raw or roasted	Netherlands
Ecuador	Cash crop	Coffee, coffee husks and skins and coffee substitutes	United States
Germany	Cereal	Barley	Germany
Libya	Fruit	Citrus fruit, fresh or dried	Saudi Arabia
France	Fruit	Citrus fruit, fresh or dried	Germany
Somalia	Cash crop	Coffee, coffee husks and skins and coffee substitutes	Germany
Russian Federation	Cereal	Wheat and meslin	Armenia
Côte d'Ivoire	Cash crop	Cocoa beans, whole or broken, raw or roasted	Netherlands
Bulgaria	Fruit	Grapes, fresh or dried	Germany
El Salvador	Fruit	Bananas, including plantains, fresh or dried	United States
Dominican Republic	Fruit	Dates, figs, pineapple, avocado, guava, fresh or dried	United States
Nepal	Cereal	Rice	Iran, Islamic Rep.
France	Fruit	Apples, pears and quinces, fresh	Germany
Syrian Arab Republic	Vegetable	Tomatoes, fresh or chilled	Syrian Arab Republic
Uzbekistan	Cereal	Wheat and meslin	Azerbaijan
Uganda	Cash crop	Tea	Pakistan
Kazakhstan	Vegetable	Vegetables, leguminous dried, shelled	Turkey
Vietnam	Cereal	Rice	France
China	Vegetable	Vegetables nes, fresh or chilled	Japan
Thailand	Cash crop	Coffee, coffee husks and skins and coffee substitutes	Japan
Côte d'Ivoire	Cash crop	Cocoa beans, whole or broken, raw or roasted	Germany
India	Cash crop	Tea	Russian Federation
Spain	Vegetable	Tomatoes, fresh or chilled	France
United States	Vegetable	Tomatoes, fresh or chilled	United States
Senegal	Fruit	Dates, figs, pineapple, avocado, guava, fresh or dried	Burkina Faso
China	Vegetable	Vegetables, leguminous dried, shelled	India
South Africa	Fruit	Bananas, including plantains, fresh or dried	South Africa
Tanzania	Cash crop	Tea	South Africa
Indonesia	Vegetable	Vegetables nes, fresh or chilled	Singapore
Nigeria	Vegetable	Onions, shallots, garlic, leeks, etc., fresh or chilled	Ghana
Niger	Cash crop	Cocoa beans, whole or broken, raw or roasted	Barbados
Costa Rica	Cash crop	Coffee, coffee husks and skins and coffee substitutes	United States
Germany	Vegetable	Tomatoes, fresh or chilled	Germany
India	Cash crop	Nutmeg, mace and cardamons	India
Colombia	Cash crop	Coffee, coffee husks and skins and coffee substitutes	Germany
Vietnam	Fruit	Bananas, including plantains, fresh or dried	Japan
Germany	Cereal	Wheat and meslin	Germany
Hungary	Cereal	Wheat and meslin	Spain
China	Cereal	Wheat and meslin	Egypt, Arab Rep.
Uganda	Cash crop	Tea	Kenya
Egypt, Arab Rep.	Cash crop	Locust beans, seaweed, sugar beet, cane, for food	Germany
Mali	Cereal	Rice	Mali
Romania	Cereal	Maize (corn)	Romania
Malaysia	Vegetable	Manioc, arrowroot, salep etc, fresh, dried, sago pith	China
China	Fruit	Fruit, dried, nes, dried fruit and nut mixtures	Russian Federation
Iraq	Fruit	Nuts except coconut, brazil and cashew, fresh or dried	Germany
Kenya	Fruit	Coconuts, Brazil nuts and cashew nuts, fresh or dried	India
Kenya	Cash crop	Coffee, coffee husks and skins and coffee substitutes	Switzerland
Poland	Cereal	Maize (corn)	Egypt, Arab Rep.
Brazil	Cash crop	Soya beans	China
China	Cereal	Rice	Philippines
Zimbabwe	Cereal	Maize (corn)	Zimbabwe
South Africa	Cash crop	Tea	South Africa

ARMENIA

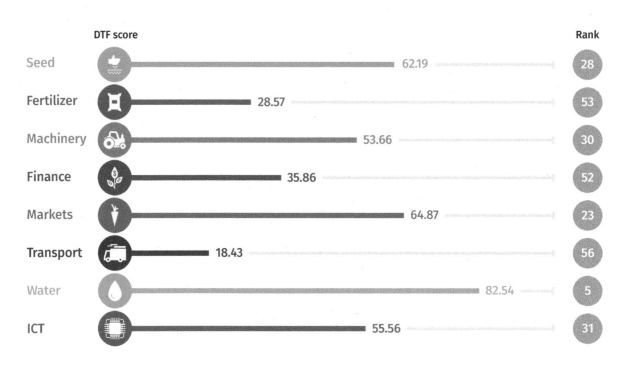

DTF score		Rank
Seed	62.19	28
Fertilizer	28.57	53
Machinery	53.66	30
Finance	35.86	52
Markets	64.87	23
Transport	18.43	56
Water	82.54	5
ICT	55.56	31

SEED[a] | DTF Score 62.19 ◇ Rank 28

Plant breeding index (0-10)	8.0
Variety registration index (0-8)	6.5
Time to register new variety (days)	587
Cost to register new variety (% income per capita)	18.5
Seed quality control index (0-12)	2.0

FERTILIZER | DTF Score 28.57 ◇ Rank 53

Fertilizer registration index (0-7)	0.0
Time to register a new fertilizer product (days)	N/A
Cost to register a new fertilizer product (% income per capita)	N/A
Quality control of fertilizer index (0-7)	2.0
Importing & distributing fertilizer index (0-7)	6.0

MACHINERY | DTF Score 53.66 ◇ Rank 30

Tractor operation index (0-5)	0.5
Time to register a tractor (days)	3
Cost to register a tractor (% income per capita)	0.3
Tractor testing and standards index (0-8)	5.0
Time to obtain type approval (days)	No practice
Cost to obtain type approval (% income per capita)	No practice
Tractor import index (0-5)	5.0

FINANCE | DTF Score 35.86 ◇ Rank 52

Branchless Banking

Agent banking index (0-5)	0.0
E-money index (0-4)	3.8

Movable Collateral

Warehouse receipts index (0-5)	0.0
Doing Business - getting credit index (0-8)	4.0

Non-bank Lending Institutions

Microfinance institutions index (0-7)	0.0
Financial cooperatives index (0-7)	5.0

MARKETS | DTF Score 64.87 ◇ Rank 23

Producer organizations index (0-13)	9.3
Plant protection index (0-8)	3.5
Agricultural trade index (0-9)	5.0
Documents to export agricultural goods (number)	1
Time to export agricultural goods (days)	1
Cost to export agricultural goods (% income per capita)	0.0

TRANSPORT | DTF Score 18.43 ◇ Rank 56

Trucking licenses and operations index (0-11)	2.0
Time to obtain trucking licenses (days)	N/A
Cost to obtain trucking licenses (% income per capita)	N/A
Cross-border transportation index (0-9)	5.0
Time to obtain cross-border license (days)	N/A
Cost to obtain cross-border license (% income per capita)	N/A

WATER | DTF Score 82.54 ◇ Rank 5

Integrated water resource management index (0-29)	22.5
Individual water use for irrigation index (0-20)	17.5

ICT | DTF Score 55.56 ◇ Rank 31

ICT index (0-9)	5.0

a. The indicators apply to the formal seed system only.

BANGLADESH

DTF score   **Rank**

Seed	34.27	54
Fertilizer	54.25	35
Machinery	30.44	49
Finance	56.71	23
Markets	66.10	21
Transport	45.03	45
Water	14.66	56
ICT	50.00	37

SEED[a] | DTF Score 34.27 ◇ Rank 54

Plant breeding index *(0-10)*	6.0
Variety registration index *(0-8)*	5.5
Time to register new variety *(days)*	No practice
Cost to register new variety *(% income per capita)*	No practice
Seed quality control index *(0-12)*	1.0

FERTILIZER | DTF Score 54.25 ◇ Rank 35

Fertilizer registration index *(0-7)*	4.4
Time to register a new fertilizer product *(days)*	945
Cost to register a new fertilizer product *(% income per capita)*	58.8
Quality control of fertilizer index *(0-7)*	4.5
Importing & distributing fertilizer index *(0-7)*	3.0

MACHINERY | DTF Score 30.44 ◇ Rank 49

Tractor operation index *(0-5)*	3.0
Time to register a tractor *(days)*	17
Cost to register a tractor *(% income per capita)*	8.3
Tractor testing and standards index *(0-8)*	0.3
Time to obtain type approval *(days)*	N/A
Cost to obtain type approval *(% income per capita)*	N/A
Tractor import index *(0-5)*	1.5

FINANCE | DTF Score 56.71 ◇ Rank 23

Branchless Banking

Agent banking index *(0-5)*	4.7
E-money index *(0-4)*	1.0

Movable Collateral

Warehouse receipts index *(0-5)*	3.5
Doing Business - getting credit index *(0-8)*	3.0

Non-bank Lending Institutions

Microfinance institutions index *(0-7)*	4.0
Financial cooperatives index *(0-7)*	4.0

MARKETS | DTF Score 66.10 ◇ Rank 21

Producer organizations index *(0-13)*	6.0
Plant protection index *(0-8)*	6.0
Agricultural trade index *(0-9)*	5.0
Documents to export agricultural goods *(number)*	1
Time to export agricultural goods *(days)*	1
Cost to export agricultural goods *(% income per capita)*	0.1

TRANSPORT | DTF Score 45.03 ◇ Rank 45

Trucking licenses and operations index *(0-11)*	4.5
Time to obtain trucking licenses *(days)*	3
Cost to obtain trucking licenses *(% income per capita)*	2.5
Cross-border transportation index *(0-9)*	4.0
Time to obtain cross-border license *(days)*	N/A
Cost to obtain cross-border license *(% income per capita)*	N/A

WATER | DTF Score 14.66 ◇ Rank 56

Integrated water resource management index *(0-29)*	8.5
Individual water use for irrigation index *(0-20)*	0.0

ICT | DTF Score 50.00 ◇ Rank 37

ICT index *(0-9)*	4.5

COUNTRY TABLES

a. The indicators apply to the formal seed system only.

179

BENIN

DTF score | | Rank

	DTF score	Rank
Seed	32.81	55
Fertilizer	14.58	61
Machinery	25.83	53
Finance	43.35	41
Markets	56.14	34
Transport	36.32	50
Water	43.15	38
ICT	55.56	31

SEED[a] | DTF Score 32.81 ◇ Rank 55

Plant breeding index (0-10)	5.0
Variety registration index (0-8)	4.5
Time to register new variety (days)	No practice
Cost to register new variety (% income per capita)	No practice
Seed quality control index (0-12)	3.0

FERTILIZER | DTF Score 14.58 ◇ Rank 61

Fertilizer registration index (0-7)	0.0
Time to register a new fertilizer product (days)	N/A
Cost to register a new fertilizer product (% income per capita)	N/A
Quality control of fertilizer index (0-7)	0.0
Importing & distributing fertilizer index (0-7)	3.5

MACHINERY | DTF Score 25.83 ◇ Rank 53

Tractor operation index (0-5)	0.0
Time to register a tractor (days)	N/A
Cost to register a tractor (% income per capita)	N/A
Tractor testing and standards index (0-8)	2.3
Time to obtain type approval (days)	N/A
Cost to obtain type approval (% income per capita)	N/A
Tractor import index (0-5)	5.0

FINANCE | DTF Score 43.35 ◇ Rank 41

Branchless Banking

Agent banking index (0-5)	0.0
E-money index (0-4)	3.8

Movable Collateral

Warehouse receipts index (0-5)	0.0
Doing Business - getting credit index (0-8)	4.0

Non-bank Lending Institutions

Microfinance institutions index (0-7)	4.0
Financial cooperatives index (0-7)	4.0

MARKETS | DTF Score 56.14 ◇ Rank 34

Producer organizations index (0-13)	7.5
Plant protection index (0-8)	3.0
Agricultural trade index (0-9)	4.5
Documents to export agricultural goods (number)	1
Time to export agricultural goods (days)	2
Cost to export agricultural goods (% income per capita)	1.0

TRANSPORT | DTF Score 36.32 ◇ Rank 50

Trucking licenses and operations index (0-11)	5.0
Time to obtain trucking licenses (days)	40
Cost to obtain trucking licenses (% income per capita)	19.7
Cross-border transportation index (0-9)	5.0
Time to obtain cross-border license (days)	No practice
Cost to obtain cross-border license (% income per capita)	No practice

WATER | DTF Score 43.15 ◇ Rank 38

Integrated water resource management index (0-29)	18.5
Individual water use for irrigation index (0-20)	4.5

ICT | DTF Score 55.56 ◇ Rank 31

ICT index (0-9)	5.0

a. The indicators apply to the formal seed system only.

BOLIVIA

DTF score		Rank
Seed	64.41	25
Fertilizer	39.29	45
Machinery	25.83	52
Finance	67.48	13
Markets	65.51	22
Transport	70.31	15
Water	35.52	43
ICT	58.33	30

SEED[a] | DTF Score 64.41 ◇ Rank 25

Plant breeding index *(0-10)*	7.0
Variety registration index *(0-8)*	5.0
Time to register new variety *(days)*	517
Cost to register new variety *(% income per capita)*	24.5
Seed quality control index *(0-12)*	7.0

FERTILIZER | DTF Score 39.29 ◇ Rank 45

Fertilizer registration index *(0-7)*	1.0
Time to register a new fertilizer product *(days)*	N/A
Cost to register a new fertilizer product *(% income per capita)*	N/A
Quality control of fertilizer index *(0-7)*	7.0
Importing & distributing fertilizer index *(0-7)*	3.0

MACHINERY | DTF Score 25.83 ◇ Rank 52

Tractor operation index *(0-5)*	0.5
Time to register a tractor *(days)*	No practice
Cost to register a tractor *(% income per capita)*	No practice
Tractor testing and standards index *(0-8)*	2.3
Time to obtain type approval *(days)*	N/A
Cost to obtain type approval *(% income per capita)*	N/A
Tractor import index *(0-5)*	4.5

FINANCE | DTF Score 67.48 ◇ Rank 13

Branchless Banking

Agent banking index *(0-5)*	0.0
E-money index *(0-4)*	3.7

Movable Collateral

Warehouse receipts index *(0-5)*	4.5
Doing Business - getting credit index *(0-8)*	3.0

Non-bank Lending Institutions

Microfinance institutions index *(0-7)*	6.0
Financial cooperatives index *(0-7)*	7.0

MARKETS | DTF Score 65.51 ◇ Rank 22

Producer organizations index *(0-13)*	10.8
Plant protection index *(0-8)*	4.0
Agricultural trade index *(0-9)*	5.0
Documents to export agricultural goods *(number)*	1
Time to export agricultural goods *(days)*	2
Cost to export agricultural goods *(% income per capita)*	1.9

TRANSPORT | DTF Score 70.31 ◇ Rank 15

Trucking licenses and operations index *(0-11)*	4.5
Time to obtain trucking licenses *(days)*	5
Cost to obtain trucking licenses *(% income per capita)*	0.2
Cross-border transportation index *(0-9)*	5.0
Time to obtain cross-border license *(days)*	10
Cost to obtain cross-border license *(% income per capita)*	6.2

WATER | DTF Score 35.52 ◇ Rank 43

Integrated water resource management index *(0-29)*	9.0
Individual water use for irrigation index *(0-20)*	8.0

ICT | DTF Score 58.33 ◇ Rank 30

ICT index *(0-9)*	5.3

---

a. The indicators apply to the formal seed system only.

BOSNIA AND HERZEGOVINA

DTF score · Rank

Category	DTF score	Rank
Seed	32.08	56
Fertilizer	96.16	1
Machinery	51.41	34
Finance	23.33	60
Markets	74.89	11
Transport	57.44	32
Water	81.47	6
ICT	55.56	31

SEED[a] | DTF Score 32.08 ◇ Rank 56

Plant breeding index (0-10)	7.0
Variety registration index (0-8)	2.0
Time to register new variety (days)	No practice
Cost to register new variety (% income per capita)	No practice
Seed quality control index (0-12)	4.0

FERTILIZER | DTF Score 96.16 ◇ Rank 1

Fertilizer registration index (0-7)	6.0
Time to register a new fertilizer product (days)	31
Cost to register a new fertilizer product (% income per capita)	0.5
Quality control of fertilizer index (0-7)	7.0
Importing & distributing fertilizer index (0-7)	7.0

MACHINERY | DTF Score 51.41 ◇ Rank 34

Tractor operation index (0-5)	1.0
Time to register a tractor (days)	7
Cost to register a tractor (% income per capita)	13.4
Tractor testing and standards index (0-8)	5.3
Time to obtain type approval (days)	N/A
Cost to obtain type approval (% income per capita)	N/A
Tractor import index (0-5)	5.0

FINANCE | DTF Score 23.33 ◇ Rank 60

Branchless Banking

Agent banking index (0-5)	0.0
E-money index (0-4)	0.0

Movable Collateral

Warehouse receipts index (0-5)	3.3
Doing Business - getting credit index (0-8)	6.0

Non-bank Lending Institutions

Microfinance institutions index (0-7)	0.0
Financial cooperatives index (0-7)	0.0

MARKETS | DTF Score 74.89 ◇ Rank 11

Producer organizations index (0-13)	8.5
Plant protection index (0-8)	6.0
Agricultural trade index (0-9)	6.5
Documents to export agricultural goods (number)	1
Time to export agricultural goods (days)	1
Cost to export agricultural goods (% income per capita)	0.3

TRANSPORT | DTF Score 57.44 ◇ Rank 32

Trucking licenses and operations index (0-11)	6.5
Time to obtain trucking licenses (days)	90
Cost to obtain trucking licenses (% income per capita)	6.0
Cross-border transportation index (0-9)	6.0
Time to obtain cross-border license (days)	38
Cost to obtain cross-border license (% income per capita)	6.8

WATER | DTF Score 81.47 ◇ Rank 6

Integrated water resource management index (0-29)	25.5
Individual water use for irrigation index (0-20)	15.0

ICT | DTF Score 55.56 ◇ Rank 31

ICT index (0-9)	5.0

a. The indicators apply to the formal seed system only.

ENABLING THE BUSINESS OF AGRICULTURE 2017

BURKINA FASO

DTF score | | Rank

Category	DTF score	Rank
Seed	28.96	57
Fertilizer	23.21	56
Machinery	52.63	32
Finance	43.35	41
Markets	54.63	37
Transport	72.23	12
Water	31.16	47
ICT	27.78	59

SEED[a] | DTF Score 28.96 ◇ Rank 57

Plant breeding index *(0-10)*	2.0
Variety registration index *(0-8)*	4.0
Time to register new variety *(days)*	No practice
Cost to register new variety *(% income per capita)*	No practice
Seed quality control index *(0-12)*	5.5

FERTILIZER | DTF Score 23.21 ◇ Rank 56

Fertilizer registration index *(0-7)*	0.0
Time to register a new fertilizer product *(days)*	N/A
Cost to register a new fertilizer product *(% income per capita)*	N/A
Quality control of fertilizer index *(0-7)*	3.5
Importing & distributing fertilizer index *(0-7)*	3.0

MACHINERY | DTF Score 52.63 ◇ Rank 32

Tractor operation index *(0-5)*	2.5
Time to register a tractor *(days)*	30
Cost to register a tractor *(% income per capita)*	5.6
Tractor testing and standards index *(0-8)*	3.3
Time to obtain type approval *(days)*	4
Cost to obtain type approval *(% income per capita)*	11.1
Tractor import index *(0-5)*	1.5

FINANCE | DTF Score 43.35 ◇ Rank 41

Branchless Banking

Agent banking index *(0-5)*	0.0
E-money index *(0-4)*	3.8

Movable Collateral

Warehouse receipts index *(0-5)*	0.0
Doing Business - getting credit index *(0-8)*	4.0

Non-bank Lending Institutions

Microfinance institutions index *(0-7)*	4.0
Financial cooperatives index *(0-7)*	4.0

MARKETS | DTF Score 54.63 ◇ Rank 37

Producer organizations index *(0-13)*	9.8
Plant protection index *(0-8)*	2.0
Agricultural trade index *(0-9)*	5.0
Documents to export agricultural goods *(number)*	2
Time to export agricultural goods *(days)*	2
Cost to export agricultural goods *(% income per capita)*	2.2

TRANSPORT | DTF Score 72.23 ◇ Rank 12

Trucking licenses and operations index *(0-11)*	4.5
Time to obtain trucking licenses *(days)*	1
Cost to obtain trucking licenses *(% income per capita)*	3.0
Cross-border transportation index *(0-9)*	5.0
Time to obtain cross-border license *(days)*	1
Cost to obtain cross-border license *(% income per capita)*	3.3

WATER | DTF Score 31.16 ◇ Rank 47

Integrated water resource management index *(0-29)*	13.0
Individual water use for irrigation index *(0-20)*	3.5

ICT | DTF Score 27.78 ◇ Rank 59

ICT index *(0-9)*	2.5

a. The indicators apply to the formal seed system only.

COUNTRY TABLES

183

BURUNDI

SUB-SAHARAN AFRICA
LOW INCOME

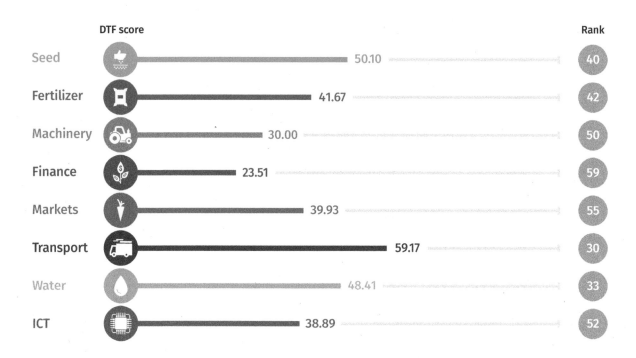

DTF score | | Rank

Seed	50.10	40
Fertilizer	41.67	42
Machinery	30.00	50
Finance	23.51	59
Markets	39.93	55
Transport	59.17	30
Water	48.41	33
ICT	38.89	52

SEED[a] | DTF Score 50.10 ◇ Rank 40

Plant breeding index (0-10)	9.0
Variety registration index (0-8)	3.5
Time to register new variety (days)	No practice
Cost to register new variety (% income per capita)	No practice
Seed quality control index (0-12)	8.0

FERTILIZER | DTF Score 41.67 ◇ Rank 42

Fertilizer registration index (0-7)	3.0
Time to register a new fertilizer product (days)	No practice
Cost to register a new fertilizer product (% income per capita)	No practice
Quality control of fertilizer index (0-7)	4.0
Importing & distributing fertilizer index (0-7)	4.0

MACHINERY | DTF Score 30.00 ◇ Rank 50

Tractor operation index (0-5)	2.5
Time to register a tractor (days)	No practice
Cost to register a tractor (% income per capita)	No practice
Tractor testing and standards index (0-8)	0.0
Time to obtain type approval (days)	N/A
Cost to obtain type approval (% income per capita)	N/A
Tractor import index (0-5)	5.0

FINANCE | DTF Score 23.51 ◇ Rank 59

Branchless Banking

Agent banking index (0-5)	0.0
E-money index (0-4)	0.0

Movable Collateral

Warehouse receipts index (0-5)	0.0
Doing Business - getting credit index (0-8)	1.0

Non-bank Lending Institutions

Microfinance institutions index (0-7)	5.0
Financial cooperatives index (0-7)	4.0

MARKETS | DTF Score 39.93 ◇ Rank 55

Producer organizations index (0-13)	7.0
Plant protection index (0-8)	3.0
Agricultural trade index (0-9)	3.0
Documents to export agricultural goods (number)	4
Time to export agricultural goods (days)	4
Cost to export agricultural goods (% income per capita)	3.1

TRANSPORT | DTF Score 59.17 ◇ Rank 30

Trucking licenses and operations index (0-11)	3.0
Time to obtain trucking licenses (days)	1
Cost to obtain trucking licenses (% income per capita)	4.6
Cross-border transportation index (0-9)	6.0
Time to obtain cross-border license (days)	1
Cost to obtain cross-border license (% income per capita)	76.9

WATER | DTF Score 48.41 ◇ Rank 33

Integrated water resource management index (0-29)	8.5
Individual water use for irrigation index (0-20)	13.5

ICT | DTF Score 38.89 ◇ Rank 52

ICT index (0-9)	3.5

a. The indicators apply to the formal seed system only.

ENABLING THE BUSINESS OF AGRICULTURE 2017

184

CAMBODIA

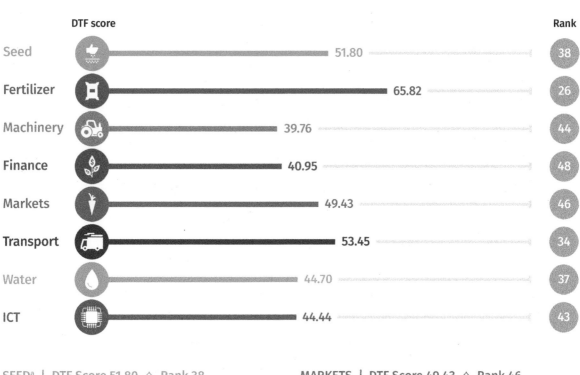

	DTF score	Rank
Seed	51.80	38
Fertilizer	65.82	26
Machinery	39.76	44
Finance	40.95	48
Markets	49.43	46
Transport	53.45	34
Water	44.70	37
ICT	44.44	43

SEED[a] | DTF Score 51.80 ◇ Rank 38

Plant breeding index *(0-10)*	8.0
Variety registration index *(0-8)*	2.0
Time to register new variety *(days)*	407
Cost to register new variety *(% income per capita)*	17.3
Seed quality control index *(0-12)*	3.0

FERTILIZER | DTF Score 65.82 ◇ Rank 26

Fertilizer registration index *(0-7)*	3.4
Time to register a new fertilizer product *(days)*	152
Cost to register a new fertilizer product *(% income per capita)*	107.8
Quality control of fertilizer index *(0-7)*	5.0
Importing & distributing fertilizer index *(0-7)*	4.0

MACHINERY | DTF Score 39.76 ◇ Rank 44

Tractor operation index *(0-5)*	2.5
Time to register a tractor *(days)*	14
Cost to register a tractor *(% income per capita)*	22.5
Tractor testing and standards index *(0-8)*	0.3
Time to obtain type approval *(days)*	N/A
Cost to obtain type approval *(% income per capita)*	N/A
Tractor import index *(0-5)*	5.0

FINANCE | DTF Score 40.95 ◇ Rank 48

Branchless Banking

Agent banking index *(0-5)*	3.6
E-money index *(0-4)*	0.0

Movable Collateral

Warehouse receipts index *(0-5)*	0.0
Doing Business - getting credit index *(0-8)*	7.0

Non-bank Lending Institutions

Microfinance institutions index *(0-7)*	6.0
Financial cooperatives index *(0-7)*	0.0

MARKETS | DTF Score 49.43 ◇ Rank 46

Producer organizations index *(0-13)*	8.8
Plant protection index *(0-8)*	3.0
Agricultural trade index *(0-9)*	5.5
Documents to export agricultural goods *(number)*	2
Time to export agricultural goods *(days)*	6
Cost to export agricultural goods *(% income per capita)*	5.2

TRANSPORT | DTF Score 53.45 ◇ Rank 34

Trucking licenses and operations index *(0-11)*	4.0
Time to obtain trucking licenses *(days)*	8
Cost to obtain trucking licenses *(% income per capita)*	37.0
Cross-border transportation index *(0-9)*	5.0
Time to obtain cross-border license *(days)*	7
Cost to obtain cross-border license *(% income per capita)*	22.5

WATER | DTF Score 44.70 ◇ Rank 37

Integrated water resource management index *(0-29)*	16.5
Individual water use for irrigation index *(0-20)*	6.5

ICT | DTF Score 44.44 ◇ Rank 43

ICT index *(0-9)*	4.0

a. The indicators apply to the formal seed system only.

185

CAMEROON

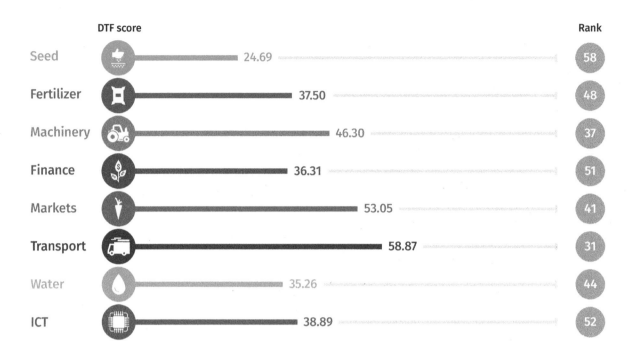

DTF score	Rank

	DTF score	Rank
Seed	24.69	58
Fertilizer	37.50	48
Machinery	46.30	37
Finance	36.31	51
Markets	53.05	41
Transport	58.87	31
Water	35.26	44
ICT	38.89	52

SEED[a] | DTF Score 24.69 ◇ Rank 58

Plant breeding index (0-10)	3.0
Variety registration index (0-8)	3.5
Time to register new variety (days)	No practice
Cost to register new variety (% income per capita)	No practice
Seed quality control index (0-12)	3.0

FERTILIZER | DTF Score 37.50 ◇ Rank 48

Fertilizer registration index (0-7)	0.0
Time to register a new fertilizer product (days)	N/A
Cost to register a new fertilizer product (% income per capita)	N/A
Quality control of fertilizer index (0-7)	3.5
Importing & distributing fertilizer index (0-7)	6.0

MACHINERY | DTF Score 46.30 ◇ Rank 37

Tractor operation index (0-5)	2.5
Time to register a tractor (days)	No practice
Cost to register a tractor (% income per capita)	No practice
Tractor testing and standards index (0-8)	6.5
Time to obtain type approval (days)	90
Cost to obtain type approval (% income per capita)	270.7
Tractor import index (0-5)	2.0

FINANCE | DTF Score 36.31 ◇ Rank 51

Branchless Banking

Agent banking index (0-5)	0.0
E-money index (0-4)	1.0

Movable Collateral

Warehouse receipts index (0-5)	0.0
Doing Business - getting credit index (0-8)	4.0

Non-bank Lending Institutions

Microfinance institutions index (0-7)	5.0
Financial cooperatives index (0-7)	5.0

MARKETS | DTF Score 53.05 ◇ Rank 41

Producer organizations index (0-13)	10.0
Plant protection index (0-8)	4.0
Agricultural trade index (0-9)	2.0
Documents to export agricultural goods (number)	1
Time to export agricultural goods (days)	8
Cost to export agricultural goods (% income per capita)	0.7

TRANSPORT | DTF Score 58.87 ◇ Rank 31

Trucking licenses and operations index (0-11)	5.8
Time to obtain trucking licenses (days)	65
Cost to obtain trucking licenses (% income per capita)	2.3
Cross-border transportation index (0-9)	7.0
Time to obtain cross-border license (days)	60
Cost to obtain cross-border license (% income per capita)	1.4

WATER | DTF Score 35.26 ◇ Rank 44

Integrated water resource management index (0-29)	4.5
Individual water use for irrigation index (0-20)	11.0

ICT | DTF Score 38.89 ◇ Rank 52

ICT index (0-9)	3.5

a. The indicators apply to the formal seed system only.

CHILE

OECD HIGH INCOME
HIGH INCOME

DTF score

Category	DTF score	Rank
Seed	61.77	29
Fertilizer	26.79	54
Machinery	54.70	28
Finance	42.62	46
Markets	76.41	9
Transport	44.44	46
Water	55.17	28
ICT	72.22	15

SEED[a] | DTF Score 61.77 ◇ Rank 29

Plant breeding index (0-10)	9.0
Variety registration index (0-8)	6.0
Time to register new variety (days)	848
Cost to register new variety (% income per capita)	12.5
Seed quality control index (0-12)	4.0

FERTILIZER | DTF Score 26.79 ◇ Rank 54

Fertilizer registration index (0-7)	0.0
Time to register a new fertilizer product (days)	N/A
Cost to register a new fertilizer product (% income per capita)	N/A
Quality control of fertilizer index (0-7)	3.5
Importing & distributing fertilizer index (0-7)	4.0

MACHINERY | DTF Score 54.70 ◇ Rank 28

Tractor operation index (0-5)	4.0
Time to register a tractor (days)	4
Cost to register a tractor (% income per capita)	0.6
Tractor testing and standards index (0-8)	0.0
Time to obtain type approval (days)	N/A
Cost to obtain type approval (% income per capita)	N/A
Tractor import index (0-5)	5.0

FINANCE | DTF Score 42.62 ◇ Rank 46

Branchless Banking

Agent banking index (0-5)	0.0
E-money index (0-4)	1.0

Movable Collateral

Warehouse receipts index (0-5)	3.5
Doing Business - getting credit index (0-8)	6.0

Non-bank Lending Institutions

Microfinance institutions index (0-7)	0.0
Financial cooperatives index (0-7)	6.0

MARKETS | DTF Score 76.41 ◇ Rank 9

Producer organizations index (0-13)	6.0
Plant protection index (0-8)	7.0
Agricultural trade index (0-9)	7.5
Documents to export agricultural goods (number)	1
Time to export agricultural goods (days)	1
Cost to export agricultural goods (% income per capita)	0.0

TRANSPORT | DTF Score 44.44 ◇ Rank 46

Trucking licenses and operations index (0-11)	3.0
Time to obtain trucking licenses (days)	N/A
Cost to obtain trucking licenses (% income per capita)	N/A
Cross-border transportation index (0-9)	5.0
Time to obtain cross-border license (days)	7
Cost to obtain cross-border license (% income per capita)	0.0

WATER | DTF Score 55.17 ◇ Rank 28

Integrated water resource management index (0-29)	17.5
Individual water use for irrigation index (0-20)	10.0

ICT | DTF Score 72.22 ◇ Rank 15

ICT index (0-9)	6.5

a. The indicators apply to the formal seed system only.

COLOMBIA

DTF score   **Rank**

Category	DTF score	Rank
Seed	63.19	27
Fertilizer	81.58	8
Machinery	38.16	45
Finance	92.10	1
Markets	70.08	17
Transport	73.92	10
Water	85.52	3
ICT	88.89	9

SEED[a] | DTF Score 63.19 ◇ Rank 27

Plant breeding index *(0-10)*	9.0
Variety registration index *(0-8)*	4.0
Time to register new variety *(days)*	591
Cost to register new variety *(% income per capita)*	53.4
Seed quality control index *(0-12)*	6.5

FERTILIZER | DTF Score 81.58 ◇ Rank 8

Fertilizer registration index *(0-7)*	6.0
Time to register a new fertilizer product *(days)*	45
Cost to register a new fertilizer product *(% income per capita)*	7.8
Quality control of fertilizer index *(0-7)*	6.0
Importing & distributing fertilizer index *(0-7)*	4.0

MACHINERY | DTF Score 38.16 ◇ Rank 45

Tractor operation index *(0-5)*	1.5
Time to register a tractor *(days)*	2
Cost to register a tractor *(% income per capita)*	1.1
Tractor testing and standards index *(0-8)*	0.3
Time to obtain type approval *(days)*	N/A
Cost to obtain type approval *(% income per capita)*	N/A
Tractor import index *(0-5)*	3.0

FINANCE | DTF Score 92.10 ◇ Rank 1

Branchless Banking

Agent banking index *(0-5)*	4.5
E-money index *(0-4)*	3.7

Movable Collateral

Warehouse receipts index *(0-5)*	5.0
Doing Business - getting credit index *(0-8)*	8.0

Non-bank Lending Institutions

Microfinance institutions index *(0-7)*	5.0
Financial cooperatives index *(0-7)*	7.0

MARKETS | DTF Score 70.08 ◇ Rank 17

Producer organizations index *(0-13)*	9.1
Plant protection index *(0-8)*	6.0
Agricultural trade index *(0-9)*	6.0
Documents to export agricultural goods *(number)*	2
Time to export agricultural goods *(days)*	4
Cost to export agricultural goods *(% income per capita)*	0.4

TRANSPORT | DTF Score 73.92 ◇ Rank 10

Trucking licenses and operations index *(0-11)*	8.0
Time to obtain trucking licenses *(days)*	60
Cost to obtain trucking licenses *(% income per capita)*	3.2
Cross-border transportation index *(0-9)*	7.0
Time to obtain cross-border license *(days)*	15
Cost to obtain cross-border license *(% income per capita)*	0.8

WATER | DTF Score 85.52 ◇ Rank 3

Integrated water resource management index *(0-29)*	23.5
Individual water use for irrigation index *(0-20)*	18.0

ICT | DTF Score 88.89 ◇ Rank 9

ICT index *(0-9)*	8.0

a. The indicators apply to the formal seed system only.

CÔTE D'IVOIRE

DTF score		Rank
Seed	60.20	30
Fertilizer	39.29	45
Machinery	47.44	35
Finance	60.37	18
Markets	31.67	60
Transport	68.00	19
Water	25.60	49
ICT	61.11	22

SEED[a] | DTF Score 60.20 ◇ Rank 30

Plant breeding index *(0-10)*	6.0
Variety registration index *(0-8)*	6.5
Time to register new variety *(days)*	368
Cost to register new variety *(% income per capita)*	137.2
Seed quality control index *(0-12)*	3.0

FERTILIZER | DTF Score 39.29 ◇ Rank 45

Fertilizer registration index *(0-7)*	0.0
Time to register a new fertilizer product *(days)*	N/A
Cost to register a new fertilizer product *(% income per capita)*	N/A
Quality control of fertilizer index *(0-7)*	5.0
Importing & distributing fertilizer index *(0-7)*	6.0

MACHINERY | DTF Score 47.44 ◇ Rank 35

Tractor operation index *(0-5)*	1.5
Time to register a tractor *(days)*	N/A
Cost to register a tractor *(% income per capita)*	N/A
Tractor testing and standards index *(0-8)*	6.7
Time to obtain type approval *(days)*	18
Cost to obtain type approval *(% income per capita)*	40.5
Tractor import index *(0-5)*	1.5

FINANCE | DTF Score 60.37 ◇ Rank 18

Branchless Banking

Agent banking index *(0-5)*	0.0
E-money index *(0-4)*	3.9

Movable Collateral

Warehouse receipts index *(0-5)*	5.0
Doing Business - getting credit index *(0-8)*	4.0

Non-bank Lending Institutions

Microfinance institutions index *(0-7)*	4.0
Financial cooperatives index *(0-7)*	4.0

MARKETS | DTF Score 31.67 ◇ Rank 60

Producer organizations index *(0-13)*	7.5
Plant protection index *(0-8)*	2.0
Agricultural trade index *(0-9)*	2.0
Documents to export agricultural goods *(number)*	3
Time to export agricultural goods *(days)*	11
Cost to export agricultural goods *(% income per capita)*	3.1

TRANSPORT | DTF Score 68.00 ◇ Rank 19

Trucking licenses and operations index *(0-11)*	5.0
Time to obtain trucking licenses *(days)*	3
Cost to obtain trucking licenses *(% income per capita)*	15.0
Cross-border transportation index *(0-9)*	5.0
Time to obtain cross-border license *(days)*	2
Cost to obtain cross-border license *(% income per capita)*	3.9

WATER | DTF Score 25.60 ◇ Rank 49

Integrated water resource management index *(0-29)*	10.5
Individual water use for irrigation index *(0-20)*	3.0

ICT | DTF Score 61.11 ◇ Rank 22

ICT index *(0-9)*	5.5

a. The indicators apply to the formal seed system only.

COUNTRY TABLES

189

DENMARK

DTF score | | Rank

Category	DTF score	Rank
Seed	85.32	3
Fertilizer	92.23	3
Machinery	81.82	8
Finance	45.83	37
Markets	78.82	6
Transport	88.89	3
Water	60.91	24
ICT	94.44	6

SEED[a] | DTF Score 85.32 ◇ Rank 3

Plant breeding index (0-10)	9.0
Variety registration index (0-8)	7.0
Time to register new variety (days)	690
Cost to register new variety (% income per capita)	7.4
Seed quality control index (0-12)	12.0

FERTILIZER | DTF Score 92.23 ◇ Rank 3

Fertilizer registration index (0-7)	6.4
Time to register a new fertilizer product (days)	31
Cost to register a new fertilizer product (% income per capita)	0.4
Quality control of fertilizer index (0-7)	6.5
Importing & distributing fertilizer index (0-7)	6.0

MACHINERY | DTF Score 81.82 ◇ Rank 8

Tractor operation index (0-5)	2.0
Time to register a tractor (days)	No data
Cost to register a tractor (% income per capita)	0.1
Tractor testing and standards index (0-8)	7.0
Time to obtain type approval (days)	No data
Cost to obtain type approval (% income per capita)	No data
Tractor import index (0-5)	5.0

FINANCE | DTF Score 45.83 ◇ Rank 37

Branchless Banking

Agent banking index (0-5)	N/A
E-money index (0-4)	3.8

Movable Collateral

Warehouse receipts index (0-5)	0.0
Doing Business - getting credit index (0-8)	7.0

Non-bank Lending Institutions

Microfinance institutions index (0-7)	N/A
Financial cooperatives index (0-7)	0.0

MARKETS | DTF Score 78.82 ◇ Rank 6

Producer organizations index (0-13)	6.5
Plant protection index (0-8)	7.0
Agricultural trade index (0-9)	7.0
Documents to export agricultural goods (number)	0
Time to export agricultural goods (days)	0
Cost to export agricultural goods (% income per capita)	0.0

TRANSPORT | DTF Score 88.89 ◇ Rank 3

Trucking licenses and operations index (0-11)	10.8
Time to obtain trucking licenses (days)	30
Cost to obtain trucking licenses (% income per capita)	0.0
Cross-border transportation index (0-9)	9.0
Time to obtain cross-border license (days)	30
Cost to obtain cross-border license (% income per capita)	0.0

WATER | DTF Score 60.91 ◇ Rank 24

Integrated water resource management index (0-29)	23.0
Individual water use for irrigation index (0-20)	8.5

ICT | DTF Score 94.44 ◇ Rank 6

ICT index (0-9)	8.5

a. The indicators apply to the formal seed system only.

EGYPT, ARAB REP.

MIDDLE EAST & NORTH AFRICA
LOWER MIDDLE INCOME

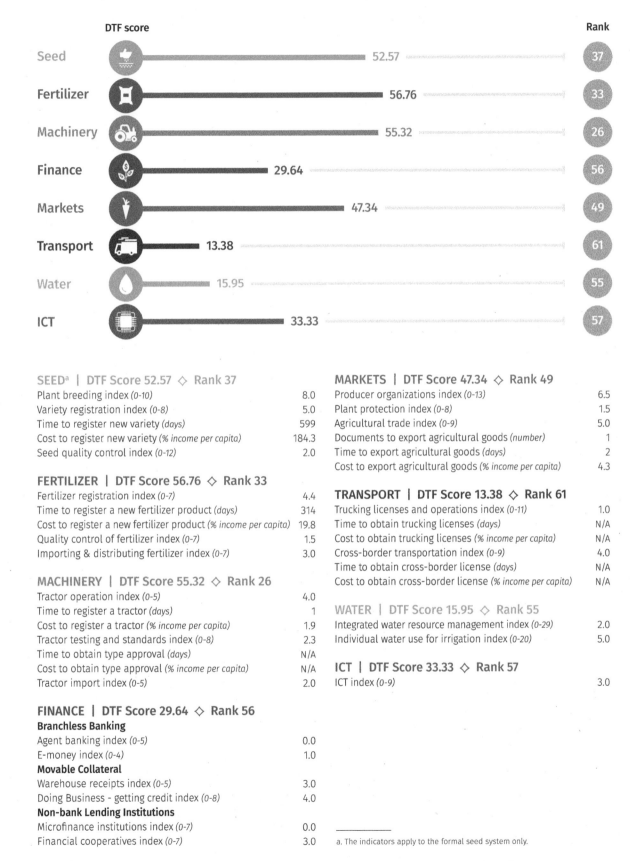

DTF score		Rank
Seed	52.57	37
Fertilizer	56.76	33
Machinery	55.32	26
Finance	29.64	56
Markets	47.34	49
Transport	13.38	61
Water	15.95	55
ICT	33.33	57

SEED[a] | DTF Score 52.57 ◇ Rank 37
Plant breeding index *(0-10)*	8.0
Variety registration index *(0-8)*	5.0
Time to register new variety *(days)*	599
Cost to register new variety *(% income per capita)*	184.3
Seed quality control index *(0-12)*	2.0

FERTILIZER | DTF Score 56.76 ◇ Rank 33
Fertilizer registration index *(0-7)*	4.4
Time to register a new fertilizer product *(days)*	314
Cost to register a new fertilizer product *(% income per capita)*	19.8
Quality control of fertilizer index *(0-7)*	1.5
Importing & distributing fertilizer index *(0-7)*	3.0

MACHINERY | DTF Score 55.32 ◇ Rank 26
Tractor operation index *(0-5)*	4.0
Time to register a tractor *(days)*	1
Cost to register a tractor *(% income per capita)*	1.9
Tractor testing and standards index *(0-8)*	2.3
Time to obtain type approval *(days)*	N/A
Cost to obtain type approval *(% income per capita)*	N/A
Tractor import index *(0-5)*	2.0

FINANCE | DTF Score 29.64 ◇ Rank 56
Branchless Banking
Agent banking index *(0-5)*	0.0
E-money index *(0-4)*	1.0

Movable Collateral
Warehouse receipts index *(0-5)*	3.0
Doing Business - getting credit index *(0-8)*	4.0

Non-bank Lending Institutions
Microfinance institutions index *(0-7)*	0.0
Financial cooperatives index *(0-7)*	3.0

MARKETS | DTF Score 47.34 ◇ Rank 49
Producer organizations index *(0-13)*	6.5
Plant protection index *(0-8)*	1.5
Agricultural trade index *(0-9)*	5.0
Documents to export agricultural goods *(number)*	1
Time to export agricultural goods *(days)*	2
Cost to export agricultural goods *(% income per capita)*	4.3

TRANSPORT | DTF Score 13.38 ◇ Rank 61
Trucking licenses and operations index *(0-11)*	1.0
Time to obtain trucking licenses *(days)*	N/A
Cost to obtain trucking licenses *(% income per capita)*	N/A
Cross-border transportation index *(0-9)*	4.0
Time to obtain cross-border license *(days)*	N/A
Cost to obtain cross-border license *(% income per capita)*	N/A

WATER | DTF Score 15.95 ◇ Rank 55
Integrated water resource management index *(0-29)*	2.0
Individual water use for irrigation index *(0-20)*	5.0

ICT | DTF Score 33.33 ◇ Rank 57
ICT index *(0-9)*	3.0

a. The indicators apply to the formal seed system only.

ETHIOPIA

SUB-SAHARAN AFRICA
LOW INCOME

DTF score | | Rank

Seed	51.07	39
Fertilizer	19.64	59
Machinery	55.95	25
Finance	52.96	27
Markets	45.69	51
Transport	66.89	21
Water	46.94	34
ICT	11.11	62

ENABLING THE BUSINESS OF AGRICULTURE 2017

192

SEED[a] | DTF Score 51.07 ◇ Rank 39

Plant breeding index (0-10)	6.0
Variety registration index (0-8)	4.5
Time to register new variety (days)	620
Cost to register new variety (% income per capita)	77.8
Seed quality control index (0-12)	4.0

FERTILIZER | DTF Score 19.64 ◇ Rank 59

Fertilizer registration index (0-7)	1.0
Time to register a new fertilizer product (days)	N/A
Cost to register a new fertilizer product (% income per capita)	N/A
Quality control of fertilizer index (0-7)	4.5
Importing & distributing fertilizer index (0-7)	0.0

MACHINERY | DTF Score 55.95 ◇ Rank 25

Tractor operation index (0-5)	3.5
Time to register a tractor (days)	2
Cost to register a tractor (% income per capita)	1.9
Tractor testing and standards index (0-8)	4.3
Time to obtain type approval (days)	No practice
Cost to obtain type approval (% income per capita)	No practice
Tractor import index (0-5)	3.0

FINANCE | DTF Score 52.96 ◇ Rank 27

Branchless Banking

Agent banking index (0-5)	4.6
E-money index (0-4)	0.0

Movable Collateral

Warehouse receipts index (0-5)	5.0
Doing Business - getting credit index (0-8)	1.0

Non-bank Lending Institutions

Microfinance institutions index (0-7)	4.0
Financial cooperatives index (0-7)	4.0

MARKETS | DTF Score 45.69 ◇ Rank 51

Producer organizations index (0-13)	10.6
Plant protection index (0-8)	1.0
Agricultural trade index (0-9)	3.5
Documents to export agricultural goods (number)	3
Time to export agricultural goods (days)	3
Cost to export agricultural goods (% income per capita)	2.5

TRANSPORT | DTF Score 66.89 ◇ Rank 21

Trucking licenses and operations index (0-11)	4.0
Time to obtain trucking licenses (days)	1
Cost to obtain trucking licenses (% income per capita)	5.5
Cross-border transportation index (0-9)	4.0
Time to obtain cross-border license (days)	1
Cost to obtain cross-border license (% income per capita)	5.5

WATER | DTF Score 46.94 ◇ Rank 34

Integrated water resource management index (0-29)	12.0
Individual water use for irrigation index (0-20)	10.5

ICT | DTF Score 11.11 ◇ Rank 62

ICT index (0-9)	1.0

a. The indicators apply to the formal seed system only. Recent research estimates that 59.3% of Ethiopian famers' households used non-commercial maize seed for planting during the 2011/2012 season. (Sheahan, M. and Barrett, C.B., 2016. Ten striking facts about agricultural input use in Sub-Saharan Africa. Food Policy.)

GEORGIA

DTF score		Rank
Seed	71.42	13
Fertilizer	68.44	21
Machinery	41.81	42
Finance	44.11	39
Markets	67.91	19
Transport	48.50	38
Water	29.83	48
ICT	94.44	6

SEED[a] | DTF Score 71.42 ◇ Rank 13

Plant breeding index *(0-10)*	9.0
Variety registration index *(0-8)*	7.0
Time to register new variety *(days)*	581
Cost to register new variety *(% income per capita)*	0.0
Seed quality control index *(0-12)*	4.0

FERTILIZER | DTF Score 68.44 ◇ Rank 21

Fertilizer registration index *(0-7)*	4.4
Time to register a new fertilizer product *(days)*	730
Cost to register a new fertilizer product *(% income per capita)*	16.7
Quality control of fertilizer index *(0-7)*	4.5
Importing & distributing fertilizer index *(0-7)*	6.0

MACHINERY | DTF Score 41.81 ◇ Rank 42

Tractor operation index *(0-5)*	0.5
Time to register a tractor *(days)*	1
Cost to register a tractor *(% income per capita)*	0.7
Tractor testing and standards index *(0-8)*	0.0
Time to obtain type approval *(days)*	N/A
Cost to obtain type approval *(% income per capita)*	N/A
Tractor import index *(0-5)*	5.0

FINANCE | DTF Score 44.11 ◇ Rank 39
Branchless Banking

Agent banking index *(0-5)*	0.0
E-money index *(0-4)*	2.0

Movable Collateral

Warehouse receipts index *(0-5)*	3.5
Doing Business - getting credit index *(0-8)*	7.0

Non-bank Lending Institutions

Microfinance institutions index *(0-7)*	0.0
Financial cooperatives index *(0-7)*	4.0

MARKETS | DTF Score 67.91 ◇ Rank 19

Producer organizations index *(0-13)*	6.5
Plant protection index *(0-8)*	5.5
Agricultural trade index *(0-9)*	6.5
Documents to export agricultural goods *(number)*	1
Time to export agricultural goods *(days)*	3
Cost to export agricultural goods *(% income per capita)*	0.3

TRANSPORT | DTF Score 48.50 ◇ Rank 38

Trucking licenses and operations index *(0-11)*	2.0
Time to obtain trucking licenses *(days)*	N/A
Cost to obtain trucking licenses *(% income per capita)*	N/A
Cross-border transportation index *(0-9)*	7.0
Time to obtain cross-border license *(days)*	3
Cost to obtain cross-border license *(% income per capita)*	0.8

WATER | DTF Score 29.83 ◇ Rank 48

Integrated water resource management index *(0-29)*	11.5
Individual water use for irrigation index *(0-20)*	4.0

ICT | DTF Score 94.44 ◇ Rank 6

ICT index *(0-9)*	8.5

a. The indicators apply to the formal seed system only.

COUNTRY TABLES

193

GHANA

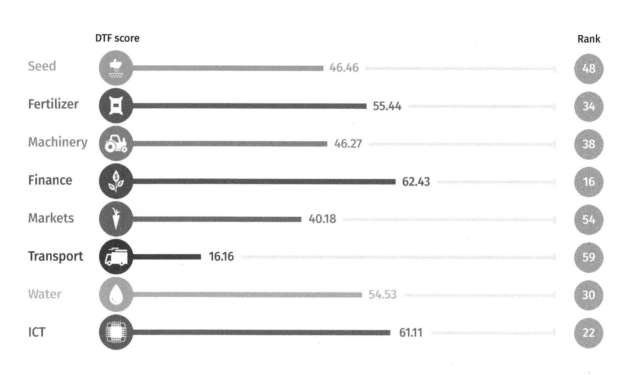

	DTF score	Rank
Seed	46.46	48
Fertilizer	55.44	34
Machinery	46.27	38
Finance	62.43	16
Markets	40.18	54
Transport	16.16	59
Water	54.53	30
ICT	61.11	22

SEED[a] | DTF Score 46.46 ◇ Rank 48

Plant breeding index (0-10)	4.0
Variety registration index (0-8)	6.0
Time to register new variety (days)	757
Cost to register new variety (% income per capita)	1091.6
Seed quality control index (0-12)	8.5

FERTILIZER | DTF Score 55.44 ◇ Rank 34

Fertilizer registration index (0-7)	3.4
Time to register a new fertilizer product (days)	231
Cost to register a new fertilizer product (% income per capita)	377.0
Quality control of fertilizer index (0-7)	5.0
Importing & distributing fertilizer index (0-7)	2.5

MACHINERY | DTF Score 46.27 ◇ Rank 38

Tractor operation index (0-5)	3.5
Time to register a tractor (days)	30
Cost to register a tractor (% income per capita)	10.1
Tractor testing and standards index (0-8)	2.0
Time to obtain type approval (days)	N/A
Cost to obtain type approval (% income per capita)	N/A
Tractor import index (0-5)	5.0

FINANCE | DTF Score 62.43 ◇ Rank 16

Branchless Banking

Agent banking index (0-5)	4.2
E-money index (0-4)	3.5

Movable Collateral

Warehouse receipts index (0-5)	0.0
Doing Business - getting credit index (0-8)	6.0

Non-bank Lending Institutions

Microfinance institutions index (0-7)	4.0
Financial cooperatives index (0-7)	5.0

MARKETS | DTF Score 40.18 ◇ Rank 54

Producer organizations index (0-13)	5.9
Plant protection index (0-8)	3.0
Agricultural trade index (0-9)	2.0
Documents to export agricultural goods (number)	3
Time to export agricultural goods (days)	No data
Cost to export agricultural goods (% income per capita)	1.0

TRANSPORT | DTF Score 16.16 ◇ Rank 59

Trucking licenses and operations index (0-11)	1.0
Time to obtain trucking licenses (days)	N/A
Cost to obtain trucking licenses (% income per capita)	N/A
Cross-border transportation index (0-9)	5.0
Time to obtain cross-border license (days)	No practice
Cost to obtain cross-border license (% income per capita)	No practice

WATER | DTF Score 54.53 ◇ Rank 30

Integrated water resource management index (0-29)	13.5
Individual water use for irrigation index (0-20)	12.5

ICT | DTF Score 61.11 ◇ Rank 22

ICT index (0-9)	5.5

a. The indicators apply to the formal seed system only.

GREECE

DTF score

Rank

	DTF score	Rank
Seed	70.43	14
Fertilizer	81.57	9
Machinery	83.39	5
Finance	85.83	4
Markets	80.65	5
Transport	71.25	14
Water	73.66	12
ICT	100.00	1

SEED[a] | DTF Score 70.43 ◇ Rank 14

Plant breeding index *(0-10)*	8.0
Variety registration index *(0-8)*	5.0
Time to register new variety *(days)*	729
Cost to register new variety *(% income per capita)*	8.7
Seed quality control index *(0-12)*	9.5

FERTILIZER | DTF Score 81.57 ◇ Rank 9

Fertilizer registration index *(0-7)*	7.0
Time to register a new fertilizer product *(days)*	186
Cost to register a new fertilizer product *(% income per capita)*	2.4
Quality control of fertilizer index *(0-7)*	6.5
Importing & distributing fertilizer index *(0-7)*	3.0

MACHINERY | DTF Score 83.39 ◇ Rank 5

Tractor operation index *(0-5)*	2.0
Time to register a tractor *(days)*	4
Cost to register a tractor *(% income per capita)*	0.1
Tractor testing and standards index *(0-8)*	7.0
Time to obtain type approval *(days)*	35
Cost to obtain type approval *(% income per capita)*	1.2
Tractor import index *(0-5)*	5.0

FINANCE | DTF Score 85.83 ◇ Rank 4

Branchless Banking

Agent banking index *(0-5)*	N/A
E-money index *(0-4)*	3.8

Movable Collateral

Warehouse receipts index *(0-5)*	4.5
Doing Business - getting credit index *(0-8)*	3.0

Non-bank Lending Institutions

Microfinance institutions index *(0-7)*	N/A
Financial cooperatives index *(0-7)*	7.0

MARKETS | DTF Score 80.65 ◇ Rank 5

Producer organizations index *(0-13)*	9.9
Plant protection index *(0-8)*	6.0
Agricultural trade index *(0-9)*	5.5
Documents to export agricultural goods *(number)*	0
Time to export agricultural goods *(days)*	0
Cost to export agricultural goods *(% income per capita)*	0.0

TRANSPORT | DTF Score 71.25 ◇ Rank 14

Trucking licenses and operations index *(0-11)*	8.8
Time to obtain trucking licenses *(days)*	60
Cost to obtain trucking licenses *(% income per capita)*	3.1
Cross-border transportation index *(0-9)*	9.0
Time to obtain cross-border license *(days)*	60
Cost to obtain cross-border license *(% income per capita)*	3.8

WATER | DTF Score 73.66 ◇ Rank 12

Integrated water resource management index *(0-29)*	27.5
Individual water use for irrigation index *(0-20)*	10.5

ICT | DTF Score 100.00 ◇ Rank 1

ICT index *(0-9)*	9.0

a. The indicators apply to the formal seed system only.

GUATEMALA

DTF score		Rank
Seed	64.04	26
Fertilizer	80.36	10
Machinery	18.83	57
Finance	55.89	24
Markets	72.15	14
Transport	18.31	58
Water	10.34	58
ICT	63.89	21

SEED[a] | DTF Score 64.04 ◇ Rank 26

Plant breeding index (0-10)	5.0
Variety registration index (0-8)	4.5
Time to register new variety (days)	166
Cost to register new variety (% income per capita)	1.9
Seed quality control index (0-12)	6.0

FERTILIZER | DTF Score 80.36 ◇ Rank 10

Fertilizer registration index (0-7)	4.8
Time to register a new fertilizer product (days)	113
Cost to register a new fertilizer product (% income per capita)	1.2
Quality control of fertilizer index (0-7)	7.0
Importing & distributing fertilizer index (0-7)	3.5

MACHINERY | DTF Score 18.83 ◇ Rank 57

Tractor operation index (0-5)	0.0
Time to register a tractor (days)	N/A
Cost to register a tractor (% income per capita)	N/A
Tractor testing and standards index (0-8)	0.3
Time to obtain type approval (days)	N/A
Cost to obtain type approval (% income per capita)	N/A
Tractor import index (0-5)	4.5

FINANCE | DTF Score 55.89 ◇ Rank 24

Branchless Banking

Agent banking index (0-5)	4.5
E-money index (0-4)	1.0

Movable Collateral

Warehouse receipts index (0-5)	4.5
Doing Business - getting credit index (0-8)	7.0

Non-bank Lending Institutions

Microfinance institutions index (0-7)	0.0
Financial cooperatives index (0-7)	3.0

MARKETS | DTF Score 72.15 ◇ Rank 14

Producer organizations index (0-13)	7.0
Plant protection index (0-8)	6.0
Agricultural trade index (0-9)	6.5
Documents to export agricultural goods (number)	1
Time to export agricultural goods (days)	1
Cost to export agricultural goods (% income per capita)	0.2

TRANSPORT | DTF Score 18.31 ◇ Rank 58

Trucking licenses and operations index (0-11)	3.2
Time to obtain trucking licenses (days)	N/A
Cost to obtain trucking licenses (% income per capita)	N/A
Cross-border transportation index (0-9)	4.0
Time to obtain cross-border license (days)	N/A
Cost to obtain cross-border license (% income per capita)	N/A

WATER | DTF Score 10.34 ◇ Rank 58

Integrated water resource management index (0-29)	6.0
Individual water use for irrigation index (0-20)	0.0

ICT | DTF Score 63.89 ◇ Rank 21

ICT index (0-9)	5.8

a. The indicators apply to the formal seed system only.

HAITI

DTF score   **Rank**

Indicator	DTF score	Rank
Seed	10.00	61
Fertilizer	21.43	58
Machinery	41.79	43
Finance	32.65	54
Markets	35.58	57
Transport	7.83	62
Water	12.20	57
ICT	44.44	43

SEED[a] | DTF Score 10.00 ◇ Rank 61

Plant breeding index *(0-10)*	4.0
Variety registration index *(0-8)*	0.0
Time to register new variety *(days)*	No practice
Cost to register new variety *(% income per capita)*	No practice
Seed quality control index *(0-12)*	0.0

FERTILIZER | DTF Score 21.43 ◇ Rank 58

Fertilizer registration index *(0-7)*	0.0
Time to register a new fertilizer product *(days)*	N/A
Cost to register a new fertilizer product *(% income per capita)*	N/A
Quality control of fertilizer index *(0-7)*	0.0
Importing & distributing fertilizer index *(0-7)*	6.0

MACHINERY | DTF Score 41.79 ◇ Rank 43

Tractor operation index *(0-5)*	2.5
Time to register a tractor *(days)*	5
Cost to register a tractor *(% income per capita)*	40.8
Tractor testing and standards index *(0-8)*	0.3
Time to obtain type approval *(days)*	N/A
Cost to obtain type approval *(% income per capita)*	N/A
Tractor import index *(0-5)*	5.0

FINANCE | DTF Score 32.65 ◇ Rank 54

Branchless Banking

Agent banking index *(0-5)*	3.7
E-money index *(0-4)*	1.0

Movable Collateral

Warehouse receipts index *(0-5)*	0.0
Doing Business - getting credit index *(0-8)*	2.0

Non-bank Lending Institutions

Microfinance institutions index *(0-7)*	0.0
Financial cooperatives index *(0-7)*	5.0

MARKETS | DTF Score 35.58 ◇ Rank 57

Producer organizations index *(0-13)*	4.5
Plant protection index *(0-8)*	0.0
Agricultural trade index *(0-9)*	No data
Documents to export agricultural goods *(number)*	1
Time to export agricultural goods *(days)*	No data
Cost to export agricultural goods *(% income per capita)*	1.6

TRANSPORT | DTF Score 7.83 ◇ Rank 62

Trucking licenses and operations index *(0-11)*	1.0
Time to obtain trucking licenses *(days)*	N/A
Cost to obtain trucking licenses *(% income per capita)*	N/A
Cross-border transportation index *(0-9)*	2.0
Time to obtain cross-border license *(days)*	N/A
Cost to obtain cross-border license *(% income per capita)*	N/A

WATER | DTF Score 12.20 ◇ Rank 57

Integrated water resource management index *(0-29)*	2.0
Individual water use for irrigation index *(0-20)*	3.5

ICT | DTF Score 44.44 ◇ Rank 43

ICT index *(0-9)*	4.0

a. The indicators apply to the formal seed system only. Recent research estimates that 94.7% of the seed used by farmers in Haiti in 2010 were sourced in the informal seed sector. (McGuire, S. and Sperling, L., 2016. Seed systems smallholder farmers use. Food Security, 8(1), pp.179-195.)

COUNTRY TABLES

197

INDIA

DTF score

Rank

Category	DTF score	Rank
Seed	66.60	21
Fertilizer	69.59	18
Machinery	59.56	21
Finance	66.10	15
Markets	52.53	43
Transport	41.22	49
Water	17.63	53
ICT	66.67	18

SEED[a] | DTF Score 66.60 ◇ Rank 21

Plant breeding index *(0-10)*	8.0
Variety registration index *(0-8)*	6.0
Time to register new variety *(days)*	397
Cost to register new variety *(% income per capita)*	98.7
Seed quality control index *(0-12)*	4.5

FERTILIZER | DTF Score 69.59 ◇ Rank 18

Fertilizer registration index *(0-7)*	5.0
Time to register a new fertilizer product *(days)*	804
Cost to register a new fertilizer product *(% income per capita)*	171
Quality control of fertilizer index *(0-7)*	3.5
Importing & distributing fertilizer index *(0-7)*	7.0

MACHINERY | DTF Score 59.56 ◇ Rank 21

Tractor operation index *(0-5)*	3.5
Time to register a tractor *(days)*	7
Cost to register a tractor *(% income per capita)*	0.2
Tractor testing and standards index *(0-8)*	3.8
Time to obtain type approval *(days)*	270
Cost to obtain type approval *(% income per capita)*	604.4
Tractor import index *(0-5)*	4.5

FINANCE | DTF Score 66.10 ◇ Rank 15

Branchless Banking

Agent banking index *(0-5)*	4.9
E-money index *(0-4)*	3.8

Movable Collateral

Warehouse receipts index *(0-5)*	5.0
Doing Business - getting credit index *(0-8)*	5.0

Non-bank Lending Institutions

Microfinance institutions index *(0-7)*	0.0
Financial cooperatives index *(0-7)*	3.0

MARKETS | DTF Score 52.53 ◇ Rank 43

Producer organizations index *(0-13)*	6.2
Plant protection index *(0-8)*	6.0
Agricultural trade index *(0-9)*	4.5
Documents to export agricultural goods *(number)*	3
Time to export agricultural goods *(days)*	8
Cost to export agricultural goods *(% income per capita)*	2.0

TRANSPORT | DTF Score 41.22 ◇ Rank 49

Trucking licenses and operations index *(0-11)*	9.3
Time to obtain trucking licenses *(days)*	8
Cost to obtain trucking licenses *(% income per capita)*	24.0
Cross-border transportation index *(0-9)*	2.0
Time to obtain cross-border license *(days)*	N/A
Cost to obtain cross-border license *(% income per capita)*	N/A

WATER | DTF Score 17.63 ◇ Rank 53

Integrated water resource management index *(0-29)*	9.5
Individual water use for irrigation index *(0-20)*	0.5

ICT | DTF Score 66.67 ◇ Rank 18

ICT index *(0-9)*	6.0

a. The indicators apply to the formal seed system only.

ITALY

OECD HIGH INCOME
HIGH INCOME

	DTF score	Rank
Seed	81.55	4
Fertilizer	85.09	6
Machinery	71.41	11
Finance	81.07	6
Markets	81.85	4
Transport	86.31	4
Water	74.09	10
ICT	94.44	6

SEED[a] | DTF Score 81.55 ◇ Rank 4
Plant breeding index (0-10)	10.0
Variety registration index (0-8)	5.5
Time to register new variety (days)	624
Cost to register new variety (% income per capita)	5.6
Seed quality control index (0-12)	10.5

FERTILIZER | DTF Score 85.09 ◇ Rank 6
Fertilizer registration index (0-7)	6.0
Time to register a new fertilizer product (days)	450
Cost to register a new fertilizer product (% income per capita)	11.2
Quality control of fertilizer index (0-7)	6.5
Importing & distributing fertilizer index (0-7)	6.0

MACHINERY | DTF Score 71.41 ◇ Rank 11
Tractor operation index (0-5)	2.0
Time to register a tractor (days)	6
Cost to register a tractor (% income per capita)	0.4
Tractor testing and standards index (0-8)	7.0
Time to obtain type approval (days)	170
Cost to obtain type approval (% income per capita)	No data
Tractor import index (0-5)	5.0

FINANCE | DTF Score 81.07 ◇ Rank 6
Branchless Banking
Agent banking index (0-5)	N/A
E-money index (0-4)	3.8

Movable Collateral
Warehouse receipts index (0-5)	4.5
Doing Business - getting credit index (0-8)	3.0

Non-bank Lending Institutions
Microfinance institutions index (0-7)	N/A
Financial cooperatives index (0-7)	6.0

MARKETS | DTF Score 81.85 ◇ Rank 4
Producer organizations index (0-13)	8.8
Plant protection index (0-8)	7.0
Agricultural trade index (0-9)	6.5
Documents to export agricultural goods (number)	0
Time to export agricultural goods (days)	0
Cost to export agricultural goods (% income per capita)	0.0

TRANSPORT | DTF Score 86.31 ◇ Rank 4
Trucking licenses and operations index (0-11)	9.8
Time to obtain trucking licenses (days)	30
Cost to obtain trucking licenses (% income per capita)	0.7
Cross-border transportation index (0-9)	9.0
Time to obtain cross-border license (days)	30
Cost to obtain cross-border license (% income per capita)	0.2

WATER | DTF Score 74.09 ◇ Rank 10
Integrated water resource management index (0-29)	20.5
Individual water use for irrigation index (0-20)	15.5

ICT | DTF Score 94.44 ◇ Rank 6
ICT index (0-9)	8.5

a. The indicators apply to the formal seed system only.

199

JORDAN

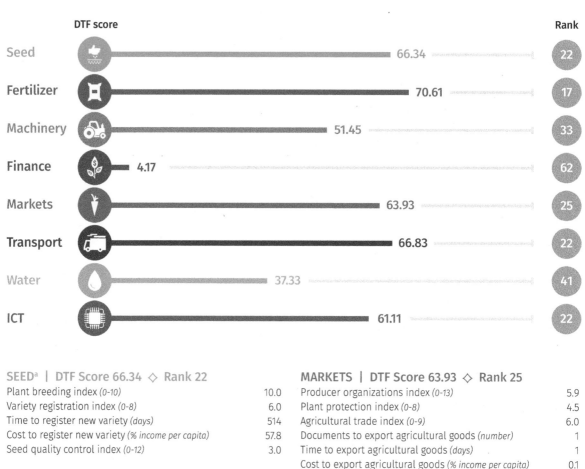

DTF score		Rank
Seed	66.34	22
Fertilizer	70.61	17
Machinery	51.45	33
Finance	4.17	62
Markets	63.93	25
Transport	66.83	22
Water	37.33	41
ICT	61.11	22

SEED[a] | DTF Score 66.34 ◇ Rank 22

Plant breeding index (0-10)	10.0
Variety registration index (0-8)	6.0
Time to register new variety (days)	514
Cost to register new variety (% income per capita)	57.8
Seed quality control index (0-12)	3.0

FERTILIZER | DTF Score 70.61 ◇ Rank 17

Fertilizer registration index (0-7)	4.4
Time to register a new fertilizer product (days)	45
Cost to register a new fertilizer product (% income per capita)	0.9
Quality control of fertilizer index (0-7)	3.5
Importing & distributing fertilizer index (0-7)	5.0

MACHINERY | DTF Score 51.45 ◇ Rank 33

Tractor operation index (0-5)	4.0
Time to register a tractor (days)	1
Cost to register a tractor (% income per capita)	20.2
Tractor testing and standards index (0-8)	1.2
Time to obtain type approval (days)	N/A
Cost to obtain type approval (% income per capita)	N/A
Tractor import index (0-5)	4.5

FINANCE | DTF Score 4.17 ◇ Rank 62

Branchless Banking

Agent banking index (0-5)	0.0
E-money index (0-4)	1.0

Movable Collateral

Warehouse receipts index (0-5)	0.0
Doing Business - getting credit index (0-8)	0.0

Non-bank Lending Institutions

Microfinance institutions index (0-7)	0.0
Financial cooperatives index (0-7)	0.0

MARKETS | DTF Score 63.93 ◇ Rank 25

Producer organizations index (0-13)	5.9
Plant protection index (0-8)	4.5
Agricultural trade index (0-9)	6.0
Documents to export agricultural goods (number)	1
Time to export agricultural goods (days)	1
Cost to export agricultural goods (% income per capita)	0.1

TRANSPORT | DTF Score 66.83 ◇ Rank 22

Trucking licenses and operations index (0-11)	4.5
Time to obtain trucking licenses (days)	4
Cost to obtain trucking licenses (% income per capita)	15.5
Cross-border transportation index (0-9)	5.0
Time to obtain cross-border license (days)	4
Cost to obtain cross-border license (% income per capita)	0.5

WATER | DTF Score 37.33 ◇ Rank 41

Integrated water resource management index (0-29)	11.5
Individual water use for irrigation index (0-20)	7.0

ICT | DTF Score 61.11 ◇ Rank 22

ICT index (0-9)	5.5

a. The indicators apply to the formal seed system only.

KAZAKHSTAN

DTF score		Rank
Seed	53.65	35
Fertilizer	73.14	15
Machinery	81.44	9
Finance	36.73	50
Markets	70.84	16
Transport	19.44	55
Water	65.73	18
ICT	61.11	22

SEED[a] | DTF Score 53.65 ◇ Rank 35

Plant breeding index (0-10)	10.0
Variety registration index (0-8)	6.5
Time to register new variety (days)	No practice
Cost to register new variety (% income per capita)	No practice
Seed quality control index (0-12)	4.0

FERTILIZER | DTF Score 73.14 ◇ Rank 15

Fertilizer registration index (0-7)	2.9
Time to register a new fertilizer product (days)	246
Cost to register a new fertilizer product (% income per capita)	11.7
Quality control of fertilizer index (0-7)	5.0
Importing & distributing fertilizer index (0-7)	6.5

MACHINERY | DTF Score 81.44 ◇ Rank 9

Tractor operation index (0-5)	2.5
Time to register a tractor (days)	10
Cost to register a tractor (% income per capita)	0.0
Tractor testing and standards index (0-8)	6.2
Time to obtain type approval (days)	15
Cost to obtain type approval (% income per capita)	6.9
Tractor import index (0-5)	5.0

FINANCE | DTF Score 36.73 ◇ Rank 50

Branchless Banking

Agent banking index (0-5)	0.0
E-money index (0-4)	1.0

Movable Collateral

Warehouse receipts index (0-5)	4.5
Doing Business - getting credit index (0-8)	5.0

Non-bank Lending Institutions

Microfinance institutions index (0-7)	0.0
Financial cooperatives index (0-7)	3.0

MARKETS | DTF Score 70.84 ◇ Rank 16

Producer organizations index (0-13)	10.5
Plant protection index (0-8)	5.5
Agricultural trade index (0-9)	7.0
Documents to export agricultural goods (number)	3
Time to export agricultural goods (days)	5
Cost to export agricultural goods (% income per capita)	0.6

TRANSPORT | DTF Score 19.44 ◇ Rank 55

Trucking licenses and operations index (0-11)	3.7
Time to obtain trucking licenses (days)	N/A
Cost to obtain trucking licenses (% income per capita)	N/A
Cross-border transportation index (0-9)	4.0
Time to obtain cross-border license (days)	N/A
Cost to obtain cross-border license (% income per capita)	N/A

WATER | DTF Score 65.73 ◇ Rank 18

Integrated water resource management index (0-29)	20.0
Individual water use for irrigation index (0-20)	12.5

ICT | DTF Score 61.11 ◇ Rank 22

ICT index (0-9)	5.5

---

a. The indicators apply to the formal seed system only.

KENYA

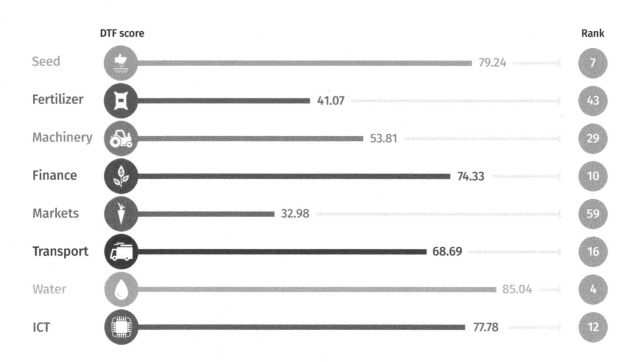

	DTF score		Rank
Seed		79.24	7
Fertilizer	41.07		43
Machinery	53.81		29
Finance		74.33	10
Markets	32.98		59
Transport		68.69	16
Water		85.04	4
ICT		77.78	12

SEED[a] | DTF Score 79.24 ◇ Rank 7

Plant breeding index *(0-10)*	10.0
Variety registration index *(0-8)*	7.0
Time to register new variety *(days)*	322
Cost to register new variety *(% income per capita)*	123.2
Seed quality control index *(0-12)*	6.0

FERTILIZER | DTF Score 41.07 ◇ Rank 43

Fertilizer registration index *(0-7)*	1.5
Time to register a new fertilizer product *(days)*	N/A
Cost to register a new fertilizer product *(% income per capita)*	N/A
Quality control of fertilizer index *(0-7)*	4.0
Importing & distributing fertilizer index *(0-7)*	6.0

MACHINERY | DTF Score 53.81 ◇ Rank 29

Tractor operation index *(0-5)*	2.5
Time to register a tractor *(days)*	7
Cost to register a tractor *(% income per capita)*	2.0
Tractor testing and standards index *(0-8)*	2.7
Time to obtain type approval *(days)*	N/A
Cost to obtain type approval *(% income per capita)*	N/A
Tractor import index *(0-5)*	5.0

FINANCE | DTF Score 74.33 ◇ Rank 10

Branchless Banking

Agent banking index *(0-5)*	4.2
E-money index *(0-4)*	4.0

Movable Collateral

Warehouse receipts index *(0-5)*	0.0
Doing Business - getting credit index *(0-8)*	5.0

Non-bank Lending Institutions

Microfinance institutions index *(0-7)*	7.0
Financial cooperatives index *(0-7)*	7.0

MARKETS | DTF Score 32.98 ◇ Rank 59

Producer organizations index *(0-13)*	6.9
Plant protection index *(0-8)*	1.5
Agricultural trade index *(0-9)*	3.5
Documents to export agricultural goods *(number)*	4
Time to export agricultural goods *(days)*	4
Cost to export agricultural goods *(% income per capita)*	5.6

TRANSPORT | DTF Score 68.69 ◇ Rank 16

Trucking licenses and operations index *(0-11)*	3.5
Time to obtain trucking licenses *(days)*	1
Cost to obtain trucking licenses *(% income per capita)*	2.2
Cross-border transportation index *(0-9)*	6.0
Time to obtain cross-border license *(days)*	10
Cost to obtain cross-border license *(% income per capita)*	14.9

WATER | DTF Score 85.04 ◇ Rank 4

Integrated water resource management index *(0-29)*	22.5
Individual water use for irrigation index *(0-20)*	18.5

ICT | DTF Score 77.78 ◇ Rank 12

ICT index *(0-9)*	7.0

a. The indicators apply to the formal seed system only. Recent research estimates that 82.3% of the seed used by farmers in Kenya in 2011 were sourced in the informal seed sector. (McGuire, S. and Sperling, L., 2016. Seed systems smallholder farmers use. Food Security, 8(1), pp.179-195.)

KOREA, REP.

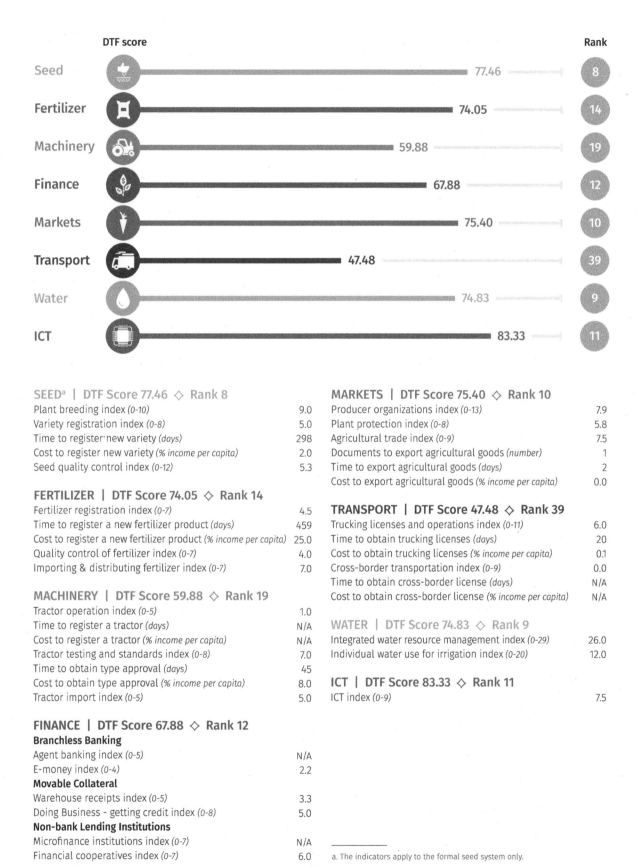

DTF score		Rank
Seed	77.46	8
Fertilizer	74.05	14
Machinery	59.88	19
Finance	67.88	12
Markets	75.40	10
Transport	47.48	39
Water	74.83	9
ICT	83.33	11

SEED[a] | DTF Score 77.46 ◇ Rank 8

Plant breeding index *(0-10)*	9.0
Variety registration index *(0-8)*	5.0
Time to register new variety *(days)*	298
Cost to register new variety *(% income per capita)*	2.0
Seed quality control index *(0-12)*	5.3

FERTILIZER | DTF Score 74.05 ◇ Rank 14

Fertilizer registration index *(0-7)*	4.5
Time to register a new fertilizer product *(days)*	459
Cost to register a new fertilizer product *(% income per capita)*	25.0
Quality control of fertilizer index *(0-7)*	4.0
Importing & distributing fertilizer index *(0-7)*	7.0

MACHINERY | DTF Score 59.88 ◇ Rank 19

Tractor operation index *(0-5)*	1.0
Time to register a tractor *(days)*	N/A
Cost to register a tractor *(% income per capita)*	N/A
Tractor testing and standards index *(0-8)*	7.0
Time to obtain type approval *(days)*	45
Cost to obtain type approval *(% income per capita)*	8.0
Tractor import index *(0-5)*	5.0

FINANCE | DTF Score 67.88 ◇ Rank 12

Branchless Banking

Agent banking index *(0-5)*	N/A
E-money index *(0-4)*	2.2

Movable Collateral

Warehouse receipts index *(0-5)*	3.3
Doing Business - getting credit index *(0-8)*	5.0

Non-bank Lending Institutions

Microfinance institutions index *(0-7)*	N/A
Financial cooperatives index *(0-7)*	6.0

MARKETS | DTF Score 75.40 ◇ Rank 10

Producer organizations index *(0-13)*	7.9
Plant protection index *(0-8)*	5.8
Agricultural trade index *(0-9)*	7.5
Documents to export agricultural goods *(number)*	1
Time to export agricultural goods *(days)*	2
Cost to export agricultural goods *(% income per capita)*	0.0

TRANSPORT | DTF Score 47.48 ◇ Rank 39

Trucking licenses and operations index *(0-11)*	6.0
Time to obtain trucking licenses *(days)*	20
Cost to obtain trucking licenses *(% income per capita)*	0.1
Cross-border transportation index *(0-9)*	0.0
Time to obtain cross-border license *(days)*	N/A
Cost to obtain cross-border license *(% income per capita)*	N/A

WATER | DTF Score 74.83 ◇ Rank 9

Integrated water resource management index *(0-29)*	26.0
Individual water use for irrigation index *(0-20)*	12.0

ICT | DTF Score 83.33 ◇ Rank 11

ICT index *(0-9)*	7.5

---

a. The indicators apply to the formal seed system only.

COUNTRY TABLES

203

KYRGYZ REPUBLIC

DTF score | Rank

	DTF score	Rank
Seed	36.44	53
Fertilizer	69.38	19
Machinery	64.98	14
Finance	78.61	8
Markets	72.60	13
Transport	18.43	56
Water	46.21	36
ICT	44.44	43

SEED[a] | DTF Score 36.44 ◇ Rank 53

Plant breeding index (0-10)	7.0
Variety registration index (0-8)	4.0
Time to register new variety (days)	970
Cost to register new variety (% income per capita)	219.4
Seed quality control index (0-12)	2.0

FERTILIZER | DTF Score 69.38 ◇ Rank 19

Fertilizer registration index (0-7)	3.8
Time to register a new fertilizer product (days)	357
Cost to register a new fertilizer product (% income per capita)	21.4
Quality control of fertilizer index (0-7)	4.0
Importing & distributing fertilizer index (0-7)	6.0

MACHINERY | DTF Score 64.98 ◇ Rank 14

Tractor operation index (0-5)	3.0
Time to register a tractor (days)	2
Cost to register a tractor (% income per capita)	1.5
Tractor testing and standards index (0-8)	5.5
Time to obtain type approval (days)	No practice
Cost to obtain type approval (% income per capita)	No practice
Tractor import index (0-5)	5.0

FINANCE | DTF Score 78.61 ◇ Rank 8
Branchless Banking

Agent banking index (0-5)	4.1
E-money index (0-4)	3.5

Movable Collateral

Warehouse receipts index (0-5)	3.5
Doing Business - getting credit index (0-8)	6.0

Non-bank Lending Institutions

Microfinance institutions index (0-7)	5.0
Financial cooperatives index (0-7)	6.0

MARKETS | DTF Score 72.60 ◇ Rank 13

Producer organizations index (0-13)	8.5
Plant protection index (0-8)	5.5
Agricultural trade index (0-9)	6.5
Documents to export agricultural goods (number)	1
Time to export agricultural goods (days)	1
Cost to export agricultural goods (% income per capita)	0.7

TRANSPORT | DTF Score 18.43 ◇ Rank 56

Trucking licenses and operations index (0-11)	2.0
Time to obtain trucking licenses (days)	N/A
Cost to obtain trucking licenses (% income per capita)	N/A
Cross-border transportation index (0-9)	5.0
Time to obtain cross-border license (days)	N/A
Cost to obtain cross-border license (% income per capita)	N/A

WATER | DTF Score 46.21 ◇ Rank 36

Integrated water resource management index (0-29)	21.0
Individual water use for irrigation index (0-20)	4.0

ICT | DTF Score 44.44 ◇ Rank 43

ICT index (0-9)	4.0

a. The indicators apply to the formal seed system only.

LAO PDR

EAST ASIA & PACIFIC
LOWER MIDDLE INCOME

DTF score   **Rank**

Category	DTF score	Rank
Seed	20.94	59
Fertilizer	65.70	27
Machinery	14.83	59
Finance	41.07	47
Markets	55.17	35
Transport	64.38	26
Water	40.95	40
ICT	27.78	59

SEED[a] | DTF Score 20.94 ◇ Rank 59

Plant breeding index (0-10)	4.0
Variety registration index (0-8)	3.5
Time to register new variety (days)	No practice
Cost to register new variety (% income per capita)	No practice
Seed quality control index (0-12)	0.0

FERTILIZER | DTF Score 65.70 ◇ Rank 27

Fertilizer registration index (0-7)	3.4
Time to register a new fertilizer product (days)	No data
Cost to register a new fertilizer product (% income per capita)	0.5
Quality control of fertilizer index (0-7)	5.0
Importing & distributing fertilizer index (0-7)	3.0

MACHINERY | DTF Score 14.83 ◇ Rank 59

Tractor operation index (0-5)	1.0
Time to register a tractor (days)	No practice
Cost to register a tractor (% income per capita)	No practice
Tractor testing and standards index (0-8)	0.3
Time to obtain type approval (days)	N/A
Cost to obtain type approval (% income per capita)	N/A
Tractor import index (0-5)	2.5

FINANCE | DTF Score 41.07 ◇ Rank 47

Branchless Banking

Agent banking index (0-5)	0.0
E-money index (0-4)	1.0

Movable Collateral

Warehouse receipts index (0-5)	0.0
Doing Business - getting credit index (0-8)	4.0

Non-bank Lending Institutions

Microfinance institutions index (0-7)	6.0
Financial cooperatives index (0-7)	6.0

MARKETS | DTF Score 55.17 ◇ Rank 35

Producer organizations index (0-13)	7.0
Plant protection index (0-8)	4.5
Agricultural trade index (0-9)	6.0
Documents to export agricultural goods (number)	2
Time to export agricultural goods (days)	3
Cost to export agricultural goods (% income per capita)	4.8

TRANSPORT | DTF Score 64.38 ◇ Rank 26

Trucking licenses and operations index (0-11)	6.5
Time to obtain trucking licenses (days)	37
Cost to obtain trucking licenses (% income per capita)	6.1
Cross-border transportation index (0-9)	5.0
Time to obtain cross-border license (days)	30
Cost to obtain cross-border license (% income per capita)	0.3

WATER | DTF Score 40.95 ◇ Rank 40

Integrated water resource management index (0-29)	16.5
Individual water use for irrigation index (0-20)	5.0

ICT | DTF Score 27.78 ◇ Rank 59

ICT index (0-9)	2.5

---

a. The indicators apply to the formal seed system only.

LIBERIA

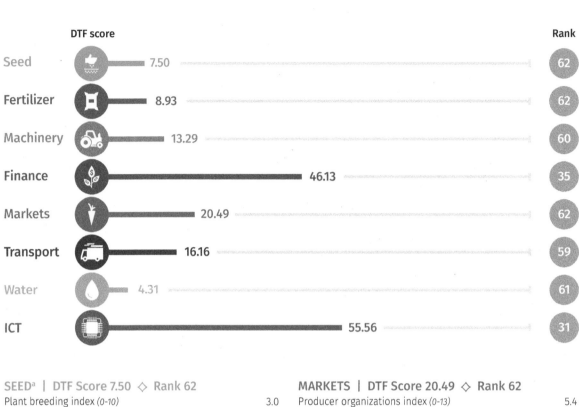

DTF score / Rank

	DTF score	Rank
Seed	7.50	62
Fertilizer	8.93	62
Machinery	13.29	60
Finance	46.13	35
Markets	20.49	62
Transport	16.16	59
Water	4.31	61
ICT	55.56	31

SEED[a] | DTF Score 7.50 ◇ Rank 62

Plant breeding index (0-10)	3.0
Variety registration index (0-8)	0.0
Time to register new variety (days)	No practice
Cost to register new variety (% income per capita)	No practice
Seed quality control index (0-12)	0.0

FERTILIZER | DTF Score 8.93 ◇ Rank 62

Fertilizer registration index (0-7)	0.0
Time to register a new fertilizer product (days)	N/A
Cost to register a new fertilizer product (% income per capita)	N/A
Quality control of fertilizer index (0-7)	0.0
Importing & distributing fertilizer index (0-7)	2.5

MACHINERY | DTF Score 13.29 ◇ Rank 60

Tractor operation index (0-5)	1.0
Time to register a tractor (days)	5
Cost to register a tractor (% income per capita)	92.1
Tractor testing and standards index (0-8)	0.3
Time to obtain type approval (days)	N/A
Cost to obtain type approval (% income per capita)	N/A
Tractor import index (0-5)	0.0

FINANCE | DTF Score 46.13 ◇ Rank 35

Branchless Banking

Agent banking index (0-5)	0.0
E-money index (0-4)	4.0

Movable Collateral

Warehouse receipts index (0-5)	0.0
Doing Business - getting credit index (0-8)	5.0

Non-bank Lending Institutions

Microfinance institutions index (0-7)	4.0
Financial cooperatives index (0-7)	4.0

MARKETS | DTF Score 20.49 ◇ Rank 62

Producer organizations index (0-13)	5.4
Plant protection index (0-8)	0.0
Agricultural trade index (0-9)	2.0
Documents to export agricultural goods (number)	4
Time to export agricultural goods (days)	7
Cost to export agricultural goods (% income per capita)	No data

TRANSPORT | DTF Score 16.16 ◇ Rank 59

Trucking licenses and operations index (0-11)	1.0
Time to obtain trucking licenses (days)	N/A
Cost to obtain trucking licenses (% income per capita)	N/A
Cross-border transportation index (0-9)	5.0
Time to obtain cross-border license (days)	No practice
Cost to obtain cross-border license (% income per capita)	No practice

WATER | DTF Score 4.31 ◇ Rank 61

Integrated water resource management index (0-29)	2.5
Individual water use for irrigation index (0-20)	0.0

ICT | DTF Score 55.56 ◇ Rank 31

ICT index (0-9)	5.0

a. The indicators apply to the formal seed system only.

MALAWI

DTF score   **Rank**

Category	DTF score	Rank
Seed	45.30	50
Fertilizer	39.83	44
Machinery	56.67	23
Finance	58.27	20
Markets	56.86	33
Transport	46.44	41
Water	65.56	19
ICT	41.67	50

SEED[a] | DTF Score 45.30 ◇ Rank 50

Plant breeding index *(0-10)*	5.0
Variety registration index *(0-8)*	5.5
Time to register new variety *(days)*	579
Cost to register new variety *(% income per capita)*	2038.1
Seed quality control index *(0-12)*	6.0

FERTILIZER | DTF Score 39.83 ◇ Rank 44

Fertilizer registration index *(0-7)*	3.5
Time to register a new fertilizer product *(days)*	913
Cost to register a new fertilizer product *(% income per capita)*	3030.5
Quality control of fertilizer index *(0-7)*	4.5
Importing & distributing fertilizer index *(0-7)*	3.0

MACHINERY | DTF Score 56.67 ◇ Rank 23

Tractor operation index *(0-5)*	4.0
Time to register a tractor *(days)*	15
Cost to register a tractor *(% income per capita)*	8.3
Tractor testing and standards index *(0-8)*	5.0
Time to obtain type approval *(days)*	240
Cost to obtain type approval *(% income per capita)*	428.6
Tractor import index *(0-5)*	3.0

FINANCE | DTF Score 58.27 ◇ Rank 20

Branchless Banking

Agent banking index *(0-5)*	2.5
E-money index *(0-4)*	3.8

Movable Collateral

Warehouse receipts index *(0-5)*	0.0
Doing Business - getting credit index *(0-8)*	5.0

Non-bank Lending Institutions

Microfinance institutions index *(0-7)*	5.0
Financial cooperatives index *(0-7)*	5.0

MARKETS | DTF Score 56.86 ◇ Rank 33

Producer organizations index *(0-13)*	9.0
Plant protection index *(0-8)*	3.0
Agricultural trade index *(0-9)*	4.5
Documents to export agricultural goods *(number)*	1
Time to export agricultural goods *(days)*	1
Cost to export agricultural goods *(% income per capita)*	2.8

TRANSPORT | DTF Score 46.44 ◇ Rank 41

Trucking licenses and operations index *(0-11)*	5.5
Time to obtain trucking licenses *(days)*	1
Cost to obtain trucking licenses *(% income per capita)*	5.5
Cross-border transportation index *(0-9)*	4.0
Time to obtain cross-border license *(days)*	N/A
Cost to obtain cross-border license *(% income per capita)*	N/A

WATER | DTF Score 65.56 ◇ Rank 19

Integrated water resource management index *(0-29)*	17.0
Individual water use for irrigation index *(0-20)*	14.5

ICT | DTF Score 41.67 ◇ Rank 50

ICT index *(0-9)*	3.8

---

a. The indicators apply to the formal seed system only. Recent research estimates that 68.8% of the seed used by farmers in Malawi in 2011 were sourced in the informal seed sector. (McGuire, S. and Sperling, L., 2016. Seed systems smallholder farmers use. Food Security, 8(1), pp.179-195.)

COUNTRY TABLES

207

MALAYSIA

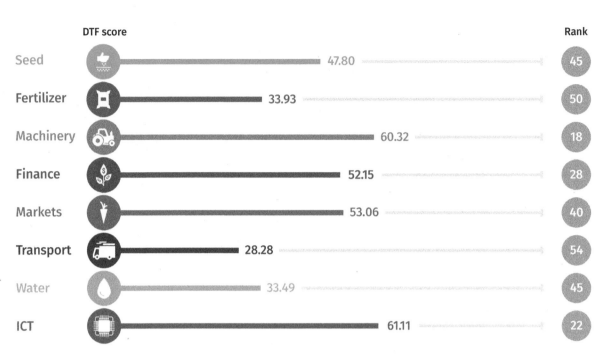

	DTF score		Rank
Seed		47.80	45
Fertilizer		33.93	50
Machinery		60.32	18
Finance		52.15	28
Markets		53.06	40
Transport		28.28	54
Water		33.49	45
ICT		61.11	22

SEED[a] | DTF Score 47.80 ◇ Rank 45

Plant breeding index (0-10)	9.0
Variety registration index (0-8)	3.0
Time to register new variety (days)	561
Cost to register new variety (% income per capita)	7.0
Seed quality control index (0-12)	0.0

FERTILIZER | DTF Score 33.93 ◇ Rank 50

Fertilizer registration index (0-7)	0.0
Time to register a new fertilizer product (days)	N/A
Cost to register a new fertilizer product (% income per capita)	N/A
Quality control of fertilizer index (0-7)	3.5
Importing & distributing fertilizer index (0-7)	6.0

MACHINERY | DTF Score 60.32 ◇ Rank 18

Tractor operation index (0-5)	4.5
Time to register a tractor (days)	7
Cost to register a tractor (% income per capita)	0.2
Tractor testing and standards index (0-8)	2.7
Time to obtain type approval (days)	N/A
Cost to obtain type approval (% income per capita)	N/A
Tractor import index (0-5)	4.5

FINANCE | DTF Score 52.15 ◇ Rank 28

Branchless Banking

Agent banking index (0-5)	4.4
E-money index (0-4)	3.8

Movable Collateral

Warehouse receipts index (0-5)	0.0
Doing Business - getting credit index (0-8)	6.0

Non-bank Lending Institutions

Microfinance institutions index (0-7)	0.0
Financial cooperatives index (0-7)	4.0

MARKETS | DTF Score 53.06 ◇ Rank 40

Producer organizations index (0-13)	4.9
Plant protection index (0-8)	4.0
Agricultural trade index (0-9)	3.5
Documents to export agricultural goods (number)	2
Time to export agricultural goods (days)	No data
Cost to export agricultural goods (% income per capita)	0.0

TRANSPORT | DTF Score 28.28 ◇ Rank 54

Trucking licenses and operations index (0-11)	5.2
Time to obtain trucking licenses (days)	44
Cost to obtain trucking licenses (% income per capita)	4.2
Cross-border transportation index (0-9)	0.0
Time to obtain cross-border license (days)	N/A
Cost to obtain cross-border license (% income per capita)	N/A

WATER | DTF Score 33.49 ◇ Rank 45

Integrated water resource management index (0-29)	10.0
Individual water use for irrigation index (0-20)	6.5

ICT | DTF Score 61.11 ◇ Rank 22

ICT index (0-9)	5.5

a. The indicators apply to the formal seed system only.

MALI

SUB-SAHARAN AFRICA
LOW INCOME

DTF score		Rank

Category	DTF score	Rank
Seed	36.99	52
Fertilizer	66.76	23
Machinery	8.83	61
Finance	43.35	41
Markets	51.78	44
Transport	45.05	44
Water	24.44	50
ICT	38.89	52

SEED[a] | DTF Score 36.99 ◇ Rank 52

Plant breeding index (0-10)	4.0
Variety registration index (0-8)	5.0
Time to register new variety (days)	No practice
Cost to register new variety (% income per capita)	No practice
Seed quality control index (0-12)	5.0

FERTILIZER | DTF Score 66.76 ◇ Rank 23

Fertilizer registration index (0-7)	4.5
Time to register a new fertilizer product (days)	90
Cost to register a new fertilizer product (% income per capita)	124.4
Quality control of fertilizer index (0-7)	3.5
Importing & distributing fertilizer index (0-7)	4.5

MACHINERY | DTF Score 8.83 ◇ Rank 61

Tractor operation index (0-5)	0.0
Time to register a tractor (days)	N/A
Cost to register a tractor (% income per capita)	N/A
Tractor testing and standards index (0-8)	0.3
Time to obtain type approval (days)	N/A
Cost to obtain type approval (% income per capita)	N/A
Tractor import index (0-5)	2.0

FINANCE | DTF Score 43.35 ◇ Rank 41

Branchless Banking

Agent banking index (0-5)	0.0
E-money index (0-4)	3.8

Movable Collateral

Warehouse receipts index (0-5)	0.0
Doing Business - getting credit index (0-8)	4.0

Non-bank Lending Institutions

Microfinance institutions index (0-7)	4.0
Financial cooperatives index (0-7)	4.0

MARKETS | DTF Score 51.78 ◇ Rank 44

Producer organizations index (0-13)	8.0
Plant protection index (0-8)	2.0
Agricultural trade index (0-9)	5.5
Documents to export agricultural goods (number)	1
Time to export agricultural goods (days)	2
Cost to export agricultural goods (% income per capita)	4.1

TRANSPORT | DTF Score 45.05 ◇ Rank 44

Trucking licenses and operations index (0-11)	3.5
Time to obtain trucking licenses (days)	3
Cost to obtain trucking licenses (% income per capita)	3.8
Cross-border transportation index (0-9)	5.0
Time to obtain cross-border license (days)	No practice
Cost to obtain cross-border license (% income per capita)	No practice

WATER | DTF Score 24.44 ◇ Rank 50

Integrated water resource management index (0-29)	12.0
Individual water use for irrigation index (0-20)	1.5

ICT | DTF Score 38.89 ◇ Rank 52

ICT index (0-9)	3.5

---

a. The indicators apply to the formal seed system only.

209

MEXICO

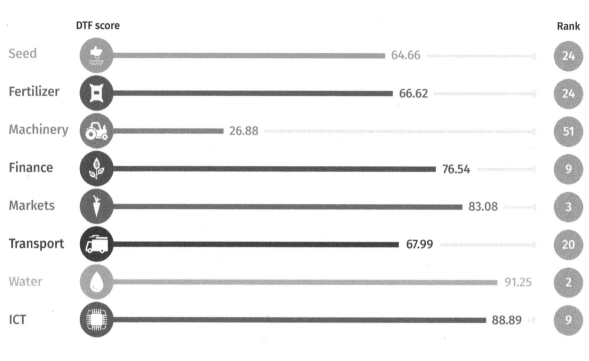

	DTF score	Rank
Seed	64.66	24
Fertilizer	66.62	24
Machinery	26.88	51
Finance	76.54	9
Markets	83.08	3
Transport	67.99	20
Water	91.25	2
ICT	88.89	9

SEED[a] | DTF Score 64.66 ◇ Rank 24

Plant breeding index *(0-10)*	8.0
Variety registration index *(0-8)*	5.0
Time to register new variety *(days)*	621
Cost to register new variety *(% income per capita)*	16.2
Seed quality control index *(0-12)*	7.0

FERTILIZER | DTF Score 66.62 ◇ Rank 24

Fertilizer registration index *(0-7)*	6.0
Time to register a new fertilizer product *(days)*	765
Cost to register a new fertilizer product *(% income per capita)*	11.5
Quality control of fertilizer index *(0-7)*	4.0
Importing & distributing fertilizer index *(0-7)*	4.5

MACHINERY | DTF Score 26.88 ◇ Rank 51

Tractor operation index *(0-5)*	1.0
Time to register a tractor *(days)*	No data
Cost to register a tractor *(% income per capita)*	No data
Tractor testing and standards index *(0-8)*	3.0
Time to obtain type approval *(days)*	N/A
Cost to obtain type approval *(% income per capita)*	N/A
Tractor import index *(0-5)*	2.5

FINANCE | DTF Score 76.54 ◇ Rank 9

Branchless Banking

Agent banking index *(0-5)*	4.2
E-money index *(0-4)*	0.0

Movable Collateral

Warehouse receipts index *(0-5)*	4.5
Doing Business - getting credit index *(0-8)*	8.0

Non-bank Lending Institutions

Microfinance institutions index *(0-7)*	6.0
Financial cooperatives index *(0-7)*	7.0

MARKETS | DTF Score 83.08 ◇ Rank 3

Producer organizations index *(0-13)*	9.8
Plant protection index *(0-8)*	7.0
Agricultural trade index *(0-9)*	7.5
Documents to export agricultural goods *(number)*	1
Time to export agricultural goods *(days)*	1
Cost to export agricultural goods *(% income per capita)*	0.3

TRANSPORT | DTF Score 67.99 ◇ Rank 20

Trucking licenses and operations index *(0-11)*	7.5
Time to obtain trucking licenses *(days)*	30
Cost to obtain trucking licenses *(% income per capita)*	4.0
Cross-border transportation index *(0-9)*	5.0
Time to obtain cross-border license *(days)*	30
Cost to obtain cross-border license *(% income per capita)*	3.1

WATER | DTF Score 91.25 ◇ Rank 2

Integrated water resource management index *(0-29)*	29.0
Individual water use for irrigation index *(0-20)*	16.5

ICT | DTF Score 88.89 ◇ Rank 9

ICT index *(0-9)*	8.0

a. The indicators apply to the formal seed system only.

MOROCCO

DTF score   **Rank**

	DTF score	Rank
Seed	67.87	20
Fertilizer	32.14	51
Machinery	60.33	17
Finance	29.00	57
Markets	64.22	24
Transport	79.89	8
Water	76.59	8
ICT	66.67	18

SEED[a] | DTF Score 67.87 ◇ Rank 20
Plant breeding index *(0-10)*	10.0
Variety registration index *(0-8)*	4.5
Time to register new variety *(days)*	584
Cost to register new variety *(% income per capita)*	18.1
Seed quality control index *(0-12)*	6.5

FERTILIZER | DTF Score 32.14 ◇ Rank 51
Fertilizer registration index *(0-7)*	0.0
Time to register a new fertilizer product *(days)*	N/A
Cost to register a new fertilizer product *(% income per capita)*	N/A
Quality control of fertilizer index *(0-7)*	5.5
Importing & distributing fertilizer index *(0-7)*	3.5

MACHINERY | DTF Score 60.33 ◇ Rank 17
Tractor operation index *(0-5)*	0.5
Time to register a tractor *(days)*	1
Cost to register a tractor *(% income per capita)*	1.3
Tractor testing and standards index *(0-8)*	5.0
Time to obtain type approval *(days)*	31
Cost to obtain type approval *(% income per capita)*	272.0
Tractor import index *(0-5)*	3.0

FINANCE | DTF Score 29.00 ◇ Rank 57
Branchless Banking
Agent banking index *(0-5)*	2.6
E-money index *(0-4)*	1.0

Movable Collateral
Warehouse receipts index *(0-5)*	3.0
Doing Business - getting credit index *(0-8)*	3.0

Non-bank Lending Institutions
Microfinance institutions index *(0-7)*	0.0
Financial cooperatives index *(0-7)*	0.0

MARKETS | DTF Score 64.22 ◇ Rank 24
Producer organizations index *(0-13)*	6.8
Plant protection index *(0-8)*	6.5
Agricultural trade index *(0-9)*	5.0
Documents to export agricultural goods *(number)*	2
Time to export agricultural goods *(days)*	4
Cost to export agricultural goods *(% income per capita)*	0.5

TRANSPORT | DTF Score 79.89 ◇ Rank 8
Trucking licenses and operations index *(0-11)*	6.2
Time to obtain trucking licenses *(days)*	6
Cost to obtain trucking licenses *(% income per capita)*	0.0
Cross-border transportation index *(0-9)*	6.0
Time to obtain cross-border license *(days)*	1
Cost to obtain cross-border license *(% income per capita)*	0.0

WATER | DTF Score 76.59 ◇ Rank 8
Integrated water resource management index *(0-29)*	20.5
Individual water use for irrigation index *(0-20)*	16.5

ICT | DTF Score 66.67 ◇ Rank 18
ICT index *(0-9)*	6.0

a. The indicators apply to the formal seed system only.

MOZAMBIQUE

DTF score		Rank
Seed	65.68	23
Fertilizer	38.93	47
Machinery	34.58	47
Finance	55.10	25
Markets	59.52	30
Transport	54.91	33
Water	63.36	21
ICT	61.11	22

SEED[a] | DTF Score 65.68 ◇ Rank 23

Plant breeding index (0-10)	8.0
Variety registration index (0-8)	6.0
Time to register new variety (days)	582
Cost to register new variety (% income per capita)	86.2
Seed quality control index (0-12)	6.0

FERTILIZER | DTF Score 38.93 ◇ Rank 47

Fertilizer registration index (0-7)	3.4
Time to register a new fertilizer product (days)	No practice
Cost to register a new fertilizer product (% income per capita)	No practice
Quality control of fertilizer index (0-7)	4.0
Importing & distributing fertilizer index (0-7)	3.5

MACHINERY | DTF Score 34.58 ◇ Rank 47

Tractor operation index (0-5)	0.5
Time to register a tractor (days)	20
Cost to register a tractor (% income per capita)	14.6
Tractor testing and standards index (0-8)	2.3
Time to obtain type approval (days)	N/A
Cost to obtain type approval (% income per capita)	N/A
Tractor import index (0-5)	4.5

FINANCE | DTF Score 55.10 ◇ Rank 25

Branchless Banking

Agent banking index (0-5)	3.9
E-money index (0-4)	1.0

Movable Collateral

Warehouse receipts index (0-5)	3.8
Doing Business - getting credit index (0-8)	2.0

Non-bank Lending Institutions

Microfinance institutions index (0-7)	4.0
Financial cooperatives index (0-7)	5.0

MARKETS | DTF Score 59.52 ◇ Rank 30

Producer organizations index (0-13)	8.1
Plant protection index (0-8)	5.0
Agricultural trade index (0-9)	5.0
Documents to export agricultural goods (number)	1
Time to export agricultural goods (days)	7
Cost to export agricultural goods (% income per capita)	2.0

TRANSPORT | DTF Score 54.91 ◇ Rank 33

Trucking licenses and operations index (0-11)	5.0
Time to obtain trucking licenses (days)	3
Cost to obtain trucking licenses (% income per capita)	19.5
Cross-border transportation index (0-9)	5.0
Time to obtain cross-border license (days)	3
Cost to obtain cross-border license (% income per capita)	58.5

WATER | DTF Score 63.36 ◇ Rank 21

Integrated water resource management index (0-29)	15.0
Individual water use for irrigation index (0-20)	15.0

ICT | DTF Score 61.11 ◇ Rank 22

ICT index (0-9)	5.5

a. The indicators apply to the formal seed system only.

MYANMAR

EAST ASIA & PACIFIC
LOWER MIDDLE INCOME

DTF score   **Rank**

Category	DTF score	Rank
Seed	54.60	34
Fertilizer	61.64	30
Machinery	2.83	62
Finance	22.92	61
Markets	42.33	53
Transport	30.19	51
Water	2.59	62
ICT	50.00	37

SEED[a] | DTF Score 54.60 ◇ Rank 34

Plant breeding index (0-10)	7.0
Variety registration index (0-8)	3.0
Time to register new variety (days)	306
Cost to register new variety (% income per capita)	26.6
Seed quality control index (0-12)	3.0

FERTILIZER | DTF Score 61.64 ◇ Rank 30

Fertilizer registration index (0-7)	4.4
Time to register a new fertilizer product (days)	41
Cost to register a new fertilizer product (% income per capita)	7.3
Quality control of fertilizer index (0-7)	3.0
Importing & distributing fertilizer index (0-7)	3.0

MACHINERY | DTF Score 2.83 ◇ Rank 62

Tractor operation index (0-5)	0.0
Time to register a tractor (days)	N/A
Cost to register a tractor (% income per capita)	N/A
Tractor testing and standards index (0-8)	0.3
Time to obtain type approval (days)	N/A
Cost to obtain type approval (% income per capita)	N/A
Tractor import index (0-5)	0.5

FINANCE | DTF Score 22.92 ◇ Rank 61

Branchless Banking
Agent banking index (0-5)	0.0
E-money index (0-4)	1.0

Movable Collateral
Warehouse receipts index (0-5)	0.0
Doing Business - getting credit index (0-8)	1.0

Non-bank Lending Institutions
Microfinance institutions index (0-7)	3.0
Financial cooperatives index (0-7)	4.0

MARKETS | DTF Score 42.33 ◇ Rank 53

Producer organizations index (0-13)	6.5
Plant protection index (0-8)	0.0
Agricultural trade index (0-9)	5.0
Documents to export agricultural goods (number)	2
Time to export agricultural goods (days)	4
Cost to export agricultural goods (% income per capita)	1.2

TRANSPORT | DTF Score 30.19 ◇ Rank 51

Trucking licenses and operations index (0-11)	1.5
Time to obtain trucking licenses (days)	7
Cost to obtain trucking licenses (% income per capita)	0.1
Cross-border transportation index (0-9)	1.0
Time to obtain cross-border license (days)	N/A
Cost to obtain cross-border license (% income per capita)	N/A

WATER | DTF Score 2.59 ◇ Rank 62

Integrated water resource management index (0-29)	1.5
Individual water use for irrigation index (0-20)	0.0

ICT | DTF Score 50.00 ◇ Rank 37

ICT index (0-9)	4.5

a. The indicators apply to the formal seed system only.

COUNTRY TABLES

213

NEPAL

DTF score		Rank
Seed	47.31	46
Fertilizer	45.46	41
Machinery	47.21	36
Finance	46.31	34
Markets	60.60	28
Transport	29.77	52
Water	22.97	52
ICT	44.44	43

SEED[a] | DTF Score 47.31 ◇ Rank 46

Plant breeding index (0-10)	4.0
Variety registration index (0-8)	5.5
Time to register new variety (days)	611
Cost to register new variety (% income per capita)	0.0
Seed quality control index (0-12)	1.0

FERTILIZER | DTF Score 45.46 ◇ Rank 41

Fertilizer registration index (0-7)	3.4
Time to register a new fertilizer product (days)	1125
Cost to register a new fertilizer product (% income per capita)	645.2
Quality control of fertilizer index (0-7)	5.0
Importing & distributing fertilizer index (0-7)	3.5

MACHINERY | DTF Score 47.21 ◇ Rank 36

Tractor operation index (0-5)	3.0
Time to register a tractor (days)	2
Cost to register a tractor (% income per capita)	4.6
Tractor testing and standards index (0-8)	0.3
Time to obtain type approval (days)	N/A
Cost to obtain type approval (% income per capita)	N/A
Tractor import index (0-5)	4.0

FINANCE | DTF Score 46.31 ◇ Rank 34

Branchless Banking

Agent banking index (0-5)	3.6
E-money index (0-4)	1.0

Movable Collateral

Warehouse receipts index (0-5)	0.0
Doing Business - getting credit index (0-8)	3.0

Non-bank Lending Institutions

Microfinance institutions index (0-7)	4.0
Financial cooperatives index (0-7)	6.0

MARKETS | DTF Score 60.60 ◇ Rank 28

Producer organizations index (0-13)	6.9
Plant protection index (0-8)	4.0
Agricultural trade index (0-9)	6.0
Documents to export agricultural goods (number)	2
Time to export agricultural goods (days)	2
Cost to export agricultural goods (% income per capita)	0.7

TRANSPORT | DTF Score 29.77 ◇ Rank 52

Trucking licenses and operations index (0-11)	4.0
Time to obtain trucking licenses (days)	2
Cost to obtain trucking licenses (% income per capita)	38.2
Cross-border transportation index (0-9)	3.0
Time to obtain cross-border license (days)	N/A
Cost to obtain cross-border license (% income per capita)	N/A

WATER | DTF Score 22.97 ◇ Rank 52

Integrated water resource management index (0-29)	1.0
Individual water use for irrigation index (0-20)	8.5

ICT | DTF Score 44.44 ◇ Rank 43

ICT index (0-9)	4.0

_____

a. The indicators apply to the formal seed system only.

NETHERLANDS

OECD HIGH INCOME
HIGH INCOME

DTF score | | Rank

	DTF score	Rank
Seed	88.00	1
Fertilizer	83.33	7
Machinery	81.83	7
Finance	61.31	17
Markets	87.61	1
Transport	76.47	9
Water	64.27	20
ICT	100.00	1

SEED[a] | DTF Score 88.00 ◇ Rank 1

Plant breeding index (0-10)	9.0
Variety registration index (0-8)	7.0
Time to register new variety (days)	556
Cost to register new variety (% income per capita)	13.7
Seed quality control index (0-12)	12.0

FERTILIZER | DTF Score 83.33 ◇ Rank 7

Fertilizer registration index (0-7)	5.0
Time to register a new fertilizer product (days)	N/A
Cost to register a new fertilizer product (% income per capita)	N/A
Quality control of fertilizer index (0-7)	6.5
Importing & distributing fertilizer index (0-7)	6.0

MACHINERY | DTF Score 81.83 ◇ Rank 7

Tractor operation index (0-5)	2.0
Time to register a tractor (days)	1
Cost to register a tractor (% income per capita)	0.1
Tractor testing and standards index (0-8)	7.0
Time to obtain type approval (days)	No data
Cost to obtain type approval (% income per capita)	No data
Tractor import index (0-5)	5.0

FINANCE | DTF Score 61.31 ◇ Rank 17

Branchless Banking

Agent banking index (0-5)	N/A
E-money index (0-4)	2.8

Movable Collateral

Warehouse receipts index (0-5)	2.5
Doing Business - getting credit index (0-8)	3.0

Non-bank Lending Institutions

Microfinance institutions index (0-7)	N/A
Financial cooperatives index (0-7)	5.0

MARKETS | DTF Score 87.61 ◇ Rank 1

Producer organizations index (0-13)	8.0
Plant protection index (0-8)	8.0
Agricultural trade index (0-9)	8.0
Documents to export agricultural goods (number)	0
Time to export agricultural goods (days)	0
Cost to export agricultural goods (% income per capita)	0.0

TRANSPORT | DTF Score 76.47 ◇ Rank 9

Trucking licenses and operations index (0-11)	9.8
Time to obtain trucking licenses (days)	56
Cost to obtain trucking licenses (% income per capita)	0.9
Cross-border transportation index (0-9)	9.0
Time to obtain cross-border license (days)	56
Cost to obtain cross-border license (% income per capita)	0.9

WATER | DTF Score 64.27 ◇ Rank 20

Integrated water resource management index (0-29)	23.5
Individual water use for irrigation index (0-20)	9.5

ICT | DTF Score 100.00 ◇ Rank 1

ICT index (0-9)	9.0

---

a. The indicators apply to the formal seed system only.

COUNTRY TABLES

215

NICARAGUA

DTF score   **Rank**

Category	DTF score	Rank
Seed	47.92	44
Fertilizer	78.20	11
Machinery	33.03	48
Finance	45.94	36
Markets	66.29	20
Transport	51.56	36
Water	61.98	23
ICT	44.44	43

SEED[a] | DTF Score 47.92 ◇ Rank 44

Plant breeding index *(0-10)*	7.0
Variety registration index *(0-8)*	6.5
Time to register new variety *(days)*	650
Cost to register new variety *(% income per capita)*	786.9
Seed quality control index *(0-12)*	3.0

FERTILIZER | DTF Score 78.20 ◇ Rank 11

Fertilizer registration index *(0-7)*	4.8
Time to register a new fertilizer product *(days)*	28
Cost to register a new fertilizer product *(% income per capita)*	82.5
Quality control of fertilizer index *(0-7)*	7.0
Importing & distributing fertilizer index *(0-7)*	3.5

MACHINERY | DTF Score 33.03 ◇ Rank 48

Tractor operation index *(0-5)*	1.0
Time to register a tractor *(days)*	10
Cost to register a tractor *(% income per capita)*	5.6
Tractor testing and standards index *(0-8)*	0.0
Time to obtain type approval *(days)*	N/A
Cost to obtain type approval *(% income per capita)*	N/A
Tractor import index *(0-5)*	3.5

FINANCE | DTF Score 45.94 ◇ Rank 36
Branchless Banking

Agent banking index *(0-5)*	3.6
E-money index *(0-4)*	1.0

Movable Collateral

Warehouse receipts index *(0-5)*	4.3
Doing Business - getting credit index *(0-8)*	3.0

Non-bank Lending Institutions

Microfinance institutions index *(0-7)*	0.0
Financial cooperatives index *(0-7)*	4.0

MARKETS | DTF Score 66.29 ◇ Rank 20

Producer organizations index *(0-13)*	9.4
Plant protection index *(0-8)*	6.0
Agricultural trade index *(0-9)*	4.5
Documents to export agricultural goods *(number)*	2
Time to export agricultural goods *(days)*	2
Cost to export agricultural goods *(% income per capita)*	1.4

TRANSPORT | DTF Score 51.56 ◇ Rank 36

Trucking licenses and operations index *(0-11)*	8.0
Time to obtain trucking licenses *(days)*	7
Cost to obtain trucking licenses *(% income per capita)*	4.5
Cross-border transportation index *(0-9)*	4.0
Time to obtain cross-border license *(days)*	N/A
Cost to obtain cross-border license *(% income per capita)*	N/A

WATER | DTF Score 61.98 ◇ Rank 23

Integrated water resource management index *(0-29)*	20.0
Individual water use for irrigation index *(0-20)*	11.0

ICT | DTF Score 44.44 ◇ Rank 43

ICT index *(0-9)*	4.0

a. The indicators apply to the formal seed system only.

NIGER

DTF score | | Rank

Category	DTF score	Rank
Seed	45.42	49
Fertilizer	25.00	55
Machinery	20.83	55
Finance	43.01	45
Markets	53.11	39
Transport	68.20	17
Water	41.85	39
ICT	44.44	43

SEED[a] | DTF Score 45.42 ◇ Rank 49

Plant breeding index (0-10)	4.0
Variety registration index (0-8)	8.0
Time to register new variety (days)	No practice
Cost to register new variety (% income per capita)	No practice
Seed quality control index (0-12)	5.0

FERTILIZER | DTF Score 25.00 ◇ Rank 55

Fertilizer registration index (0-7)	0.0
Time to register a new fertilizer product (days)	N/A
Cost to register a new fertilizer product (% income per capita)	N/A
Quality control of fertilizer index (0-7)	3.0
Importing & distributing fertilizer index (0-7)	3.5

MACHINERY | DTF Score 20.83 ◇ Rank 55

Tractor operation index (0-5)	0.0
Time to register a tractor (days)	N/A
Cost to register a tractor (% income per capita)	N/A
Tractor testing and standards index (0-8)	0.3
Time to obtain type approval (days)	N/A
Cost to obtain type approval (% income per capita)	N/A
Tractor import index (0-5)	5.0

FINANCE | DTF Score 43.01 ◇ Rank 45

Branchless Banking

Agent banking index (0-5)	0.0
E-money index (0-4)	3.8

Movable Collateral

Warehouse receipts index (0-5)	0.0
Doing Business - getting credit index (0-8)	4.0

Non-bank Lending Institutions

Microfinance institutions index (0-7)	4.0
Financial cooperatives index (0-7)	4.0

MARKETS | DTF Score 53.11 ◇ Rank 39

Producer organizations index (0-13)	8.0
Plant protection index (0-8)	2.0
Agricultural trade index (0-9)	5.0
Documents to export agricultural goods (number)	1
Time to export agricultural goods (days)	2
Cost to export agricultural goods (% income per capita)	2.4

TRANSPORT | DTF Score 68.20 ◇ Rank 17

Trucking licenses and operations index (0-11)	4.5
Time to obtain trucking licenses (days)	2
Cost to obtain trucking licenses (% income per capita)	9.6
Cross-border transportation index (0-9)	5.0
Time to obtain cross-border license (days)	1
Cost to obtain cross-border license (% income per capita)	9.6

WATER | DTF Score 41.85 ◇ Rank 39

Integrated water resource management index (0-29)	10.5
Individual water use for irrigation index (0-20)	9.5

ICT | DTF Score 44.44 ◇ Rank 43

ICT index (0-9)	4.0

a. The indicators apply to the formal seed system only.

COUNTRY TABLES

217

NIGERIA

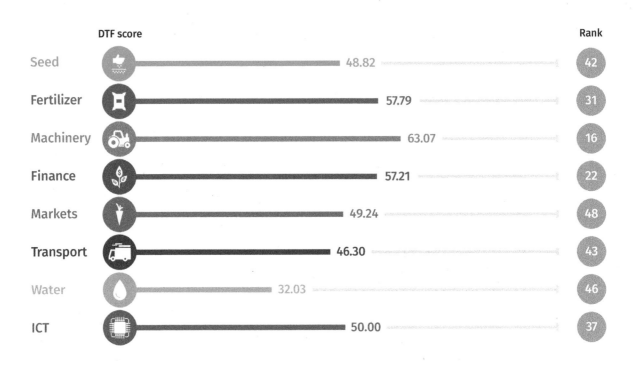

	DTF score	Rank
Seed	48.82	42
Fertilizer	57.79	31
Machinery	63.07	16
Finance	57.21	22
Markets	49.24	48
Transport	46.30	43
Water	32.03	46
ICT	50.00	37

SEED[a] | DTF Score 48.82 ◇ Rank 42

Plant breeding index *(0-10)*	3.0
Variety registration index *(0-8)*	5.5
Time to register new variety *(days)*	367
Cost to register new variety *(% income per capita)*	197.9
Seed quality control index *(0-12)*	3.0

FERTILIZER | DTF Score 57.79 ◇ Rank 31

Fertilizer registration index *(0-7)*	4.0
Time to register a new fertilizer product *(days)*	225
Cost to register a new fertilizer product *(% income per capita)*	6.0
Quality control of fertilizer index *(0-7)*	3.0
Importing & distributing fertilizer index *(0-7)*	3.0

MACHINERY | DTF Score 63.07 ◇ Rank 16

Tractor operation index *(0-5)*	0.5
Time to register a tractor *(days)*	14
Cost to register a tractor *(% income per capita)*	9.9
Tractor testing and standards index *(0-8)*	5.7
Time to obtain type approval *(days)*	105
Cost to obtain type approval *(% income per capita)*	99.0
Tractor import index *(0-5)*	5.0

FINANCE | DTF Score 57.21 ◇ Rank 22

Branchless Banking	3.7
Agent banking index *(0-5)*	3.8
E-money index *(0-4)*	
Movable Collateral	0.0
Warehouse receipts index *(0-5)*	6.0
Doing Business - getting credit index *(0-8)*	
Non-bank Lending Institutions	4.0
Microfinance institutions index *(0-7)*	3.0
Financial cooperatives index *(0-7)*	

MARKETS | DTF Score 49.24 ◇ Rank 48

Producer organizations index *(0-13)*	7.0
Plant protection index *(0-8)*	2.0
Agricultural trade index *(0-9)*	4.0
Documents to export agricultural goods *(number)*	2
Time to export agricultural goods *(days)*	7
Cost to export agricultural goods *(% income per capita)*	0.5

TRANSPORT | DTF Score 46.30 ◇ Rank 43

Trucking licenses and operations index *(0-11)*	3.5
Time to obtain trucking licenses *(days)*	1
Cost to obtain trucking licenses *(% income per capita)*	1.4
Cross-border transportation index *(0-9)*	5.0
Time to obtain cross-border license *(days)*	No practice
Cost to obtain cross-border license *(% income per capita)*	No practice

WATER | DTF Score 32.03 ◇ Rank 46

Integrated water resource management index *(0-29)*	13.5
Individual water use for irrigation index *(0-20)*	3.5

ICT | DTF Score 50.00 ◇ Rank 37

ICT index *(0-9)*	4.5

a. The indicators apply to the formal seed system only. Recent research estimates that 76% of Nigerian famers' households used non-commercial maize seed for planting during 2010/2011 season. (Sheahan, M. and Barrett, C.B., 2016. Ten striking facts about agricultural input use in Sub-Saharan Africa. Food Policy.)

PERU

DTF score		Rank
Seed	72.49	10
Fertilizer	30.36	52
Machinery	18.50	58
Finance	86.67	2
Markets	61.28	27
Transport	84.75	5
Water	73.79	11
ICT	72.22	15

SEED[a] | DTF Score 72.49 ◇ Rank 10

Plant breeding index *(0-10)*	7.0
Variety registration index *(0-8)*	5.0
Time to register new variety *(days)*	357
Cost to register new variety *(% income per capita)*	21.3
Seed quality control index *(0-12)*	8.0

FERTILIZER | DTF Score 30.36 ◇ Rank 52

Fertilizer registration index *(0-7)*	0.0
Time to register a new fertilizer product *(days)*	N/A
Cost to register a new fertilizer product *(% income per capita)*	N/A
Quality control of fertilizer index *(0-7)*	2.5
Importing & distributing fertilizer index *(0-7)*	6.0

MACHINERY | DTF Score 18.50 ◇ Rank 58

Tractor operation index *(0-5)*	0.0
Time to register a tractor *(days)*	N/A
Cost to register a tractor *(% income per capita)*	N/A
Tractor testing and standards index *(0-8)*	1.0
Time to obtain type approval *(days)*	N/A
Cost to obtain type approval *(% income per capita)*	N/A
Tractor import index *(0-5)*	4.0

FINANCE | DTF Score 86.67 ◇ Rank 2

Branchless Banking

Agent banking index *(0-5)*	4.3
E-money index *(0-4)*	3.7

Movable Collateral

Warehouse receipts index *(0-5)*	5.0
Doing Business - getting credit index *(0-8)*	8.0

Non-bank Lending Institutions

Microfinance institutions index *(0-7)*	7.0
Financial cooperatives index *(0-7)*	3.0

MARKETS | DTF Score 61.28 ◇ Rank 27

Producer organizations index *(0-13)*	9.2
Plant protection index *(0-8)*	5.0
Agricultural trade index *(0-9)*	6.0
Documents to export agricultural goods *(number)*	2
Time to export agricultural goods *(days)*	11
Cost to export agricultural goods *(% income per capita)*	0.7

TRANSPORT | DTF Score 84.75 ◇ Rank 5

Trucking licenses and operations index *(0-11)*	7.5
Time to obtain trucking licenses *(days)*	3
Cost to obtain trucking licenses *(% income per capita)*	0.4
Cross-border transportation index *(0-9)*	7.0
Time to obtain cross-border license *(days)*	7
Cost to obtain cross-border license *(% income per capita)*	0.0

WATER | DTF Score 73.79 ◇ Rank 11

Integrated water resource management index *(0-29)*	22.5
Individual water use for irrigation index *(0-20)*	14.0

ICT | DTF Score 72.22 ◇ Rank 15

ICT index *(0-9)*	6.5

---

a. The indicators apply to the formal seed system only. Recent research estimates that 92.8% of the maize seed used for planting during the 2010/2011 season in Peru were non-certified seed. (Lapeña, I., 2012. La Nueva Legislación de Semillas y sus implicancias para la agricultura familiar en el Perú. Serie de Política y Derecho Ambiental. Sociedad Peruana de Derecho Ambiental, (26).)

PHILIPPINES

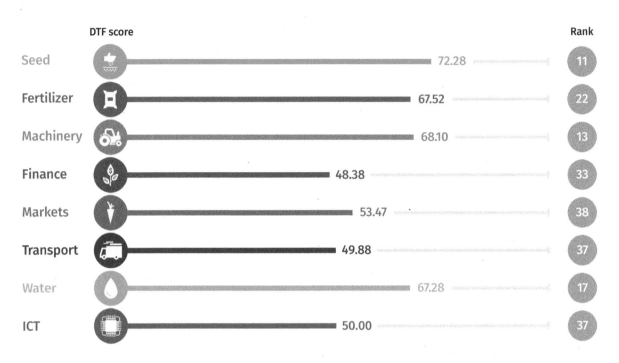

DTF score		Rank
Seed	72.28	11
Fertilizer	67.52	22
Machinery	68.10	13
Finance	48.38	33
Markets	53.47	38
Transport	49.88	37
Water	67.28	17
ICT	50.00	37

SEED[a] | DTF Score 72.28 ◇ Rank 11
Plant breeding index *(0-10)*	10.0
Variety registration index *(0-8)*	6.5
Time to register new variety *(days)*	570
Cost to register new variety *(% income per capita)*	1.5
Seed quality control index *(0-12)*	5.3

FERTILIZER | DTF Score 67.52 ◇ Rank 22
Fertilizer registration index *(0-7)*	4.4
Time to register a new fertilizer product *(days)*	134
Cost to register a new fertilizer product *(% income per capita)*	9.2
Quality control of fertilizer index *(0-7)*	4.5
Importing & distributing fertilizer index *(0-7)*	3.5

MACHINERY | DTF Score 68.10 ◇ Rank 13
Tractor operation index *(0-5)*	2.0
Time to register a tractor *(days)*	11
Cost to register a tractor *(% income per capita)*	0.0
Tractor testing and standards index *(0-8)*	5.2
Time to obtain type approval *(days)*	30
Cost to obtain type approval *(% income per capita)*	12.6
Tractor import index *(0-5)*	3.0

FINANCE | DTF Score 48.38 ◇ Rank 33
Branchless Banking
Agent banking index *(0-5)*	0.0
E-money index *(0-4)*	3.6

Movable Collateral
Warehouse receipts index *(0-5)*	4.5
Doing Business - getting credit index *(0-8)*	2.0

Non-bank Lending Institutions
Microfinance institutions index *(0-7)*	0.0
Financial cooperatives index *(0-7)*	6.0

MARKETS | DTF Score 53.47 ◇ Rank 38
Producer organizations index *(0-13)*	5.5
Plant protection index *(0-8)*	2.0
Agricultural trade index *(0-9)*	5.5
Documents to export agricultural goods *(number)*	1
Time to export agricultural goods *(days)*	2
Cost to export agricultural goods *(% income per capita)*	0.0

TRANSPORT | DTF Score 49.88 ◇ Rank 37
Trucking licenses and operations index *(0-11)*	5.5
Time to obtain trucking licenses *(days)*	235
Cost to obtain trucking licenses *(% income per capita)*	3.8
Cross-border transportation index *(0-9)*	5.0
Time to obtain cross-border license *(days)*	No practice
Cost to obtain cross-border license *(% income per capita)*	No practice

WATER | DTF Score 67.28 ◇ Rank 17
Integrated water resource management index *(0-29)*	18.0
Individual water use for irrigation index *(0-20)*	14.5

ICT | DTF Score 50.00 ◇ Rank 37
ICT index *(0-9)*	4.5

---

a. The indicators apply to the formal seed system only.

POLAND

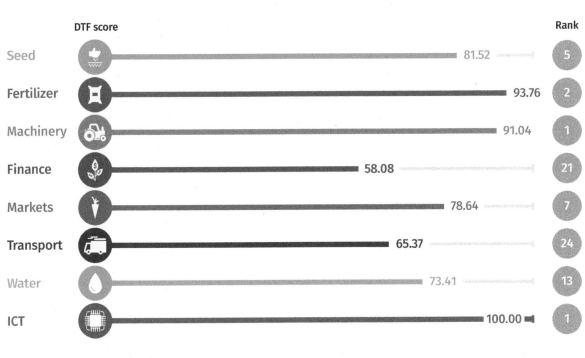

	DTF score		Rank
Seed		81.52	5
Fertilizer		93.76	2
Machinery		91.04	1
Finance		58.08	21
Markets		78.64	7
Transport		65.37	24
Water		73.41	13
ICT		100.00	1

SEED[a] | DTF Score 81.52 ◇ Rank 5

Plant breeding index *(0-10)*	10.0
Variety registration index *(0-8)*	5.5
Time to register new variety *(days)*	699
Cost to register new variety *(% income per capita)*	15.2
Seed quality control index *(0-12)*	11.5

FERTILIZER | DTF Score 93.76 ◇ Rank 2

Fertilizer registration index *(0-7)*	7.0
Time to register a new fertilizer product *(days)*	60
Cost to register a new fertilizer product *(% income per capita)*	15.7
Quality control of fertilizer index *(0-7)*	6.5
Importing & distributing fertilizer index *(0-7)*	6.0

MACHINERY | DTF Score 91.04 ◇ Rank 1

Tractor operation index *(0-5)*	5.0
Time to register a tractor *(days)*	2
Cost to register a tractor *(% income per capita)*	0.4
Tractor testing and standards index *(0-8)*	7.0
Time to obtain type approval *(days)*	60
Cost to obtain type approval *(% income per capita)*	220.5
Tractor import index *(0-5)*	5.0

FINANCE | DTF Score 58.08 ◇ Rank 21

Branchless Banking

Agent banking index *(0-5)*	4.1
E-money index *(0-4)*	3.8

Movable Collateral

Warehouse receipts index *(0-5)*	0.0
Doing Business - getting credit index *(0-8)*	7.0

Non-bank Lending Institutions

Microfinance institutions index *(0-7)*	0.0
Financial cooperatives index *(0-7)*	6.0

MARKETS | DTF Score 78.64 ◇ Rank 7

Producer organizations index *(0-13)*	8.8
Plant protection index *(0-8)*	7.8
Agricultural trade index *(0-9)*	4.5
Documents to export agricultural goods *(number)*	0
Time to export agricultural goods *(days)*	0
Cost to export agricultural goods *(% income per capita)*	0.0

TRANSPORT | DTF Score 65.37 ◇ Rank 24

Trucking licenses and operations index *(0-11)*	8.8
Time to obtain trucking licenses *(days)*	90
Cost to obtain trucking licenses *(% income per capita)*	1.7
Cross-border transportation index *(0-9)*	9.0
Time to obtain cross-border license *(days)*	90
Cost to obtain cross-border license *(% income per capita)*	19.4

WATER | DTF Score 73.41 ◇ Rank 13

Integrated water resource management index *(0-29)*	23.0
Individual water use for irrigation index *(0-20)*	13.5

ICT | DTF Score 100.00 ◇ Rank 1

ICT index *(0-9)*	9.0

a. The indicators apply to the formal seed system only.

ROMANIA

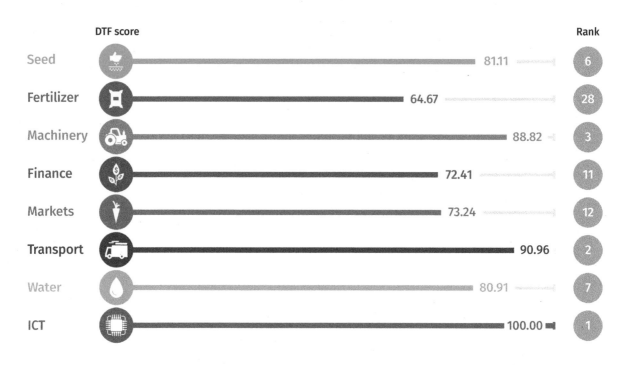

	DTF score	Rank
Seed	81.11	6
Fertilizer	64.67	28
Machinery	88.82	3
Finance	72.41	11
Markets	73.24	12
Transport	90.96	2
Water	80.91	7
ICT	100.00	1

SEED[a] | DTF Score 81.11 ◇ Rank 6

Plant breeding index *(0-10)*	10.0
Variety registration index *(0-8)*	5.5
Time to register new variety *(days)*	654
Cost to register new variety *(% income per capita)*	23.2
Seed quality control index *(0-12)*	11.0

FERTILIZER | DTF Score 64.67 ◇ Rank 28

Fertilizer registration index *(0-7)*	4.8
Time to register a new fertilizer product *(days)*	1205
Cost to register a new fertilizer product *(% income per capita)*	46.3
Quality control of fertilizer index *(0-7)*	6.5
Importing & distributing fertilizer index *(0-7)*	3.0

MACHINERY | DTF Score 88.82 ◇ Rank 3

Tractor operation index *(0-5)*	5.0
Time to register a tractor *(days)*	30
Cost to register a tractor *(% income per capita)*	0.4
Tractor testing and standards index *(0-8)*	8.0
Time to obtain type approval *(days)*	30
Cost to obtain type approval *(% income per capita)*	7.7
Tractor import index *(0-5)*	5.0

FINANCE | DTF Score 72.41 ◇ Rank 11

Branchless Banking

Agent banking index *(0-5)*	3.4
E-money index *(0-4)*	3.8

Movable Collateral

Warehouse receipts index *(0-5)*	5.0
Doing Business - getting credit index *(0-8)*	7.0

Non-bank Lending Institutions

Microfinance institutions index *(0-7)*	0.0
Financial cooperatives index *(0-7)*	6.0

MARKETS | DTF Score 73.24 ◇ Rank 12

Producer organizations index *(0-13)*	7.3
Plant protection index *(0-8)*	6.5
Agricultural trade index *(0-9)*	5.0
Documents to export agricultural goods *(number)*	0
Time to export agricultural goods *(days)*	0
Cost to export agricultural goods *(% income per capita)*	0.0

TRANSPORT | DTF Score 90.96 ◇ Rank 2

Trucking licenses and operations index *(0-11)*	9.8
Time to obtain trucking licenses *(days)*	15
Cost to obtain trucking licenses *(% income per capita)*	2.0
Cross-border transportation index *(0-9)*	9.0
Time to obtain cross-border license *(days)*	15
Cost to obtain cross-border license *(% income per capita)*	2.0

WATER | DTF Score 80.91 ◇ Rank 7

Integrated water resource management index *(0-29)*	23.0
Individual water use for irrigation index *(0-20)*	16.5

ICT | DTF Score 100.00 ◇ Rank 1

ICT index *(0-9)*	9.0

---

a. The indicators apply to the formal seed system only.

RUSSIAN FEDERATION

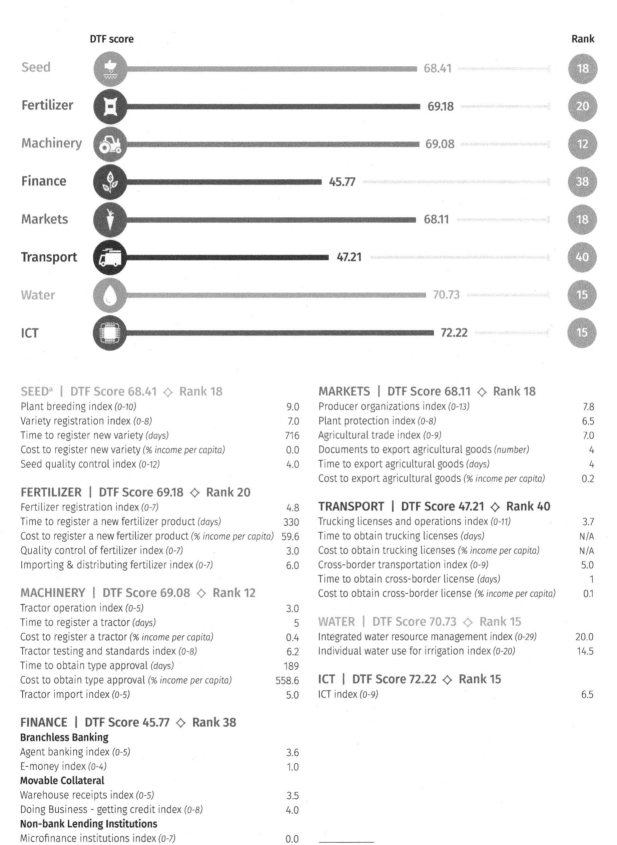

DTF score	Rank
Seed	68.41	18
Fertilizer	69.18	20
Machinery	69.08	12
Finance	45.77	38
Markets	68.11	18
Transport	47.21	40
Water	70.73	15
ICT	72.22	15

SEED[a] | DTF Score 68.41 ◇ Rank 18

Plant breeding index *(0-10)*	9.0
Variety registration index *(0-8)*	7.0
Time to register new variety *(days)*	716
Cost to register new variety *(% income per capita)*	0.0
Seed quality control index *(0-12)*	4.0

FERTILIZER | DTF Score 69.18 ◇ Rank 20

Fertilizer registration index *(0-7)*	4.8
Time to register a new fertilizer product *(days)*	330
Cost to register a new fertilizer product *(% income per capita)*	59.6
Quality control of fertilizer index *(0-7)*	3.0
Importing & distributing fertilizer index *(0-7)*	6.0

MACHINERY | DTF Score 69.08 ◇ Rank 12

Tractor operation index *(0-5)*	3.0
Time to register a tractor *(days)*	5
Cost to register a tractor *(% income per capita)*	0.4
Tractor testing and standards index *(0-8)*	6.2
Time to obtain type approval *(days)*	189
Cost to obtain type approval *(% income per capita)*	558.6
Tractor import index *(0-5)*	5.0

FINANCE | DTF Score 45.77 ◇ Rank 38

Branchless Banking

Agent banking index *(0-5)*	3.6
E-money index *(0-4)*	1.0

Movable Collateral

Warehouse receipts index *(0-5)*	3.5
Doing Business - getting credit index *(0-8)*	4.0

Non-bank Lending Institutions

Microfinance institutions index *(0-7)*	0.0
Financial cooperatives index *(0-7)*	4.0

MARKETS | DTF Score 68.11 ◇ Rank 18

Producer organizations index *(0-13)*	7.8
Plant protection index *(0-8)*	6.5
Agricultural trade index *(0-9)*	7.0
Documents to export agricultural goods *(number)*	4
Time to export agricultural goods *(days)*	4
Cost to export agricultural goods *(% income per capita)*	0.2

TRANSPORT | DTF Score 47.21 ◇ Rank 40

Trucking licenses and operations index *(0-11)*	3.7
Time to obtain trucking licenses *(days)*	N/A
Cost to obtain trucking licenses *(% income per capita)*	N/A
Cross-border transportation index *(0-9)*	5.0
Time to obtain cross-border license *(days)*	1
Cost to obtain cross-border license *(% income per capita)*	0.1

WATER | DTF Score 70.73 ◇ Rank 15

Integrated water resource management index *(0-29)*	20.0
Individual water use for irrigation index *(0-20)*	14.5

ICT | DTF Score 72.22 ◇ Rank 15

ICT index *(0-9)*	6.5

---

a. The indicators apply to the formal seed system only.

RWANDA

DTF score | | Rank

Seed	20.21	60
Fertilizer	52.58	38
Machinery	43.37	41
Finance	80.63	7
Markets	49.30	47
Transport	62.70	27
Water	50.00	32
ICT	41.67	50

SEED[a] | DTF Score 20.21 ◇ Rank 60

Plant breeding index (0-10)	6.0
Variety registration index (0-8)	1.0
Time to register new variety (days)	No practice
Cost to register new variety (% income per capita)	No practice
Seed quality control index (0-12)	1.0

FERTILIZER | DTF Score 52.58 ◇ Rank 38

Fertilizer registration index (0-7)	1.9
Time to register a new fertilizer product (days)	730
Cost to register a new fertilizer product (% income per capita)	2.0
Quality control of fertilizer index (0-7)	4.0
Importing & distributing fertilizer index (0-7)	4.5

MACHINERY | DTF Score 43.37 ◇ Rank 41

Tractor operation index (0-5)	2.5
Time to register a tractor (days)	2
Cost to register a tractor (% income per capita)	153.7
Tractor testing and standards index (0-8)	1.5
Time to obtain type approval (days)	N/A
Cost to obtain type approval (% income per capita)	N/A
Tractor import index (0-5)	5.0

FINANCE | DTF Score 80.63 ◇ Rank 7

Branchless Banking

Agent banking index (0-5)	3.7
E-money index (0-4)	3.9

Movable Collateral

Warehouse receipts index (0-5)	3.5
Doing Business - getting credit index (0-8)	8.0

Non-bank Lending Institutions

Microfinance institutions index (0-7)	5.0
Financial cooperatives index (0-7)	5.0

MARKETS | DTF Score 49.30 ◇ Rank 47

Producer organizations index (0-13)	9.0
Plant protection index (0-8)	0.5
Agricultural trade index (0-9)	3.0
Documents to export agricultural goods (number)	1
Time to export agricultural goods (days)	1
Cost to export agricultural goods (% income per capita)	0.0

TRANSPORT | DTF Score 62.70 ◇ Rank 27

Trucking licenses and operations index (0-11)	5.0
Time to obtain trucking licenses (days)	7
Cost to obtain trucking licenses (% income per capita)	21.5
Cross-border transportation index (0-9)	6.0
Time to obtain cross-border license (days)	1
Cost to obtain cross-border license (% income per capita)	28.6

WATER | DTF Score 50.00 ◇ Rank 32

Integrated water resource management index (0-29)	14.5
Individual water use for irrigation index (0-20)	10.0

ICT | DTF Score 41.67 ◇ Rank 50

ICT index (0-9)	3.8

a. The indicators apply to the formal seed system only.

SENEGAL

DTF score		Rank
Seed	52.80	36
Fertilizer	17.86	60
Machinery	25.15	54
Finance	43.35	41
Markets	54.65	36
Transport	51.57	35
Water	35.73	42
ICT	50.00	37

SEED[a] | DTF Score 52.80 ◇ Rank 36

Plant breeding index (0-10)	7.0
Variety registration index (0-8)	5.5
Time to register new variety (days)	561
Cost to register new variety (% income per capita)	708.5
Seed quality control index (0-12)	5.5

FERTILIZER | DTF Score 17.86 ◇ Rank 60

Fertilizer registration index (0-7)	0.0
Time to register a new fertilizer product (days)	N/A
Cost to register a new fertilizer product (% income per capita)	N/A
Quality control of fertilizer index (0-7)	1.0
Importing & distributing fertilizer index (0-7)	4.0

MACHINERY | DTF Score 25.15 ◇ Rank 54

Tractor operation index (0-5)	1.0
Time to register a tractor (days)	5
Cost to register a tractor (% income per capita)	0.6
Tractor testing and standards index (0-8)	0.3
Time to obtain type approval (days)	N/A
Cost to obtain type approval (% income per capita)	N/A
Tractor import index (0-5)	0.5

FINANCE | DTF Score 43.35 ◇ Rank 41

Branchless Banking

Agent banking index (0-5)	0.0
E-money index (0-4)	3.8

Movable Collateral

Warehouse receipts index (0-5)	0.0
Doing Business - getting credit index (0-8)	4.0

Non-bank Lending Institutions

Microfinance institutions index (0-7)	4.0
Financial cooperatives index (0-7)	4.0

MARKETS | DTF Score 54.65 ◇ Rank 36

Producer organizations index (0-13)	7.8
Plant protection index (0-8)	3.5
Agricultural trade index (0-9)	4.0
Documents to export agricultural goods (number)	2
Time to export agricultural goods (days)	3
Cost to export agricultural goods (% income per capita)	3.8

TRANSPORT | DTF Score 51.57 ◇ Rank 35

Trucking licenses and operations index (0-11)	6.8
Time to obtain trucking licenses (days)	12
Cost to obtain trucking licenses (% income per capita)	2.8
Cross-border transportation index (0-9)	5.0
Time to obtain cross-border license (days)	No practice
Cost to obtain cross-border license (% income per capita)	No practice

WATER | DTF Score 35.73 ◇ Rank 42

Integrated water resource management index (0-29)	5.5
Individual water use for irrigation index (0-20)	10.5

ICT | DTF Score 50.00 ◇ Rank 37

ICT index (0-9)	4.5

a. The indicators apply to the formal seed system only.

SERBIA

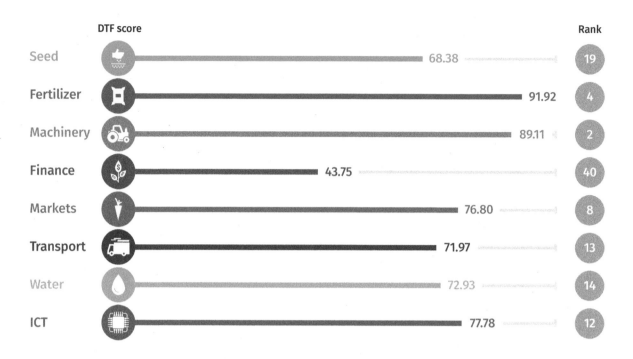

	DTF score		Rank
Seed		68.38	19
Fertilizer		91.92	4
Machinery		89.11	2
Finance	43.75		40
Markets		76.80	8
Transport		71.97	13
Water		72.93	14
ICT		77.78	12

SEED[a] | DTF Score 68.38 ◇ Rank 19

Plant breeding index *(0-10)*	8.0
Variety registration index *(0-8)*	5.0
Time to register new variety *(days)*	604
Cost to register new variety *(% income per capita)*	0.4
Seed quality control index *(0-12)*	7.0

FERTILIZER | DTF Score 91.92 ◇ Rank 4

Fertilizer registration index *(0-7)*	5.8
Time to register a new fertilizer product *(days)*	22
Cost to register a new fertilizer product *(% income per capita)*	5.3
Quality control of fertilizer index *(0-7)*	6.0
Importing & distributing fertilizer index *(0-7)*	7.0

MACHINERY | DTF Score 89.11 ◇ Rank 2

Tractor operation index *(0-5)*	3.0
Time to register a tractor *(days)*	2
Cost to register a tractor *(% income per capita)*	5.6
Tractor testing and standards index *(0-8)*	8.0
Time to obtain type approval *(days)*	30
Cost to obtain type approval *(% income per capita)*	2.7
Tractor import index *(0-5)*	5.0

FINANCE | DTF Score 43.75 ◇ Rank 40

Branchless Banking	0.0
Agent banking index *(0-5)*	4.0
E-money index *(0-4)*	
Movable Collateral	5.0
Warehouse receipts index *(0-5)*	5.0
Doing Business - getting credit index *(0-8)*	
Non-bank Lending Institutions	0.0
Microfinance institutions index *(0-7)*	0.0
Financial cooperatives index *(0-7)*	

MARKETS | DTF Score 76.80 ◇ Rank 8

Producer organizations index *(0-13)*	7.0
Plant protection index *(0-8)*	7.0
Agricultural trade index *(0-9)*	6.5
Documents to export agricultural goods *(number)*	1
Time to export agricultural goods *(days)*	2
Cost to export agricultural goods *(% income per capita)*	0.2

TRANSPORT | DTF Score 71.97 ◇ Rank 13

Trucking licenses and operations index *(0-11)*	6.5
Time to obtain trucking licenses *(days)*	30
Cost to obtain trucking licenses *(% income per capita)*	1.6
Cross-border transportation index *(0-9)*	7.0
Time to obtain cross-border license *(days)*	30
Cost to obtain cross-border license *(% income per capita)*	4.3

WATER | DTF Score 72.93 ◇ Rank 14

Integrated water resource management index *(0-29)*	22.0
Individual water use for irrigation index *(0-20)*	14.0

ICT | DTF Score 77.78 ◇ Rank 12

ICT index *(0-9)*	7.0

a. The indicators apply to the formal seed system only.

SPAIN

DTF score		Rank
Seed	86.65	2
Fertilizer	91.10	5
Machinery	83.23	6
Finance	86.67	3
Markets	87.08	2
Transport	91.70	1
Water	94.53	1
ICT	100.00	1

SEED[a] | DTF Score 86.65 ◇ Rank 2

Plant breeding index *(0-10)*	10.0
Variety registration index *(0-8)*	6.0
Time to register new variety *(days)*	598
Cost to register new variety *(% income per capita)*	9.3
Seed quality control index *(0-12)*	12.0

FERTILIZER | DTF Score 91.10 ◇ Rank 5

Fertilizer registration index *(0-7)*	5.8
Time to register a new fertilizer product *(days)*	90
Cost to register a new fertilizer product *(% income per capita)*	0.0
Quality control of fertilizer index *(0-7)*	7.0
Importing & distributing fertilizer index *(0-7)*	6.0

MACHINERY | DTF Score 83.23 ◇ Rank 6

Tractor operation index *(0-5)*	4.5
Time to register a tractor *(days)*	5
Cost to register a tractor *(% income per capita)*	0.6
Tractor testing and standards index *(0-8)*	7.0
Time to obtain type approval *(days)*	451
Cost to obtain type approval *(% income per capita)*	32.2
Tractor import index *(0-5)*	5.0

FINANCE | DTF Score 86.67 ◇ Rank 3

Branchless Banking

Agent banking index *(0-5)*	N/A
E-money index *(0-4)*	3.8

Movable Collateral

Warehouse receipts index *(0-5)*	3.5
Doing Business - getting credit index *(0-8)*	5.0

Non-bank Lending Institutions

Microfinance institutions index *(0-7)*	N/A
Financial cooperatives index *(0-7)*	7.0

MARKETS | DTF Score 87.08 ◇ Rank 2

Producer organizations index *(0-13)*	10.8
Plant protection index *(0-8)*	7.8
Agricultural trade index *(0-9)*	5.5
Documents to export agricultural goods *(number)*	0
Time to export agricultural goods *(days)*	0
Cost to export agricultural goods *(% income per capita)*	0.0

TRANSPORT | DTF Score 91.70 ◇ Rank 1

Trucking licenses and operations index *(0-11)*	9.8
Time to obtain trucking licenses *(days)*	4
Cost to obtain trucking licenses *(% income per capita)*	0.2
Cross-border transportation index *(0-9)*	9.0
Time to obtain cross-border license *(days)*	25
Cost to obtain cross-border license *(% income per capita)*	0.5

WATER | DTF Score 94.53 ◇ Rank 1

Integrated water resource management index *(0-29)*	28.0
Individual water use for irrigation index *(0-20)*	18.5

ICT | DTF Score 100.00 ◇ Rank 1

ICT index *(0-9)*	9.0

a. The indicators apply to the formal seed system only.

SRI LANKA

DTF score		**Rank**

Seed — 47.10 — **47**

Fertilizer — 53.82 — **36**

Machinery — 46.18 — **39**

Finance — 28.67 — **58**

Markets — 33.85 — **58**

Transport — 42.43 — **48**

Water — 16.68 — **54**

ICT — 27.78 — **59**

SEED[a] | DTF Score 47.10 ◇ Rank 47

Plant breeding index *(0-10)*	4.0
Variety registration index *(0-8)*	3.5
Time to register new variety *(days)*	298
Cost to register new variety *(% income per capita)*	0.0
Seed quality control index *(0-12)*	2.0

FERTILIZER | DTF Score 53.82 ◇ Rank 36

Fertilizer registration index *(0-7)*	2.4
Time to register a new fertilizer product *(days)*	365
Cost to register a new fertilizer product *(% income per capita)*	3.7
Quality control of fertilizer index *(0-7)*	3.5
Importing & distributing fertilizer index *(0-7)*	3.5

MACHINERY | DTF Score 46.18 ◇ Rank 39

Tractor operation index *(0-5)*	2.5
Time to register a tractor *(days)*	3
Cost to register a tractor *(% income per capita)*	3.3
Tractor testing and standards index *(0-8)*	2.3
Time to obtain type approval *(days)*	N/A
Cost to obtain type approval *(% income per capita)*	N/A
Tractor import index *(0-5)*	3.0

FINANCE | DTF Score 28.67 ◇ Rank 58

Branchless Banking

Agent banking index *(0-5)*	0.0
E-money index *(0-4)*	3.7

Movable Collateral

Warehouse receipts index *(0-5)*	0.0
Doing Business - getting credit index *(0-8)*	3.0

Non-bank Lending Institutions

Microfinance institutions index *(0-7)*	0.0
Financial cooperatives index *(0-7)*	3.0

MARKETS | DTF Score 33.85 ◇ Rank 58

Producer organizations index *(0-13)*	6.9
Plant protection index *(0-8)*	2.0
Agricultural trade index *(0-9)*	2.5
Documents to export agricultural goods *(number)*	3
Time to export agricultural goods *(days)*	4
Cost to export agricultural goods *(% income per capita)*	7.1

TRANSPORT | DTF Score 42.43 ◇ Rank 48

Trucking licenses and operations index *(0-11)*	3.5
Time to obtain trucking licenses *(days)*	2
Cost to obtain trucking licenses *(% income per capita)*	2.7
Cross-border transportation index *(0-9)*	0.0
Time to obtain cross-border license *(days)*	N/A
Cost to obtain cross-border license *(% income per capita)*	N/A

WATER | DTF Score 16.68 ◇ Rank 54

Integrated water resource management index *(0-29)*	7.5
Individual water use for irrigation index *(0-20)*	1.5

ICT | DTF Score 27.78 ◇ Rank 59

ICT index *(0-9)*	2.5

---

a. The indicators apply to the formal seed system only.

ENABLING THE BUSINESS OF AGRICULTURE 2017

SUDAN

DTF score		Rank

Seed	49.34	41
Fertilizer	23.21	56
Machinery	54.87	27
Finance	33.93	53
Markets	30.56	61
Transport	43.36	47
Water	10.17	59
ICT	33.33	57

SEED[a] | DTF Score 49.34 ◇ Rank 41

Plant breeding index *(0-10)*	8.0
Variety registration index *(0-8)*	4.5
Time to register new variety *(days)*	654
Cost to register new variety *(% income per capita)*	620.7
Seed quality control index *(0-12)*	4.5

FERTILIZER | DTF Score 23.21 ◇ Rank 56

Fertilizer registration index *(0-7)*	0.0
Time to register a new fertilizer product *(days)*	N/A
Cost to register a new fertilizer product *(% income per capita)*	N/A
Quality control of fertilizer index *(0-7)*	3.5
Importing & distributing fertilizer index *(0-7)*	3.0

MACHINERY | DTF Score 54.87 ◇ Rank 27

Tractor operation index *(0-5)*	2.5
Time to register a tractor *(days)*	7
Cost to register a tractor *(% income per capita)*	29.8
Tractor testing and standards index *(0-8)*	5.3
Time to obtain type approval *(days)*	45
Cost to obtain type approval *(% income per capita)*	146.6
Tractor import index *(0-5)*	1.5

FINANCE | DTF Score 33.93 ◇ Rank 53

Branchless Banking

Agent banking index *(0-5)*	0.0
E-money index *(0-4)*	2.0

Movable Collateral

Warehouse receipts index *(0-5)*	0.0
Doing Business - getting credit index *(0-8)*	2.0

Non-bank Lending Institutions

Microfinance institutions index *(0-7)*	5.0
Financial cooperatives index *(0-7)*	4.0

MARKETS | DTF Score 30.56 ◇ Rank 61

Producer organizations index *(0-13)*	6.5
Plant protection index *(0-8)*	1.5
Agricultural trade index *(0-9)*	No data
Documents to export agricultural goods *(number)*	2
Time to export agricultural goods *(days)*	21
Cost to export agricultural goods *(% income per capita)*	6.1

TRANSPORT | DTF Score 43.46 ◇ Rank 47

Trucking licenses and operations index *(0-11)*	1.0
Time to obtain trucking licenses *(days)*	N/A
Cost to obtain trucking licenses *(% income per capita)*	N/A
Cross-border transportation index *(0-9)*	7.0
Time to obtain cross-border license *(days)*	14
Cost to obtain cross-border license *(% income per capita)*	2.4

WATER | DTF Score 10.17 ◇ Rank 59

Integrated water resource management index *(0-29)*	3.0
Individual water use for irrigation index *(0-20)*	2.0

ICT | DTF Score 33.33 ◇ Rank 57

ICT index *(0-9)*	3.0

a. The indicators apply to the formal seed system only.

TAJIKISTAN

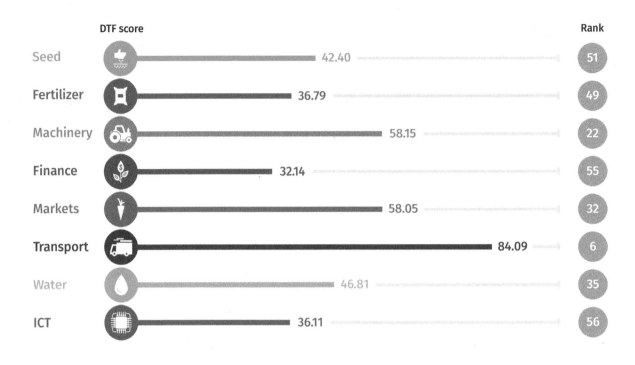

	DTF score	Rank
Seed	42.40	51
Fertilizer	36.79	49
Machinery	58.15	22
Finance	32.14	55
Markets	58.05	32
Transport	84.09	6
Water	46.81	35
ICT	36.11	56

SEED[a] | DTF Score 42.40 ◇ Rank 51

Plant breeding index (0-10)	8.0
Variety registration index (0-8)	4.5
Time to register new variety (days)	No practice
Cost to register new variety (% income per capita)	No practice
Seed quality control index (0-12)	4.0

FERTILIZER | DTF Score 36.79 ◇ Rank 49

Fertilizer registration index (0-7)	2.3
Time to register a new fertilizer product (days)	No practice
Cost to register a new fertilizer product (% income per capita)	No practice
Quality control of fertilizer index (0-7)	2.0
Importing & distributing fertilizer index (0-7)	6.0

MACHINERY | DTF Score 58.15 ◇ Rank 22

Tractor operation index (0-5)	3.0
Time to register a tractor (days)	10
Cost to register a tractor (% income per capita)	1.5
Tractor testing and standards index (0-8)	4.0
Time to obtain type approval (days)	No practice
Cost to obtain type approval (% income per capita)	No practice
Tractor import index (0-5)	5.0

FINANCE | DTF Score 32.14 ◇ Rank 55

Branchless Banking

Agent banking index (0-5)	0.0
E-money index (0-4)	1.0

Movable Collateral

Warehouse receipts index (0-5)	0.0
Doing Business - getting credit index (0-8)	2.0

Non-bank Lending Institutions

Microfinance institutions index (0-7)	7.0
Financial cooperatives index (0-7)	3.0

MARKETS | DTF Score 58.05 ◇ Rank 32

Producer organizations index (0-13)	9.0
Plant protection index (0-8)	4.5
Agricultural trade index (0-9)	5.5
Documents to export agricultural goods (number)	2
Time to export agricultural goods (days)	6
Cost to export agricultural goods (% income per capita)	4.3

TRANSPORT | DTF Score 84.09 ◇ Rank 6

Trucking licenses and operations index (0-11)	9.5
Time to obtain trucking licenses (days)	2
Cost to obtain trucking licenses (% income per capita)	0.4
Cross-border transportation index (0-9)	5.0
Time to obtain cross-border license (days)	1
Cost to obtain cross-border license (% income per capita)	5.1

WATER | DTF Score 46.81 ◇ Rank 35

Integrated water resource management index (0-29)	17.0
Individual water use for irrigation index (0-20)	7.0

ICT | DTF Score 36.11 ◇ Rank 56

ICT index (0-9)	3.3

a. The indicators apply to the formal seed system only.

TANZANIA

SUB-SAHARAN AFRICA
LOW INCOME

DTF score		Rank
Seed	68.91	17
Fertilizer	52.84	37
Machinery	44.38	40
Finance	84.85	5
Markets	37.88	56
Transport	65.13	25
Water	62.67	22
ICT	66.67	18

SEED[a] | DTF Score 68.91 ◇ Rank 17

Plant breeding index *(0-10)*	9.0
Variety registration index *(0-8)*	4.0
Time to register new variety *(days)*	333
Cost to register new variety *(% income per capita)*	65.1
Seed quality control index *(0-12)*	6.5

FERTILIZER | DTF Score 52.84 ◇ Rank 37

Fertilizer registration index *(0-7)*	3.4
Time to register a new fertilizer product *(days)*	578
Cost to register a new fertilizer product *(% income per capita)*	983.1
Quality control of fertilizer index *(0-7)*	7.0
Importing & distributing fertilizer index *(0-7)*	3.0

MACHINERY | DTF Score 44.38 ◇ Rank 40

Tractor operation index *(0-5)*	0.5
Time to register a tractor *(days)*	3
Cost to register a tractor *(% income per capita)*	20.7
Tractor testing and standards index *(0-8)*	3.5
Time to obtain type approval *(days)*	N/A
Cost to obtain type approval *(% income per capita)*	N/A
Tractor import index *(0-5)*	5.0

FINANCE | DTF Score 84.85 ◇ Rank 5

Branchless Banking

Agent banking index *(0-5)*	4.1
E-money index *(0-4)*	3.7

Movable Collateral

Warehouse receipts index *(0-5)*	4.5
Doing Business - getting credit index *(0-8)*	6.0

Non-bank Lending Institutions

Microfinance institutions index *(0-7)*	6.0
Financial cooperatives index *(0-7)*	6.0

MARKETS | DTF Score 37.88 ◇ Rank 56

Producer organizations index *(0-13)*	9.7
Plant protection index *(0-8)*	3.0
Agricultural trade index *(0-9)*	3.0
Documents to export agricultural goods *(number)*	4
Time to export agricultural goods *(days)*	16
Cost to export agricultural goods *(% income per capita)*	4.3

TRANSPORT | DTF Score 65.13 ◇ Rank 25

Trucking licenses and operations index *(0-11)*	3.5
Time to obtain trucking licenses *(days)*	3
Cost to obtain trucking licenses *(% income per capita)*	4.7
Cross-border transportation index *(0-9)*	6.0
Time to obtain cross-border license *(days)*	14
Cost to obtain cross-border license *(% income per capita)*	22.0

WATER | DTF Score 62.67 ◇ Rank 22

Integrated water resource management index *(0-29)*	17.5
Individual water use for irrigation index *(0-20)*	13.0

ICT | DTF Score 66.67 ◇ Rank 18

ICT index *(0-9)*	6.0

a. The indicators apply to the formal seed system only. Recent research estimates that 70.2% of Tanzanian famers' households used non-commercial maize seed for planting during the 2010/2011 season. (Sheahan, M. and Barrett, C.B., 2016. Ten striking facts about agricultural input use in Sub-Saharan Africa. Food Policy.)

THAILAND

DTF score		Rank
Seed	56.87	32
Fertilizer	71.65	16
Machinery	56.53	24
Finance	52.11	29
Markets	44.63	52
Transport	29.08	53
Water	6.03	60
ICT	55.56	31

SEED[a] | DTF Score 56.87 ◇ Rank 32

Plant breeding index *(0-10)*	8.0
Variety registration index *(0-8)*	3.0
Time to register new variety *(days)*	327
Cost to register new variety *(% income per capita)*	7.3
Seed quality control index *(0-12)*	3.0

FERTILIZER | DTF Score 71.65 ◇ Rank 16

Fertilizer registration index *(0-7)*	5.4
Time to register a new fertilizer product *(days)*	100
Cost to register a new fertilizer product *(% income per capita)*	2.0
Quality control of fertilizer index *(0-7)*	4.5
Importing & distributing fertilizer index *(0-7)*	3.5

MACHINERY | DTF Score 56.53 ◇ Rank 24

Tractor operation index *(0-5)*	3.0
Time to register a tractor *(days)*	1
Cost to register a tractor *(% income per capita)*	0.2
Tractor testing and standards index *(0-8)*	1.8
Time to obtain type approval *(days)*	N/A
Cost to obtain type approval *(% income per capita)*	N/A
Tractor import index *(0-5)*	5.0

FINANCE | DTF Score 52.11 ◇ Rank 29
Branchless Banking

Agent banking index *(0-5)*	3.4
E-money index *(0-4)*	3.5

Movable Collateral

Warehouse receipts index *(0-5)*	3.8
Doing Business - getting credit index *(0-8)*	2.0

Non-bank Lending Institutions

Microfinance institutions index *(0-7)*	0.0
Financial cooperatives index *(0-7)*	4.0

MARKETS | DTF Score 44.63 ◇ Rank 52

Producer organizations index *(0-13)*	5.0
Plant protection index *(0-8)*	3.0
Agricultural trade index *(0-9)*	4.5
Documents to export agricultural goods *(number)*	3
Time to export agricultural goods *(days)*	6
Cost to export agricultural goods *(% income per capita)*	0.7

TRANSPORT | DTF Score 29.08 ◇ Rank 53

Trucking licenses and operations index *(0-11)*	5.0
Time to obtain trucking licenses *(days)*	45
Cost to obtain trucking licenses *(% income per capita)*	0.8
Cross-border transportation index *(0-9)*	0.0
Time to obtain cross-border license *(days)*	No practice
Cost to obtain cross-border license *(% income per capita)*	No practice

WATER | DTF Score 6.03 ◇ Rank 60

Integrated water resource management index *(0-29)*	3.5
Individual water use for irrigation index *(0-20)*	0.0

ICT | DTF Score 55.56 ◇ Rank 31

ICT index *(0-9)*	5.0

a. The indicators apply to the formal seed system only.

TURKEY

DTF score		Rank
Seed	72.07	12
Fertilizer	74.10	13
Machinery	88.69	4
Finance	49.06	32
Markets	59.95	29
Transport	62.61	28
Water	24.14	51
ICT	55.56	31

SEED[a] | DTF Score 72.07 ◇ Rank 12

Plant breeding index *(0-10)*	6.0
Variety registration index *(0-8)*	6.5
Time to register new variety *(days)*	646
Cost to register new variety *(% income per capita)*	28.8
Seed quality control index *(0-12)*	10.0

FERTILIZER | DTF Score 74.10 ◇ Rank 13

Fertilizer registration index *(0-7)*	5.4
Time to register a new fertilizer product *(days)*	50
Cost to register a new fertilizer product *(% income per capita)*	1.7
Quality control of fertilizer index *(0-7)*	5.0
Importing & distributing fertilizer index *(0-7)*	3.5

MACHINERY | DTF Score 88.69 ◇ Rank 4

Tractor operation index *(0-5)*	4.5
Time to register a tractor *(days)*	2
Cost to register a tractor *(% income per capita)*	2.4
Tractor testing and standards index *(0-8)*	6.7
Time to obtain type approval *(days)*	90
Cost to obtain type approval *(% income per capita)*	102.1
Tractor import index *(0-5)*	5.0

FINANCE | DTF Score 49.06 ◇ Rank 32

Branchless Banking

Agent banking index *(0-5)*	0.0
E-money index *(0-4)*	3.4

Movable Collateral

Warehouse receipts index *(0-5)*	5.0
Doing Business - getting credit index *(0-8)*	3.0

Non-bank Lending Institutions

Microfinance institutions index *(0-7)*	0.0
Financial cooperatives index *(0-7)*	5.0

MARKETS | DTF Score 59.95 ◇ Rank 29

Producer organizations index *(0-13)*	5.1
Plant protection index *(0-8)*	7.0
Agricultural trade index *(0-9)*	4.0
Documents to export agricultural goods *(number)*	3
Time to export agricultural goods *(days)*	3
Cost to export agricultural goods *(% income per capita)*	0.4

TRANSPORT | DTF Score 62.61 ◇ Rank 28

Trucking licenses and operations index *(0-11)*	8.7
Time to obtain trucking licenses *(days)*	4
Cost to obtain trucking licenses *(% income per capita)*	83.5
Cross-border transportation index *(0-9)*	7.0
Time to obtain cross-border license *(days)*	6
Cost to obtain cross-border license *(% income per capita)*	334.1

WATER | DTF Score 24.14 ◇ Rank 51

Integrated water resource management index *(0-29)*	14.0
Individual water use for irrigation index *(0-20)*	0.0

ICT | DTF Score 55.56 ◇ Rank 31

ICT index *(0-9)*	5.0

---

a. The indicators apply to the formal seed system only.

UGANDA

DTF score | | **Rank**

Category	DTF score	Rank
Seed	57.82	31
Fertilizer	46.75	40
Machinery	53.21	31
Finance	50.30	31
Markets	50.44	45
Transport	68.17	18
Water	58.58	26
ICT	61.11	22

SEED[a] | DTF Score 57.82 ◇ Rank 31

Plant breeding index *(0-10)*	7.0
Variety registration index *(0-8)*	5.5
Time to register new variety *(days)*	523
Cost to register new variety *(% income per capita)*	0.0
Seed quality control index *(0-12)*	3.0

FERTILIZER | DTF Score 46.75 ◇ Rank 40

Fertilizer registration index *(0-7)*	3.4
Time to register a new fertilizer product *(days)*	663
Cost to register a new fertilizer product *(% income per capita)*	215.3
Quality control of fertilizer index *(0-7)*	4.0
Importing & distributing fertilizer index *(0-7)*	2.0

MACHINERY | DTF Score 53.21 ◇ Rank 31

Tractor operation index *(0-5)*	2.0
Time to register a tractor *(days)*	9
Cost to register a tractor *(% income per capita)*	16.3
Tractor testing and standards index *(0-8)*	5.0
Time to obtain type approval *(days)*	No practice
Cost to obtain type approval *(% income per capita)*	No practice
Tractor import index *(0-5)*	5.0

FINANCE | DTF Score 50.30 ◇ Rank 31

Branchless Banking

Agent banking index *(0-5)*	0.0
E-money index *(0-4)*	1.0

Movable Collateral

Warehouse receipts index *(0-5)*	5.0
Doing Business - getting credit index *(0-8)*	5.0

Non-bank Lending Institutions

Microfinance institutions index *(0-7)*	5.0
Financial cooperatives index *(0-7)*	3.0

MARKETS | DTF Score 50.44 ◇ Rank 45

Producer organizations index *(0-13)*	6.9
Plant protection index *(0-8)*	3.0
Agricultural trade index *(0-9)*	4.0
Documents to export agricultural goods *(number)*	3
Time to export agricultural goods *(days)*	4
Cost to export agricultural goods *(% income per capita)*	0.3

TRANSPORT | DTF Score 68.17 ◇ Rank 18

Trucking licenses and operations index *(0-11)*	4.5
Time to obtain trucking licenses *(days)*	1
Cost to obtain trucking licenses *(% income per capita)*	5.9
Cross-border transportation index *(0-9)*	6.0
Time to obtain cross-border license *(days)*	2
Cost to obtain cross-border license *(% income per capita)*	29.9

WATER | DTF Score 58.58 ◇ Rank 26

Integrated water resource management index *(0-29)*	11.5
Individual water use for irrigation index *(0-20)*	15.5

ICT | DTF Score 61.11 ◇ Rank 22

ICT index *(0-9)*	5.5

a. The indicators apply to the formal seed system only. Recent research estimates that 63.4% of Ugandan famers' households used non-commercial maize seed for planting during the 2010/2011 season. (Sheahan, M. and Barrett, C.B., 2016. Ten striking facts about agricultural input use in Sub-Saharan Africa. Food Policy.)

UKRAINE

DTF score | | **Rank**

	DTF score	Rank
Seed	56.44	33
Fertilizer	57.62	32
Machinery	63.75	15
Finance	53.27	26
Markets	61.35	26
Transport	46.42	42
Water	54.61	29
ICT	44.44	43

SEED[a] | DTF Score 56.44 ◇ Rank 33

Plant breeding index *(0-10)*	8.0
Variety registration index *(0-8)*	5.0
Time to register new variety *(days)*	714
Cost to register new variety *(% income per capita)*	25.4
Seed quality control index *(0-12)*	3.0

FERTILIZER | DTF Score 57.62 ◇ Rank 32

Fertilizer registration index *(0-7)*	4.8
Time to register a new fertilizer product *(days)*	325
Cost to register a new fertilizer product *(% income per capita)*	845.8
Quality control of fertilizer index *(0-7)*	3.0
Importing & distributing fertilizer index *(0-7)*	6.0

MACHINERY | DTF Score 63.75 ◇ Rank 15

Tractor operation index *(0-5)*	0.5
Time to register a tractor *(days)*	6
Cost to register a tractor *(% income per capita)*	2.2
Tractor testing and standards index *(0-8)*	4.8
Time to obtain type approval *(days)*	No data
Cost to obtain type approval *(% income per capita)*	219.7
Tractor import index *(0-5)*	5.0

FINANCE | DTF Score 53.27 ◇ Rank 26

Branchless Banking

Agent banking index *(0-5)*	3.1
E-money index *(0-4)*	1.0

Movable Collateral

Warehouse receipts index *(0-5)*	5.0
Doing Business - getting credit index *(0-8)*	6.0

Non-bank Lending Institutions

Microfinance institutions index *(0-7)*	0.0
Financial cooperatives index *(0-7)*	4.0

MARKETS | DTF Score 61.35 ◇ Rank 26

Producer organizations index *(0-13)*	8.4
Plant protection index *(0-8)*	4.5
Agricultural trade index *(0-9)*	5.0
Documents to export agricultural goods *(number)*	3
Time to export agricultural goods *(days)*	5
Cost to export agricultural goods *(% income per capita)*	0.9

TRANSPORT | DTF Score 46.42 ◇ Rank 42

Trucking licenses and operations index *(0-11)*	2.0
Time to obtain trucking licenses *(days)*	N/A
Cost to obtain trucking licenses *(% income per capita)*	N/A
Cross-border transportation index *(0-9)*	7.0
Time to obtain cross-border license *(days)*	10
Cost to obtain cross-border license *(% income per capita)*	3.2

WATER | DTF Score 54.61 ◇ Rank 29

Integrated water resource management index *(0-29)*	15.0
Individual water use for irrigation index *(0-20)*	11.5

ICT | DTF Score 44.44 ◇ Rank 43

ICT index *(0-9)*	4.0

a. The indicators apply to the formal seed system only.

COUNTRY TABLES

235

URUGUAY

DTF score		Rank
Seed	76.46	9
Fertilizer	65.88	25
Machinery	20.00	56
Finance	59.07	19
Markets	71.68	15
Transport	72.33	11
Water	59.40	25
ICT	50.00	37

SEED[a] | DTF Score 76.46 ◇ Rank 9

Plant breeding index (0-10)	10.0
Variety registration index (0-8)	4.0
Time to register new variety (days)	305
Cost to register new variety (% income per capita)	5.0
Seed quality control index (0-12)	8.3

FERTILIZER | DTF Score 65.88 ◇ Rank 25

Fertilizer registration index (0-7)	4.0
Time to register a new fertilizer product (days)	11
Cost to register a new fertilizer product (% income per capita)	12.6
Quality control of fertilizer index (0-7)	4.5
Importing & distributing fertilizer index (0-7)	3.0

MACHINERY | DTF Score 20.00 ◇ Rank 56

Tractor operation index (0-5)	0.0
Time to register a tractor (days)	N/A
Cost to register a tractor (% income per capita)	N/A
Tractor testing and standards index (0-8)	0.0
Time to obtain type approval (days)	N/A
Cost to obtain type approval (% income per capita)	N/A
Tractor import index (0-5)	5.0

FINANCE | DTF Score 59.07 ◇ Rank 19

Branchless Banking

Agent banking index (0-5)	3.7
E-money index (0-4)	3.5

Movable Collateral

Warehouse receipts index (0-5)	4.3
Doing Business - getting credit index (0-8)	3.0

Non-bank Lending Institutions

Microfinance institutions index (0-7)	0.0
Financial cooperatives index (0-7)	5.0

MARKETS | DTF Score 71.68 ◇ Rank 15

Producer organizations index (0-13)	10.1
Plant protection index (0-8)	4.5
Agricultural trade index (0-9)	5.5
Documents to export agricultural goods (number)	1
Time to export agricultural goods (days)	2
Cost to export agricultural goods (% income per capita)	0.2

TRANSPORT | DTF Score 72.33 ◇ Rank 11

Trucking licenses and operations index (0-11)	5.5
Time to obtain trucking licenses (days)	2
Cost to obtain trucking licenses (% income per capita)	0.0
Cross-border transportation index (0-9)	6.0
Time to obtain cross-border license (days)	33
Cost to obtain cross-border license (% income per capita)	0.0

WATER | DTF Score 59.40 ◇ Rank 25

Integrated water resource management index (0-29)	18.5
Individual water use for irrigation index (0-20)	11.0

ICT | DTF Score 50.00 ◇ Rank 37

ICT index (0-9)	4.5

a. The indicators apply to the formal seed system only.

VIETNAM

DTF score		Rank

	DTF score	Rank
Seed	48.31	43
Fertilizer	74.87	12
Machinery	74.18	10
Finance	51.19	30
Markets	58.34	31
Transport	79.99	7
Water	58.53	27
ICT	77.78	12

SEED[a] | DTF Score 48.31 ◇ Rank 43

Plant breeding index (0-10)	6.0
Variety registration index (0-8)	5.0
Time to register new variety (days)	901
Cost to register new variety (% income per capita)	406.2
Seed quality control index (0-12)	5.0

FERTILIZER | DTF Score 74.87 ◇ Rank 12

Fertilizer registration index (0-7)	6.0
Time to register a new fertilizer product (days)	15
Cost to register a new fertilizer product (% income per capita)	5.2
Quality control of fertilizer index (0-7)	5.0
Importing & distributing fertilizer index (0-7)	3.0

MACHINERY | DTF Score 74.18 ◇ Rank 10

Tractor operation index (0-5)	2.0
Time to register a tractor (days)	10
Cost to register a tractor (% income per capita)	3.5
Tractor testing and standards index (0-8)	4.3
Time to obtain type approval (days)	11
Cost to obtain type approval (% income per capita)	0.5
Tractor import index (0-5)	5.0

FINANCE | DTF Score 51.19 ◇ Rank 30

Branchless Banking

Agent banking index (0-5)	0.0
E-money index (0-4)	3.0

Movable Collateral

Warehouse receipts index (0-5)	0.0
Doing Business - getting credit index (0-8)	6.0

Non-bank Lending Institutions

Microfinance institutions index (0-7)	5.0
Financial cooperatives index (0-7)	6.0

MARKETS | DTF Score 58.34 ◇ Rank 31

Producer organizations index (0-13)	8.3
Plant protection index (0-8)	5.5
Agricultural trade index (0-9)	3.5
Documents to export agricultural goods (number)	2
Time to export agricultural goods (days)	3
Cost to export agricultural goods (% income per capita)	1.9

TRANSPORT | DTF Score 79.99 ◇ Rank 7

Trucking licenses and operations index (0-11)	5.0
Time to obtain trucking licenses (days)	3
Cost to obtain trucking licenses (% income per capita)	0.5
Cross-border transportation index (0-9)	7.0
Time to obtain cross-border license (days)	2
Cost to obtain cross-border license (% income per capita)	0.5

WATER | DTF Score 58.53 ◇ Rank 27

Integrated water resource management index (0-29)	18.0
Individual water use for irrigation index (0-20)	11.0

ICT | DTF Score 77.78 ◇ Rank 12

ICT index (0-9)	7.0

a. The indicators apply to the formal seed system only.

COUNTRY TABLES

237

ZAMBIA

DTF score		Rank
Seed	69.36	16
Fertilizer	52.29	39
Machinery	35.01	46
Finance	66.22	14
Markets	45.92	50
Transport	66.59	23
Water	67.93	16
ICT	61.11	22

SEED[a] | DTF Score 69.36 ◇ Rank 16

Plant breeding index (0-10)	8.0
Variety registration index (0-8)	5.5
Time to register new variety (days)	544
Cost to register new variety (% income per capita)	70.1
Seed quality control index (0-12)	8.0

FERTILIZER | DTF Score 52.29 ◇ Rank 39

Fertilizer registration index (0-7)	2.9
Time to register a new fertilizer product (days)	210
Cost to register a new fertilizer product (% income per capita)	226.6
Quality control of fertilizer index (0-7)	3.5
Importing & distributing fertilizer index (0-7)	2.5

MACHINERY | DTF Score 35.01 ◇ Rank 46

Tractor operation index (0-5)	0.5
Time to register a tractor (days)	16
Cost to register a tractor (% income per capita)	7.6
Tractor testing and standards index (0-8)	0.3
Time to obtain type approval (days)	N/A
Cost to obtain type approval (% income per capita)	N/A
Tractor import index (0-5)	5.0

FINANCE | DTF Score 66.22 ◇ Rank 14

Branchless Banking

Agent banking index (0-5)	0.0
E-money index (0-4)	3.8

Movable Collateral

Warehouse receipts index (0-5)	5.0
Doing Business - getting credit index (0-8)	6.0

Non-bank Lending Institutions

Microfinance institutions index (0-7)	5.0
Financial cooperatives index (0-7)	4.0

MARKETS | DTF Score 45.92 ◇ Rank 50

Producer organizations index (0-13)	10.3
Plant protection index (0-8)	2.0
Agricultural trade index (0-9)	5.0
Documents to export agricultural goods (number)	4
Time to export agricultural goods (days)	9
Cost to export agricultural goods (% income per capita)	2.4

TRANSPORT | DTF Score 66.59 ◇ Rank 23

Trucking licenses and operations index (0-11)	4.5
Time to obtain trucking licenses (days)	46
Cost to obtain trucking licenses (% income per capita)	4.2
Cross-border transportation index (0-9)	6.0
Time to obtain cross-border license (days)	1
Cost to obtain cross-border license (% income per capita)	7.8

WATER | DTF Score 67.93 ◇ Rank 16

Integrated water resource management index (0-29)	22.0
Individual water use for irrigation index (0-20)	12.0

ICT | DTF Score 61.11 ◇ Rank 22

ICT index (0-9)	5.5

a. The indicators apply to the formal seed system only.

ZIMBABWE

DTF score | | Rank

	DTF score	Rank
Seed	69.65	15
Fertilizer	61.86	29
Machinery	59.81	20
Finance	38.75	49
Markets	52.99	42
Transport	62.27	29
Water	52.28	31
ICT	38.89	52

SEED[a] | DTF Score 69.65 ◇ Rank 15

Plant breeding index *(0-10)*	10.0
Variety registration index *(0-8)*	4.0
Time to register new variety *(days)*	607
Cost to register new variety *(% income per capita)*	41.2
Seed quality control index *(0-12)*	8.5

FERTILIZER | DTF Score 61.86 ◇ Rank 29

Fertilizer registration index *(0-7)*	4.4
Time to register a new fertilizer product *(days)*	15
Cost to register a new fertilizer product *(% income per capita)*	15.9
Quality control of fertilizer index *(0-7)*	3.0
Importing & distributing fertilizer index *(0-7)*	3.0

MACHINERY | DTF Score 59.81 ◇ Rank 20

Tractor operation index *(0-5)*	4.5
Time to register a tractor *(days)*	3
Cost to register a tractor *(% income per capita)*	18.8
Tractor testing and standards index *(0-8)*	4.7
Time to obtain type approval *(days)*	N/A
Cost to obtain type approval *(% income per capita)*	N/A
Tractor import index *(0-5)*	4.0

FINANCE | DTF Score 38.75 ◇ Rank 49

Branchless Banking

Agent banking index *(0-5)*	0.0
E-money index *(0-4)*	0.0

Movable Collateral

Warehouse receipts index *(0-5)*	3.5
Doing Business - getting credit index *(0-8)*	5.0

Non-bank Lending Institutions

Microfinance institutions index *(0-7)*	4.0
Financial cooperatives index *(0-7)*	3.0

MARKETS | DTF Score 52.99 ◇ Rank 42

Producer organizations index *(0-13)*	7.5
Plant protection index *(0-8)*	2.0
Agricultural trade index *(0-9)*	No data
Documents to export agricultural goods *(number)*	1
Time to export agricultural goods *(days)*	No data
Cost to export agricultural goods *(% income per capita)*	1.2

TRANSPORT | DTF Score 62.27 ◇ Rank 29

Trucking licenses and operations index *(0-11)*	5.5
Time to obtain trucking licenses *(days)*	5
Cost to obtain trucking licenses *(% income per capita)*	14.7
Cross-border transportation index *(0-9)*	4.0
Time to obtain cross-border license *(days)*	7
Cost to obtain cross-border license *(% income per capita)*	17.6

WATER | DTF Score 52.28 ◇ Rank 31

Integrated water resource management index *(0-29)*	18.0
Individual water use for irrigation index *(0-20)*	8.5

ICT | DTF Score 38.89 ◇ Rank 52

ICT index *(0-9)*	3.5

a. The indicators apply to the formal seed system only. Recent research estimates that 77.3% of the seed used by farmers in Zimbabwe in 2009 were sourced in the informal seed sector. (McGuire, S. and Sperling, L., 2016. Seed systems smallholder farmers use. Food Security, 8(1), pp.179-195.)

COUNTRY TABLES

239

Local Experts

GLOBAL

Africa Legal Network

AGCO

Axiata Group Berhad

Bayer Animal Health

Boehringer Ingelheim Animal
Health GmbH

Cargill

Centil Law

Ceva Santé Animale

Choong Ang Vaccine
Laboratories Co., Ltd. (CAVAC)

CIRAD

Comité Européen
des groupements de
constructeurs du machinisme
agricole (CEMA)

ComCashew/GIZ

Deutsche Gesellschaft
für Internationale
Zusammenarbeit GmbH (GIZ)

DFDL Law Group

DLA Piper

Elanco Animal Health

Food and Agriculture
Organization of the United
Nations

Freshfel Europe

Grata International

HealthforAnimals

Hester Biosciences Limited

HM.Clause

International Co-operative
Alliance (ICA)

International Fertilizer
Association (IFA)

International Fertilizer
Development Center (IFDC)

International Grain Trade
Coalition (IGTC)

International Road Transport
Union (IRU) - Global
Partnership for Sustainable
Transport (GPST)

International Water
Management Institute (IWMI)

International Women's Coffee
Alliance (IWCA)

John Deere

KWS

Limagrain

Merck Animal Health

Merial Ltd.

Monsanto

Oikocredit

Olam International

One Acre Fund

Seed Co

Sociedad Química y Minera
(SQM)

Soil Health Consortia for
Eastern and Southern Africa

Syngenta

The Regional Environmental
Center for Central and Eastern
Europe (REC)

Tractors and Farm Equipment
Ltd.

Trammo

UNDP

Virbac

Yara

Zoetis

ARMENIA

AM Law Firm

Armenian State Agrarian
University

Center for Agribusiness
and Rural Development
Foundation (CARD)

Central Bank of Armenia

Green Lane Agricultural
Assistance

Hrashk Aygi LLC

Mentis Law PLC

Regional Environmental
Centre for the Caucasus

Republic of Armenia Ministry
of Nature Protection

Scientific Center of
Agrobiotechnology

Scientific Center of Vegetable
and Industrial Crops

State Committee of Water
Economy of the Ministry of
Agriculture of the Republic of
Armenia

Prudence CJSC
Nerses Aghababyan

SpecMash LLC
Vladimir Akopov

Unitrans
Heghine Armenyan

Alvina Avagyan

Fruit Armenia OJSC
Anna Avagyan

ACBA Credit Agricole Bank
CJSC
Angelika Baghramyan

Agrarian Farmer's Association
of Armenia
Hrachia Berberyan

Center for Agribusiness and
Rural Development (CARD)
Sergey Chakhmakhchyan

SEF International UCO LLC
Hovhannes Chamsaryan

Hester Biosciences Limited
Rajiv Gandhi

"Green Lad" LLC
Tigran Gharajyan

Fruit Armenia OJSC
Gor Gharibyan

Scientific Center of Soil,
Agrochemistry and
Melioration
Hunan Ghazaryan

Scientific Centre of Drug and
Medical Technology Expertise
(SCDMTE)
Lilit Ghazaryan

Euroterm
Vahe Ghazaryan

Ministry of Agriculture of the
Republic of Armenia
Vardan Ghushchyan

Ayele NGO
Erik Grigoryan

Scientific Center of Soil,
Agrochemistry and
Melioration
Robert Grigozyan

Yerevan State University
Heghine Hakhverdyan

Association of International
Road Carriers of Armenia
(AIRCA)
Herbert Hambardzumyan

Armenia Tree Project
Arthur Harutyunyan

Healthy Garden Cooperative
Gevorg Harutyunyan

Fruit Armenia OJSC
Hovik Hovhannisyan

K-Telecom VivaCell-MTS
Ralf Iirikyan

Ministry of Transport and
Communication
Arman Karapetyan

Armenia Tree Project
Lucineh Kassarjian

CARD Agro Service
Artak Khachatryan

Scientific Center of Soil,
Agrochemistry and
Melioration
Samvel Kroyan

Artagro LLC
Arthur Ktrakyan

SEF International UCO LLC
Arsen Kuchukyan

Scientific Center of Soil,
Agrochemistry and
Melioration
Albert Markosyan

DS Logistics
Davit Marutyan

National Centre for Legislative
Regulation PIU
Gnel Mayilyan

Fruit Armenia OJSC
Elena Mizzoyan

Scientific Center of Soil,
Agrochemistry and
Melioration
Anzhela Mkrtchyan

SpecMash LLC
Ashot Mnatsakanyan

Prudence CJSC
Edward Mouradian

Ministry of Agriculture of the
Republic of Armenia
Artur Nikoyan

Trans Logistic Caucasus LLC
Egishe Ovannisyan

Ministry of Agriculture of the
Republic of Armenia
Anahit Ovsenyan

National Academy of Sciences
Davit Pipoyan

Prudence CJSC
Karine Pogosyan

Armenia Tree Project
Alla Sahakyan

Ministry of Agriculture of the
Republic of Armenia
Samvel Sahakyan

Armenian National University of Architecture and Construction
Vilik Sargsyan

Ayele NGO
Nane Shahnazaryajn

Environmental Impact Monitoring Center
Gayane Shahnazaryan

Siatrans Logistic
Artur Stepanyan

International Center for Agribusiness Research and Education
Vardan Urutyan

Karine Yesayan

BANGLADESH

ACI Limited

Axiata Group Berhad

Bengal Overseas Ltd.

Rajdhani Enterprise

East West Seeds India Pvt. Ltd.
Habib Abdur Rahman

Eastern Bank Ltd.
Nafis Ahmed

Bangladesh Agricultural Development Corporation (BADC)
Aziz AKM Abdul

Mega Pharma Limited
Md. Nurul Alam

Bangladesh Agricultural Research Council
S. M. Khorshed Alam

WAVE Foundation
Mohsin Ali

Lal Teer Seed Limited
Mahbub Anam

Lal Teer Seed Limited
Shah Mohammad Arefin

Legacy Legal Corporate
Jennifer Ashraf

Department of Agricultural Extension (DAE)
Anjan Chandra Mandal

Hester Biosciences Limited
Rajiv Gandhi

Dr. Kamal Hossain & Associates
Moin Ghani

The Premier Bank Limited
Shamim Habib

Advance Animal Science Co. Ltd.
Aminul Haque

Gentry Pharmaceuticals Limited
Lutful Hoque

Md. Sirajul Hoque

Department of Agricultural Extension (DAE)
Monir Hosen

WAVE Foundation
Anwar Hossain

Md. Moqbul Hossain

Mohammad Iqbal Hossain

S Hossain & Associates
Sanwar Hossain

Eastern Bank Ltd.
Ali Reza Iftekhar

Bangladesh Chemical Industries Corporation
Mohammed Iqbal

Power Social Enterprises Ltd.
Md. Nazrul Islam

ASA
Md. Hamidul Islam

Bangladesh Fruits, Vegetables & Allied Products Exporters Association
Md. Monjurul Islam

Bangladesh Chemical Industries Corporation
Monirul Islam

Bangladesh Bank
Nazrul Islam

Gentry Pharmaceuticals Limited
Reajul Islam

Bangladesh Chemical Industries Corporation
Saidul Islam

Eastern Bank Ltd.
Saiful Islam

International Fertilizer Development Center (IFDC)
Ishrat Jahan

Metal (Pvt.) Ltd.
Humayun Kabir

Dhaka District Judge Court
Hossain Md. Nazmul Karim

University of Malaya
Mohammad Ershadul Karim

Raihan Khalid & Associates
Abu Raihan M. Khalid

Bangladesh Bank
Md. Enamul Karim Khan

Advance Animal Science Co. Ltd.
Munzur Murshid Khan

Bangladesh Rice Research Institute
Md. Maniruzzaman

HSBC
François de Maricourt

Choong Ang Vaccine Laboratories Co., Ltd. (CAVAC)
Juver Membrebe

Lal Teer Seed Limited
Abdul Awal Mintoo

Advance Animal Science Co. Ltd.
Ahmed Moinuddin Khandker Moyeenudin

Eastern Bank Ltd.
Usman Rashed Muyeen

Ministry of Agriculture
Md. Nasiruzzaman

Bangladesh Bank
Abu Farah Md. Nasser

Advance Animal Science Co. Ltd.
Nazmina

Bangladesh Chemical Industries Corporation
Mostafizur Rahman Patwary

Legacy Legal Corporate
Tameem Rahman

Gentry Pharmaceuticals Limited
Tuwhidur Rahman

S Hossain & Associates
Sheikh Rajib

ACI Ltd.
Subrata Ranjan Das

Ministry of Agriculture
Abdur Razzaque

Lal Teer Seed Limited
M Abdur Razzaque

Bangladesh Agricultural Research Institute
Kshirode C Roy

Bangladesh Agricultural Research Institute
Arun Saha

Department of Agricultural Extension (DAE)
Shoumen Saha

Bangladesh Agricultural Research Council
Md. Salam

Milky Way Shipping Lines (Pvt.) Ltd.
Mohammad Solaiman

M.S. Aleya Enterprise Ltd.
Md. Mostafa Talukder

Bangladesh Bank
Md. Amir Uddin

NN Agro Trade
Md. Nazim Uddin

Microcredit Regulatory Authority
Mohammad Yakub Hossain

Milky Way Shipping Lines (Pvt.) Ltd.
Golam Zilani

BENIN

Université d'Abomey-Calavi
Enoch G. Achigan-Dako

ComCashew/GIZ
William Agyekum Acquah

Université d'Abomey-Calavi
Appolinaire Adandonon

Pierre Adisso

CNS-Maïs/PPAAO Bénin INRAB
Adolphe Adjanohoun

ComCashew/GIZ
Mary Adzanyo

Cabinet Agbantou
Saïdou Agbantou

Ministère de l'Agriculture, de l'Elevage et de la Pêche
Ludovic Franck Agbayahoun

Autorité de Régulation des Communications Electroniques et de la Poste (ARCEP)
Géraud-Constant Ahokpossi

Bénin Gold Cashew Industries
Michel Kouvi Akognon

Cabinet Rafikou A. Alabi
Agnila Rafikou Alabi

Centrale d'Achat des Intrants Agricoles (CAIA)
Yessoufou Alamon

Almo et Fils
Mohamed Alitonou

Direction Générale de l'Eau
Tchokpohoué Allomasso

Djima Aly

Cabinet Rafikou A. Alabi
Aum Rockas Amoussouvi

GID SARL Géomatique, Ingénierie et Développement
S. Judicaël Azon

Direction Générale de l'Eau
Félix Azonsi

Olaogou Phirmin Biaou

Cabinet d'avocats de Maître Chiba Pulchérie Natabou
David Binouyo

Orabank Benin
Nicole Bopke

Orabank Benin
Hervé Borna

Université d'Abomey-Calavi
Augustin Chabossou

Senaigroup
Senakpon Tadjou Clotoe

Association PEBCo-BETHESDA
François Coco

Université d'Agriculture de Kétou
Jean Timothée Claude Codjia

CNS-Maïs/PPAAO Bénin INRAB
Romuald A. Dossou

Orabank Benin
Modeste Elegbede

Ministère de l'Agriculture, de l'Elevage et de la Pêche
Felix Gbaguidi

Senaigroup
Romain Gbodogbe

Ministère de l'Agriculture, de l'Elevage et de la Pêche
Victorin Gbogbo

Antoine Loffa Homeky

Université d'Abomey-Calavi
Carlos A. Houdegbe

Cabinet Agbantou
Marcel Hounnou

Cabinet Agbantou
Silas Hounsounou

*Agence de Développement de
la Mécanisation Agricole*
Guy Omer C. Hountondji

Kesse & Associates
Kesse Ekwueme Ilodi

DHL Courier
Onwuegbu Jiaji

*Ministère de l'Agriculture, de
l'Elevage et de la Pêche*
Guillaume Kimba

*African Climate Policy Centre
(ACPC) – UN Economic
Commission for Africa*
Baba A. Rivaldo Kpadonou

*Ministère de l'Agriculture, de
l'Elevage et de la Pêche*
Byll Orou Kperou Gado

Emmanuel Lougbegnon

*Institut National des
Recherches Agricoles du
Bénin (INRAB)*
Toussaint Mikpon

*Groupement des Exploitants
Agricoles du Bénin*
Franck Monkoun

AgroBénin
Hervé Nankpan

*Cabinet d'avocats de Maître
Chiba Pulchérie Natabou*
Chiba Pulchérie Natabou

Bioversity International
Sognigbe N'Danikou

*Ministère de l'Agriculture, de
l'Elevage et de la Pêche*
Charafa Olahanmi

Global Veterinary Agency
Carlos Quenum

ComCashew/GIZ
Mohamed Issaka Salifou

*Laboratoire d'Analyse
Régionale et d'Expertise
Sociale*
Gansari Sanni

Université de Parakou
Emmanuel Tôn'dénan Sekloka

*Laboratoire d'Analyse
Régionale et d'Expertise
Sociale*
Afouda Servais Alix

Café logistique
Gabriel Sounouvou

*Action pour la Promotion des
Initiatives Communautaires*
Alidou Takpara

Association PEBCo-BETHESDA
Pascal Tamegnon

Association PEBCo-BETHESDA
Bignon Elvis Espérat Tossa

SSEI Logistique et Transport
Komabou Tozo

Orabank Benin
Marie-Lydie Vigan

Bioversity International
Raymond Vodouhe

ComCashew/GIZ
Rita Weidinger

CNS-Maïs/PPAAO Bénin INRAB
Chabi Gouro Yallou

Cajou Bénin Export
Karl Affo Yenakpon

*Ministère de l'Agriculture, de
l'Elevage et de la Pêche*
Cosme Zinse

BOLIVIA

*Cooperativa de Ahorro y
Crédito Jesús Nazareno, Ltda.*

*Instituto Nacional de
Innovación Agropecuaria y
Forestal (INIAF)*

*Servicio Nacional de Sanidad
Agropecuaria e Inocuidad
Alimentaria (SENASAG)*

Yara

*Entidad Ejecutora de Medio
Ambiente y Agua (EMAGUA) –
Ministerio de Medio Ambiente
y Agua (MMAyA)*
Jacques Alcoba Barba

Sistemas de Riego Valley S.A.
Isaac Alfaro

*Universidad Mayor de San
Simón*
Mercedes Alvarez

Sistemas de Riego Valley S.A.
Rolando Aparicio

Previt S.R.L.
Francisco Balanza

Previt S.R.L.
Luis Balanza

*Becerra de la Roca Donoso &
Asociados S.R.L.*
Mauricio Becerra de la Roca
Donoso

*Sociedad Industrial y
Comercial de Riego y
Agricultura Sicra Ltda.*
Gonzalo Blanco

C.R. & F. Rojas Abogados
José Manuel Canelas Schütt

*Becerra de la Roca Donoso &
Asociados S.R.L.*
Ibling Chavarria

*Universidad Mayor de San
Andrés*
René Chipana Rivera

C.R. & F. Rojas Abogados
Sergio José Dávila Zeballos

*Asociación de Proveedores de
Insumos Agropecuarios (APIA)*
María Reina Durán Achával

*Cámara de Exportadores
Camex Bolivia*
Beatriz Espinoza Calderón

Armando Ferrufino
Coqu.eugniot

*Fundación para el Desarrollo
Tecnológico Agropecuario de
los Valles*
Miguel Florido

Indacochea & Asociados
Úrsula Font

*Entidad Ejecutora de Medio
Ambiente y Agua (EMAGUA) –
Ministerio de Medio Ambiente
y Agua (MMAyA)*
María Eugenia Gamboa Nina

*Deutsche Gesellschaft
für Internationale
Zusammenarbeit GmbH (GIZ)*
Humberto Gandarillas
Antezana

Hester Biosciences Limited
Rajiv Gandhi

*Banco de Desarrollo
Productivo*
Iván Garrón

*Instituto Nacional de
Innovación Agropecuaria y
Forestal (INIAF)*
Edwin Iquize Villca

*Sociedad Industrial y
Comercial de Riego y
Agricultura Sicra Ltda.*
Cesar Iriarte Salaues

*Deutsche Gesellschaft
für Internationale
Zusammenarbeit GmbH (GIZ)*
Christopher Klinnert

AG Logistics S.R.L. Bolivia
Fabrizio Leigue Rioja

Indacochea & Asociados
Ichín Ma

MARCAL Consultores
Sergio Diego Martínez
Calbimonte

*Deutsche Gesellschaft
für Internationale
Zusammenarbeit GmbH (GIZ)*
Hernán Montaño Gonzales

Estudio Moreno Baldivieso
Ramiro Moreno Baldivieso

Estudio Moreno Baldivieso
Andrés Moreno Gutiérrez

Estudio Moreno Baldivieso
Luis Moreno Gutiérrez

Estudio Moreno Baldivieso
Rodrigo Moreno Gutiérrez

*Deutsche Gesellschaft
für Internationale
Zusammenarbeit GmbH (GIZ)*
Jimmy Navarro Scott

*Aagro Consultora Mercados
Bolivianos*
Alberto Ospital

*Blackwood Consulting Corp /
Abogados*
Hugo Alvaro Otero Gambarte

*Instituto Nacional de
Innovación Agropecuaria y
Forestal (INIAF)*
Álvaro Otondo Maldonado

Agrónomo
Jaime Palenque

Nibol Ltda.
Dorian Pereyra

*Viceministerio de
Telecomunicaciones*
Gustavo Leandro Pozo Vargas

AG Logistics S.R.L. Bolivia
Silvia Quevedo

*Quintanilla, Soria & Nishizaw
Soc. Civ.*
Gabriel Ribera Requena

Fundación PROINPA
Wilfredo Rojas

C.R. & F. Rojas Abogados
Diego Fernando Rojas Moreno

*Universidad Mayor de San
Simón*
Ana María Romero

Monsanto Bolivia
Alejandro Rossi

*Helvetas Swiss
Intercooperation*
Carlos Saavedra

*Fundación para el Desarrollo
Tecnológico Agropecuario de
los Valles*
Claudia Sainz

*Salame, Tejada & Asociados
Soc. Civ.*
Iván Salame
González-Aramayo

*Viceministerio de
Telecomunicaciones*
Ariel Salvatierra

*Ministerio de Desarrollo Rural
y Tierras*
Lucio Tito Villca

William Torrez

Urenda Abogados S.C.
Manuel Urenda

*Asociación de Proveedores de
Insumos Agropecuarios (APIA)*
Marco Villarroel

BOSNIA AND
HERZEGOVINA

*Banking Agency of the
Republic of Srpska*

Spaho Law Office

*Ministry of Agriculture, Water
Management and Forestry of
the Federation of Bosnia and
Herzegovina*
Eldin Alikadić

University of Banja Luka
Marina Antić

*Ministry of Foreign Trade and
Economic Relations of Bosnia
and Herzegovina*
Gorana Bašević

Bašo d.o.o.
Nermin Bašić

Spaho Law Office
Jesenko Behlilović

*Ministry of Foreign Trade and
Economic Relations of Bosnia
and Herzegovina*
Fahro Belko

Sajić Advokatska Firma
Ognjen Bogdanić

EU-LINK
Slavko Bogdanović

Sjemenarna d.o.o.
Ivan Bošnjak

Administration of Bosnia and Herzegovina for Plant Health Protection
Mirjana Brzica

Hydro-Engineering Institute Sarajevo
Selma Čengić

United Nations Development Programme
Jovanka Cetković

United Nations Development Program
Raduška Cupać

University of Sarajevo
Hamid Čustović

Dars Voće d.o.o.
Nikola Daka

Ministry of Agriculture, Water Management and Forestry of the Federation of Bosnia and Herzegovina
Dragana Divković

Administration of Bosnia and Herzegovina for Plant Health Protection
Ivana Djerić

Marić & Co. Law Firm
Amina Djugum

Ministry of Agriculture, Forestry and Water Management of Republic of Srpska
Nenad Djukić

The Customs Sector of the Indirect Tax Authority
Miro Džakula

Hester Biosciences Limited
Rajiv Gandhi

Saračević and Gazibegović Lawyers (SGL)
Adis Gazibegović

Bios
Adis Hodžić

Huskić Law Office
Nusmir Huskić

Ministry of Agriculture, Water Management and Forestry of the Federation of Bosnia and Herzegovina
Alma Imamović

Spaho Law Office
Admir Jusufbegović

University of Banja Luka
Danijela Kondić

Banking Agency of the Federation of Bosnia and Herzegovina (FBA)
Edvard Kotorić

Administration of Bosnia and Herzegovina for Plant Health Protection
Sladjana Kreštalica

AgroDar s.p.z
Aldin Kuduzović

Hydro-Engineering Institute Sarajevo
Tarik Kupusović

Esad Mahir

Saračević and Gazibegović Lawyers (SGL)
Harun Nović

Ministry of Agriculture, Water Management and Forestry of the Federation of Bosnia and Herzegovina
Halil Omanović

Ziraat Bank
Ensar Osmić

University of Banja Luka
Nataša Pašalić

Saračević and Gazibegović Lawyers (SGL)
Saida Porović

Administration of Bosnia and Herzegovina for Plant Health Protection
Radenko Radović

Sajić Advokatska Firma
Aleksandar Sajić

Saračević and Gazibegović Lawyers (SGL)
Emina Saračević

MKF Lider
Džavid Sefjović

University of Sarajevo
Selim Škaljić

Ministry of Foreign Trade and Economic Relations of Bosnia and Herzegovina
Admir Softić

Spaho Law Office
Emir Spaho

Spaho Law Office
Mehmed Spaho

Sajić Advokatska Firma
Dragan Stijak

Agricom d.o.o.
Murat Suljć

Regional Environmental Center for Central and Eastern Europe (REC)
Lejla Šuman

Agricom d.o.o.
Mirza Tahirović

Land Registry Office of the Sarajevo Municipal Court
Ekrem Tošić

Transkop doo
Dejan Žepić

AgroMehanika d.o.o.
Ivana Zlopaša

BURKINA FASO

Lexconsult

ComCashew/GIZ
William Agyekum Acquah

ComCashew/GIZ
Mary Adzanyo

United Bank for Africa Burkina (UBA Burkina)
Valentin Akue

Graine SARL
Boureima Bado

Sotria-B S.A.R.L
Soumahila Bamba

Autorité du Bassin de la Volta
Eléonore Bélemlilga

Fisconsult-Bitié & Associés
Adama Bitié

Société Nationale d'aménagement du Territoire et de l'Equipement Rurale
Tassére Bouda

CB Énergie
Arnaud Chabanne

Ministère de l'Eau, des Aménagements Hydrauliques et de l'Assainissement
Moustapha Congo

Rémi Coulibaly

Association TIN BA
Yempabou Coulidiati

Laafi Sira Kwieogo LSK
Boureima Dambre

Société de Commercialisation et Transit
Yaya Dembélé

Société de Développement du Pôle de Développement de Bagré (Bagrêpôle)
Mamadou Cellou Diallo

Ministère des Infrastructures, du Désenclavement et des Transports
Mamadou Diallo

Hester Biosciences Limited
Rajiv Gandhi

Université de Ouagadougou
Amidou Garane

Chambre de Commerce et d'Industrie du Burkina Faso (CCI BF)
Djakaridja Gnamou

Institut de l'Environnement et de Recherches Agricoles (INERA)
Zacharia Gnankambary

Telecel Faso
Philippe Goabga

United Bank for Africa Burkina (UBA Burkina)
Innocent K. Hien

Ministère de l'Agriculture et des Aménagements Hydrauliques
Aline Kaboré

UMECAP
Fodié Kébé

FAGRI
Issaka Kolga

Fisconsult-Bitié & Associés
Akim Dramane Konaté

Sotria-B S.A.R.L
Minata Koné

Organisation des Transporteurs Routiers du Faso (OTRAF)
Issoufou Maïga

Direction Générale des Ressources en Eau
Nadine Naré/Ouérécé

Union Nationale des Producteurs d'Anacarde
Eloi Nombré

Cabinet d'Avocats M. Kopiho
H.Lamoussa Ouattara

Ministère de l'Agriculture et des Aménagements Hydrauliques
Moussa Ouattara

Programme de Renforcement de la Gouvernance Locale Administrative (PRGLA)
Moussa Ouedraogo

Relwendé Marc Ouedraogo

Direction Générale de l'Aménagement du Territoire et de l'Appui à la Décentralisation (DGAT)
Souleymane Ouedraogo

Société de Développement du Pôle de Développement de Bagré (Bagrépôle)
Yacouba Ouedraogo

Fédération Nationale des Industries de l'Agroalimentaire et de Transformation du Burkina (FIAB)
Dieudonné Pakodtogo

Société Nationale d'Aménagement du Territoire et de l'Equipement Rurale
Pierre Sanon

Centre d'Arbitrage de Médiation et Conciliation de Ouagadougou (CAMC-O)
G. Moussa Savadogo

Ministère des Enseignements Secondaire et Supérieur
Mahamadou Sawadogo

Service national des Semences du Burkina Faso
Abdoulaye R. Semdé

Organisation des Transporteurs Routiers du Faso (OTRAF)
El Hadj Kassoum K. Simpore

Ministère de l'Agriculture et des Aménagements Hydrauliques
Mariam Some

ComCashew/GIZ
Youssoufou Sore

Bureau National des Sols (BUNASOL) du Burkina Faso
Ibrahima Sory

Ministère de l'Agriculture de l'Hydraulique et des Recherches Halieutiques
Evariste Tapsoba

Chambre de Commerce et d'Industrie du Burkina Faso (CCI BF)
Franck Tapsoba

GGTI Motors
Issaka Tapsoba

Pan African Institute for
Development
Norbert François Tchouaffé
Tchiadje

Ministère de l'Agriculture
de l'Hydraulique et des
Recherches Halieutiques
Salif Tentica

Ministère de l'Eau, des
Aménagements Hydrauliques
et de l'Assainissement
Karim Traore

Ministère de l'Agriculture
et des Aménagements
Hydrauliques
Seydina Oumar Traore

ComCashew/GIZ
Rita Weidinger

Laafi Sira Kwieogo LSK
Seydou Soungalo Yameogo

ETY GTZ
Jean Pierre Yaméogo

Chambre de Commerce et
d'Industrie du Burkina Faso
(CCI BF)
Emmanuel Yoda

Agro Productions
Jonas Yogo

Direction Générale des
Aménagements et du
Développement de l'Irrigation
(DGADI)
Adolphe Zangre

Partenariat National de l'Eau
Léila Nakié Zerbo

United Bank for Africa
Burkina (UBA Burkina)
Safiatou Zonou

BURUNDI

Ministère de l'Eau, de
l'Environnement, de
l'Aménagement du Territoire
et de l'Urbanisme

bLive Solutions
Eloge Bapfunya

Muyango Law Firm
Jean-Claude Barakamfitiye

One Acre Fund
Leger Bruggeman

Autorité de Régulation de la
Filière Café (ARFIC)
Marius Bucumi

Projet d'Appui à
l'Intensification et à la
Valorisation Agricoles du
Burundi (PAIVA-B)
Daniel Burinkio

International Fertilizer
Development Center (IFDC)
Leone Comin

FSTE Fonds de Solidarité
des Travailleurs de
l'Enseignement
Bernard Désiré Ntavumba

Ministère de l'Agriculture et
de l'Élevage
Prosper Dodiko

Hester Biosciences Limited
Rajiv Gandhi

PAIOSA - Institutional
and operational support
programme for the
agricultural sector
Patrick Henri

Seed Co., Ltd.
Noëlla Isine

Terimbere Société de
Transport
Emmanuel Karikurubu

Ministère de l'Agriculture et
de l'Élevage
Lucien Masabarakiza

Association for Peace and
Human Rights
Camille Munezero

Institut des Sciences
Agronomiques du Burundi
(ISABU)
Dieudonné Nahimana

Compagnie de Gérance du
Coton
Pierre Claver Nahimana

Confédération des
associations des producteurs
agricoles pour le
développement (CAPAD)
Jean Marie Ndayishimiye

Ministère de l'Eau, de
l'Environnement, de
l'Aménagement du Territoire
et de l'Urbanisme
Emmanuel Ndorimana

Ministère de l'Agriculture et
de l'Élevage
Schadrack Nduwimana

SOGESTAL Kirimiro
Samuel Nibitanga

Société de Commercialisation
des Intrants Agricoles et des
Services Divers (SOCEASED)
Fiston Nikiza

Christian Aid
Emery Ninganza

Service du Catalogue National
des espèces et variétés
végétales
Désiré Niragira

bLive Solutions
Brice Niyondiko

MUTEC
Fabien Niyongere

PAIOSA - Institutional
and operational support
programme for the
agricultural sector
Etienne Niyonzima

Le Programme National pour
la Sécurité Alimentaire et
le Développement Rural de
l'Imbo et du Moso
Gérard Niyungeko

Banque de la République du
Burundi
Simplice Nsabiyumva

Emmanuel Nshimirimana

International Fertilizer
Development Center (IFDC)
Alexis Ntamavukiro

Association des transporteurs
internationaux du Burundi
(ATiB)
Eric Ntangaro

AgriProFocus
Jean Paul Nzosaba

Seed Co
Kasaija Patrick Banage

Bureau Burundais de
Normalisation
Eric Ruracenyeka

Chambre Sectorielle des
Transporteurs et Transitaires
du Burundi
Aimé Rwankineza Uwimana

Ministère de l'Agriculture et
de l'Élevage
Eliakim Sakayoya

Banque Commerciale du
Burundi (Bancobu)
Gaspard Sindayigaya

PAIOSA - Institutional
and operational support
programme for the
agricultural sector
Jorre Vleminckx

CAMBODIA

Axiata Group Berhad

Sithisak Law office

Telecommunication Regulator
of Cambodia (TRC)

Ministry of Agriculture,
Forestry and Fisheries
Saruth Chan

Angkor Green Investment and
Development Co., Ltd.
Sopheak Chan

Ministry of Agriculture,
Forestry and Fisheries
Sinh Chao

Ministry of Agriculture,
Forestry and Fisheries
Saintdona Chea

Amret
Ly Cheapiseth

Cambodia Trucking
Association (CAMTA)
Sok Chheang

Ministry of Agriculture,
Forestry and Fisheries
Meng Chhun

Hester Biosciences Limited
Rajiv Gandhi

National Bank of Cambodia
Bomakara Heng

P&A Asia Law Firm
Pagnawat Heng

UNDP
Phearanich Hing

Bun & Associates
Sophealeak Ing

E@A Consultant Firm
Ham Kimkong

Institute of Technology of
Cambodia (ITC)
Sarann Ly

HBS Law Firm & Consultants
Tayseng Ly

Choong Ang Vaccine
Laboratories Co., Ltd. (CAVAC)
Juver Membrebe

Royal University of Agriculture
Sarom Men

P&A Asia Law Firm
Sovannith Nget

Ministry of Agriculture,
Forestry and Fisheries
Op Pich

P&A Asia Law Firm
Allen Prak

Seng Hong Heng Import
Export & Transport Co., Ltd.
Hi Seng Sam

Cambodia Development
Resource Institute (CDRI)
Sreymom Sam
Channa Samorn

Co-operative Association of
Cambodia (CAC)
Vong Sarinda

German Cooperative and
Raiffeisen Confederation
(DGRV) Cambodia
Hardy Schneider

RMA Group (Cambodia)
Michael Sela Keo

Kong Hour Rice Mill Import
Export Co., Ltd.
Leanhour Seng

Kong Hour Rice Mill Import
Export Co., Ltd.
Thyse Seng

Amru Rice (Cambodia)
Co., Ltd.
Saran Song

Amret
Seng Sophin Pou Sovann

Chungpor Taing Co., Ltd.
Chung Por Taing

Multico MS (Cambodia) Co.,
Ltd.
Hartono Tiodora

Bayon Heritage Holding
Group Co., Ltd.
Chan Vannak

DFDL
Daniel Wein

CAMEROON

Advans Cameroun S.A

Gifama SARL

Ministère de l'Elevage, des
Pêches et des Industries
Animales
Ahmadou Alkaissou

Centre National d'Etudes
et d'Experimentation du
Machinisme Agricole
Raphael Ambassa-kiki

Albert Apan

Conseil Interprofessionnel Des
Societes D'Assainissement Au
Cameroun (CISAC)
Ndjib Bahoya

Centurion Law Group
Carine Bella Foe

Jing & Partners
Bayee Besong

Comité des Pesticides
d'Afrique Centrale
Benoît Bouato

Centurion Law Group
Keseena Chengadu

Express Cargo Sarl
Benga Nomen Christopher

Yannick Wilfreid Djemeni

National d'Etudes et
d'Experimentation du
Machinisme Agricole
Georges Ela Ela

Centre National d'Etudes
et d'Experimentation du
Machinisme Agricole
Ernest Ela Evina

Centurion Law Group
Leopoldo Jeremias Esesa Mba
Ada

Centurion Law Group
William Fonkeng

Fimex International SA
Christian Fosso

Ministère de l'Elevage, des
Pêches et des Industries
Animales
Zéphyrin Fotso Kamnga

Hester Biosciences Limited
Rajiv Gandhi

Ministère de l'Agriculture et
du Développement Rural
François Gandji

Albert Ichakou

Jing & Partners
Paul T. Jing

LANAVET
Jean-Philippe Kazi

Zangue and Partners
Bertrand Kuimo

Transport Expert
Christophe Magloire Lessouga
Etoundi

Agence de Régulation des
Télécommunications
Jean René Loumou Nono

Projet d'Amélioration de la
Competitivité Agricole
Guy Parfait Maga

Comité des Pesticides
d'Afrique Centrale
Josian Edson Maho Yalen

Evelyne Mandessi Bell
Law Firm
Evelyne Mandessi Bell

Cameroon
Centurion Law Group
Carl Mbeng

African Cocoa & Coffee
Farmers' Marketing
Organization - ACCFMO
Sylvanus Ngene Nekenja

Pierre Marie Ngnike

IRAD - Institut de
recherche agricole pour le
développement
Eddy Léonard Ngonkeu
Mangaptche

GIC AGRIPO - Agriculteurs
Professionnels du Cameroun
Adeline Ngo-Samnick

GIC AGRIPO - Agriculteurs
Professionnels du Cameroun
Emilienne Ngo-Samnick

Chede Cooperative Union Ltd.
(CHEDE)
Michael Njume Ebong

Caatech CAM Ltd.
Hauxstable Nomen

GIC AGRIPO - Agriculteurs
Professionnels du Cameroun
Pascal Nondjock

Union Bank of Cameroon
Victor Noumoue

Clinique Vet La Faune Du
Centre
Françoise Chantal Ntsama
Ayangma

Comité des Pesticides
d'Afrique Centrale
Salomon Nyassé

Pan African Institute for
Development
Norbert François Tchouaffé
Tchiadje

Institut de Recherches
Géologiques et Minières
(IRGM)
Fantong Wilson Yetoh

International Institute of
Tropical Agriculture (IITA)
Cameroon
Martin Yemefack

Zangue and Partners
Serges Zangue

GHR Consulting
Emmanuel Zogo

CHILE

Servicio Agrícola y Ganadero
(SAG)

Soquimich Comercial S.A. SQM

Servicio Agrícola y Ganadero
(SAG)
Alejandra Aburto

Aurora Amigo Vasquez

Araya & Cía. Abogados
Jorge Arab

Araya & Cía. Abogados
Matías Araya

Universidad de Concepción
Jose Luis Arumi

Servicio Agrícola y Ganadero
(SAG)
Rodrigo Astete Rocha

Grasty Quintana Majlis & Cía.
Catalina Baeza

Bahamondez, Alvarez &
Zegers Ltda.
Felipe Bahamondez

Barros & Errázuriz Abogados
Pedro Pablo Ballivian Searle

Ministerio de Agricultura
Carlos Barrientos

Brokering Abogados
Marlene Brokering
Schumacher

Carey y Cía. Ltda.
Guillermo Carey

Francisco Caroca Diaz

Alessandri Abogados
Felipe Cousiño

Araya & Cía. Abogados
Inés De Ros Casacuberta

POCH
Romina Echaíz

Cubillos Evans Abogados
Rafael Fernández

Ministerio de Agricultura
Rodrigo Figueroa

Gajardo & Rodríguez
Abogados
Patricio Gajardo

Hester Biosciences Limited
Rajiv Gandhi

Pamela Grandon

German Illanes

DIAgua Derecho e Ingeniería
del Agua
Pablo Jaeger Cousiño

Pablo Manríquez León

Ing. Recursos Naturales
Renovables
Denisse Márquez

Carey y Cía. Ltda.
Eduardo Martin

Universidad de Chile
Eduardo Martínez

Carey y Cía. Ltda.
Raúl Mazzarella

Ministerio de Agricultura
Víctor Medina

Carey y Cía. Ltda.
Felipe Meneses

Servicio Agrícola y Ganadero
(SAG)
Roberto Mir

Brokering Abogados
Angelina Morales

Araya & Cía. Abogados
Sebastián Norris

Daniela Olfos

Instituto Nacional
de Investigaciones
Agropecuarias (INIA)
Fernando Ortega

José Manuel Ortíz Alonso

Ministerio de Agricultura
Rodrigo Pérez

Francisco Pichott

Grasty Quintana Majlis & Cía.
Hugo Prieto

Bahamondez, Alvarez &
Zegers Ltda.
Cynthia Provoste

Philippi Prietocarrizosa & Uría
María Paz Pulgar

Oficina de Estudios y Políticas
Agrarias (ODEPA)
Eduardo Ramirez

Carey y Cía. Ltda.
Julio Recordon

Ministerio del Medio
Ambiente
Jaime Rovira

Carey y Cía. Ltda.
Miguel Saldivia

Transportes Cono Sur y Cía.
S.L.
Oscar Aurelio Santamaria
Osses

Servicio Agrícola y Ganadero
(SAG)
Alvaro Sepúlveda Luque

Carey y Cía. Ltda.
Alfonso Silva

Cooperativa de Riego
Cristian Soto

Universidad de Chile
Gerardo Soto Mundaca

Araya & Cía. Abogados
Alejandra Tagle

Marcel Thevenot - Sills

Alessandri Abogados
Alicia Undurraga Pellegrini

Carey y Cía. Ltda.
Rafael Vergara

Grasty Quintana Majlis & Cía.
Lucy Young

Araya & Cía. Abogados
Gabriela Zepeda

COLOMBIA

Federación Nacional de
Cafeteros de Colombia

Instituto Colombiano
Agropecuario (ICA)

Ministerio de Transporte

Yara

Asociación Nacional de
Médicos Veterinarios de
Colombia (AMEVEC)
Víctor Acero

Instituto Geográfico Agustín
Codazzi
Germán Darío Álvarez Lucero

Garrigues
Nicolás Angulo Rodríguez

Comercial de Riegos Ltda.
Felipe Ardila

Philippi, Prietocarrizosa y Uría
Isabella Ariza Murillo

Fabian Bedoya

Corporación Ecoversa
Javier Tomás Blanco Freja

Garrigues
Roberto Borrás Polanía

Ministerio de Ambiente y Desarrollo Sostenible
Ximena Carranza Hernández

Geomarine Ingenieros Consultores
Andrés Felipe Carvajal

Parra Rodríguez Sanín S.A.S.
Alejandro Castilla

Parra Rodríguez Sanín S.A.S.
Carlos Andrés Castilla

DLA Piper Martínez Neira Abogados
Juan Sebastián Celis

Federacion Nacional de Comerciantes de Colombia (FENALCO)
Sara Cristina Illidge

Cruz & Asociados
Julián Camilo Cruz González

Asociación Colombiana de Propiedad Intelectual
Juan Carlos Cuesta Quintero

Centro Internacional de Agricultura Tropical
Daniel Debouck

Maria Luisa Eslava

Asociación Colombiana de Propiedad Intelectual
Raisha Gamba

Hester Biosciences Limited
Rajiv Gandhi

Garrigues
Camilo Gantiva Hidalgo

Philippi, Prietocarrizosa y Uría
Juan Fernando Gaviria Guzmán

Brigard & Urrutia Abogados S.A.S
Juan Camilo Gómez

Ivanagro S.A.
Fredy Alberto Gómez Bustamante

Ministerio de Ambiente y Desarrollo Sostenible
Francisco Gómez Montes

Gelber Gutiérrez Palacio

Asociación Nacional de Empresas Transportadoras de Carga por Carretera (ASECARGA)
Jairo Herrera Murillo

DLA Piper Martínez Neira Abogados
Luis Eduardo Hoffmann Delvalle

Superintendencia Financiera de Colombia
Samir Alejandro Kiuhan Vásquez

DLA Piper Martínez Neira Abogados
Andrea Londoño

Ministerio de Ambiente y Desarrollo Sostenible
Margarita Lopera

Ministerio de Agricultura y Desarrollo Rural
Nelson Enrique Lozano Castro

Jhon Mármol

DLA Piper Martínez Neira Abogados
Camilo Martínez Beltrán

CasaToro Automotriz S.A.
Hernan Mejía

Brigard & Urrutia Abogados S.A.S
Sergio Michelsen

Universidad Distrital Francisco José de Caldas
Ivonne Astrid Moreno Horta

Parra Rodríguez Sanín S.A.S.
Francisco Javier Morón López

José Lloreda Camacho & Co
Juan Manuel Ojeda

Ministerio de Ambiente y Desarrollo Sostenible
Carlos Augusto Ospina Bravo

Instituto Geográfico Agustín Codazzi
Julio Cesar Palacios Rodríguez

Johnier Pavas

Centro Internacional de Agricultura Tropical
Michael Peters

Ministerio de Ambiente y Desarrollo Sostenible
Andrés Pinilla

Instituto de Investigación y Desarrollo en Agua Potable, Saneamento Básico y Conservación del Recurso Hídrico
Inés Restrepo Tarquino

Parra Rodríguez Sanín S.A.S.
Bernardo Rodríguez Ossa

Ministerio de Ambiente y Desarrollo Sostenible
Paula Andrea Rojas

Garrigues
Adriana Rojas Tamayo

Brigard & Urrutia Abogados S.A.S
Esteban Rubio

Corporación Ecoversa
Gloria Helena Sanclemente Zea

Instituto Colombiano Agropecuário (ICA)
Mc Allister Tafur Garzón

José Lloreda Camacho & Co
Gustavo Tamayo

Philippi, Prietocarrizosa y Uría
Javier Valle Zayas

Invasa Maquinaria S.A.S.
Jorge Vargas

Brigard & Urrutia Abogados S.A.S
Lina Vargas

Holland & Knight
José Vicente Zapata Lugo

María Jimena Zuluaga Villegas

CÔTE D'IVOIRE

Advans

BK & Associés
Elisabeth Aho

Générale de Produits Agricoles (GPA)
Kouamé Ahoussou

PolyPompes Ivoire
Aka Alexandre Allouko

Ministère d'Etat et de l'Agriculture, Direction des Productions Vivrières et de la Sécurité Alimentaire
Bertin Anon

Olam Ivoire Sarl
Augustin Apetey

Générale de Produits Agricoles (GPA)
Kamel Assaf

Générale de Produits Agricoles (GPA)
Yannick Assouma

Agence Nationale d'Appui au Développement Rural
Evrard Yao Attoh

BK & Associés
Eric Bably

Afrique Emergence et Investissements SA
Fahan Bamba

Ministère de l'Environnement, de la Salubrité Urbaine et du Développement Durable
Marina Céline Bayeba

INADIS (Inter Afrique Negoce Et Distribution)
Jules Bayile

CFAO Equipement
Kahou Boehi Bi

Olam Ivoire Sarl
Arouna Coulibaly

Ministère de l'Economie Numérique et de la Poste
Ibrahim Coulibaly

Ministère de l'Economie Numérique et de la Poste
Henri Danon

Cabinet Jean-François Chauveau
Guillaume Dauchez

Ministère de l'Economie Numérique et de la Poste
Dadie Roger Dede

Ministère des Ressources Animales et Halieutiques
Cisse Diarra

ANASEMCI - Association nationale des semenciers de Côte d'Ivoire
Azi Leopold Diby

Ministère de l'Agriculture
Kouadio Jean Esse

Syndicat National des Transporteurs Professionnels de Côte d'Ivoire
Soumaila Fofana

Hester Biosciences Limited
Rajiv Gandhi

Proparcom
Aude Viviane Goulivas-Calle

BK & Associés
Simplice Houphouët

Université Félix Houphouët-Boigny
Jean Patrice Jourda

Ministère des Ressources Animales et Halieutiques
Louis Ketremindie

Centre National de Recherche Agronomique (CNRA)
Edmond Kouablan Koffi

Oikocredit
Yves Komaclo

Société Coopérative Anouanzè-Douekoue
Kan Marcel Konan

Ministère des Transports
Yao Godefroy Konan

Ministère d'Etat et de l'Agriculture, Direction des Productions Vivrières et de la Sécurité Alimentaire
Lucien Kouamé

Générale de Produits Agricoles (GPA)
Olivier Kouamé

Syndicat National des Transporteurs Professionnels de Côte d'Ivoire
Koné Mery

Côte d'Ivoire Agri
Jean Thierry Oura

BK & Associés
Eléonore Pokou

Oikocredit
Solène Prince Agbodjan

Oikocredit
Frank Rubio

Orange
Lacina Soumahoro

Commission de l'Union Economique et Monétaire Ouest Africaine (UEMOA)
Assiongbon Têko-Agbo

Ministère de l'Environnement, de la Salubrité Urbaine et du Développement Durable
Yannick Alain Troupah

Ministère des Transports
Roger Tia Yangba

Ministère de l'Environnement, de la Salubrité Urbaine et du Développement Durable
Kahantayé Aude Zeta

DENMARK

Danish AgriFish Agency

Danish Agro

Yara

Technical University of Denmark (DTU)
Peter Bauer-Gottwein

DAKOFO (The Danish Grain- and Feed-Trade Association)
Asbjørn Børsting

Danish Medicines Agency
Asbjørn Brandt

Danish AgriFish Agency
Merete Buus

Technical University of Denmark (DTU)
Claus Davidsen

Johansson & Kalstrup
Flemming Davidsen

Danish Seed Council
Nils Elmegaard

Aalborg University (AAU)
Stig Enemark

Hester Biosciences Limited
Rajiv Gandhi

Danish Society for Nature Conservation
Susanne Herfelt

Geological Survey of Denmark and Greenland (GEUS)·
Anker Lajer Højberg

Horten Advokatpartnerselskab
Poul Hvilsted

Limagrain (Denmark)
Thomas Bisgaard Jacobsen

The Danish Nature Agency
Eva Juul Jensen

Geological Survey of Denmark and Greenland (GEUS)
Lisbeth Flindt Jørgensen

Kammeradvokaten/Law Firm Poul Schmith
Jakob Kamby

COWI A/S
Ulf Kjellerup

Danish AgriFish Agency
Birgitte Lund

Bech-Bruun
Louise Lundsby Wessel

Danish Society for Nature Conservation
Rikke Lundsgaard

Søholt Gods
Inger Mikkelsen

Bech-Bruun
Jes Anker Mikkelsen

ITD Trade Association for the Danish Road Transport of Goods
Jacob Christian Nielsen

Yara
Mogens Nielsen

Danish Transport and Construction Agency
Jan Persson

Holst, Advokater
Sanaz Ranjbaran

Danish Energy Agency
Rikke Rosenmejer

DAKOFO (The Danish Grain- and Feed-Trade Association)
Claus Saabye Erichsen

Bruun & Hjejle Law Firm
Jakob Echwald Sevel

Danish AgriFish Agency
Jørgen Søgaard Hansen

Danish AgriFish Agency
Maria Lillie Sonne

Aalborg University (AAU)
Esben Munk Sorensen

Holst, Advokater
Jakob Sørensen

Bech-Bruun
Per Speyer Mellemgaard

Gorrissen Federspiel
Michael Steen Jensen

Rønne & Lundgren
Andreas Tamasauskas

Rønne & Lundgre
Ian Tokley

Horten Advokatpartnerselskab
Mads Broe Trustrup

EGYPT, ARAB REP.

Sharkawy & Sarhan Law Firm

United Hybrid International

Nacita Company
Naguib Abadir

Fayoum University
Mahmoud Mohamed Ali Abdel-Azim

Arab Company for Agricultural Production
Ahmed Abdelhamid

Tanta Motors
Amr Aboufreikha

Tahoun Law Office
Moamen Adel
Walid Aly

Tarek Aoun

AGREEN - Green Egypt for Agricultural Investment Co
Ali Ashour

Agricultural Engineering Research Institute
Samar Attaher

United Hybrid International
Mostafa Badr

Matouk Bassiouny
Mahmoud Bassiouny

Hegazy & Associates
Muhammad El Haggan

Shalakany Law Office
Emad El Shalakany

Agricultural Engineering Research Institute
Ahmed El-Behery

National Water Research Center
Talaat El-Gamal

Tahoun Law Office
Ahmed Elkady

Ministry of Agriculture and Land Reclamation
Islam Farahat

Sharkawy & Sarhan Law Firm
Ahmad Farghal

Baker & McKenzie
Aya Fasih

Hester Biosciences Limited
Rajiv Gandhi

Baker & McKenzie
Mohamed Ghannam

Shalakany Law Office
Nada Hafez

El Waha Mining & Fertilizers - Wamfert
Ahmed Hamdy El Maadawy

Hegazy & Associates
Walid Hegazy

Agricultural Engineering Research Institute
Rania Ibrahim

Orange Egypt
Sherif Issa

Sharkawy & Sarhan Law Firm
Omar Khattab

Baker & McKenzie
Ahmed Omar

Ministry of Agriculture and Land Reclamation
Shaza Omar

Tahoun Law Office
Maged Said

Nubafarm
Mohamed Shaban

Shalakany Law Office
Khaled Sherif

Soliman, Hashish & Partners
Frédéric Soliman

Tahoun Law Office
Nermine Tahoun

Hegazy & Associates
Phil Zager

ETHIOPIA

Ethiopian Agricultural Transformation Agency (ATA)
Birkneh Abebe

Ministry of Agriculture and Natural Resources
Mulugeta Abera

Ministry of Water, Irrigation and Energy
Kifle Alemayehu

Ethiopian Institute of Agricultural Research
Melaku Alemu

Habtamu Assefa

Ministry of Agriculture and Natural Resources
Weldehawariat Assefa

Ministry of Environment, Forest and Climate Change
Addissu Gebremedhin Atsibha

Ethiopia Commodity Exchange
Abenet Bekele

Ministry of Agriculture and Natural Resources
Abebaw Belay

Moenco Quality Machinery Branch
Ashetu Biruk

International Center for Agricultural Research in the Dry Areas (ICARDA)
Zewdie Bishaw

HD Ethiopian Coffee Trading PLC
Dawit Daniel

Ethiopian Agricultural Business Corporation
Maru Degefa

National Bank of Ethiopia
Solomon Desta

Ethiopian Biodiversity Institute
Motuma Didita

Ethiopian Road Transport Authority
Yibeltal Dubale

International Water Management Institute (IWMI)
Teklu Erkossa

Hester Biosciences Limited
Rajiv Gandhi

International Water Management Institute (IWMI)
Gebrehaweria Gebregziabher

Ethiopian Coffee Growers and Exporters Association
Yilma Gebrekidan

Moenco Quality Machinery Branch
Alehegn Gebru

Civet Coffee International Trading Enterprise
Teklay Glibanos

Ministry of Water, Irrigation and Energy
Semunesh Golla

Addis Ababa University
Seifu Kebede Gurmessa

International Water Management Institute (IWMI)
Fitsum Hagos

International Water Management Institute (IWMI)
Alemseged Tamiru Haile

International Water Management Institute (IWMI)
Amare Haileslassie

Haftom Kesete Kahsay

Teshome Gabre-Mariam Bokan Law Office
Mahlet Kassa

Ethiopian Agricultural Transformation Agency (ATA)
Samuel Keno

Ministry of Environment, Forest and Climate Change
Selam Kidane Abebe

Ethiopian Agricultural Transformation Agency (ATA)
Henok Melaku

Bekure Melesse

Ministry of Water, Irrigation and Energy
Bayu Nuru Mohammed

Kedir Musema

Ethiopian Institute of Agricultural Research
Tilahun Nebi

Teshome Gabre-Mariam Bokan Law Office
Obsa Shiferaw

Ethiopian Agricultural Transformation Agency (ATA)
Kefyalew Sisay

Ethiopian Agricultural Transformation Agency (ATA)
Addisu Tadege

IWCA – Ethiopia Chapter
Emebet Tafesse Bitew

Genet Tassew

Ministry of Water, Irrigation and Energy
Sisay Teklu

Ethiopian Institute of Agricultural Research
Fentahun Mengistu Tiruneh

Bahir Dar University-Institute of Land Administration
Daniel Weldegebriel Ambaye

Mesfin Tafesse & Associates
Mekidem Yehiyes

YA Coffee Roasters
Sara Yirga Woldegerima

GEORGIA

Agrimatco

International Road and Transport Union (IRU)

GT Group Ltd.
Giorgi Abjandadze

National Environmental Agency
Marine Arabidze

Georgian Farmers Union
Raul Babunashvili

Ministry of Environment and Natural Resources Protection, Water Resources Management Service
Eliso Barnovi

Georgian Trans Expedition Ltd.
Levan Berdzenishvili

BLC Law Office
Nino Bolkvadze

National Food Agency
Asmat Buachidze

Scientific Research Center of Agriculture
Mirian Chokheli

National Food Agency
Levan Dumbadze

JSC MFO Crystal
Malkhaz Dzadzua

Terra DeNovo LLC
David Egiashvili

Isragreen Ltd.
Irakli Eradze

Isragreen Ltd.
Levan Gachechiladze

Hester Biosciences Limited
Rajiv Gandhi

National Food Agency
Marina Ghvinepadze

Dechert LLP
Archil Giorgadze

EXPERTO Consulting
Ludovic Girod

National Environmental Agency
Gizo Gogichaishvili

Agromotors
Akaki Gogsadze

Business Legal Bureau (BLB)
Nino Gotsireli

LPA Law Firm
Nana Gurgenidze

Dechert LLP
Nana Gvazava

Legal Partners Associated (LPA) LLC
Jaba Gvelebiani

Dechert LLP
Tamar Jikia

EXPERTO Consulting
Gvantsa Kakhurashvili

BLC Law Office
Levan Kantaria

Business Legal Bureau (BLB)
David Khaindrava

Dechert LLP
Ana Kostava

Agricom LLC
Ketevan Kublashvili

Alliance Group Holdings
Aieti Kukava

BLC Law Office
Ketti Kvartskhava

Ministry of Environment and Natural Resources Protection, Water Resources Management Service
Mariam Makarova

Georgian National Communications Commission
Tamar Marghania

Dechert LLP
Nicola Mariani

Aleksandr Moseshvili

Business Legal Bureau (BLB)
Maya Mtsariashvili

Association for Farmers Rights Defense, AFRD-EUFRAS Georgia
Kakha Nadiradze

Ethic Capital
Levan Nanskani

National Food Agency
Bezhan Rekhviashvili

Isragreen Ltd.
Ilya Shapira

Mechanization LLC
Paata Shekeladze

Georgian Farmers' Association
Edvard Shermadini

EXPERTO Consulting
Keti Sidamonidze

Association of Flour Producers of Georgia
Levan Silagava

Georgian National Communications Commission
Rati Skhirtladze

Santa Trans International Transport
Mamuka Tevzadze

LPA Law Firm
Tamar Tsitsishvili

Business Legal Bureau (BLB)
Mariam Vashakidze

FINCA Bank
Vusal Verdiyev

FINCA Bank
David Zarandia

GHANA

Wuni Zaligu Development Association
Ziblim Abdul-Karim

SARI - The Savanna Agricultural Research Institute
Mashark S Abdulai

Ministry of Food and Agriculture (MoFA)
Ebenezer Aboagye

Council for Scientific and Industrial Research (CSIR)
Lawrence Aboagye Misa

Institute of Agricultural Research
Kwame Afreh-Nuamah

USAID Feed the Future
Maxwell Agbenorhevi

Environmental Protection Agency (EPA)
Florence Agyei-Martey

ÆLEX
Akinloye Ajayi

William Amanfu

Ministry of Food and Agriculture, Agricultural Engineering Services Directorate
Kate Amegatcher

Environmental Protection Agency (EPA)
Daniel S. Amlalo

Ministry of Food and Agriculture (MoFA)
Imoro Amoro

Water Resources Commission
Ben Yah Ampomah

National Communications Authority
Robert Apaya

E.A.L.C. (Estelle Appiah Legislative Counsel)
Estelle Appiah

Savanna Seed Services Company Limited
Adingtingah Apullah Patrick

ÆLEX
Beverly Asamoah

University of Ghana
Isaac Asante

African Fertilizer and Agribusiness Partnership (AFAP)
Isaac Asare

ÆLEX
Soji Awogbade

Joseph Adongo Awuni

Robin-Huws Barnes

Pan-African Savings & Loans
Kwaku D. Berchie

Ministry of Food and Agriculture (MoFA)
Kyofa Boamah

Kwame Nkrumah University of Science and Technology, Agricultural Engineering Department
Emmanuel Y.H. Bobobee

Olam Ghana Limited
Eric Asare Botwe

Ministry of Food & Agriculture, Agricultural Engineering Services Directorate
George K.A. Brantuo

R.A.Codjoe Law Offices
Raymond Codjoe

Ghana Irrigation Development Authority (GIDA)
Francis Danquah Ohemeng

Darko, Keli-Delataa & Co.
John Darko

Hester Biosciences Limited
Rajiv Gandhi

Environmental Protection
Agency (EPA)
Peace Gbeckor- Kove

University of Ghana
Kwame Gyan

Centre for Human Rights,
University of Pretoria
Michael Gyan Nyarko

Seed Producers Association of
Ghana (SEEDPAG)
Thomas Havor

Crown Transport & Logistics Ltd.
Ghassan Husseini

National Communications
Authority
Rahmata Issahaq-Pelpuo

M&B Seeds
Ben Kemetse

Kimathi & Partners
Augustine Kidisil

Kimathi & Partners
Kimathi Kuenyehia

Kimathi & Partners
Sefakor Kuenyehia

Reindorf Chambers
Kizzita Mensah

Mercer & Company
Andrew Mercer

Water Resources Commission
Eric Muala

Mercer & Company
Kwabena Nimakoh

Institute of Agricultural
Research
George Nkansah Oduro

Olam Ghana Limited
Kennedy Ntoso

Kimathi & Partners
Sarpong Odame

Plant Protection and
Regulatory Services
Directorate (PPRSD) - Ghana
Samuel Okyere

Mercer & Company
Jeffrey Osei Mensah

Private Transport Association
of Ghana
Asamoah Owusu-Akyaw

Ghana Investment Fund for
Electronic Communications
-GIFEC
Philip Prempeh

Reindorf Chambers
Kweki Quaynor Ahlijah

Elizabeth Tetteh
Elizabeth Rosebud Afua Alifo
Tetteh

Olam Ghana Limited
Isaac Sackey

Ministry of Food and
Agriculture (MoFA)
Simeon Salakpi

Environmental Protection
Agency (EPA)
Lovelace Sarpong

Pan-African Savings & Loans
Felix Yartey

Mercer & Company
Ebenezer Yaw Gyamerah

Kwame Nkrumah University of
Science and Technology
Eric Yeboah

Foresight Generation Club
Albert Yeboah Obeng

GREECE

Z & A Consulting Engineers

Greek Biotope / Wetland
Centre (EKBY)
Eftyhia Alexandridou

Panhellenic Exporters
Association (PEA)
Nikolaos Archontis

Machinery Importers' -
Representatives' Association
(MIRA)
Savvas Balouktsis

World Wildlife Fund
Georgios Chasiotis

NOMOS Law Firm
Georgios Chatzigiannakis

Zepos & Yannopoulos Law
Firm
Sofia Chatzigiannidou

I.K. Rokas & Partners
Maria Demirakou

Ministry of Rural Development
and Food
Gerasimos Dendrinos

KG Law Firm
Sotirios Douklias

KG Law Firm
Elizabeth Eleftheriades

Ministry of Rural Development
and Food
Ioannis Fermantzis

National Bank of Greece
Kyriaki Flesiopoulou

Ministry of Rural Development
and Food
Maria Fotiadou-Talidourou

GEFRA
George Frangistas

Hester Biosciences Limited
Rajiv Gandhi

National and Kapodistrian
University of Athens
Maria Gavouneli

NOMOS Law Firm
Constantine Hadjiyannakis

National Technical University
of Athens
Maria Kapetanaki

Koutalidis Law Firm
Ioannis Kaptanis

Margaropoulos & Associates -
Scientia Legis Law Firm
Kyriaki Karakasi

Hellenic Telecommunications
and Post Commission (EETT)
Ioanna Kontopoulou

Koutalidis Law Firm
Nikos Koritsas

Hellenic Agricultural
Organization "DEMETER"
Evangelos Korpetis

OTE S.A
Ilias Kotsopoulos

Hellagrolip S.A.
Theodora Kouloura

Public Power Corporation S.A.
Ioannis Kouvopoulos

Yara Hellas S.A.
Nikos Kyriakidis

Ilias G. Anagnostopoulos Law
firm
Persa Lampropoulou

Hellenic Telecommunications
and Post Commission (EETT)
Evagelia Liakopoulou

Zeus Kiwi SA
Christina Manossis

Margaropoulos & Associates -
Scientia Legis Law Firm
Nikolaos K. Margaropoulos

Michalopoulou & Associates
Ioanna Michalopoulou

National Technical University
of Athens
Maria Mimikou

Geodis Calberson GE
Anthony Narlis

Ministry of Rural Development
and Food
Maria Oikonomou

Zepos & Yannopoulos Law
Firm
Stefanos Panayiotopoulos

Koutalidis Law Firm
Effie Papoutsi

Incofruit-Hellas
George Polychronakis

National Technical University
of Athens
Alexandros Psomas

I.K. Rokas & Partners
Ioannis Rokas

KG Law Firm
Konstantinos Serdaris

KEPA-ANEM
Neoklis Stamkos

Ministry of Rural Development
and Food
Komninos Stougiannidis

I.K. Rokas & Partners
Harris Synodinos

Cooperative Bank of Karditsa
Panagiotis Tournavitis

OTE S.A
Nadia Trata

KG Law Firm
Kimon Tsakiris

Ministry of Environment,
Energy & Climate Change
Vassiliki Maria Tzatzaki

V.ATTIS Business Consulting
Ltd.
Eleftherios Vagenas

NOMOS Law Firm
Maria Vastaroucha

Vrysopoulos Law Offices
Socrates Vrysopoulos

Greece
Koutalidis Law Firm
Nikos Xenoyiannis

GUATEMALA

Asociación Gremio Químico

Berger, Pemueller &
Asociados

Disagro Maquinaria

GremiAgro

Superintendencia de Bancos
de Guatemala

Ministerio de Ambiente y
Recursos Naturales
Alvaro René Aceituno Ibañez

Semillas S.A.
Jesús Alcázar Andrade

Asociación de Organizaciones
de los Cuchumatanes
(ASOCUCH)
Sergio Romeo Alonzo Recinos

Arias & Muñoz
Jorge Luis Arenales de la Roca

Duwest
Pedro Arias

Asociación SHARE
David Arrivillaga

Carrillo & Asociados
Axel Beteta

Ministerio de Ambiente y
Recursos Naturales
Maritza Yaneth Campos
Fuentes

QIL+4 Abogados
Alejandro Cofiño

Cordón Ovalle & Asociados
Carlos Roberto Cordón
Krumme

Bufete Olivero S.A.
Pablo Antonio Coronado
Bonilla

Ministerio de Economía de
Guatemala
Maura de Muralles

Ministerio de Ambiente y
Recursos Naturales
Nestor Francisco Fajardo
Herrera

Organismo Internacional
Regional de Sanidad
Agropecuaria (OIRSA)
Lauriano Figueroa

Especialista en Sostenibilidad
Ambiental y Agronegocios
Giovanni Fernando García
Barrios

Doingtrade Guatemala S.L.
Christian Josué Girón Carreto

Bufete Olivero S.A.
Enrique Goicolea

Asociación SHARE
Guillermo González

Superintendencia de Bancos de Guatemala
Roberto Giovanni González

Técnica Universal, S.A. (Tecun Guatemala)
Herver López

Maquinaria y Equipos S.A.
Miguel Manzo

Instituto de Ciencia y Tecnología Agrícola (ICTA)
María de los Angeles Mérida Gúzman

Bufete Olivero S.A.
Maria Haydee Monge

Aragón & Aragón
Lizeth Morales

Ministerio de Ambiente y Recursos Naturales
Ernesto Moscoso

Aragón & Aragón
Pedro Aragón Muñoz

Superintendencia de Bancos de Guatemala
Karla Gabriela Muñoz

Bufete Olivero S.A.
Stefano Olivero

Bufete Olivero S.A.
Raúl Andrés Olivero Arroyo

Serca S.A.
Víctor Orantes

Ministerio de Ambiente y Recursos Naturales
Olivia Orellana Alas

Instituto de Ciencia y Tecnología Agrícola (ICTA)
Albaro Dionel Orellana Polanco

Ministerio de Agricultura, Ganadería y Alimentación
Guillermo Austreberto Ortiz Aldana

Bufete Olivero S.A.
Manuel Pérez

Carrillo & Asociados
Mélida Pineda

Ana Gabriela Platero Midence

Frutas Tropicales de Guatemala S.A. (FRUTESA)
Gloria Elena Polanco

Dirección General de Transportes
Alfredo Porres

Ministerio de Ambiente y Recursos Naturales
Ricardo Galiazo Serrano Amaya

QIL+4 Abogados
María Isabel Sierra Dávila

Duwest
Cristina Son

Duwest
Armando Soto

Superintendencia de Bancos de Guatemala
Jorge Eduardo Soto Guzmán

ARTLEX - Attorneys at Law
Enrique Toledo-Cotera

ARTLEX - Attorneys at Law
Enrique Toledo-Fernandez

HAITI

National transport services S.A. (NATRANS S.A)

Société de coopération pour le développement international (SOCODEVI)

Truck Out Services

Northwater Consulting
James K. Adamson

Cabinet Jude Baptiste et Associés
Jude Baptiste

Cabinet Lissade
Michelle Bien-Aimé

Jean-Marie Binette

Agronomes et Vétérinaires Sans Frontières
Marie Bonnard

Ministère de l'Agriculture, des Resources Naturelles et du Développement Rural
Montès Charles

Banque de la République d'Haiti
Robinson Charles

Ministère de l'Agriculture, des Ressources Naturelles et du Développement Rural
Pierre Frisner Clerveus

Darbouco
Jehan H. Dartigue

Ministère de l'Agriculture, des Ressources Naturelles et du Développement Rural
Pierre Guito Laurore

Ministère de l'Agriculture, des Resources Naturelles et du Développement Rural
Alix Jacques

Cabinet Lissade
Nephtalie Jacques

Foratech Environnement
Gerald Jean-Baptiste

Banque de la République d'Haiti
Jean Armand Mondelis

FAO
Aloys Nizigiyimana

Jérôme Pennec

Ministère de l'Agriculture, des Resources Naturelles et du Développement Rural
Emmanuel Prophète

Concordia University School of Law
Ryan Stoa

Cabinet Lissade
Salim Succar

INDIA

Agra Mandi

Agricultural and Processed Food Products Export Development Authority (APEDA)

Geo-Chem Labs

Maharashtra State Agricultural Marketing Board

National Bank for Agriculture and Rural Development

Odisha State Agriculture Marketing Board

SGS India

Uttar Pradesh State Agriculture Markets Board

Vimta Laboratories

Ankit Trading Company
Ankit Agarwal

Laxmi Trading Company
Harish Agarwal

University of Delhi
Akash Anand

National Agricultural Cooperative Marketing Federation of India Ltd. (NAFED)
Bhaviya Anand

Syngenta India Ltd.
Seetharam Annadana

M.V. Kini & Co.
Nivedita Atre

Indian Farmers Fertiliser Cooperative Limited (IFFCO)
U.S. Awasthi

Suryoday Micro Finance Limited
R Baskar Babu

Uttar Pradesh State Cooperative Bank
Akhilesh Kumar Bajpai

M/s. Bal Roadlines
Daya Singh Bal

M/s. Bal Roadlines
Malkit Bal

M/s. Bal Roadlines
Ranjit Singh Bal

M.K. Exports
Manoj Barai

Maharashtra Hybrid Seeds Company Private Limited (Mahyco)
Rajendra Barwale

Indian Council of Agricultural Research (ICAR)
Shashikumar Bhalla

Trilegal
Ashish Bhan

Phoenix Legal
Aditya Bhargava

Hammurabi & Solomon
Shweta Bharti

Basant Agro Tech
Akshay Bhartia

Specstra Inc.
Smita Bhatia

National Federation of State Cooperative Banks
Subrahmanyam Bhima

Raghavendra Birur Kalleshappa

Tractors and Farm Equipment Ltd.
Vijayakumar Browning

The Fertiliser Association of India
Tapan Chanda

India Tineta Pharma Pvt. Ltd.
Vipin Chandan

Nippon Express
Rishi Chauhan

Ratnagiri Seeds and Farm
Neeraj Choubey

Delhi Test House
Sonia Chugh

Ministry of Road Transport & Highways
Abhay Damle

Commissionerate of Agriculture, Maharashtra
Krushnarao Deshmukh

Pradeep Deshmukh

Yashodeep Deshmukh

Globion India Private Limited
Dibyendu Kumar Dey

Indian Council of Agricultural Research (ICAR)
Shiv Kumar Dhyani

Lucknow Cargo Packers & Movers
Vijay Dixit

Suryoday Micro Finance Limited
Yogesh Dixit

National Bureau of Plant Genetic Resources
S.C. Dubey

INDIALAW Practitioners LLP
Sneha Dubey

Uttar Pradesh Cooperative Department
S.C. Dwivedi

INDIALAW Practitioners LLP
Varsha G.S.

Hester Biosciences Limited
Rajiv Gandhi

Ankit Trading Company
Sunil Garg

State Institute for Management of Agriculture
Mukesh Gautam

Translational Research Platform for Veterinary Biologicals (TRPVB)
Dhinakar Raj Gopal

TMT Law Practice
Swati Gore

National Seed Association of India
Kalyan Goswami

All India Transporter's Welfare Association
R.K. Gulati

Zodiac Pharma
Ramyakeerthi Gundlapalle

M/s. Indore Agra Roadways(Regd.)
Devendra Gupta

All India Motor Transport Congress (AIMTC)
Naveen Kumar Gupta

University of Delhi
Neeraj Gupta

Hammurabi & Solomon
Rashmi Gupta

The Amritsar Transport Company (PVT.) Ltd.
S. K. Gupta

Regional Plant Quarantine Organization (Maharashtra)
K L Gurjar

National Federation of State Cooperative Banks
Hanamashetti J.S.

National Federation of State Cooperative Banks (NAFSCOB)
Hanamashetti J.S.

Sinha, AZB & Partners
Rishabhdev Jain

M/s. Indore Agra Roadways(Regd.)
Prashant Dev Jengaria

M/s. Indore Agra Roadways(Regd.)
Preeti Jengaria

Jhyamlal Jajodia

Ministry of Agriculture and Farmers' Welfare
Vijay Kumar N. Kale

Yara
Sanjiv Kanwar

Deepak Fertilizers
S. Kartik

National Collateral Management Services Limited (NCML)
Sanjay Kaul

Trilegal
Richa Kaushal

Tractors and Farm Equipment Ltd.
T. R. Kesavan

Neeraj Associates
Sunayana Khare

Cargo Carriers (India) Limited
Raman Khosla

Mahindra
Kislay Kishor

Technik Corp Industries Pvt Ltd.
Ashish Kishore

Nupur Heights Private Limited
Arunesh Kishorepuria

Ministry of Agriculture and Farmers' Welfare
Ashwani Kumar

Neeraj Associates
Neeraj Kumar

Kautilya Legal Solutions
Nishant Kumar

Karu Kirana Shop
Prabhat Kumar

Drinking Water Expert
Ravindra Kumar

International Co-operative Alliance (ICA)
Santosh Kumar

Central Integrated Pest Management Centre, Uttar Pradesh
Umesh Kumar

Indian Farmers Fertiliser Cooperative Limited (IFFCO)
Yogendra Kumar

Beejsheetal Research Pvt. Ltd.
Nandkumar Kunchge

Microchem Silliker Lab
Ajit Lagoo

Ministry of Chemicals and Fertilizers
Sushil K Lohani

All India Motor Transport Congress (AIMTC)
Amrit Lal Madan

Pithampur Bombay Roadways
Amrit Lal Madan

Chambers of Ritin Rai
Jayant Malik

INDIALAW Practitioners LLP
J. Mandakini

TMT Law Practice
Purvasha Mansharamani

Sinha, AZB & Partners
Pallavi Meena

Khushi Ram Behari Lal (KRBL)
Rakesh Mehrotra

Choong Ang Vaccine Laboratories Co., Ltd. (CAVAC)
Juver Membrebe

Chandragupt Institute of Management Patna
Babu Lal Mishra

S.K.Tractors
Suneel Mishra

Bihar Agricultural Marketing Board
Sushil Kumar Mishra

Swastik Transport Corporation
Rajkumar Misra

Ministry of Road Transport & Highways
Sanjay Mitra

TMT Law Practice
Kaushik Moitra

Ministry of Road Transport & Highways
Leena Nandan Tariq

Nisamuddin Khan

LT Foods Ltd.
J.S. Oberoi

INDIALAW Practitioners LLP
Shiju P V

Department of Agriculture and Farmers Empowerment (Govt. of Odisha)
Pradeep Paikray

Panda Associates
K.N. Panda

Odisha Byabasayee Mahasangh
Sudhakar Panda

Government of Odisha
Susanta Kumar Panda

Yara
Binaya Kumar Parida
Mubeen Patel

Shri Bahubali Transport
Mahesh Patil

Global AgriSystem
Gokul Patnaik

Globion India Private Limited
Sunil Kumar Peram

Office of the Transport Commissioner, Uttar Pradesh State
Ganga Phal

RallyMark Legal
Rupendra Porwal

College of Agriculture, Dapoli
S. S. Prabhudesai

Co-operative House Building & Finance Corporation Ltd.
Bhagwati Prasad

Coromandel
Ravi Prasad

John Deere
Sunny Prasad

Retired Associate Professor, WALMI, Aurangabad
Pradeep Purandare

Chambers of Ritin Rai
Ritin Rai

Mahindra
Ramesh Ramachandran

Centre for Sustainable Agriculture
G. V. Ramanjaneyulu

Alivira Animal Health Ltd.
Rupesh Rane

Orissa State Seeds Corporation Limited
Joyti Ranjan Misra

Centre for Technology Alternatives for Rural Areas
Bakul Rao

Chambers of Ritin Rai
Prateek Rath

Radhakrishna Foodland Pvt. Ltd.
Bipin Reghunathan

M.V. Kini & Co.
Els Reynaers

Indian Farmers Fertiliser Cooperative Limited (IFFCO)
Arabinda Roy

Ministry of Commerce & Industry, Government of India
S.P. Roy

Pune District Central Cooperative Bank
Sanjaykumar S. Bhosale

Sohan Lal Commodity Management Pvt Ltd.
Sandeep Sabharwal

All India Transporter's Welfare Association
Deepak Sachdeva

Olam Agro India Ltd.
Sanjay Sacheti

Maharashtra State, Office of the Transport Commissioner
Satish B. Sahasrabudhe

Chandragupt Institute of Management Patna
Debabrata Samanta

Regional Plant Quarantine Organization (Maharashtra)
N Sathyanarayana

Neeraj Associates
Rishi Saxena

Coromandel
Sanjay Saxena

TransportMitra Services Private Ltd.
Mahima Semwal

Confederation of Indian Industry
Ankur Seth

Mahindra
Sagar Shah

Global AgriSystem
S.K. Sharma

Phoenix Legal
Yashna Shrawani

Global AgriSystem
B.K. Sikka

All India Transporter's Welfare Association
Pradeep Singal

Bihar Truck Owners Association
Bhanu Sekhar Prasad Singh

Indian Council of Agricultural Research (ICAR)
Kanchan Kumar Singh

Suraj Cropsciences Ltd.
P.P Singh

UP Seed Development Corp.
Rishi Raj Singh

DNA Agri Seeds Pvt. Ltd.
S.P Singh

International Co-operative Alliance (ICA)
Savitri Singh

Phoenix Legal
Sawant Singh

Agricultural Machinery
Manufacturers Association
(AMMA-India)
Surendra Singh

Tata Chemicals Limited
Narendra Kumar Singhal

LT Foods Ltd.
Ashutosh Kumar Sinha

Ranu Sinha

Sinha, AZB & Partners
Shuchi Sinha

Sinha, AZB & Partners
Pragya Sood

Agriculture Directorate
C.P Srivastava

*National Federation of State
Cooperative Banks (NAFSCOB)*
Bhima Subrahmanyam

*All India Rice Exporters
Association (AIREA)*
R. Sundaresan

*Maharashtra Agro Industries
Development Corporation*
Dilip Suryagan

Zodiac Pharma
Tara Chand Tak

University of Delhi
Usha Tandon

*Mulla & Mulla & Craigie Blunt
& Caroe*
Shardul J. Thacker

*State Level Farm Machinery
Training and Testing Institute*
Anand Tripathi

*Ministry of Agriculture and
Farmers' Welfare*
Prabhat Verma

Reserve Bank of India
N. S. Vishwanathan

*Seed Industries Association of
Maharashtra*
S.D. Wankhede

*Tata Institute of Social
Sciences (TISS)*
Sachin Warghade

Globion India Private Limited
Niraj Warke

ITALY

Assomela

DANDRIA Studio Legale
Angela Addessi

*Gianni, Origoni, Grippo,
Cappelli & Partners*
Luca Amicarelli

University of Catania
Alessandro Ancarani

*Gianni, Origoni, Grippo,
Cappelli & Partners*
Camilla Andreini

*Cleary Gottlieb Steen &
Hamilton LLP*
Gianluca Atzori

Megaris Ltd.
Renato Benintendi

Genio Civile Catania
Sonia Berretta

Rete Semi Rurali
Riccardo Bocci

*Regional Agency for
Agriculture and Forestry
(ERSAF), Lombardy Region*
Stefano Brenna

Biolchim S.P.A.
Leonardo Cacioppo

Sapienza University of Rome
Federico Caporale

*Gianni, Origoni, Grippo,
Cappelli & Partners*
Antonella Capria

DLA Piper
Germana Cassar

Jones Day
Bruno Castellini

*Regional Agency for
Agriculture and Forestry
(ERSAF), Lombardy Region*
Beniamino Cavagna

*Regional Agency for
Agriculture and Forestry
(ERSAF)*
Mariangela Ciampitti

*Orrick, Herrington & Sutcliffe
LLP*
Daniele Consolo

Uniontrasporti
Iolanda Conte

DANDRIA Studio Legale
Gennaro d'Andria

NCTM Studio Legale Associato
Ada Lucia De Cesaris

*Council for Agricultural
Research and Agricultural
Economics Analysis (CREA)*
Flavio Roberto De Salvador

Piselli & Partners
Gianni Marco Di Paolo

*Council for Agricultural
Research and Agricultural
Economics Analysis (CREA)*
Petra Engel

*Ministry of Agriculture,
Alimentation and Forestry
Policies (MiPAAF)*
Bruno Caio Faraglia

Pavia e Ansaldo
Elena Felici

Union Transporti
Antonello Fontanili

*Ministry of Agricultural, Food
and Forestry Policies*
Antonio Frattarelli

*Italian National Institute for
Environmental Protection and
Research (ISPRA)*
Fiorenzo Fumanti

Hester Biosciences Limited
Rajiv Gandhi

DANDRIA Studio Legale
Serena Guglielmo

*National Research Council
Institute of Biosciences and
Bioresources (CNR-IBBR)*
Gaetano Laghetti

NCTM Studio Legale Associato
Francesca Leonelli

DLA Piper
Andrea Leonforte

Limagrain Italy
Elisa Lombardi

*Orrick, Herrington & Sutcliffe
LLP*
Simone Lucatello

*Italian National Institute for
Environmental Protection and
Research (ISPRA)*
Stefano Lucci

*Italian National Institute for
Environmental Protection and
Research (ISPRA)*
Anna Luise

*National Research Council
Institute of Biosciences and
Bioresources (CNR-IBBR)*
Benedetta Margiotta

University of Udine
Antonio Massarutto

*Gianni, Origoni, Grippo,
Cappelli & Partners*
Luna Maria Mignosa

Pavia e Ansaldo
Luca Montolivo

*Italian National Institute for
Environmental Protection and
Research (ISPRA)*
Michele Munafò

*Fondazione Eni Enrico Mattei
(FEEM)*
Jaroslav Mysiak

Biolchim S.P.A.
Barbara Novak

Jones Day
Tommaso Pepe

*Fondazione Eni Enrico Mattei
(FEEM)*
Carlos Dionisio Pèrez Blanco

*FederUNACOMA (Italian
Agricultural Machinery
Manufacturers Federation)*
Marco Pezzini

*National Research Council
Institute of Biosciences and
Bioresources (CNR-IBBR)*
Domenico Pignone

Piselli & Partners
Emilia Piselli

Piselli & Partners
Pierluigi Piselli

Piselli & Partners
Ioana Pricopi

*FederUNACOMA (Italian
Agricultural Machinery
Manufacturers Federation)*
Ing Fabio Ricci

University of Catania
Giuseppe Rossi

*Gianni, Origoni, Grippo,
Cappelli & Partners*
Edward Ruggeri

*Fondazione Eni Enrico Mattei
(FEEM)*
Silvia Santato

Legance Avvocati Associati
Luca Geninatti Satè

*Ministry of Agriculture,
Alimentation and Forestry
Policies (MiPAAF)*
Federico Sòrgoni

Jones Day
Francesco Squerzoni

Svlitana Stepanuik

Limagrain Italy
Luciano Tosi

*National Research Council
Institute of Biosciences and
Bioresources (CNR-IBBR)*
Giovanni Giuseppe Vendramin

Legance Avvocati Associati
Alice Villari

Nicola Zanotelli

JORDAN

*The Jordan Exporters and
Producers Association for
Fruit and Vegetables (JEPA)*

Abbassi Law Office
Alaa Abbassi

*Jordan Tractor & Equipment
Co*
Emad Abu Baker

Ministry of Environment
Izzat Abu Hammra

*Jordan Cooperative
Corporation*
Dina Abul Ghanam

Ministry of Agriculture
Ahmad Akour

*J.R.C. Advocates & Legal
Consultants*
Main Al Kurdi

Barcelona Seeds
Raed Mohammad Al Qatanani

Ministry of Environment
Ahmad Al Qatarneh

*Jordan University of Science
and Technology*
Munir Al Rusan

*Land Transport Regulatory
Commission*
Khawla Al-Aboushi

Ministry of Agriculture
Emad Alawad

Al Qawafel Agro
Mohammad Al-Bess

*International Business Legal
Associates*
Eman Aldabbas

*Telecommunications
Regulatory Commission*
Abdullmalik Al-Eassawi

ENABLING THE BUSINESS OF AGRICULTURE 2017

252

Ministry of Agriculture
Nada Al-Frihat

Water Authority of Jordan
Rashed Alhadidi

HM Clause (Jordan)
Nabeel Alkhatib

Telecommunications
Regulatory Commission
Al-Ansari Almashakbeh

Jordan Valley Authority
Nassra Almaslah

The National Center for
Agricultural Research and
Extension (NCARE)
Nasab Alrawashdeh

Ministry of Agriculture
Monther Alrefai

The National Center for
Agricultural Research and
Extension (NCARE)
Jamal Alrusheidat

Central Bank of Jordan
Ghadeer Alsmadi

Ministry of Agriculture
Hazim Al-Smadi

The National Center for
Agricultural Research and
Extension (NCARE)
Maha Al-Syouf

Ministry of Agriculture
Khaled Al-Talafih

Central Bank of Jordan
Fadi Al-Tayyan

Jordan Tractor & Equipment
Co
Amin Amireh

Amosh Legal Services &
Arbitration
Ibrahem Amosh

Naqel Transport & Investment
Barter Company
Jamal Abu Amro

Ali Sharif Zu'bi Advocates and
Legal Consultants
Mohammad Amro

Ministry of Agriculture
Kholoud Aranki

Faidi Law Firm
Howayda Arikat

Ali Sharif Zu'bi Advocates and
Legal Consultants
Khaled Asfour

HM Clause (Jordan)
Tom Atens

Jordan Tractor & Equipment
Co
Gladys Daccache

HM Clause (Jordan)
Ala'a Dweik

Fresh Yield International
Basil El-Deek

Faidi Law Firm
Ahmad Faidi

Hester Biosciences Limited
Rajiv Gandhi

Eversheds
Lana Habash

Land Transport Regulatory
Commission
Zuhair Hattar

Ali Sharif Zu'bi Advocates and
Legal Consultants
Lubna Hawamdeh

German Jordanian University
Muna Hindiyeh

Jaradat & Associates
Abdullah Jaradat

The University of Jordan
Emad Karablieh

Ali Sharif Zu'bi Advocates and
Legal Consultants
Rakan Kawar

Ali Sharif Zu'bi Advocates and
Legal Consultants
Layan Khrais

Arab Potash Company
Rashing Lubani

Atwan & Partners
Yazan Mansour

Central Bank of Jordan
Aya Maraqa

The National Center for
Agricultural Research and
Extension (NCARE)
Naem Mazahrih

Ali Sharif Zu'bi Advocates and
Legal Consultants
Luma Mdanat

Choong Ang Vaccine
Laboratories Co., Ltd. (CAVAC)
Juver Membrebe

Jordan Tractor & Equipment
Co
Hazem Momani

Central Bank of Jordan
Adnan Naji

Jordan Valley Authority
Ghassan Obeidat

Ali Sharif Zu'bi Advocates and
Legal Consultants
Majdi Salaita

HM Clause (Jordan)
Moayad Salameh

Arab Potash Company
Jafar Salem

The University of Jordan
Amer Salman

Kemapco Arab Fertilizers &
Chemicals Industries Ltd.
Bishara Sayegh

The National Center for
Agricultural Research and
Extension (NCARE)
Yahya Shakhatreh

Ministry of Environment
Belal Shqarin

Telfah Trading Company
Sami Telfah

Suhail Wahsheh

Ali Sharif Zu'bi Advocates and
Legal Consultants
Kareem Zureikat

KAZAKHSTAN

Coms Trade LLP

Delta Bank

MFO "Arnur Credit", LLP

Ministry of Information
and Communication of the
Republic of Kazakhstan

The Ministry of Agriculture of
Kazakhstan

Grata International
Lola Abdukhalykova

Centil Law (formerly Colibri
Law)
Zhanar Abdullayeva

MUGAN
Ilgar Agalar

Bank Kassa Nova
Leila Akiltayeva

The Ministry of Agriculture of
Kazakhstan
Zhanargul Aytumkanbetova

Kazphosphate LLC
Erik Baimurzaev

Grata International
Assel Batyrbayeva

Institute of Botany and
Phytointroduction
Sergei Chekalin

Grata International
Shaimerden Chikanaev

Institute of Botany and
Phytointroduction
Liliya Dimeyeva

Hester Biosciences Limited
Rajiv Gandhi

Grata International
Zarina Iskakova

Grata International
Marina Kahiani

Meirambek Karazhigitov

The Ministry of Agriculture of
Kazakhstan
Nurlan Serikbayevich Karimov

Bank Kassa Nova
Nurlan Kosakov

Kazakhstan
Agro Star Grain LLC
Oleg Kunayev

Grata International
Leila Makhmetova

Olzha Holding
Eduard Matveev

Institute of Botany and
Phytointroduction
Tansari Murtazayeva

Asian Credit Fund
Dzhalol Murzakhmetov

Ministry of Agriculture
Marat Saduov

Bank Astana
Lyazzat Sagyndykova

Kcell JSC
Irina Shol

Linkage & Mind
Saida Shukurova

Korvet Agro
Emiliya Sim

Institute of Botany and
Phytointroduction
Gulnara Sitpaeva

Daua
Yerkin T. Saiduldin

Chim Service LLP
Yuriy Nikolaevich Tyuleikin

Bank Astana
Daniyar Uspanov

Kazakh Research Institute of
Agriculture and Plant Growing
Minura Yessimbekova

Kazphosphate LLC
Darhan Zekenov

Dentons Kazakhstan, LLP
Vassiliy Zenov

Centre for Sustainable
Production and Consumption
Zulfira Zikrina

KENYA

East Africa Tea Trade
Association

Advanta Seed International
Asfaw Ageru

HM Clause Kenya Limited
Sebastian Alix

Kenya Tea Development
Agency
John Bett

B.M. Musau & Co. Advocates
Mathias Botany

Jomo Kenyatta University of
Agriculture and Technology
Henry Bwisa

Erid Chelangat

University of Eldoret
Michael Chelulei

Grace Chilande

Seed Co. Limited
John Derera

Hester Biosciences Limited
Rajiv Gandhi

Gumbo & Associates
Erick Gumbo

FSD Kenya
Francis Gwer

Coulson Harney Advocates
Richard Harney

Kenya Agricultural
Productivity Project (KAPP)
Edwin Ikitoo

National Environment
Management Authority
Joyce Imende

Coulson Harney Advocates
Dominic Indokhomi

Land O'Lakes Inc.
Ignatius Kahiu

Kaplan & Stratton
Sarah Kiarie-Muia

Kenya Plant Health
Inspectorate Service (KEPHIS)
Esther Kimani

World Agroforestry Center
(ICRAF)
Zakayo Kinyanjui

B.M. Musau & Co. Advocates
Evelyn Kyania

Kenya Seed Company
Alphonse Laboso

Eric Maghas Tegei

Kenya Agricultural and
Livestock Research
Organization (KALRO)
Nesbert Mangale

Maseno University
Dominic Marera

National Environment
Management Authority
Catherine Mbaisi

East African Seed Company -
Kenya
Nicholas Mengich

World Agroforestry Center
(ICRAF)
Alice Muchugi

Kenya Agricultural and
Livestock Research
Organization (KALRO)
Anne Muriuki

B.M. Musau & Co. Advocates
Benjamin Musau

African Conservation Tillage
Network (ACT)
Weldon Mutai

AGMARK
James Mutonyi

Cargill Kenya Limited
Ralph Mwadime

South Eastern Kenya
University
Moses Mwangi

Cooper K-Brands Limited
Jeremiah Mwangu

Egerton University
Lenah Nakhone

MEA Fertilizers
Daniel Ndegwa

Kenya Plant Health
Inspectorate Service (KEPHIS)
Faith Ndunge

Cooper K-Brands Limited
Charles Ndungu

Igeria & Ngugi Advocates
Benson Ngugi

Gikera & Vadgama Advocates
Michael Njiguna

Kenya Agricultural and
Livestock Research

Organization (KALRO)
Desterio Nyamongo

Nile Basin Initiative
John Rao Nyaoro

Kenya Plant Health
Inspectorate Service (KEPHIS)
Ivan Obare

Egerton University
Gilbert Obati

ELYMEDICARE PHARMACY
Elly Obonyo

Chemagro International
Limited
Henry Ogola

John Omiti

Kaplan & Stratton
Phillip Onyango

Gikera & Vadgama Advocates
Stephen Ouma

Jomo Kenyatta University of
Agriculture and Technology
Robert Owino

Global Water Partnership
George Sanga

Coulson Harney Advocates
John Syekei

Gikera & Vadgama Advocates
Punit Vadgama

Reinder van de Meer

Kenya Veterinary Vaccines
Production Institute
(KEVEVAPI)
Jane Wachira

Ethical Tea Partnership Ltd.
Joseph Wagurah

Gumbo & Associates
Collins Wanjala

Coulson Harney Advocates
Nerima Were

B.M. Musau & Co. Advocates
Edmond Wesonga

KOREA, REP.

Animal and Plant Quarantine
Agency

Asia Seed Co., Ltd.

Chobi Co., Ltd.

Chungnam National
University

Foundation of Agri. Tech,
Commercialization & Transfer
(FACT)

FSS Financial Supervisory
Service

Korea Deposit Insurance
Corporation

LS Mtron

Ministry of Agriculture, Food
and Rural Affairs

Ministry of Environment

NH Trading Co., Ltd.

Nongsan Trading Co., Ltd.

Nongwoo Bio Co., Ltd.

Optipharm Corp.

Pungnong Co., Ltd.

Rural Development
Administration National
Institute of Agricutural Sciences

Bae Kim & Lee LLC
Jong Sik Bang

Lee & Ko
Seung Hoon Choi

National Agricultural
Cooperative Federation (NACF)
Noelle Compton

Water Management
Information System
Center, Ministry of Land,
Infrastructure, and Transport
Hyun Gyo Jung

National Agricultural
Cooperative Federation (NACF)
Gwangseog Hong

Korea International Trade
Association (KITA), Jeonbuk
Center
Sungchul Hwang

Kim & Chang
In Hwan Jun

Tong Yang Moolsan -
Machinery Division
Youngsun Kang

Korea Environment Institute (KEI)
Hojeong Kim

Kim & Chang
Hyun-Yong Leo Kim

Seoul National University
Kyeong Uk Kim

Yulchon LLC
Kyoung Yeon Kim

KOLEE E&L Corp.
Martin Ko

Korea Environment Institute
(KEI)
Byung Kook Lee

Lee & Ko
Han Kyung Lee

Korea Development Institute
Hojun Lee

Kim & Chang
James Geechul Lee

Korea Rural Community
Corporation (KRC)
Sung-Hee Lee

Dongcheon Foundation
Takgon Lee

Kim & Chang
Yoon Jeong Lee

Yulchon LLC
Young Jo Lee

Samsung C&T
Stanislav Pak

Syngenta
Hee Young Park

Lee & Ko
Keum Sub Park

Korea Real Estate Research
Institute
Sungkyu Park

Lee & Ko
John Pool

TYM
HyunBin Shin

Bae Kim & Lee LLC
Wook Yoo

Kim & Chang
Tae Hyun Yoon

Lee & Ko
Won Yoon

Yulchon LLC
Yonghee Yoon

KYRGYZ REPUBLIC

CJSC Agrimatco Ltd.

State Communications Agency
under the Government of
Kyrgyz Republic

ARIS
Azizbek Abdiev

Mol Tushum
Ilyas Abdirashit

International Center for Soil
Fertility and Agricultural
Development
Dilshod Abdulhamidov

Lorenz International Law Firm
Myrzagul Aidaralieva

Ministry of Agriculture and
Melioration of the Kyrgyz
Republic
Makhmira Akhmetova

Kompanion Financial Group
Ulanbek Akimkanov

Lorenz International Law Firm
Niyaz Aldashev

Kompanion Financial Group
Damir Alymbek

State Inspectorate for
Veterinary and Phytosanitary
Safety
Ruslan F. Beishenkulov

International Fertilizer
Development Center
Hiqmet Demiri

OJSC "Commercial Bank
KYRGYZSTAN"
Ruslan Derbishev

Lorenz International Law Firm
Samara Dumanaeva

Department of Cadastre and
Registration of Rights on
Immovable Property under
the State Registration Service
of Kyrgyz Republic
Bakytbek Dzhusupbekov

Hester Biosciences Limited
Rajiv Gandhi

Ulita LLC
Vasiliy Gorbachev

Seed Association of Kyrgyzstan
Abdul Hakim Islamov

Mol Tushum
Abdirashit Halmurzaev

Lorenz International Law Firm
Kymbat Ibakova

Kompanion Financial Group
Bolot Ibraimov

State Inspectorate for Veterinary and Phytosanitary Safety
Bolot Jumanaliev

UofLE "Association of Suppliers (Producers and Distributors)"
Marat Keldibek uulu

Lorenz International Law Firm
Evgeny Kim

Salym Finance
Mirlan Kulov

UNDP
Talaibek Makeev

Association of the International Road Transport Operators of the Kyrgyz Republic (AIRTO-KR)
Beknazar Mamytov

State Inspectorate for Veterinary and Phytosanitary Safety
Adyl Nurbaev

Seed Support Project
Rutgar Persson

State Agency on Environment Protection and Forestry under the Government of the Kyrgyz Republic
Asel Raimkulova

Rijk Zwaan Kyrgyz Republic
Aibek Rasidov

Ministry of Agriculture and Melioration of the Kyrgyz Republic
Ekaterina Sakhvaeva

Kompanion Financial Group
Jamil Sargymbaeva

Foreign Investors Association
Iskender Sharsheyev

Kisa
Iurii Sukhinin

Mol·Tushum
Patta Tajibaev

Credit Union ABN
Maria Taranchieva

State Seed Testing Agency of the Kyrgyz Republic
Dmitri Ten

Lorenz International Law Firm
Jibek Tenizbaeva

CJSC Atrium Holding
Baktybek Tumonbaev

Uran Tursunaliev

UofLE "Association of Suppliers (Producers and Distributors)"
Gulnara Uskenbaeva

LAO PDR

C.S. Transport Co., Ltd.

CTI Logistics Co., Ltd.

Outspan Bolovens Limited (OBL)

Tilleke & Gibbins Lao Co., Ltd.

Bank of the Lao PDR
Santi Bounleuth

Lao Law & Consultancy Group
Siri Boutdakham

Agroforex Company
Francis Chagnaud

Sypha Chanthavong

Lao Premier International Law Office
Nawika Charoenkitchatorn

DFDL
Agnès Couriol

Lao Premier International Law Office
Bounyong Dalasone

TABI -The Agro-Biodiversity Initiative
Christopher Flint

Ministry of Natural Resources and Environment
Phousavanh Fongkhamdeng

International Water Management Institute (IWMI)
Oulavanh Keovilignavong

CPC-Bolaven Plateau Coffee Producers Cooperative
Tobe Khamphankeothavee

UNU Institute for Integrated Management of Material Fluxes and Resources (UNU-FLORES)
Mathew Kurian

The Living Land Company
Laut Lee

Philippe Leperre

Khankeo Oupravanh

Thavisith Phanakhone

Department of Agriculture Extension and Cooperatives (DAEC), Ministry of Agriculture and Forestry
Sengchanh Phetkhounluang

Microfinance Association
Pamouane Phetthany

Ministry of Agriculture and Forestry
Yatkeo Phoumidalyvanh

Bank of the Lao PDR
Visone Saysongkham

Sinouk Coffee
Sinouk Sisombat

Viladeth Sisoulath

Ministry of Natural Resources and Environment
Phingsaliao Sithiengtham

Department of Agriculture Extension and Cooperatives (DAEC), Ministry of Agriculture and Forestry
Viengkham Sodahak

Phounsavat Souphida

KP Co., Ltd.
Khambor Sypaseuth

Lao Premier International Law Office
Arpon Tunjumras

Department of Livestock and Fisheries, Ministry of Agriculture and Forestry
Sounthone Vongthilath

LIBERIA

Bolloré Africa Logistics

BRAC-LBR
Mainuddin Ahmed

Central Bank of Liberia (CBL)
Jay Brown

J.D Tranding, Inc.
Steve B. Davis

Liberia Revenue Authority
Isabel Diggs

Liberia Revenue Authority
Max Teah Duncan

WARCIP Liberia
Bildi Elliot

GLS Business
Gabriel Fadairo

Farmers Union Network of Liberia
Josephine Francis

Access Bank
Vezele Gbogie

Ministry of Transport
Erasmus Gongar

Gro Green
Ralph Hamm

Price Trading Inc.
Charles Hopkins

Liberia Produce Marketing Corporation (LPMC)
Kenneth Kafumba

Liberia Revenue Authority
Eric Kamara

Central Bank of Liberia (CBL)
Mussah Kamara

BRAC-LBR
Tapan Kumar Karmaker

Gro Green
Prince T. Kollie

Omega Supply Chain
Abdallah Mansour

Access Bank
Friederike Moeller

Agro Inc.
Tupin Morgan

World Council of Credit Unions (WOCCU)
Patrick Muriuki

J.D Tranding, Inc.
Ben T. Nyepon

Wienco Liberia, Ltd.
Samuel Oduro Asare

Environmental Protection Agency of the Republic of Liberia
Levi Z. Piah

Premier Resource
Ansu Sirleaf

Premier Resource
Mohamed Sirleaf

Ministry of Agriculture
Sizi Z. Subah

Liberia Telecommunications Authority
Joe Sumo

Liberia Telecommunications Authority
Kolubahzizi T. Howard

Environmental Protection Agency of the Republic of Liberia
Jerry T. Toe

Liberia Telecommunications Authority
T. Emmanuel Tomah

Liberation Cocoa
Sheikh A. Turay

Environmental Protection Agency of the Republic of Liberia
Johansen T. Voker

Greenfield Liberia Inc.
Hussein Wazni

CARI - Central Agricultural Research Institute
Walter Wiles

Liberia Telecommunications Authority
Harry T. Yuan, Sr.

MALAWI

Cargo Management Logistics Ltd.

Department of Land Resources Conservation

Malawi Investment and Trade Centre (MITC)

Ministry of Transport and Public Works

Opportunity Bank Malawi

James Finlay (Blantyre) Ltd.
Chipulumutso Bakali

Agricultural Trading Company Ltd.
Christopher Beya

One Acre Fund
Joshua Cauthen

Centre for Environmental Policy & Advocacy
William Chadza

Knight & Knight
Noel Chalamanda

Sukambizi Association Trust
Austin Changazi

Mike Chigowo

Savjani & Co.
Ricky Chingota

Patrick Mphatso Chinguwo

Reserve Bank of Malawi
Mtchaisi Chintengo

Pharmacy, Medicines and
Poisons Board (PMPB)
Edwin Chipala

Seed Services Unit,
Department of Agricultural
Research Services
James Chipole

Agricultural Trading Company
Ltd.
George Chisembe

Cranfield University
Brighton Chunga

AGRA
Asseta Diallo

Hester Biosciences Limited
Rajiv Gandhi

Peacock Seeds
Felix E. Jumbe

Lilongwe University of
Agriculture & Natural
Resources (LUANAR)
Vernom Kabambe

Pharmacy, Medicines and
Poisons Board (PMPB)
Godfrey Kadewele

Kalima Attorneys
Justin Kalima

Ministry of Agriculture,
Irrigation and Water
Development, Department of
Agricultural Research Services
David Kamangira

Ministry of Agriculture,
Irrigation and Water
Development, Department of
Water Resources
Sidney Kamtukule

Ministry of Transport and
Public Works, Department
of Road Traffic Safety and
Services
Anne Kandoje

Shire Rver Basin Management
Program
Rex M. Kanjedza

Chisomo Kapulula

Lilongwe University of
Agriculture & Natural
Resources (LUANAR)
Samson Katengeza

Ministry of Agriculture,
Irrigation and Water
Development
Hendrex Wycliffe
Kazembe-Phiri

Ministry of Agriculture,
Irrigation and Water
Development
Sangwani Khosa

Seed Trade Association of
Malawi (STAM)
John Lungu

ETC Agro Tractors and
Implements Ltd.
Madhu Madaka

Biodiversity Conservation
Initiative
Leonard Manda

Felix Mangani

M-Livestock Consultants
Lawrence Matiasi

Environmental Affairs
Department
John Mawenda

James Finlay (Blantyre) Ltd.
Ross McDonald

Lilongwe University of
Agriculture & Natural
Resources (LUANAR)
Wezi Mhango

Biodiversity Conservation
Initiative
Godwin Mkamanga

Department of Agricultural
Research Services
Chandiona Munthali

Reserve Bank of Malawi
Hains Munthali

Malawi Communications
Regulatory Authority (MACRA)
Patrick Bennett Musiyapo

Seed Services Unit,
Department of Agricultural
Research Services
Hastings Musopole

Ministry of Agriculture,
Irrigation and Water
Development
Readwell P. Musopole

Lilongwe University of
Agriculture & Natural
Resources (LUANAR)
Macdonald L. Mwinjilo

Reserve Bank of Malawi
Fund Mzama

AHL Group
Oliver Nakom

Kwame Ngwira

BVM Enterprises
Poya Njoka

George Nthache

Ministry of Agriculture,
Irrigation and Water
Development
Machpherson Nthara

Ministry of Agriculture,
Irrigation and Water
Development, Department of
Agricultural Research Services
Austin Phiri

Seed Co
Dellings Phiri

Ministry of Agriculture,
Irrigation and Water
Development, Department of
Agricultural Research Services
Lawrent Pungulani

Ministry of Transport and
Public Works, Department
of Road Traffic Safety and
Services
Andrew Sandula

Seed-Tech
Wilson Shaba

Seed Co
Settie Simwawa

Ministry of Agriculture,
Irrigation and Water
Development, Department of
Agricultural Research Services
Charles Singano

MALAYSIA

Axiata Group Berhad

Bank Negara Malaysia

Green World Genetics Sdn.
Bhd.

International Islamic
University - Malaysia

Malaysia Co-operative
Societies Commission of
Malaysia

Malaysian Communications
and Multimedia Commission

Universiti Kebangsaan
Malaysia

Sime Kubota Sdn. Bhd.
Abd Halim Abd Karim

Wong & Partners
Faez Abdul Razak

Shearn Delamore & Co.
Dhinesh Bhaskaran

Tay & Partners
Hong Yun Chang

Tay & Partners
Pei Yin Chuar

Malaysian Transport Institute
(MITRANS)
Nasruddin Faisol

Hester Biosciences Limited
Rajiv Gandhi

Shook Lin & Bok
Julian George

Behn Meyer Agricare (M) Sdn.
Bhd.
Albert Heng

Tay & Partners
Wei En Hoong

Juruukur Tanahair
Shahabuddin Ibrahim

Malaysian Transport Institute
(MITRANS)
Harlina Suzana Jaafar

Shearn Delamore & Co.
Meyven Khor

Shearn Delamore & Co.
Christina Kow

Wong & Partners
Mark Lim

Union Harvest Sdn. Bhd.
Mohd Tohit Liri

Academy of Sciences Malaysia
Chia Hur Loh

Shearn Delamore & Co.
Krystle Lui

IGS Consultant
Che Abdullah Md. Rejab

Department of Aboriginal
Development
Md. Daud Md. Zin

Chooi & Company
David Ong

Shook Lin & Bok
Jalalullahl Othman

Ging Yang Siew

Shook Lin & Bok
Ainin Wan Salleh

Tay & Partners
Joe Yee Yap

MALI

Africa Trade & Industry
system

Orange Mali

Syngenta Foundation

SCS International
Marlène Amegankpoe

Sasakawa Africa Association
Abou Berthe

Coordination Nationale des
Organisations Paysannes
Abdramane Bouare

MicroCred
Fanta Dembele

SCS International
Moussa Syvlain Diakité

Direction Nationale du Génie
Rural
Hantlé Diarra

Ministère du Développement
rural, Office de protection des
végétaux
Lassana Sylvestre Diarra

Ministère de l'Agriculture
Alhouseïni Hamo Dicko

Mali Protection des Cultures
(M.P.C)
Messotigui Diomande

SFN/ABN
M. Djibrilla

Hester Biosciences Limited
Rajiv Gandhi

USC Canada
Abdrahamane Goïta

Sidi Keïta

Institut d'Economie
Rurale (IER), Ministère de
l'Agriculture de l'Elevage et de
la Pêche
Hamidou Konare

Institut d'Economie
Rurale (IER), Ministère de
l'Agriculture de l'Elevage et de
la Pêche
Mama Koné

Housseini Maiga

Cabinet d'Avocats Nassar et Collaborateurs
Eric Nassar

Arc En Ciel SARL
Amadou Ongoiba

Autorité Malienne de Régulation des Télécommunications/TIC et des Postes (AMRTP)
Samba Sow

Arc En Ciel SARL
Moctar Oumar Tall

Mali Protection des Cultures (M.P.C)
Moussa Tekete

Oumar Tounkara

Coordination Nationale des Usagers des Ressources Naturelles du Bassin Niger
Nouradine Zakaria Toure

Vesta Industries
Amadou Traoré

MEXICO

Transcooler México
Alejandro Aboytes

Comisión Nacional para el Conocimiento y Uso de la Biodiversidad (CONABIO)
Francisca Acevedo

Comisión Nacional Forestal (CONAFOR)
José Armando Alanís de la Rosa

Comisión Nacional para el Conocimiento y Uso de la Biodiversidad (CONABIO)
Vicente Arriaga Martínez

Basham, Ringe y Correa S.C.
Mariana Arrieta Maza

Jáuregui y Del Valle S.C.
Luis Alberto Balderas Fernández

Basham, Ringe y Correa S.C.
Rodolfo Barrreda Alvarado

Iniciativa para el Desarrollo Ambiental y Sustentable S.C.
Daniel Basurto González

Foliego
José Carlos Bautista

BGBG Abogados
Carlos A. Bello Hernández

Denisse Blanck

Jones Day
Paulina Bracamontes Belmonte

Instituto Tecnológico Superior de Felipe Carrillo Puerto
Diego Ramon Briceño Domínguez

Comisión Nacional para el Conocimiento y Uso de la Biodiversidad (CONABIO)
Caroline Nicole Laura Burgeff D'Hondt

Gonzalez Calvillo S.C.
Leopoldo Burguete-Stanek

Greenberg Traurig LLP
Pablo Callarisa

White & Case LLP
Antonio Cárdenas Arriola

Comisión Nacional Forestal (CONAFOR)
Jesús Carrasco Gómez

Cervantes Sainz Abogados
Luis A. Cervantes Muñiz

Comisión Nacional del Agua
Claudia Esther Coria-Bustos Pérez

Fideicomisos Instituidos en Relacion con la Agricultura-FIRA
José Antonio Cortés Barrientos

AGROVANT
Mercedes Cortés Sánchez

Pronatura México A.C.
Eduardo Cota Corona

Instituto Tecnológico Superior de Felipe Carrillo Puerto
Ivonne Cruz

Bufete de la Garza S.C.
José Mario De la Garza Marroquín

BGBG Abogados
Carlos J. Díaz Sobrino

BGBG Abogados
David Duran Molina

Asociación Mexicana de Semilleros
Alejandra Elizalde

Banco de México
Alan Elizondo

González Calvillo S.C.
Luis Alberto Esparza Romero

Basham, Ringe y Correa S.C.
Ricardo Evangelista García

López García Cano Abogados S.C.
Arturo Flores

Ritch, Mueller, Heather y Nicolau S.C.
Leopoldo Fragoso Montes

BGBG Abogados
Miguel Gallardo Guerra

Fideicomisos Instituidos en Relacion con la Agricultura-FIRA
Rafael Gamboa González

Hester Biosciences Limited
Rajiv Gandhi

Centro Mexicano de Derecho Ambiental (CEMDA)
Gisselle García Manning

Ritch, Mueller, Heather y Nicolau S.C.
Héctor A. Garza Cervera

Ritch, Mueller, Heather y Nicolau S.C.
Alessandra Gaytán

Vera y Asociados
Daniel Gómez

González & Asociados
José Juan González Márquez

Comisión Nacional para el Conocimiento y Uso de la Biodiversidad (CONABIO)
Fabiola Alejandra González Páez

Servicio Nacional de Inspección y Certificación de Semillas (SNICS)
Rosalinda González Santos

Jáuregui y Del Valle S.C.
Haydeé Montserrat González Tavira

Govea, Mercado Béjar S.C.
Javier Govea Soria

Von Wobeser y Sierra S.C.
Edmond Frederic Grieger Escudero

Financiera Nacional de Desarrollo Agropecuario, Rural, Forestal y Pesquero
Flor de Luz Guadalupe Hernández Barrios

Fideicomisos Instituidos en Relacion con la Agricultura-FIRA
José Onésimo Hernández Bello

Bufete de la Garza S.C.
Edgar Hernández Castillo

Govea, Mercado Béjar S.C.
Sergio Eduardo Herrera Torres

Comisión Nacional para el Conocimiento y Uso de la Biodiversidad (CONABIO)
Elleli Huerta

Comisión Nacional del Agua
Orlando Jaimes Martínez

Ritch, Mueller, Heather y Nicolau S.C.
Mario Enrique Juarez Noguera

Lapisa S.A. de C.V.
Paul Tonatiuh Justo Juárez

Jones Day
Jimena Kuri Izquierdo

Romo Paillés Abogados
Marco Antonio Larios Escalante

Comisión Nacional para el Conocimiento y Uso de la Biodiversidad (CONABIO)
Jorge Larson Guerra

López García Cano Abogados S.C.
Juan Fernando López

Von Wobeser y Sierra S.C.
Sofía López Casarrubias

Bufete de la Garza S.C.
Rodrigo López González

Asociación Nacional de Comercializadores de Fertilizantes
Juan Fernando Martinez

Comisión Nacional del Agua
Grisell Medina Laguna

Moreno Rodríguez y Asoc. S.C
Gerardo Moheno Gallardo

Dirección General de Sanidad Vegetal
Ana Lilia Montealegre Lara

Financiera Nacional de Desarrollo Agropecuario, Rural, Forestal y Pesquero
Antonio Eliceo Mora Téllez

White & Case LLP
Pedro Morales Gomez

Moreno Rodríguez y Asoc., S.C
José Rodrigo Moreno Rodríguez

Cervantes Sainz Abogados
Paulina Morfin

Automotriz Agrícola e Industrial Saturno S.A de C.V.
Mario Muñiz Flores

Comisión Nacional para el Conocimiento y Uso de la Biodiversidad (CONABIO)
Oswaldo Oliveros Galindo

White & Case LLP
Pilar Orozco Fernández

Greenberg Traurig LLP
Fernando Osante

Jones Day
José Jesús Pérez Alcántar

Servicio Nacional de Inspección y Certificación de Semillas (SNICS)
Felipe de Jesús Pérez de la Cerda

Servicio Nacional de Inspección y Certificación de Semillas (SNICS)
Julio César Pérez de la Cerda

Greenberg Traurig LLP
Arturo Pérez Estrada

Comisión Nacional para el Conocimiento y Uso de la Biodiversidad (CONABIO)
Rosa Maricel Portilla Alonso

Romo Paillés Abogados
Dario Preisser Rentería

Asociación Mexicana de Semilleros A.C.
Mario Puente Raya

Comisión Nacional Forestal (CONAFOR)
Francisco Quiroz Acosta

Comisión Nacional Forestal (CONAFOR)
Jorge Rescala Pérez

Romo Paillés Abogados
Maria Esther Rey Carrillo

Moreno Rodríguez y Asoc. S.C
Daniel Fernando Reyes Morales

Jurídica Especialistas de Occidente
Isaías Rivera Rodríguez

Fideicomisos Instituidos en Relacion con la Agricultura-FIRA
Carlos Ernesto Rodríguez Gómez

Iniciativa para el Desarrollo Ambiental y Sustentable S.C.
Edith Romero Juárez

Romo Paillés Abogados
Rafael Romo Corzo

Ritch, Mueller, Heather y Nicolau S.C.
Alejandra Sosa

Jones Day
Héctor R. Tinoco Jaramillo

Asesoría Biofarmacéutica Especializada
Héctor Tinoco-García

Greenberg Traurig LLP
Luis Torres

Garrigues México S.C.
Roberto Torres

Comisión Nacional del Agua
Dalia Aide Treviño Paz

Centro Mexicano de Derecho Ambiental (CEMDA)
Adriana Trigueros Hernández

Dirección General de Sanidad Vegetal
Francisco Javier Trujillo Arriaga

Casas Sombra y Pos Cosecha
Marino Valerio

Govea, Mercado Béjar S.C.
Nomar Uriel Valladares Castaño

Centro Mexicano de Derecho Ambiental (CEMDA)
Anaid Velasco

Confederación Nacional de Propietarios Rurales
Jaime Vences

Vera y Asociados
Luis Vera Morales

Servicio Nacional de Inspección y Certificación de Semillas (SNICS)
Manuel Rafael Villa Issa

Transporte.mx
Clemente Villalpando

López García Cano Abogados S.C.
Andoni Zurita

MOROCCO

Bayer Crop Science

HHH - Avocats

INRA - Institut National de Recherche Agricole

Ministère de l'Agriculture et de la Pêche Maritime

Ministère de l'Energie, des Mines, de l'Eau et de l'Environnement

SONACOS - Société Nationale de Commercialisation des Semences

Association Professionnelle du Transport et de la logistique du Nord (URTL Nord)
El Mootamid Abbad Andaloussi

Groupe Delassus
Madid Abdelilah

Sayarh & Menjra Cabinet d'Avocats
Mohamed Ali Abou Ali

RESING
Mohamed Aboufirass

Mohamed Akchati

Ministère de l'Economie et des Finances
Aziz Alouane

Khadija Arif

Institut Agronomique et Vétérinaire Hassan II
El Houssain Baali

Dris Barik

AGIP
Sofia Bekkali

Association Marocaine des Importateurs du Matériel Agricole (AMIMA)
Chakib Ben El Khadir

Ahmed Bentouhami

Ministère de l'Equipement, du Transport et de la Logistique
Lala Bahija Boucetta

Maroc Agroveto Holding
Hanane Boumehdi

Institut Agronomique et Vétérinaire Hassan II
El Hassane Bourarach

Groupe Delassus
Rabab Choukrallah

Adamas Avocats associés
Pauline Coune

Adamas Avocats associés
Philippe de Richoufftz

Office National de Sécurité Sanitaire des Produits Alimentaires (ONSSA)
Amina El Ghafki

Ministère de l'Economie et des Finances
Abdelaziz El Jai

Figes
Lamya El Mernissi

Figes
Mohamed El Mernissi

Institut Agronomique et Vétérinaire Hassan II
Moha El-Ayachi

Hester Biosciences Limited
Rajiv Gandhi

Association Marocaine des Importateurs du Matériel Agricole (AMIMA)
Nima Guitouni

HHH - Avocats
Zohra Hasnaoui

HHH - Avocats
Radja Hjiaj

HHH - Avocats
Ahmad Hussein

Charaf Corporation
Amine Kandil

GIAC TRANSLOG
Mohamed Karaouane

Agence Nationale de Réglementation des Télécommunications (ANRT)
Samira Khallouk

Université Chouaib Doukkali, Faculté des Sciences
Kamal Labbassi

Socopim Premium Group
Aziz Mchich

Sayarh & Menjra Cabinet d'Avocats
Mehdi Megzari

Université Hassan II-Casablanca
Mohamed Ali Mekouar

Fédération Interprofessionnelle Marocaine de production et d'exportation des Fruits et Légumes
Ahmed Mouflih

Centre de Travaux Agricole de Berchid
Mohamed Nebras

Sayarh & Menjra Cabinet d'Avocats
Omar Sayarh

Association des Freight Forwarders du Maroc
Rachid Tahri

Ministère de l'Economie et des Finances
Hicham Talby

Maroc Agroveto Holding
Faouzi Talhi

Houria Tazi Sadeq

MOZAMBIQUE

John Deere (Pty) Ltd. – Sub Saharan Africa

Lonagro Moçambique, Lda.

Pannar

Agricultural Research Institute of Mozambique (IIAM)
Suzie Aly

SOCREMO - Banco de Microfinanças, SARL
Ben Botha

Grace Chilande

Paulo Ferreira

Caixa Comunitária de Microfinanças
Italino Francisco

MC&A Sociedad de Advogados R.L
Pedro Gonçalves Paes

Barloworld Agriculture
Tom Holloway

Couto, Graça & Associados (CGA)
Cristina Hunguana

JLA Advogados
Zara Jamal

Eduardo Mondlane University
Dinis Juizo

Transportes Lalgy
Luis Junaide Lalgy

African Fertilizer and Agribusiness Partnership (AFAP)
Alcides Lampiao

Fernanda Lopes & Associados Advogados
Fernanda Lopes

Ministry of Agriculture (MINAG)
Anastacio Luis

Astros
Elcidio Madeira

Agricultural Research Institute of Mozambique (IIAM)
Ricardo Maria

ESM Partners, Lda.
Espirito Santo Monjane

Bordalo Mouzinho

Agricultural Research Institute of Mozambique (IIAM)
Paulino Munisse

Terra Firma Lda
Simon Norfolk

Caixa Comunitária de Microfinanças
Marino José Pascoal

Caixa Comunitaria de Microfinancas
Enoque Raimundo Changamo

AgriFocus
Fernando Sequeira

Companhia do Vanduzi
Amos Ubisse

Adriaan van den Dries

Fernanda Lopes & Associados Advogados
Joaquim Vilanculos

Autoridade Moçambicana de Fertilizantes (AMOFERT)
Carlos Zandamela

MYANMAR

Duane Morris & Selvam LLP

Myanmar Livestock Federation

Guiding Star Mon News Journal
Ko Ko Aung

DB Schenker
Nay Aung

Myanmar Containers Truck Association (MCTA)
U Thet Aung

UN Habitat
Myint Aye

Matthew Baird

DFDL
Viacheslav Baksheev

DFDL
Jaime Casanova

Hester Biosciences Limited
Rajiv Gandhi

DFDL
William Greenlee

Convenience Prosperity Co.,
Ltd.
Gerhard Hartzenberg

Harmony Myanmar Agro
Group Co, Ltd.
Min Aung Hein

Swanyee Group
U Than Win Hlaing

San Tin Htar
Nang Sang Hom

Golden Plain Agricultural
Products Cooperative Society
Limited
Kywe Htay

Hercules Logistics
Win Htike

SGS (Myanmar) Limited
Aung Kyaw Htoo

Posts and
Telecommunications
Department
Than Htun Aung

Allen & Gledhill (Myanmar)
Co., Ltd.
Ayush Jhunjhunwala

State Agricultural Institute
Lay Lay Khaing

Allen & Gledhill (Myanmar)
Co., Ltd.
Eugene Kuan

Rakhine Coastal Region
Conservation Association
(RCA)
Maung Kyi

Ministry of Agriculture,
Livestock and Irrigation
San Kyi

Allen & Gledhill (Myanmar)
Co., Ltd.
Jun Yee Lee

Shan Maw Myae Co., Ltd.
Nyan Lin

Ministry of Agriculture,
Livestock and Irrigation
U Han Thein Maung

Choong Ang Vaccine
Laboratories Co., Ltd. (CAVAC)
Juver Membrebe

DFDL
Nay Chi Min Maung

Swanyee Group
Zaw Min Sein

Hercules Logistics
Aung Min Thein

Myanmar International
Freight Forwarders
Association
Aung Khin Myint

Yezin Agricultural University
(YAU)
Theingi Myint

Shan Maw Myae Co., Ltd.
U Myo Myint

DFDL
Mya Myint Zu

Deloitte
Aung Myo Lwin

Myanmar Containers Truck
Association (MCTA)
U Tin Myo Win

Myanmar Containers Truck
Association (MCTA)
U Soe Naing

Allen & Gledhill (Myanmar)
Co., Ltd.
Minn Naing Oo

Green Avenue Consult
Myanmar
Robert Htun Nwe

Myanmar International
Consultants (MMIC), Ltd.
Myo Nyunt

Deloitte
Nwe Oo Mon

Mon-Region Social
Development Network (MSDN)
Hlaing Hteik Soe

Forest Resource Environment
Development And
Conservation Association
(FREDA)
Khin Lay Swe

ActionAid
Boon Thein

DFDL
Ei Ei Thein

Village Integrated
Development Association
San Thein

Mon-Region Social
Development Network (MSDN)
Kyaw Thi Ha

Mon-Region Social
Development Network (MSDN)
Sein Ti

San Tin Htar
Shwe Zin Toe Hla

Wageningen UR
Joep van den Broek

NEPAL

Allied Law Services
Chandramani Adhikari

Sharad Adhikari

Institute for Sustainable
Agriculture Nepal (INSAN)
Kiran Amatya

Nirdhan Utthan Bank
Iswar Atreya

Shangrila Agro World
Tara Baskota

Nepal Agricultural Research
Council (NARC)
Bhola Basnet

Community Self Reliance
Centre (CSRC)
Jagat Basnet

National Cooperative Bank
Limited (NCBL)
Upendra Dahal

Chhetry & Associates P.C.
Samindra Dhowj G.C

Hester Biosciences Limited
Rajiv Gandhi

Bioversity International
Devendra Gauchan

Alternative Herbal Products
(AHP)
Govinda Ghimire

Trade and Export Promotion
Center
Ishwari Prasad Ghimire

Nepal Agricultural Research
Council (NARC)
Krishna Hari Ghimire

PSM Global Consultants Pvt.
Ltd.
Madhab Raj Ghimire

United States Environmental
Protection Agency (EPA)
Santosh Raj Ghimire

Bal Krishna Joshi

National Cooperative Bank
Limited (NCBL)
Saroj Joshi

Pradhan, Ghimire and
Associates Pvt. Ltd.
Aadittya Kansakar

Kathmandu University
Bishal Khanal

PSM Global Consultants Pvt. Ltd.
Damodar Khanal

Nepal Agricultural Research
Council (NARC)
Ujjawal Kushwaha

Shangrila Agro World
Lobsang Lama

Agro Enterprise Centre (FNCCI)
Pradip Maharjan

Choong Ang Vaccine
Laboratories Co., Ltd. (CAVAC)
Juver Membrebe

Institute for Sustainable
Agriculture Nepal (INSAN)
Puspa Lal Moktan

Nirdhan Utthan Bank
Janardan Dev Pant

Institute of Agriculture and
Animal Science
Krishna Kumar Pant

Nepal Agricultural Research
Council (NARC)
Krishna Prasad Paudyal

Prachanda Pradhan

Plant Protection Directorate,
Ministry of Agricultural
Development
Rajiv Das Rajbhandari

Plant Protection Directorate,
Ministry of Agricultural
Development
Dilli Ram Sharma

Post Harvest Management
Directorate, Ministry of
Agricultural Development
Sabnam Shivakoti

Suva Transport
Dipesh Shrestha

Ministry of Science,
Technology and Environment
Jagdish Bhakta Shrestha

Vishokarma Auto Mart
Shiva Shrestha

Trade and Export Promotion
Center
Rajendra Singh

Ministry of Agricultural
Development
Madhusudan Singh Basnyat

Nepalese Telecommunications
Authority (NTA) - Rural
Telecommunication Section
Ambar Sthapit

Puwa Mai Alaichi Nursery
Firm
Nanda Kumar Subba

Nepal Herbs and Herbal
Products Association
(NEHHPA)
Yubraj Subedi

Bandevi Vet Pharma
Dibesh Thapa

Plant Protection Directorate,
Ministry of Agricultural
Development
Dinesh Babu Tiwari

Department of Agriculture
Rajendra Uprety

Nepal Agricultural Research
Council (NARC)
Shree Prasad Vista

NETHERLANDS

Dutch Federation of
Agricultural Machinery
Producers (FEDECOM)

Ministry of Infrastructure and
the Environment

The Greenery

Vallenduuk Advokaten

Limagrain Europe
Huub Beelen

Centre for Genetic Resources,
the Netherlands (CGN)
Martin Brink

Panteia BV
Arnaud Burgess

Norton Rose Fulbright LLP
Nikolai de Koning

Culterra
Leon Fock

Hester Biosciences Limited
Rajiv Gandhi

Utrecht University
Herman Kasper Gilissen

Van Iperen International
Joanne Grafton

Naktuinbouw
Kees Jan Groenewoud

Kadaster
Linda Heerdt

Utrecht University
Andrea Keessen

Naktuinbouw
Henk Lange

AKD
Yorko Langerak

Norton Rose Fulbright LLP
Floortje Nagelkerke

Ministry of Economic Affairs
Najim Ouelaouch

Stibbe N.V.
Rogier Raas

Stibbe N.V.
Soeradj Ramsanjhal

Adrianus Rijk

St. Thomas University School of Law
Keith Rizzardi

Kadaster
Ruben Roes

Naktuinbouw
Ad Toussaint

Seeds and Plant Propagation Material, Ministry of Economic Affairs
Marien Valstar

Van Iperen International
Erik Van den Bergh

AKD
Gerrit van der Veen

Utrecht University
Willemijn van Doorn-Hoekveld

Naktuinbouw
Kees Van Ettekoven

Centre for Genetic Resources, the Netherlands (CGN)
Theo van Hintum

Norton Rose Fulbright LLP
Gijs van Leeuwen

Utrecht University
Helena van Rijswick

Naktuinbouw
John van Ruiten

GroentenFruit Huis
Peter Verbaas

Centre for Genetic Resources, the Netherlands (CGN)
Bert Visser

Stibbe N.V.
Jaap Willeumier

Kadaster
Rik (H.J.) Wouters

NICARAGUA

AGROFORMA·

Asociación de Productores y Exportadores de Nicaragua

CISA AGRO

Comisión Nacional de Microfinanzas

CATIE
Amílcar Aguilar Carrillo

Semillas S.A.
Jesús Alcázar Andrade

CATIE
Estela Clotilde Alemán Mercado

García & Bodán Attorneys & Counsellors at Law
María Alejandra Aubert

Universidad Nacional Agraria
Álvaro Benavides González

Olam Nicaragua S.A.
Emerson Carlos

Formunica
Lizbeth Castillo

Federación de Cooperativas para el Desarrollo (FECODESA R.L.)
Blanca Castro Briones

Maquipos S.A.
Jorge Luis Centeno B.

ChamAgro
William Chamorro

Agrovet Market Animal Health
Isaac Antonio Chavarría Irias

Organismo Internacional Regional de Sanidad Agropecuaria
Juan Agustín Chavarría V

Olam Nicaragua S.A.
Alba Cruz

Universidad Nacional de Ingeniería (UNI)
Sergio Gámez Guerrero

Hester Biosciences Limited
Rajiv Gandhi·

García & Bodán Attorneys & Counsellors at Law
Terencio García Montenegro

Olam Nicaragua S.A.
Alfonso González

García & Bodán Attorneys & Counsellors at Law
Denisse Gutiérrez

CAFENICA
Martha Estela Gutiérrez Cruz

Federación de Cooperativas para el Desarrollo (FECODESA R.L.)
Rolando Herrera Torrez

Instituto Nicaragüense de Telecomunicaciones y Correos (TELCOR)
Edmundo Lacayo Castillo

Rodolfo Jose Lacayo Ubau

Olam Nicaragua S.A.
Martha Leiva

CAFENICA
Ligia López

Red de Agua y Saneamiento de Nicaragua (RASNIC)
Xiomara del Socorro Medrano

Paula Novo

Olam Nicaragua S.A.
Andrés Ospina Mejía

Federación de Cooperativas para el Desarrollo (FECODESA R.L.)
Adolfo Javier Pasquier Luna

García & Bodán Attorneys & Counsellors at Law
Jessica Porras

CAFENICA
Ruben Poveda

Revetsa
Walter Ramos

Arias & Muñoz
Ana Teresa Rizo

University of Northern Colorado
Sarah Romano

Consortium Taboada & Asociados
Alfonso José Sandino Granera

CISA AGRO
Carlos Fernando Vargas Montealegre

PROCOCER R.L.
Roberto Villegas

Eduardo Zamora

Naym Zamora

Café Nor
Frederik Zeuthen

NIGERIA

La Fayette Microfinance Bank

Federal Ministry of Agriculture and Rural Development
Ahmed Adekunle

Jackson, Etti & Edu
Morenike Ademiju

Olam Nigeria
Green Ademola

Federal Ministry of Agriculture and Rural Development
Majasan Ademola

HT - Agro
Yomi Adeniyi

Technical Centre for Agricultural and Rural Cooperation (CTA)
Matthew Adetunji

Jackson, Etti & Edu
Adekunle Adewale

Armajaro Nigeria Limited
Tokunbo Adewale Toriola

Cocoa Association of Nigeria
Segun Adewumi Olusegun

Sefton Fross
Oluwatobi Adeyemo

IFDC
Feyikemi Adurogbangba

ÆLEX
Akinloye Ajayi

Renascence Legal Practitioners and Arbitrators
Olatubosun Akanmidu

National Centre for Genetic Resources and Biotechnology (NACGRAB)
Sunday E. Aladele

National Centre for Genetic Resources and Biotechnology (NACGRAB)
Olabisi Alamu

Templars
Solomon Alo

Etisalat
Valentine Amadi

Babura Microfinance Bank Limited
Manir Aminu

Nigerian Communications Commission (NCC)
Josephine Amuwa

Sefton Fross
Olayemi Anyanechi

DFID-Propcom Maikarfi
Oluwatosin Ariyo

Aluko & Oyebode
Ina Arome

Federal Ministry of Agriculture and Rural Development
Mabel Arwoh-Ajumobi

University of Nigeria
Charles Asadu

IITA - West Africa
Robert Asiedu

Heritage Bank Limited
Olugbenga Awe

ÆLEX
Soji Awogbade

National Water Resources Institute
Olusanjo Bamgboye

Hadejia Jama'are Komadugu Yobe Basin Trust Fund
Hassan Bdliya

Bayer CropScience Nigeria
Akongs Dankande

Etisalat
Ibrahim Dikko

WEIR
Gabriel Ekanem

Federal Ministry of Agriculture and Rural Development
Adamu Eloji

George Etomi and Partners
George Etomi

Aulic Nigeria Limited
Nick Ezeh

Templars
Mojisola Fashola

Hester Biosciences Limited
Rajiv Gandhi

Ecobank Nigeria
Ayorinde Ishola

Aluko & Oyebode
Oyinkansola Karunwi

Ahmadu Bello University
Muhammed Tawfiq Ladan

David Olakunle Ladipo II

Aluko & Oyebode
Oghogho Makinde

G. Elias & Co.
Bibitayo Mimiko

Continental Logistics Limited
Mike Mornu

*Agricultural Research Council
of Nigeria*
Yarama Dakwa Ndirpaya

*Federal Ministry of Water
Resources*
Felicia Irima Ngaji-Usibe

Ridan Farms Kuje
Perpetual Nkechi Nwali

Ecobank Nigeria
Peter Obah

Templars
Chike Obianwu

Sefton Fross
Enovwor Odukuye

*National Agricultural Seed
Council*
Philip O. Ojo

*Potato Farmers Association of
Nigeria (POFAN)*
Daniel Okafor

*Seed Certification Quality
Control, NASC*
Sunday Folarin Okelola

ÆLEX
Nicola Okolo

Brass Fertilizer
Ben Okoye

Aluko & Oyebode
Jesutofunmi Olabenjo

*Renascence Legal
Practitioners and Arbitrators*
Oluwaseun Olanrewaju

George Etomi and Partners
Akasemi Ollor

*Falus Biotech International
Nigeria Ltd.*
Adefalujo Olumide

Cellulant Nigeria Limited
Olugbenga Owolabi

George Etomi and Partners
Veronica Oyedeji

*Renascence Legal
Practitioners and Arbitrators*
Olaseni A. Oyefeso

Brass Fertilizer
Sanjay Patel

Olam Nigeria
Kazeem Salaudeen

George Etomi and Partners
Ibifuro Sekibo

*Federal University of
Agriculture, Abeokuta*
Adeyinka Sobowale

Seed Co West Africa
Elliot Tembo

*NatCom Development &
Investment Limited (Ntel)*
Damian Udeh

*Federal Ministry of Agriculture
and Rural Development*
Sadiq Umar

Bayer CropScience Nigeria
Caleb Usoh

NIGER

Negoce International Niger

*Institut National de la
Recherche Agronomique du
Niger (INRAN)*
Saidou Addam Kiari
Maman Sani Amadou

*Chambre de Commerce,
d'Industrie et d'Artisannat du
Niger*
Maliki Barhouni

*Institut National de la
Recherche Agronomique du
Niger (INRAN)*
Issoufou Adam Boukar

Ministère de l'Agriculture
Maman Chekaraou

Banque Agricole du Niger
Abdoulaye Djadah

*Direction Générale de la
Protection des Végétaux*
Abdou Alimatou Douki

*Fédération des coopératives
maraîchères du Niger (FCMN-
Niya)*
Abdoussalam Douma

Hester Biosciences Limited
Rajiv Gandhi

*Institut National de la
Recherche Agronomique du
Niger (INRAN)*
Maman Garba

*Association Nationale
des Coopératives des
Professionnels de la Filière
Oignon*
Abdoul Aziz Hanafi Cissé

*Ministère de l'Hydraulique et
de l'Assainissment*
Attahirou Ibrahim Karbo

*Direction Générale de
l'Agriculture*
Ado Kanta

FAO
Lassaad Lachaal

Avocat à la Cour
Oumarou Mainassara

*Promotion des Filières
Animales et de la Qualité-
Ministère des Resources
Animales*
Adam Kade Malam Gadjimi

FAO
Bachir Maliki

Coopec Kokari
Yahouza Maman

*Institut National de la
Recherche Agronomique du
Niger (INRAN)*
Abdoulaye Mohamadou

Banque Agricole du Niger
Maman-Lawal Mossi Bagodou

Ferme Semencière Ainoma
Aichatou A. Nasser

*Institut National de la
Recherche Agronomique du
Niger (INRAN)*
Mahamane Nasser Laouali

FAO
Judicael Pazou

Jérôme Pennec

Université de Maradi
Mahamane Saadou

FAO
Amadou Saley

Airtel Niger
Karimou Salifou

Ferme Semencière Ainoma
Mahaman Salifou

FAO
Mbodji Serigne

*Etude d'Avocats Marc Le Bihan
& Collaborateurs*
Idrissa Tchernaka

*Ministère de l'Hydraulique et
de l'Assainissment*
Abdourahamane Elhadji
Aboubacar Touraoua

Ministère des Transports
Attaoulahi Zakaouanou

PERU

*Asociación Nacional del
Transporte Terrestre de Carga
(ANATEC)*

*Cooperativa Agraria de Cafés
Especiales de Yapaz Bajo
- COPACEYBA*

Corporación L'AU 88 S.A.C.

*Instituto Nacional de
Innovación Agraria*

*Organismo Supervisor de
la Inversión Privada en
Telecomunicaciones - OSIPTEL*

Tropic-X S.A.C.

*Universidad Nacional Agraria
La Molina*

Estudio Álvarez Calderón
Fanny Patricia Aguirre Garayar

*Ministerio de Agricultura y
Riego*
José Luis Alarcón Tello

Estudio Álvarez Calderón
Alfonso Álvarez Calderón
Yrigoyen

Agrovet Market S.A.
Giovanna Anchorena

Estudio Olaechea
Christian Arauco

Ilender Corp
Mauricio Alfredo Arcelles
Porras

Estudio Ávila & Abogados
Lucia Patricia Ávila Bedrega

Estudio Ávila & Abogados
Víctor Ávila Cabrera

*Instituto Nacional de
Innovación Agraria (INIA)*
Roger Becerra Gallardo

*Rodrigo, Elías & Medrano
Abogados*
Oscar Benavides

*Estudio Torres y Torres Lara
Abogados*
Johana Benites

Estudio Avila & Abogados
Mario Camoirano Garaventa

Estudio Ferrero Abogados
Fabiola Capurro

Andina Freight S.A.C
Renatto Castro

*Ministerio de Agricultura y
Riego*
Fernando Castro Verástegui

Iriarte & Asociados
Jessica Cerna

*Payet, Rey, Cauvi, Pérez
Abogados*
Vanessa Chávarry

Ministerio del Ambiente
Milagros Coral

Rey & de los Ríos Abogados
Gustavo Victor de los Ríos
Woolls

*Lazo, De Romaña & Gagliuffi
Abogados*
Fátima de Romaña

*Rodrigo, Elías & Medrano
Abogados*
Juan Carlos Del Busto

Cooperativa Sol & Café Ltda.
Javier Domínguez

*Instituto Nacional de
Innovación Agraria*
Lucía Elsa Pajuelo Cubillas

Land Alliance
Victor Endo

*Lazo, De Romaña & Gagliuffi
Abogados*
Cinthya Leticia Escate
Ampuero

Miranda&Amado Abogados
Nelly Espinoza Campos

*Llona & Bustamante
Abogados*
María del Pilar Falcón Castro

Grupo Drogavet
Freddy Farfán

*Estudio Jurídico Monteblanco
& Asociados*
Janet Fernandez

Farvet
Manolo Fernandez

Ministerio de Agricultura y
Riego
Verónika González Riva

Sergio David Goshima Zamami

Percy Grandez Barrón

*Pontificia Universidad
Católica del Perú (PUCP)*
Jorge Armando Guevara Gil

Ilender Corp
Luis Gutiérrez

Jan Hendriks

*Universidad Nacional Agraria
La Molina*
Elizabeth Consuelo Heros
Aguilar

Estudio Olaechea
Jose Antonio Honda

Ministerio del Ambiente
Nancy Huillchuanaco

Iriarte & Asociados
Erick Americo Iriarte Ahon

Miranda & Amado Abogados
Josue Greeg Jaen Palomino

Invetsa
Edgardo Landa Barsallo

*Lazo, De Romaña & Gagliuffi
Abogados*
Julián Li

*Estudio Jurídico Monteblanco
& Asociados*
Jany Mamani

*Unión Nacional de
Transportistas Dueños de
Camiones del Perú – UNT*
Luis Alberto Marcos Bernal

*Equipo de Derecho Ambiental
- EDERA*
Carmen Nadine Márquez
Muñoz

*Ministerio de Comercio
Exterior y Turismo (MINCETUR)*
Shane Martínez del Águila

*Servicio Nacional de Sanidad
Agraria (SENASA)*
Pedro Molina

*Rodrigo, Elías & Medrano
Abogados*
Fiorella Monge

*Estudio Jurídico Monteblanco
& Asociados*
Sandro Monteblanco

*Rodrigo, Elías & Medrano
Abogados*
Carlos Monteza

*Estudio Torres y Torres Lara
Abogados*
Ernesto Alonso Naveda
Cavero

Ministerio del Ambiente
Adrian Fernando Neyra
Palomino

*Universidad Nacional de San
Antonio Abad del Cusco*
Ramiro Ortega Dueñas

*Estudio Torres y Torres Lara
Abogados*
Mauricio Paredes Contreras

*Pontificia Universidad
Católica del Perú y
Universidad Peruana de
Ciencias Aplicadas*
John Richard Pineda Galarza

*Llona & Bustamante
Abogados*
Juan Prado Bustamante

Miranda & Amado Abogados
Jose Miguel Puiggros Otero

*Estudio Jurídico Monteblanco
& Asociados*
Javier Quiniones

*Unión Nacional de
Transportistas Dueños de
Camiones del Perú – UNT*
Javier Marchese Quiroz

*Autoridad Nacional del Agua
(ANA)*
José Aurelio Ramírez Garro

C. Vet. Agro
María Violeta Ramírez Jiménez

Agrovet Market S.A.
Jimena Del Risco

America Móvil Perú S.A.C. – Claro
Juan Rivadeneyra

*Rodrigo, Elías & Medrano
Abogados*
Luis Carlos Rodrigo

Agrovet Market S.A.
Annelisse Rodríguez

Cooperativa Norandino
Clever Rojas Hernández

Oikocredit
Frank Rubio

Cámara de Comercio de Lima
Roger Rubio

*Unión Nacional de
Transportistas Dueños de
Camiones del Perú – UNT*
Raquel Salcedo

*Instituto Nacional de
Innovación Agraria (INIA)*
Rosa Angélica Sánchez Díaz

*Estudio Torres y Torres Lara
Abogados*
Karina Seminario

Ministerio del Ambiente
Manuel Silva Repetto

Ministerio del Ambiente
Natalia Soto

FAO
Gonzalo Tejada

*Rodrigo, Elías & Medrano
Abogados*
Francisco Tong

Oikocredit
Carina Torres

*Payet, Rey, Cauvi, Pérez
Abogados*
Carlos Alberto Torres Mariño

*Comité de Semillas de
Lambayeque*
Mario Valencia Hernádez

*Rodrigo, Elías & Medrano
Abogados*
Úrsula Zavala

Rey & de los Ríos Abogados
Héctor Ignacio Zúñiga Luy

PHILIPPINES

Atlas Fertilizer Corporation

*Department of Environment
and Natural Resources*

*Sycip Salazar Hernandez &
Gatmaitan*
Ruben P Acebedo II

*Dime & Eviota Law Firm
(DLDTE Law)*
Ramon Alikpala

*University of the Philippines
Los Baños*
Nestor Altoveros

*Pilipino Banana Growers and
Exporters Association Inc.
(PBGEA)*
Stephen Antig

Puno and Puno Law Offices
John Maynard G. Atotubo

*Angara Abello Concepcion
Regala & Cruz Law Offices
(ACCRALAW)*
Blesie Mae P. Bustamate

*Angara Abello Concepcion
Regala & Cruz Law Offices
(ACCRALAW)*
J. Alessandra G. Cochico

Correa Trucking
Ferdinand Correa

*Dime & Eviota Law Firm
(DLDTE Law)*
Ronald Dime

*Department of Environment
and Natural Resources*
Edwin Domingo

*Philippines Provincial Road
Management Facility (PRMF)*
Nelson Doroy

East-West Seed Company, Inc.
Bel Enriquez

Bangko Sentral ng Pilipinas
Nestor A. Espenilla, Jr.

*Philippines Provincial Road
Management Facility (PRMF)*
Ananias 'Bhong' Fernandez Jr

*Sycip Salazar Hernandez &
Gatmaitan*
Alan C Fontanosa

Hester Biosciences Limited
Rajiv Gandhi

*Agricultural Machinery Testing
and Evaluation Center*
Darwin Iaranguren

*Philippines Provincial Road
Management Facility (PRMF)*
Rex Kinder

*Sycip Salazar Hernandez &
Gatmaitan*
Rose Marie M.
King-Dominguez

*National Irrigation
Administration (NIA)*
Bonifacio Labiano

*Sycip Salazar Hernandez &
Gatmaitan*
Franco Aristotle G Larcina

*Angara Abello Concepcion
Regala & Cruz Law Offices
(ACCRALAW)*
Everlene O. Lee

*Soiltech Agricultural Products
Corporation*
Ester Lupisan

*Dime & Eviota Law Firm
(DLDTE Law)*
Marie Kris Madriaga

*Choong Ang Vaccine
Laboratories Co., Ltd. (CAVAC)*
Juver Membrebe

*Soiltech Agricultural Products
Corporation*
Dan Oñate

Puno & Peñarroyo
Gianna Maree Penalosa

Puno & Peñarroyo
Fernando S. Peñarroyo

Puno and Puno Law Offices
Roderico V. Puno

Puno & Peñarroyo
Ramiila Quinto

*Department of Information
and Communication
Technology (DICT)*
Alana Ramos

Puno and Puno Law Offices
Graciello Timothy Reyes

*Board of Agricultural
Engineering*
Ariodear C. Rico

Asia Trans International Inc.
Bong Ronquillo

*Department of Information
and Communication
Technology (DICT)*
Alberto Salvador

Puno & Peñarroyo
Edward Santiago

East-West Seed Company, Inc.
Mary Ann Sayoc

Bangko Sentral ng Pilipinas
Maria Cynthia Sison

*Soiltech Agricultural Products
Corporation*
Rene So

Agri Component Corporation
Rodolfo H. Tamayo

*Angara Abello Concepcion
Regala & Cruz Law Offices
(ACCRALAW)*
Eusebio V. Tan

POLAND

*International Cooperation
Department, Agricultural
and Food Quality Inspection
(IJHARS)*

*Kancelaria Adwokatów i
Radców Prawnych Lipiński &
Walczak s.c*

Institute of Technology and Life Sciences
Bogdan Bak

Domański Zakrzewski Palinka (DZP)
Maciej Białek

Regional Environmental Center for Central and Eastern Europe (REC)
Michał Brennek

Domański Zakrzewski Palinka (DZP)
Daniel Chojnacki

Fundusz Mikro
Magdalena Dulczewska

Hester Biosciences Limited
Rajiv Gandhi

PIMR - Industrial Institute of Agricultural Engineering
Julia Goscianska-Lowinska

Domański Zakrzewski Palinka (DZP)
Tymon Grabarczyk

Yara
Olaf Günther-Borstel

RGW Rocławski Graczyk i Wspólnicy Adwokacka Spółka Jawna
Wioletta Gwizdała

Squire Patton Boggs
Igor G. Hanas

Misiewicz, Mosek & Partners Law Office
Anna Kluczek-Kollár

Squire Patton Boggs
Rafał Kozerski

The Office for Registration of Medicinal Products, Medical Devices and Biocidal Products
Anna Kucharska

Institute of Technology and Life Sciences
Leszek Labedzki

Polska Izba Gospodarcza Maszyn i Urzadzen Rolniczych (PIGMIUR)
Patryk Lajstet

John Deere Polska Sp. z o.o.
Miroslaw Leszczynski

PIMR - Industrial Institute of Agricultural Engineering
Jan Radniecki

Wardyński & Partners
Martyna Robakowska

RGW Rocławski Graczyk i Wspólnicy Adwokacka Spółka Jawna
Wojciech Rocławski

Dentons
Ewa Rutkowska-Subocz

KWS Lochow Polska
Agnieszka Sasiadek

Dentons
Agnieszka Skorupińska

Misiewicz, Mosek & Partners Law Office
Paweł Szkodlarski

Jagiellonian University
Piotr Szwedo

WKB Wiercinski, Kwiecinski, Baehr
Sergiusz Urban

BNT Neupert Zamorska & Partnerzy sp.j.
Dominika Izabela Wagrodzka

Wardyński & Partners
Dominik Wałkowski

White & Case LLP
Grzegorz J. Wąsiewski

Kancelaria Prawna Piszcz, Norek i Wspólnicy sp.k.
Monika Witt

BNT Neupert Zamorska & Partnerzy sp.j.
Jakub Woliński

John Deere Polska Sp. z o.o.
Stanislaw Wolski

Plant Breeding and Acclimatization Institute (IHAR)
Marcin Zaczyński

Wardyński & Partners
Izabela Zielińska-Barłożek

Vetoquinol Biowet Sp. z o.o.
Wojciech Zieliński

ROMANIA

National Authority for Management and Regulation in Communications (ANCOM)

National Bank of Romania

State Institute for Variety Testing and Registration (ISTIS)

Tagiri Consulting S.R.L.

Muşat & Asociaţii
Ana Maria Abrudan

National Institute of Research Development for Machines and Installations designed to Agriculture and Food Industry
Isabela Alexandru

Almaj & Albu Attorneys at Law
Nicoleta Almaj Murariu

Reff & Associates SCA
Silvia Axinescu

Ministry of Agriculture and Rural Development
Doina Baiculescu

Almaj & Albu Attorneys at Law
Sorina Baroi

Peli Filip SCA
Cristina Barticel

Muşat & Asociaţii
Andrei Boaca

Law Office Hategan
Beatrice Bostan

Muşat & Asociaţii
Gheorghe Buta

Reff & Associates SCA
Alexandru Campean

ONV LAW

Lorena Ciobanu

Ţuca Zbârcea & Asociaţii
Sergiu Cretu

Trelea Law Office
Adrian Dorin Decianu

Muşat & Asociaţii
Monia Dobrescu

Muşat & Asociaţii
Maria Dosan

Ţuca Zbârcea & Asociaţii
Ciprian Dragomir

Peli Filip SCA
Ioan Dumitraşcu

Biris Goran Law Firm
Daniela Dunel-Stancu

Peli Filip SCA
Mădălina Fildan

Hester Biosciences Limited
Rajiv Gandhi

Muşat & Asociaţii
George Ghitu

Ţuca Zbârcea & Asociaţii
Bogdan Halcu

SC BISO Romania S.R.L.
Andreea Hincu

Law Office Hategan
Andreea Iancu

Iuliana Ionescu

Almaj & Albu Attorneys at Law
Alice Ionica

Peli Filip SCA
Mihaela Ispas

Romanian Association of Producers and Importers of Agricultural Machinery- APIMAR
Mihai Ivascu

Peli Filip SCA
Monica Lancu

ONV LAW
Catalina Raluca Lazar

Maisadour Semences Romania S.R.L.
Lucian Melut

Peli Filip SCA
Anca Mitocaru

National Sanitary Veterinary and Food Safety Authority
Rodica Morcov

SC BISO Romania S.R.L.
Costin Motoiu

Muşat & Asociaţii
Mona Muşat

Agrium - Agroport Romania S.A.
Ofelia Nalbant

KWS Seminte S.R.L.
Doriana Nitu

Muşat & Asociaţii
Andrei Ormenean

KWS Lochow Polska
Codru Paun

National Institute of Research Development for Machines and Installatiohs designed to Agriculture an
Ion Pirna

Muşat & Asociaţii
Iulian Popescu

Clifford Chance Badea SCA
Loredana Ralea

National Administration "Romanian Waters"
Adrian Riti

NTMO SPRL
Cristina Rosu Elizabeth Sarbu

Muşat & Asociaţii
Alina Solschi

KPMG
Laura Toncescu

Trelea Law Office
Cristina Trelea

A.R.C.P.A. Romanian Grain Traders Association
Vasile Varvaroi

Gabriela Vasiliu-Isac

ONV LAW
Miruna Vlad

Boanta, Gidei si Asociatii Law Firm
Krisztina Voicu

Institute for Control of Veterinary Biological Products and Medicines
Valentin Voicu

RUSSIAN FEDERATION

Ministry of Agriculture of the Russian Federation

Olam Russia

Orrick (CIS) LLC

Vavilov Institute of General Genetics
Andrei Anatolievich Pomortsev

MSU Eurasian Center on Food Security
Aleksey Belugin

Association of International Road Carriers (ASMAP)
Olga Brovkina

John Deere Rus LLC
Anatoly Chuchkov

Goltsblat BLP
Ekaterina Dedova

Beiten Burkhardt Rechtsanwälte (Attorneys-at-Law)
Ekaterina Dudina

FGBNU Rosinform Agrotech
Vyacheslav Fedorenko

Hester Biosciences Limited
Rajiv Gandhi

Syngenta
Sergey Goncharov

DLA Piper Rus Limited
Vyacheslav Khorovskiy

John Deere Rus LLC
Denis Klimanov

Valery Kolesnikov

Russian Grain Union
Aleksandr Vladimiroich
Korbut

V.V. Dokuchaev Soil Science
Institute
Daniil Kozlov

Beiten Burkhardt Rechtsanwälte
(Attorneys-at-Law)
Alexey Kuzmishin

Anton Lachinov

Russian Veterinary
Association
Sergey Lakhtyukhov

Association of International
Road Carriers (ASMAP)
Andrey Lokhov

John Deere Rus LLC
Roman Medvedev

Choong Ang Vaccine
Laboratories Co., Ltd. (CAVAC)
Juver Membrebe

Rosagromash Association
- Russian Association of
Agricultural Machinery
Producers
Natalia Negrebetskaya

Legal Company East LLC
Alexei Pulik

Legal Company East LLC
Surana Radnaeva

State Certification Authority
Belgorod
Sergei Resetnik

CMS International BV
Artem Rodin

Integrites
Pavel Rusetskiy

Integrites
Andrey Ryabinin

Korma and Rationy NN
Sergey Ivanovich Sovelyev

RWANDA

Transafrica Container
Transport Ltd.
Ndaru Abdul

KCB Bank Rwanda
Alexis Bizimana

Grace Chilande

IFDC
Jeanne d'Arc Nyaruyonga

Rwanda Mountain Tea SARL
Jean Pierre Dukuzumuremyi

Jean Rwihaniza Gapusi

Balton Rwanda Ltd.
Henry Gitau

Ministry of Agriculture and
Animal Resources
Leon Hakizamungu

Equity Juris Chambers
Casandra Kabagyema

Rwanda Natural Resources
Authority (RNRA)
Vincent de Paul Kabalisa

Equity Juris Chambers
Cynthia Kankindi

Rwanda Natural Resources
Authority (RNRA)
Dismas Karuranga

Equity Juris Chambers
Diane Kayitare

Seed Co
Roland Kayumbu

Rwanda Natural Resources
Authority (RNRA)
Boniface Mahirwe

Jean Pierre Mubiligi

Paul Joseph Mugemangango

Shagasha Tea Company
Limited
Robert Muhirwa

Rwanda Natural Resources
Authority (RNRA)
Renatha Mujawayezu

National Bank of Rwanda
Elonie Mukandoli

Oikocredit International
Geoffrey Musyoki

Rwanda Utilities Regulatory
Authority (RURA)
Jean Baptiste Mutabazi

Gisakura Tea Company
Philippe Nahayo

Rwanda Agriculture Board
(RAB)
Claver Ngaboyisonga

K-Solutions & Partners
David Ngirinshuti

Yara
Peter Ngugi

National Bank of Rwanda
Gerard Nsabimana

National Bank of Rwanda
Bernard Nsengiyumva

Innocent Nzeyimana

Seed Co
Kasaija Patrick Banage

Oikocredit
Frank Rubio

National Bank of Rwanda
Bernard Rugira

John Bosco Talemwa

Esperance Uwimana

Rwanda Agriculture Board
(RAB)
Ruganzu Vicky

SENEGAL

Amafrique Suarl

Initiative Prospective Agricole
et Rurale
Cheikh Oumar Ba

FIDES Microfinance Sénégal
Philippe Couteau

Institut Sénégalais de
Recherches Agricoles (ISRA)
Diby Dia

Crédit Mutuel du Sénégal (CMS)
Baye Djiga Diagne

Institut Sénégalais de
Recherches Agricoles
Demba Diakhate

Industries Chimiques du
Sénégal (ICS)
Alassane Diallo

Cellou Diallo

Conseil Ouest et Centre
Africain pour la Recherche et
le Développement Agricoles
(CORAF/WECARD)
Yacouba Diallo

Organisation pour la Mise
en Valeur du Fleuve Sénégal
(OMVS)
Malang Diatta

Université Cheikh Anta Diop
de Dakar (UCAD)
Moctar Diaw

Université Cheikh Anta Diop
de Dakar (UCAD)
Moustapha Diène

Bassirou Dione

Coumba Nor Thiam
Oumar Diop

ISRA (Institut Sénégalais de
Recherches Agricoles)
Pape Madiama Diop

Crédit Mutuel du Sénégal (CMS)
Cheikh Bara Diouf

Union Internationale pour
la Conservation de la Nature
(UICN)
Modou Diouf

Industries Chimiques du
Sénégal (ICS)
Santosh Dorak

Institut Sénégalais de
Recherches Agricoles (ISRA)
Alioune Fall

Institut Sénégalais de
Recherches Agricoles (ISRA)
Cheikh Alassane Fall

Hester Biosciences Limited
Rajiv Gandhi

Compagnie Agricole de Saint-
Louis du Sénégal SA (CASL)
François Grandry

Coumba Nor Thiam
Sall Ibrahima

Initiative Prospective Agricole
et Rurale
Ibrahima Ka

Ministère de l'Agriculture et
de l'Equipement Rural
Samba Ka

Ministère de l'Environnement
et du Développement Durable
Mamadou Kande

Programme Semencier
d'Afrique de l'Ouest/ West
Africa Seed Programme
(PSAO/WASP)
Adama Keita

Finkone Transit S.A.
Doudou Charles Lo

Université Cheikh Anta Diop
de Dakar (UCAD)
Hélène Diakher Madioune

Université Cheikh Anta Diop
de Dakar (UCAD)
Ibrahima Mall

Institut de Recherche pour le
Développement (IRD)
Dominique Masse

Sahélienne d'entreprise de
distribution en agrobusiness
(SEDAB SARL)
Kande Moulaye

Direction de la Protection
des Végétaux, Ministère
de l'Agriculture et de
l'Équipement Rural
Abdoulaye Ndiaye

Crédit Mutuel du Sénégal
(CMS)
Mouhamed Ndiaye

Rokhaya Ndiaye

Crédit Mutuel du Sénégal
(CMS)
Thiouba Diop Ndiaye

Ordre National des Géomètres
Experts du Sénégal (O.N.G.E.S)
Samba Ndongo

Institut Sénégalais de
Recherches Agricoles
Yacine Badiane Ndour

Cabinet d'Avocat Maître
Moustapha Ndoye
Moustapha Ndoye

Kader Fanta Ngom

Sahélienne d'entreprise de
distribution en agrobusiness
(SEDAB SARL)
Lansana Niabaly

Conseil Ouest et Centre
Africain pour la Recherche et
le Développement Agricoles
(CORAF/WECARD)
Aboubakar Njoya

TSTC Senegal
Adja Aminat Sabara Diop

Direction Générale des Impôts
et des Domaines (DGID)
Macodou Sall

Institut Sénégalais de
Recherches Agricoles (ISRA)
Moussa Sall

LPS L@w
Léon Patrice Sarr

FAO Senegal
Makhfousse Sarr

Institut Sénégalais de
Recherches Agricoles (ISRA)
Saër Sarr

Association sénégalaise pour la promotion de l'irrigation et du drainage (ASPID)
Ndongo Sène

Conseil Ouest et Centre Africain pour la Recherche et le Développement Agricoles (CORAF/WECARD)
Paul Senghor

Direction Générale des Impôts et des Domaines (DGID)
Alle Badou Sine

Matforce
Mamadou Sow

PNE Senegal
Antoine Diokel Thiaw

Cabinet Habibatou Touré
Habibatou Touré

GERA
Papa Saër Wade

CAURIE Micro Finance
André Roland Youm

LPS L@w
Ndèye Khady Youm

SERBIA

Association for Transport and Telecommunication of Chamber of Commerce and Industry of Serbia

Syngenta

Karanović & Nikolić Law Firm
Stefan Antonić

Law office of Tomislav Šunjka
Jelena Bajin

University of Novi Sad
Milena Bečelić-Tomin

AGRO-Ferticrop d.o.o.
Dragana Blagojević

EU-LINK
Slavko Bogdanović

Regulatory Agency for Electronic Comunications and Postal Services
Zoran Branković

University of Novi Sad
Božo Dalmacija

Limagrain Serbia
Aleksandar Dević

Jaroslav Černi Institute
Dušan Đurić

Ivana Filipović

Hester Biosciences Limited
Rajiv Gandhi

Ministry of Agriculture and Environmental Protection
Dragana Godjevac Obradović

Senad Hopić

Rokas International Law Firm
Nikola Ilić

Ministry of Agriculture and Environmental Protection
Maja Ječmenica

IPM - Association of Manufacturers of Tractors and Agricultural Machinery
Vaso Labović

Agricom Company Group
Strahinja Lalić

Plant Protection Directorate
Sladjana Lukić

University of Novi Sad
Milan Martinov

Yara
Stevan Mesarović

RTI DOO NOVI SAD
Goran Mickovic

Plant Protection Directorate
Nebojša Milosavljević

Opportunity Bank Serbia
Dejan Milovanović

Jaroslav Černi Institute
Miodrag Milovanović

Business Association of Agricultural Machinery Importers and Exporters – A.M.I. Novi Sad
Djordje Mišković

Agroglobe
Biljana Pavkov

Environmental Protection Agency
Filip Radović

Ministry of Agriculture and Environmental Protection
Snežana Savčić-Petrić

Ministry of Agriculture and Environmental Protection
Milena Savić Ivanov

University of Novi Sad
Lazar Savin

Limagrain Serbia
Miroslav Sidor

University of Novi Sad
Mirko Simikić

Syngenta Serbia
Pavle Sklenar

Stanković and Partners Law Office
Nebojša Stanković

Rokas International Law Firm
Vuk Stanković

Ministry of Agriculture and Environmental Protection
Slavoljub Stanojević

Milan Stefanović

Opportunity Bank Serbia
Marko Stupar

Law office of Tomislav Šunjka
Tomislav Šunjka

Genera Serbia
Dejan Tadić

AgroLink Centar
Dragan Terzić

Opportunity Bank Serbia
Ivan Tomić

Waterconsult
Miroslav Tomin

Environmental Protection Agency
Dragana Vidojević

Regulatory Agency for Electronic Comunications and Postal Services
Sanja Vukčević-Vajs

Law Office Žunić
Nemanja Žunić

Law Office Žunić
Tijana Zunić Marić

SPAIN

Ameropa

Dirección General de Sanidad de la Producción Agraria

Dirección General del Catastro

Grupo AN

John Deere Spain

Ministerio de Agricultura, Alimentación y Medio Ambiente (MAGRAMA)

Ministerio de Economía y Competividad

Ministerio de Fomento

Yara

Asociación Nacional de Maquinaria Agropecuaria, Forestal y de Espacios Verdes (ANSEMAT)
Ignacio Ruiz Abad

Serrano y Acosta Abogados
María Jesús Acosta Pina

Uría & Menéndez
Isabel Aguilar Alonso

Uría & Menéndez
Carolina Albuerne González

Ministerio de Agricultura, Alimentación y Medio Ambiente (MAGRAMA)
Victoria Montemayor Alvarado

Universidad de Murcia
Santiago Manuel Álvarez Carreño

Limagrain Ibérica, S.A.
Carlos Alvarez Fernandez

Uría & Menéndez
Francisco Arróspide Baselga

Universidad CEU Cardenal Herrera
Adela M. Aura Larios de Medrano

H.M. Clause Ibérica S.A.U.
Rafael Bonet Pertusa

Polytechnic University of Catalonia
Lucila Candela Lledó

Cobo Serrano Abogados
Diego Cobo Serrano

Cuatrecasas Gonçalves Pereira
Alberto Cortegoso Vaamonde

Semillas Guadalquivir
Olivier Crassous

Uría & Menéndez
Carlos de Cárdenas Smith

Rafael de Sádaba

J&A Garrigues, S.L.P.
Alfredo Fernández Rancaño

Hester Biosciences Limited
Rajiv Gandhi

Miguel García Carretero

Vodafone España S.A.U.
Matías González

Navatrans
Miguel Ángel González Cabrejas

Universidad de Sevilla
Nuria Hernández-Mora

Uría & Menéndez
Marta López Narváez

Cuatrecasas Gonçalves Pereira
Fernando Mínguez Hernández

Colegio Oficial de Ingenieros de Telecomunicación (COIT)
Noelia Miranda Santos

J&A Garrigues, S.L.P.
Juan Muguerza Odriozola

Ministerio de Agricultura, Alimentación y Medio Ambiente (MAGRAMA)
Don José Eugenio Naranjo Chicharro

Colegio Oficial de Ingenieros de Telecomunicación (COIT)
Adrián Nogales Escudero

Gómez-Acebo & Pombo Abogados S.L.P.
José Luis Palma Fernández

Asociación Comercial Española de Fertilizantes (ACEFER)
Juan Pardo

Cuatrecasas Gonçalves Pereira
Luis Pérez de Ayala

Estación Experimental de Aula Dei - CSIC
Enrique Playán

Arare Gestión S.L.U.
Enrique Alfonso Ramos

Cobo Serrano Abogados
Teresa Reíllo Sáez

Universidad de Alicante
Millan Requena Casanova

Cuatrecasas Gonçalves Pereira
Elicia Rodríguez Puñal

Agencia Española de Medicamentos y Productos Sanitarios (AEMPS)
Consuelo Rubio

Asociación Nacional de Obtentores Vegetales (ANOVE)
Elena Sáenz

Serrano y Acosta Abogados
Javier Serrano García

Arare Gestión S.L.U.
Enrique Alfonso Soriano

SRI LANKA

Sri Lanka Council for Agricultural Research Policy (CARP)

Janathakshan Gte Ltd.
Asoka Ajantha

Sri Lanka Water Partnership
Kusum Athukorala

Julius & Creasy
Menaka Balendra

F.J. & G. De Saram
Buwaneka Basnayake

Ceylon Grain Industries
M. Ziard Caffoor

D.L. & F. De Saram
Savantha De Saram

Ajantha De Silva

Dave Tractors & Combines (Pvt) Ltd.
Anil de Silva

University of Peradeniya
Dunu Arachchige Nimal Dharmasena

Empire Teas Pvt Ltd:
Sahampathy Dissanayake

F.J. & G. De Saram
Chamal Fernando

Asian Development Bank (ADB)
Harsha Fernando

D.L. & F. De Saram
Mayuri Fernando

Heladiv
Rohan Fernando

Hester Biosciences Limited
Rajiv Gandhi

Seed and Planting Material Development Center
D. J. L. Sunil Govinnage

The Colombo Tea Traders' Association
Hettiarachchi Hemaratne

IFAD
Anura Herath

Seed Certification & Plant Protection Center
Keerthi Hettiarachchi

Julius & Creasy
Ranila Hurulle

Ganasiri Jayaratne

Hayleys Agriculture Holdings Ltd.
Chathuranga Udayal Kumara

Vet World (PVT) Ltd.
S. Kumarathas

SANASA Federation Ltd.
Navindra Liyanaarachchi

C.I.C. Seed & Foliage
Waruna Madawanarachchi

International Water Management Institute (IWMI)
Herath Manthrithilake

D.L. & F. De Saram
Hasanthie Manukulasooriya

Choong Ang Vaccine Laboratories Co., Ltd. (CAVAC)
Juver Membrebe

D.L. & F. De Saram
Sanuji Munasinghe

Julius & Creasy
Ashwini Natesan

Sudath Perera Associates
Sudath Perera

Sri Lanka Council for Agricultural Research Policy (CARP)
Thilina Premjayanth

LIRNEasia
Rohan Samarajiva

Geethani Samarasinha

Vet World (PVT) Ltd.
K. Sancheeswaran

Sumudu Senanayake

Sudath Perera Associates
Achithri Silva

Ministry of Livestock and Rural Community Development
Aruni Tiskumara

Environment Foundation Limited (EFL)
Chamila Weerathunghe

Ministry of Livestock and Rural Community Development
Chandani Ganga Wijesinghe

SUDAN

Alpha Group

CTC Group
Muhammed Abass

Omer Abelati Law Firm
Arif Abdelsalm

Ahmed M. Adam

Central Bank of Sudan
Mohammed Ali

Aztan Law Firm
Inaam Attiq

Fews Net
Yahia Awad Elkareem

Raiba Trans Ltd.
Sarah Badreldin

Grace Chilande

University of Khartoum
Mohamed Salih Dafalla

PASED
Salah Elawad

Raiba Trans Ltd.
Shaimaa Elfadil

University of Khartoum
Elnour Elsiddig

Ministry of Agriculture and Forestry
Adil Yousif Eltaib

Alnuha Company
Moneim Elyas

CTC Group
Sami Freigoun

Hester Biosciences Limited
Rajiv Gandhi

Ministry of Animal Resources and Fisheries (MARF)
Ibtisam A. Goreish

Mahmoud Elsheikh Omer & Associates - Advocates
Asmaa Hamad Abdullatif

Emirates Islamic Bank
Amr Hamad Omar

Aztan Law Firm
Tayeb Hassabo

CTC Group
Izzeldin Hassan

Nelein Engineering & Spare Parts Co., Ltd.
Mohamed Alhadi Ibrahim

University of Bahhry
Guma Komey

Mahmoud Elsheikh Omer & Associates - Advocates
Tarig Mahmoud Elsheikh Omer

Transnile for Trade & Agriculture
Faisal Mohamed Ali

Mahmoud Elsheikh Omer & Associates - Advocates
Ehab Mohamed Fadul

Darfur Development and Reconstruction Agency (DDRA)
Harum Mukhayer

Mai Agro
Alnazeer Naser

Omer Abelati Law Firm
Nafisa Omer

Al Osman Industries
Hussam Osman

Aztan Law Firm
Malaz Osman

Central Bank of Sudan
Dalal Salih

National Telecommunications Corporation (NTC)
Sami Salih

Harvest Hybrid Seed Co.
Mahmoud Seddon

Mahmoud Elsheikh Omer & Associates - Advocates
Amel M. Sharif

Central Bank of Sudan
Mohamed Siddeg

Raiba Trans Ltd.
Vickram Swaminath

TAJIKISTAN

Committee on Environmental Protection under the Government of the Republic of Tajikistan

Delegation of the European Union to the Republic of Tajikistan

Ministry of Agriculture

Ministry of Energy and Water Resources

National Bank of Tajikistan

OJSC NEKSIGOL

Sarob

Seed Association of Tajikistan

Seed Farm Latif Murodov

Colibri Law Firm
Zhanyl Abdrakhmanova

ORO Isfara Ltd.
Firdavs Abdufattoev

Tajik Academy of Agricultural Sciences (TAAS)
Hukmatullo Ahmadov

Colibri Law Firm
Hudzhanazar Aslamshoev

State Committee for Land Management and Geodesy of the Republic of Tajikistan (SCLMG)
Mukaddas Edgorova

Institute of Agricultural Economics
Tanzila Ergasheva

Ministry of Energy and Water Resources
Raftor Eralievich Hotamov

LLC MDO "Arvand"
Shahnoz Ikromi

United States Agency for International Development (USAID)
Obid Islomov

State Unitary Enterprise Registration of Immovable Property (SUERIP)
Akram Kahorov

Association of Veterinarians of Tajikistan
Mahmadnazar Kashkuloev

Tajik Research Institute of Soil Sciences
Bobisho Kholov

ABBAT – Tajik Association of Road Transport Operators
Larisa Kislyakova

State Unitary Enterprise Registration of Immovable Property (SUERIP)
Mumin Kurbonaliev

Grata International
Nurlan Kyshtobaev

Dilnavoz Sarbozovich Malakbozov

Grata International
Kamoliddin Mukhamedov

RSUE TajikAgroLeasing
Batir Muminov

LLC MDO "Arvand"
Shoira Muzaffarovna Sadykova

Bahriddin Najmudinov

CJSC Agrotechservice
Farhod Namozov

CJSC Agrotechservice
Jalolidin Nuraliev

ENABLING THE BUSINESS OF AGRICULTURE 2017

OJSC "Agroinvestbank"
Suhrob Odinayev

National Biodiversity and
Biosafety Center
Neimatullo Safarov

Tajik Academy of Agricultural
Sciences (TAAS)
Saiddzhamol Saidov

Grata International
Kanat Seidaliev

National Association of
Derkhan Farms
Azizbek Sharipov

National Biodiversity and
Biosafety Center
Khisravshoh Shermatov

Ministry of Agriculture
Saimahmad Shohzoda

ABBAT – Tajik Association of
Road Transport Operators
Makhmadali Mirzoevich
Shokirov

Nazrisho & Mirzoev Law Firm
Sherzod Sodatkadamov

Somon Farmacevtika LLC
Shamsullo Turdiev

TANZANIA

LonAgro Tanzania Ltd.

ETC Agro Tractors and
Implements Ltd.
Praveen Chandra

Grace Chilande

Ikra Educational Training
Centre (IETC)
Rosemary Olive Mbone Enie

Hester Biosciences Limited
Rajiv Gandhi

Tanzania Truck Owners
Association
Emmanuel Kakuyu

Mkono & Co. Advocates
Evarist Kameja

Deutsche Gesellschaft
für Internationale
Zusammenarbeit GmbH (GIZ)
Sylvand Kamugisha

Tanzania Truck Owners
Association
Valeriana Kitalima

Association for Law and Advocacy
for Pastoralists (ALAPA)
Elifuraha Laltaika

Norton Rose Fulbright
Adam Lovett

Selian Agricultural Research
Institute (SARI)
Charles Lyamchai

University of Dar es Salaam
James Lyimo

Selian Agricultural Research
Institute (SARI)
Stephen Lyimo

Yara
Alexandre Macedo

Lake Rukwa Basin Water
Board
Florence H. Mahay

University of Dar es Salaam
Amos Enock Majule

Ministry of Agriculture, Food
Security and Cooperatives
Rebecca Mawishe

Tanzania Official Seed
Certification Institute (TOSCI)
Dorah May

Mkono & Co. Advocates
Kasha Mchaki

Ministry of Agriculture, Food
Security and Cooperatives
Katemani Mdilly

National Plant Genetic
Resources Centre
Margaret J. Mollel

Ministry of Agriculture, Food
Security and Cooperatives
Joyce Mosile

VELMA Law
Clara Mramba

Ministry of Agriculture, Food
Security and Cooperatives
Jubilant Mwangi

Vice President's Office
Martha Ngalowera

Julius Ningu

Ministry of Agriculture, Food
Security and Cooperatives
Twalib Njohole

John Nkoma

Bank of Tanzania
Kened Abel Nyoni

Selian Agricultural Research
Institute (SARI)
George Sayula

East African Law Chambers
Thomas Sipemba

CS Investors Ltd.
Chetna Soochak

Ministry of Agriculture, Food
Security and Cooperatives
George Swella

Selian Agricultural Research
Institute (SARI)
Rose Ubwe

Directorate of Food Safety,
Tanzania Food and Drug
Authority (TFDA)
Raymond Wigenge

VELMA Law
Nicholas Zervos

THAILAND

AIS

Bank of Thailand

Limagrain

Silk Legal Co., Ltd.

Thai Fertilizer and Agricultural
Supplies Association
Pimol Buranachon

Chandler and Thong-ek Law
Offices
Sarunporn Chaianant

Silk Legal Co., Ltd.
Jason Corbett

Chandler and Thong-ek Law
Offices
Nopamon Thevit Intralib

Department of Agricultural
Extension
Dares Kittiyopas

Sasivara Laohasurayodhin

Choong Ang Vaccine
Laboratories Co., Ltd. (CAVAC)
Juver Membrebe

HM Clause
Jack Metzelaar

Chandler and Thong-ek Law
Offices
Kobchai Nitungkorn

Raweekit Phutthithanakorn

Kasetsart University
Kobkiat Pongput

National Bureau of
Agriculture Commodity and
Food Standards
Tassnee Pradyabumrung

Royal Irrigation Department
Chaiwat Prechawit

Ministry of Agriculture and
Cooperatives
Bhumisak Rasri

Chandler and Thong-ek Law
Offices
Supattra Sathornpornnanon

Chandler and Thong-ek Law
Offices
Jessada Sawatdipong

East-West Seed Roh Limited
Sonia Song

Royal Irrigation Department
Lertchai Sri-anant

Thai Transportation &
Logistics Association
Suratin Tunyaplin

KNR Group Co., Ltd.
Praew Twatchainunt

Chandler and Thong-ek Law
Offices
Kanokkorn Viriyasutum

TURKEY

Association of International
Freight Forwarders (UND)

Sah International Transport

Aegean Agricultural Research
Institute (AARI)
Neşe Adanacioğlu

AKAN-SEL
Volkan Akan

Soil, Fertilizer and Water
Resources Central Research
Institute
Suat Akgül

Ministry of Food, Agriculture
and Livestock
Taha Asikoglu

Çakmak Avukatlık Bürosu
Nazlı Başak Ayık

Aegean Agricultural Research
Institute (AARI)
Lerzan Aykas

Barlas Law
Burçin Barlas

ADMD Mavioglu & Alkan Law
Office
Ayça Bayburan

Bicak Law office
Vahit Bicak

Caglayan & Yalcin Law Firm
Nurettin Emre Bilginoglu

Caglayan & Yalcin Law Firm
Hasan Can Caglayan

General Directorate of State
Hydraulic Works
Cuma Çakmak

University of Istanbul
Hacer Düzen

Zimas Ziraat Makinalari
Sanayi ve Ticaret A.S.
Turgut Ekinci

Barlas Law
Deniz Eren

Turkish Association of
Agricultural Machinery &
Equipment Manufacturers
(TARMAKBIR)
Baran Eriş

John Deere
Özgür Baris Eryüz

Hester Biosciences Limited
Rajiv Gandhi

Anadolu Tohum Uretim ve
Pazarlama A.
Fabrice Gaujour

Baker & McKenzie / Esin
Attorney Partnership
Dogan Gultutan

Serap Zuvin Law Offices
Cangur Gunaydin

Kubota Turkey
Cihan Gürel

Turkish Association of
Agricultural Machinery &
Equipment Manufacturers
(TARMAKBIR)
Selami Ileri

General Directorate of State
Hydraulic Works
Merve İşlek

Limagrain Tohum Islah ve
Üretim San. Tic. A.Ş
Aysegul Iyidogan

Akbank
Mehmet Karabuga

Olam Turkey
Hakan Karadag

Ministry of Transportation,
Maritime Affairs and
Communications
Taner Karakulah

John Deere
Burkay Karter

Ankara University
Süleyman Kodal

Çakmak Avukatlık Bürosu
Emre Kömürcü

Serap Zuvin Law Offices
Aybala Kurtuldu

Black Sea Exporters'
Association
Şahin Kurul

ADMD Mavioglu & Alkan Law
Office
Orhan Yavuz Mavioğlu

S.E.P. GIDA SAN VE TIC. AS
Rasim Murtazaoglu

Iskenderun Fertilizer Industry
Inc.
Cemal Olgun

Turkish Association of
Agricultural Machinery &
Equipment Manufacturers
(TARMAKBIR)
Şenol Önal

John Deere
Cem Oner

Ministry of Food, Agriculture
and Livestock
Yaşar Orhan

Çakmak Avukatlık Bürosu
Nigar Özbek

Erkunt Traktor Sanayii A.S.
Bayram Tarık Ozeler

ADMD Mavioglu & Alkan Law
Office
Afife Nazlıgül Özkan

University of Istanbul
Halil Murat Özler

Olam Turkey
Ufuk Özongun

Ministry of Food, Agriculture
and Livestock
Murat Sahin

Pekin & Pekin
Irmak Samir Yörükoğlu

Limagrain Tohum Islah ve
Üretim San. Tic. A.Ş
Cenk Saracoglu

Ministry of Food, Agriculture
and Livestock
Ali Osman Sarı

University of Istanbul
Hüseyin Selçuk

ADMD Mavioglu & Alkan Law
Office
Irmak Seymen

Ministry of Food, Agriculture
and Livestock
Serkan Soykan

General Directorate of State
Hydraulic Works
Nüvit Soylu

Baker & McKenzie / Esin
Attorney Partnership
Can Sozer

Aegean Agricultural Research
Institute (AARI)
Necla Taş

Baker & McKenzie / Esin
Attorney Partnership
Hilal Temel

Pekin & Pekin
Elif Tolunay

Serap Zuvin Law Offices
Yigitl Turker

Union of Assocation of
Groundwater Irrigation
Cooperatives
Halis Uysal

John Deere
Hakan Yildiran

Hydropolitics Association of
Turkey
Dursun Yildiz

ADMD Mavioglu & Alkan Law
Office
Ali Sina Yurtsever

Serap Zuvin Law Offices
Serap Zuvin

UGANDA

Ecosystems Green Consult

LANDnet Uganda

Ministry of Agriculture, Animal
Industry and Fisheries (MAAIF)

Ministry of Lands, Housing
and Urban Development

Ministry of Water and
Environment (MWE)

National Agro Machinery Ltd.

One Acre Fund

National Drug Authority (NDA)
Noel Aineplan

Soroti Grain Millers Ltd.
Florence Apolot

Makerere University
Richard Asaba Bagonza

CR Amanya Advocates &
Solicitors
Dorcus Bayiga

Soroti Grain Millers Ltd.
William Enyagu

Hester Biosciences Limited
Rajiv Gandhi

USAID Feed the Future
Andrew Gita

Master International Ltd.
Tumwebaze Hannington

Makerere University
Andrew Isingoma

Olam Uganda Limited
Suresh Iyer

ATACO Freight Services Ltd.
James Jolly

Uganda Soil Health
Consortium
Frederick Musisi Kabuye

Uganda Communications
Commission (UCC)
Irene Kagwa-Sewankambo

Pinnacle Enviro Consult
John Kameri Ochoko

Makerere University
Emmanuel Kasimbazi

African Union of
Conservationists
Raymond Katebaka

National Agricultural
Research Organisation
(NARO)
Kaizzi Kayuki

JT Peculiar Consult (U) Ltd.
Esther Kibodyo

Ministry of Water and
Environment (MWE)
Duncan Kikoyo

Olam Uganda Limited
Luis Lopez

Atlas Cargo System
Tabitha Luggule

Seed Co
Ingabire Marie Aimee

Heifer International
William Matovu

Balton
Agnes Mbabazi Kabwisho

Engineering Solutions (U) Ltd.
Jim Middleton

Africa Coffee Academy
Robert Mugenyi Musenze

Master International Ltd.
Roderick Mwesigye

National Union of Coffee
Agribusinesses and Farm
Enterprises
Rashida Nakabuga

Shonubi, Musoke & Co.
Hellen Nakiryowa

ISOC Uganda
Lillian Nalwoga

Seed Co
Christine Namara

National Agricultural
Research Organisation
(NARO)
Brenda Namulondo

Uganda Coffee Federation
Betty Namwagala

National Agricultural
Research Organisation
(NARO)
Angella Nansamba

UGACOF Ltd.
Kailash Natani

Elija Nkusi

Ministry of Agriculture,
Animal Industry and Fisheries
(MAAIF)
Robert Ojala

Soroti Grain Millers Ltd.
Rose Omaria

Seed Co
Kasaija Patrick Banage

Olseeden Agriculture Uganda
Limited
Samuel Powell

CR Amanya Advocates &
Solicitors
Claire Amanya Rukundo
Kakeeto

Agriworks Uganda Ltd.
Abraham Salomon

Shonubi, Musoke & Co.
Alan Shonubi

Ministry of Water and
Environment (MWE)
Callist Tindimugaya

Ministry of Agriculture,
Animal Industry and Fisheries
(MAAIF)
Ephrance Tumuboine

National Agricultural
Research Organisation
(NARO)
Wilberforce Tushemereirwe

Chemiphar (U) Ltd.
Annick Uytterhaegen

National Agricultural
Research Organisation
(NARO)
Eva Zaake

Heifer International
Joshua Zimbe

UKRAINE

National Bank of Ukraine

Ostchem

Pogorilogo Research and
Development Institute

Lavrynovych & Partners
Roman Blazhko

Astapov Lawyers International
Law Group
Eugene Blinov

Astapov Lawyers International
Law Group
Ievgenii Boiarskyi

Vasil Kisil & Partners
Alexander Borodkin

Sayenko Kharenko
Nazar Chernyavsky

Andriy Demydenko

ENGARDE Attorneys at Law
Dmytro Donenko

Ukrainian Agribusiness Club
(UCAB)
Yevgeniy Dvornik

Monsanto
Vitaliy Fedchuk

KWS
Oleksandr Fedorov

Hester Biosciences Limited
Rajiv Gandhi

KWS
Volodymyr Gopchak

CMS Cameron McKenna LLP
Olena Grabarchuk

Limagrain Ukraine LLC
Tatiana Henry

Limagrain Ukraine LLC
Oleg Khekalo

Asters
Alexey Khomyakov

Limagrain Ukraine LLC
Olga Khranovska

Ukrainian Agribusiness Club (UCAB)
Vitaliy Kordysh

Asters
Roman Kostenko

ALITUS Law Firm
Arthur Kotenko

Association of International Road Carriers of Ukraine (AsMAP)
Konstantin Kovalenko

Institute of Hydraulic Engineering and Land Reclamation
Peter Kovalenko

LLC CLAAS Ukraine
Lesia Kravchuk

Project "Capacity Development for Evidence-based Land and Agricultural Policy-Making in Ukraine"
Sergiy Kubakh

AiG Law Firm
Tatyana Kuzmenko

Yara
Vadim Levkovsky

Asters
Tamara Lukanina

Lavrynovych & Partners
Olha Lyubun

State Service for Geodesy, Cartography and Cadaster
Dmytro Makarenko

Sayenko Kharenko
Orest Matviychuk

ENGARDE Attorneys at Law
Kyrylo Medvediev

Company MAIS
Mykola Melnyk

ICT-Zahid
Michael Myaleshka

CMS Cameron McKenna LLP
Tetiana Mykhailenko

Project "Capacity Development for Evidence-based Land and Agricultural Policy-Making in Ukraine"
Denys Nizalov

GOLAW
Sergiy Oberkovych

Asters
Pavlo Odnokoz

ENGARDE Attorneys at Law
Pavlo Oliinyk

AiG Law Firm
Oksana Pakhar

Aleksey Pukha & Partners
Aleksandra Pavlenko

Aleksey Pukha & Partners
Aleksey Pukha

CMS Cameron McKenna LLP
Vitaliy Radchenko

Asters
Vadym Samoilenko

Lavrynovych & Partners
Dmytro Savchuk

Monsanto
Kateryna Shchytnyk

State Service for Geodesy, Cartography and Cadaster
Rostyslav Shmanenko

KWS
Viktoriya Taran

Yara
Sergii Topolnyi

ICT-Zahid
Roman Volkov

LLC CLAAS Ukraine
Ivan Yeremenok

Aleksey Pukha & Partners
Nataliia Zaika

Ukrainian Agribusiness Club (UCAB)
Alexander Zhemoyda

Lavrynovych & Partners
Olena Zubchenko

URUGUAY

Guyer & Regules
Anabela Aldaz

Jiménez de Aréchaga, Viana & Brause
Nicolás Herrera Alonso

CIEMSA
Fernando Bacigalupo

Guyer & Regules
Diego Baldomir

Dirección Nacional de Aguas
Lourdes Batista

INASE - Instituto Nacional de Semillas
Daniel Bayce

Bragard & Durand Abogados
Florencia Berro

Guyer & Regules
Matías Bordaberry

INASE - Instituto Nacional de Semillas
Federico Boschi

Bragard & Durand Abogados
Jean Jacques Bragard

Estudio Bado, Kuster, Zerbino & Rachetti
Graciana Buffa

INASE - Instituto Nacional de Semillas
Gerardo Camps

Estudio Bado, Kuster, Zerbino & Rachetti
Alvaro Carrau

Guyer & Regules
Florencia Castagnola

Dirección Nacional de Aguas
Rodolfo Chao

Instituto Nacional de Investigación Agropecuaria (INIA)
Federico Condón Priano

Saudu
Mauricio D'Acunti

Guyer y Regules
Javier Delgado

Guyer y Regules
Gustavo Di Genio

Corporacion de Maquinaria
Ignacio Erro

República Microfinanzas S.A.
Rosana Fernández

Estudio Bado, Kuster, Zerbino & Rachetti
Jorge Fernández Reyes

Barraca Jorge W. Erro S.A.
Marcelo Ferreira

Ministerio de Ganadería, Agricultura y Pesca
Gervasio Finozzi

Fischer & Schickendantz
Juan Federico Fischer

Guyer y Regules
Federico Florín

Fischer & Schickendantz
Federico Formento

Jiménez de Aréchaga, Viana & Brause
Laura Freiría Piñeiro

Cámara Mercantil de Productos del País
Gonzalo González Piedras

Ferrere Abogados
José María Grondona

Claro
Barbara Grunfeld

Universidad Católica del Uruguay
Rodrigo Guerra

Moreno Botta Guerra Carrau
Enrique Guerra Daneri

Universidad de la República
Jorge Hernández

Guyer y Regules
Nicolás Herrera

Ministerio de Ganadería, Agricultura y Pesca
Mariana Hill

Universidad de la República
María José Viega

INASE - Instituto Nacional de Semillas
María José Juncal

Fischer & Schickendantz
Irene Kasprzyk

Dirección Nacional de Aguas
Ximena Lacués

Corporación de Maquinaria
Felipe Lecueder

Sinervia
Miguel Lezama

Guyer & Regules
Elisa Martínez

Coswin S.A.
Winston Martínez

Bergstein Abogados
Leonardo Melos

Miguel Mosco

Universidad de la República
Juan José Olivet

Mayfer S.A.
Fernando Orique

Guyer y Regules
Marcos Payssé

Guyer & Regules
Sebastián Pérez Domínguez

Sinervia
Diego Petruccelli

Asociación Uruguaya de Caminos
Gisele Pingaro

Ferrere Abogados
María Clara Porro

Ministerio de Ganadería, Agricultura y Pesca
María Laura Rabuñade

Universidad de la República
Mercedes Rivas

Cibeles S.A.
Daniel Salada

Agronegocios del Plata
Valeria Sasso

Guyer & Regules
Santiago Theoduloz

Dirección Nacional de Aguas
Roberto Torres Castro

Fischer & Schickendantz
Juan Ignacio Troccoli

Ana María Vidal

Bergstein Abogados
Silvina Vila Guillama

Ferrere Abogados
María Eugenia Yavarone

Instituto Nacional de Investigación Agropecuaria (INIA)
María S. Zerbino

VIETNAM

Vietnam Seed Trade Association

Yara
Le Duy An

Vietnam Seed Trade Association
Tran Manh Bao

Vu Linh Chi

Plant Resources Center
Pham Hung Cuong

Trung Chinh Dao

Petrovietnam Fertilizer and
Chemicals Corporation
Sang Dau Cao

VietSeed Co., Ltd.
Tung Do Thanh

Vietnam Northern Food
Corporation - VINAFOOD 1
Quach Manh Dzung

Hester Biosciences Limited
Rajiv Gandhi

Ministry of Agriculture and
Rural Development (MARD)
Dao Ha Thanh

National University of Hanoi
Vo Hung Dang

Tilleke & Gibbins Consultants
Limited
Thomas J. Treutler

Choong Ang Vaccine
Laboratories Co., Ltd. (CAVAC)
Juver Membrebe

Nguyen Thi Ngoc Hue

Marubeni Vietnam Company
Limited
Dang Nguyen

The Dariu Foundation
Hanh Nguyen

Institute for Water and
Environment (IWE)
Nguyet Thi Nguyen

Indochine Counsel
Thi Hong Duong Nguyen

DKSH Vietnam Co., Ltd.
Tuan Diep Nguyen

Bejo Zaden
Uyen Nguyen

Van Hong Nguyen

Hiep PK Cafe
Hiep Pham

Syngenta
Thuyen Pham Quang

Yara
Mehdi Saint-Andre

Bach Giang Tran

Tilleke & Gibbins Consultants
Limited
Giang Tran

Deutsche Gesellschaft
für Internationale
Zusammenarbeit GmbH (GIZ)
Kien Tran-Mai

Center for Sustainable
Development of Water Resources
and Climate Change Adaptation
(CEWAREC)
Dao Trong Tu

TRG International
Rick Yvanovich

ZAMBIA

Africa Legal Network (ALN)

Zambia Revenue Authority

Coop Group (Z) Ltd.
Michael Chanda

Corpus Legal Practitioners
Rebecca Chansa

Zenith Business Solutions
Chisanga Perry Chansongo

Grace Chilande

Sydney Chisenga

Musa Dudhia and Co.
Madaliso Daka

AGRA
Asseta Diallo

Zambia Fertilizers
Raajendran Ganapathi

Hester Biosciences Limited
Rajiv Gandhi

NWK Agri-Services
Nsondo Hamulondo

Water Resources Management
Authority (WARMA)
Rowen Jani

Corpus Legal Practitioners
Jacqueline Jhala

Corpus Legal Practitioners
Caroline Johnstone

Department of Water Affairs
Jonathan Kampata

NASCU Zambia
William Kanyika

Chapwa Kasoma

World Wildlife Fund
Loreen Katiyo

Zambia Agricultural Research
Institute (ZARI)
Maimouna S. Abass Luangala

Corpus Legal Practitioners
Fumanikile Lungani

Export Trading Group
Andrew Lunt

Zambia Agricultural Research
Institute (ZARI)
Mutinta Malambo

Musa Dudhia and Co.
Emmanuel Manda

Corpus Legal Practitioners
Chileshe G. Mange

Musa Dudhia and Co.
Harriet Mdala

Seed Control and Certification
Institute (SCCI)
Francisco Miti

Department of Water Affairs
Ngosa Howard Mpamba

NASCU Zambia
Febian Mubuyaeta

University of Zambia
Augustine Mulolwa

Department of Forestry
Lishomwa Mulongwe

Ministry of Agriculture and
Livestock
Gregory M. Mululuma

Corpus Legal Practitioners
Muchinda Muma

NASCU Zambia
Ngosa Mumba

Zambia Agricultural Research
Institute (ZARI)
Moses Mwale

University of Zambia
Elias Mwambela

Seed Co. Zambia Ltd.
Floyd Mwiinga

Zambia Agricultural Research
Institute (ZARI)
Godfrey Mwila

Zambia Agricultural Research
Institute (ZARI)
Dickson Ng'uni

Zambia Fertilizers
Jay Pandoliker

Corpus Legal Practitioners
Mabvuto Sakala

Corpus Legal Practitioners
Abigail Shansonga

Corpus Legal Practitioners
Lupiya Simusokwe

University of Zambia
Emmanuel Tembo

TCJ Legal Practitioners
Judith Tembo

ZIMBABWE

Postal and
Telecommunications
Regulatory Authority of
Zimbabwe (POTRAZ)

William Bain & Company
Holdings Private Limited

Ministry of Agriculture,
Mechanisation and Irrigation
Development (MAMID)
Judith Banana

Cowspace Technologies (Pvt)
Ltd.
Paul Chatikobo

Department of Research and
Specialist Services
Wilfried Chifamba

University of Zimbabwe
Regis Chikowo

University of the
Witwatersrand
Claudious Chikozho

Grace Chilande

Hester Biosciences Limited
Rajiv Gandhi

LEOPACK
Dave Garnett

Hussein Ranchhod & Co
Legal Practitioners
Terence Hussein

Varichem Pharmaceuticals
Portia Kampota

WaterNet
Krasposy Kujinga

Hussein Ranchhod & Co.
Legal Practitioners
Yeukai Kundodyiwa

Dube, Manikai & Hwacha
Edwin Manikai

Dube, Manikai & Hwacha
Milanda Manjengwah

World Agroforestry Centre
Livai Matarirano

Coopers Animal Health
Morgan Matingo

Mhishi Legal Practice
Cephas Mavhondo

University of Zimbabwe
Sheunesu Mpepereki

Bellah Mpofu

Ministry of Agriculture,
Mechanisation and Irrigation
Development (MAMID)
Claid Mujaju

Mushoriwa Corporate
Attorneys
Ronald Farai Mushoriwa

Waterkings Environment
Consultancy
Webster M. Muti

Ministry of Agriculture,
Mechanisation and Irrigation
Development (MAMID)
Charles Mutimaamba

Atherstone & Cook
Arthur Mutsonziwa

Hussein Ranchhod & Co.
Legal Practitioners
Shadha Omar

Dube, Manikai & Hwacha
Mutsa Remba

Zimbabwe National Water
Authority (ZINWA)
Michael James Tumbare

Medicines Control Authority of
Zimbabwe (MCAZ)
William Wekwete

Seed Co. Limited
Denias Zaranyika